STATE OF DISAPPEARANCE

OUTSPOKEN

Series editors: Adrian Parr and Santiago Zabala

Pointed, engaging, and unafraid of controversy, books in this series articulate the intellectual stakes of pressing cultural, social, environmental, economic, and political issues that unsettle today's world. Outspoken books are disruptive: they shake things up, change how we think, and make a difference. The Outspoken series seeks above all originality of perspective, approach, and thought. It encourages the identification of novel and unexpected topics or new and transformative approaches to inescapable questions, whether written from within established disciplines or from viewpoints beyond disciplinary boundaries. Each book brings theoretical inquiry into a reciprocally revealing encounter with material realities and lived experience. This series tackles the complex challenges faced by societies the world over, rethinking politics, justice, and social change in the twenty-first century.

State of Disappearance
Edited by Brad Evans and Chantal Meza

Outspoken
A Manifesto for the Twenty-First Century
Edited by Adrian Parr and Santiago Zabala

Being Vulnerable
Contemporary Political Thought
Arne De Boever

Ecoliberation
Reimagining Resistance and the Green Scare
Jennifer D. Grubbs

Revolutionary Routines
The Habits of Social Transformation
Carolyn Pedwell

Wish I Were Here
Boredom and the Interface
Mark Kingwell

State of Disappearance

Edited by

Brad Evans and Chantal Meza

McGill-Queen's University Press
Montreal & Kingston • London • Chicago

ISBN 978-0-2280-1895-7 (cloth)
ISBN 978-0-2280-1896-4 (paper)
ISBN 978-0-2280-1952-7 (ePDF)

Legal deposit fourth quarter 2023
Bibliothèque nationale du Québec

Printed in Canada on acid-free paper that is 100% ancient forest free (100% post-consumer recycled), processed chlorine free

McGill-Queen's University Press in Montreal is on land which long served as a site of meeting and exchange amongst Indigenous Peoples, including the Haudenosaunee and Anishinabeg nations. In Kingston it is situated on the territory of the Haudenosaunee and Anishinaabek. We acknowledge and thank the diverse Indigenous Peoples whose footsteps have marked these territories on which peoples of the world now gather.

Library and Archives Canada Cataloguing in Publication

Title: State of disappearance / edited by Brad Evans and Chantal Meza.
Names: Evans, Brad (International relations), editor. | Meza, Chantal, editor, artist.
Series: Outspoken (McGill-Queen's University Press)
Description: Series statement: Outspoken | Includes bibliographical references and index.
Identifiers: Canadiana (print) 20230457274 | Canadiana (ebook) 20230457282 | ISBN 9780228018957 (cloth) | ISBN 9780228018964 (paper) | ISBN 9780228019527 (ePDF)
Subjects: LCSH: Disappeared persons. | LCSH: Violence.
Classification: LCC HV6322.S73 2023 | DDC 362.87—dc23

This book was typeset in 10/13 Sabon Pro.

Dedicated to
Alvaro Meza Hernandez & Armida C. Villanueva Rojas

Los quiero mis viejitos; gracias por todo

Contents

Artist Statement

Chantal Meza

I

If I was to say the truth, I am sure this would not be the truth for others. And so, I find it senseless to bare my experiences in words. The people who need to know my truth already do, and to the rest I give only my creations – which are, I think, the less egotistical part of me.

The truth of my experience is in there, whether easy or difficult to translate; there is not much more I would like to write about my personal closeness to enforced disappearance.

I do not exist in the realm of words when it comes to express what my life lives. It is only abstract, and it is only visual, and I have long learned not to battle nor to question it. I cannot lose those hours of dwellings. How am I supposed to express the meaning of my abstract paintings with words when the abstract is beyond the written language?

If I need to write anything about enforced disappearance, I will have to stick to the study of it, not to its poetics, because I do not consider myself a writer – just as I would not consider someone who can produce an image to be a painter. Poetry in my ability stays within my paintings; that is how I see and how I live.

II

When does one begin to feel comfortable in life? Is comfort part of our denials or simply a kind of tiredness – the tiredness of suffering? You can expose yourself to the guilt caused by the many unresolved problems in the world that haunt your steps.

Perhaps comfortableness is a type of abandonment and defeat, a fear of the consequences that, guided by ignorance or empathy, will burst not only upon us but also upon our loved ones.

Sometimes, I wonder if my current comfort is due to all this. Or to the simple belief that I deserve happiness. A happiness, I realize, cannot exist in the pain of the misfortune of others, and that is when I corner myself at one end, to contemplate, and perhaps that is why it might seem as if I live in comfort, that I have learned to escape, but the truth is that I am only looking for the transformation of dreams. One gives time the right to fade from memory what no longer requires entering; then, with life's own subtleties, one gets involved in so many other things – in the many other important reasons why to exist. So, you realize, or maybe not, that whatever was in there, no longer is. And yes, all of this will seem like an aside world, a very senile remorse. You breathe it no more because it barely appears as a sigh; there is no way to hold it. And although it does not disappear, you perceive it wandering in the fleeting flashes of light that escapes through the blinks of your tramp.

I wonder whether it is possible to forgive oneself of forgetting. And how does one know that the moment of oblivion has arrived?

The answer must be an in-between. Remember eternally while avoiding the situations that brings us back to any related memory. In any case, you end up getting involved in the same thing, and that is, that things do not disappear; they hang around in one way or another.

This is it. It's done. And then? Well, something else comes with the exposure, with the exploration of the wounds, with the spectacle of the suffering and the speech, with the promulgation of the truths that one has found, of the lies that one has hidden.

Perhaps the answer to the peace of our sorrows comes with the ventilation of our penances, with the open mouth of wisdom, or with the bitter sarcasm of our pain. We could start selling our soul, the history of our experiences, and in this way redeem all the guilt that keeps us in this nauseating state among crowds. But no, really, in there, we also find ourselves lost, more lost and entangled in the torments of our mind. We are fragmented in the air. What we do or say moves stealthily and slips into our interior, and there we wrap ourselves; we feel again. It is just us, our figures standing in the heaviness of things.

III

Where does the subject come from? Where will it find us? When? Do we go looking for it? Or is it just like a mist? Coming down from the mountain on a curious and even quiet walk? Who decides? The subject or us? Why do our lives get entangled with certain stories?

IV

When one is no more than a passenger among the bitterness of others, being an impostor seems to be the first adjective that appears. The first steps that are intersected are perhaps stumbling blocks. Then we become a sort of magnet, we have attracted injustice to our feet.

V

This road has been nothing but a million questions for me. Every time the subject of enforced disappearance appears, I see ahead of me only a vein of palpitating paths that should not be opened. The ones I have been able to open have been nothing more than torments, and if I have discovered anything, it has been a vast world of abstract images. I do not know if it is my way of seeing the world or whether these abstract forms exist because that is how they are. As I have expressed on many other occasions, this topic has taught me the power of the various ways of being silent, and it has shown me the fear and fury of horror. I have understood the reasons for this stall, of the social paralysis, or perhaps, something more like a chosen oblivion with an apparent indifference; I have felt the rage that grows among all of us in a country that suffers the violence unleashed by a vile and chilling practice designed to paralyze groups of people. When life has been stripped away and you are left with nothing but broken and outraged pieces, it no longer matters to gnaw the soul out, shout it out to others, because the pain is so great and distressing that it only burns your days with innumerable misfortunes. And that is when you wonder, where has all this pain come from? Who does one confront if no one is there to give reasons? To whom should we burst our grief if the guilty have also disappeared?

VI

Why not to catch in our words the meaninglessness of our certainties? To keep on finding a language where logic and poetry meet. The academic with its human rigour and the poetic with its human outburst. Both are pure dynamite for the devastated soul, for our overwhelmed minds, or simply for a whole. We could start by imagining ourselves on a line, guided by the weight of the void. Let us walk on this thin line, not only because it is a challenge for our intelligence and our senses but also because we can weave a thread that guides us like an umbilical cord does, or like a root that goes deep down into the earth, or maybe just like the misleading line of the mountain that we observe in the distance – a mountain that is not one traceable line but the compacted life that has risen and has been sustained through time. Walking on this line is perhaps how we can start to bring two languages together in order to create a language that is not so difficult to understand.

VII

Encountering the pain of those people who carry the crude bitterness of having a loved one disappeared or the pain of all those who accompany and encourage these families every day to move forward, to demand answers, and to redirect every second of anguish is a stab in the stomach, a dagger in the heart, and a dark mist in the mind. I know very well that there is no end when trying to express how catastrophic the practice of enforced disappearance is; it does not seem to have an end point. But even if it did have an end or even if there was a way that language and art could capture in time what the state of disappearance is and the meaning of its horror – or even a way to express beyond words or shapes and colours, beyond sounds and movements, all its voids and its damages to the soul, even then, all this human expression seems to me an accumulation of mere gratification. But perhaps you could argue that these forms of expression are a way of dealing with such issues with our egos aside. And that possibly is the small spline that opens up so that we can communicate and feel ourselves a human with the other in such a way that the painful things are left out and we are only sustained by the other's warm heart ... Is that enough?

VIII

I am still lost, and the circle keeps getting bigger and bigger with every word and every stroke of paint. If one has been gifted and cursed, then one has to do one's best. After all, pain is a big part of what constitutes life – the pain that we provoke in each other with the things that we invent and with the problems that we push out of ourselves. If art is a human creation, then we have trapped ourselves inside our own circular movements, where the senses and the mind exist within a billion vortexes that are seeking an escape. If we sometimes feel liberated, it must be through fugitive movements that trespass a vortex, but this is only to create another one.

So I will not provide an end but instead, leave these expressions open.

STATE OF DISAPPEARANCE

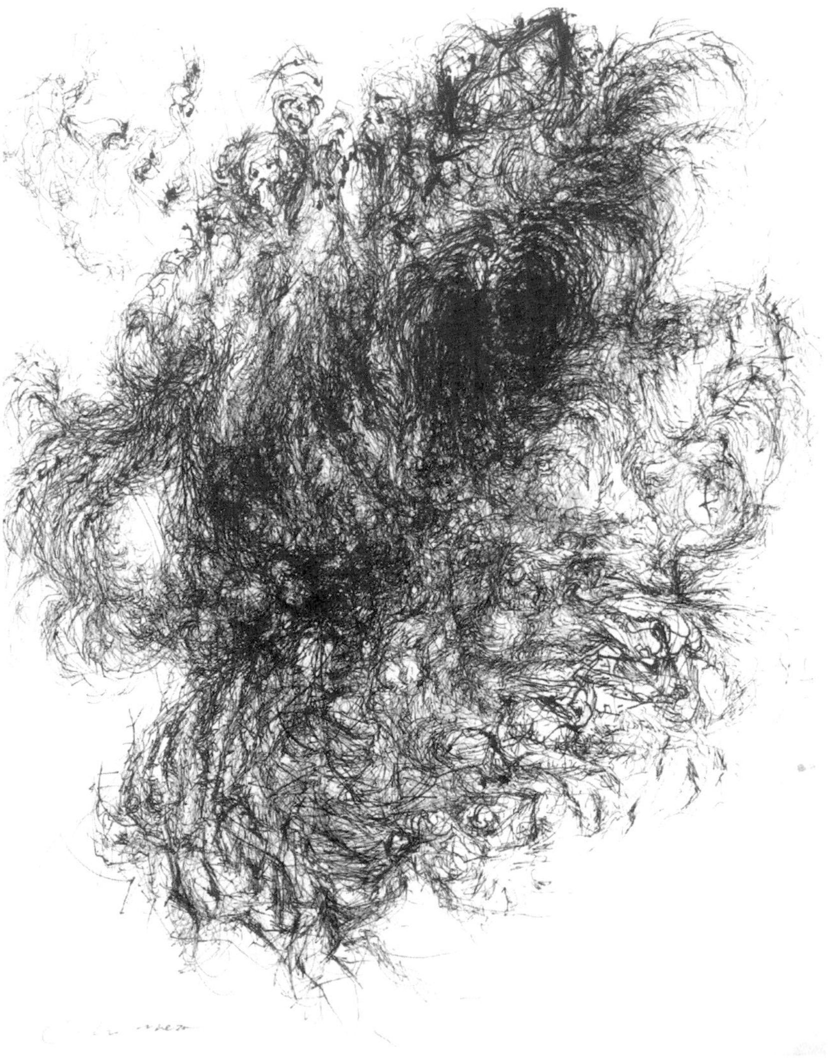

Chantal Meza, *Apparitions III*, 2017, ink on paper, 35 x 27 cm

INTRODUCTION

The Aesthetics of Disappearance

Brad Evans and Chantal Meza

One of the terrifying hallmarks of twentieth-century totalitarianism was the systematic policy of human disappearance. The ability to exterminate and vanish entire groups of people was a defining element in the dreams of total annihilation. What began in concentrated environments, such as the camps at Auschwitz or the gulags of Siberia, soon became a favoured and adapted policy brutally enforced by regimes throughout Latin America and elsewhere. During the period of dirty wars in particular, despotic regimes from Argentina through to Colombia and up into El Salvador, Guatemala, and Mexico orchestrated widespread policies that terrorized through absence, forcing entire communities to live with the perpetual nightmare of disappearance while family and friends chased unlocatable ghosts, the memory of violence being marked by actions that offered no closure. All the while, the state and its paramilitary forces provisioned their own alibis and denials, which extended the violence, often turning the blame back onto the victims. As we have learned, what these cases show is that when it comes to the psychic life of violence, there is literally more to the spectacle than meets the eye. The symbolic can be just as devastating when something is lacking or violently severed such that only the memories of the vanished remain. Living with disappearance – the denial of the disappeared to be or to ever have been able to stake a claim to life on this earth – can therefore prove to be truly unbearable, for the violence that it passes on to others after the initial act of abduction offers no kind of resolution and no prospect for recovery, assaulting the very order of time itself. How can one possibly escape from such a nightmare when love is turned into a violent haunting?

But disappearance is not just a twentieth-century problem. We can venture much farther back into the forced abduction of millions from the shores of Africa and the violence that was suffered by so many across continents and across generations. Lives that are rendered absent to some appear visible to others – the lives of husbands, wives, and children savagely pulled from the homely earth upon which they walked and thrown into a world where they were highly disposable and stripped of any claim to being part of a shared humanity.[1] Of course, the extermination was not as concentrated as the industrial forms of slaughter that would appear later, but the logic that a person's presence in space and time could be eviscerated was consistent. And let us not forget here Hannah Arendt's poignant realization that the concentration camp was not invented on European soil but emerged during the history of imperialism and had already been experimented with in places such as Cuba and South Africa.[2] Moreover, even if we leave aside the question of whether the widespread death suffered by the Indigenous peoples of the Americas due to infectious diseases was intentionally genocidal or just another instance of the "collateral damage" caused by colonization, how many genocide scholars today teach about the Californian Genocide (1849–70) that followed the annexation of Mexican lands by the United States? Just as systematic policies of kidnapping, rape, and forced separation were implemented by armed militias, so too was the Native population decimated to the point of near extinction – a population that by conservative estimates decreased from 150,000 in 1848 to 16,000 in 1900. Such bodies not only disappeared through state-sanctioned policy but have also largely disappeared from historical memory. And that is part of the continuum – or what we might rightly call "the disappearance of disappearance."

The impetus for this project comes from that region of the world. Brad spent many years in Mexico and extensively researched the conditions that gave rise to the Zapatista insurrection in 1994.[3] Influenced by the global political currents of the 1990s, which were still notably connected to the violence that had raged throughout Latin America from the late 1960s onward, critical attention notably turned to the "Indigenous question" and the centuries of persecution that Indigenous peoples had faced. Acknowledgment that they had been denied a history became part of a more normalized political discussion following the appearance of the Zapatistas from the jungles of Chiapas on New Year's Day in 1994. It also proved to be a catalyst to a wider shift in identity politics, which provided an opening not only to rethink the meaning of colonization in a rapidly globalizing world but also to account for historical injustices that still cast a dark shadow across the entire continent. Although a great deal of the focus here attended to the plight of Indigenous populations in the central and southern Americas, there was also a notable shift in critical discourse and political activism, which sought to address the legacy of reservation policies in North America with a more nuanced appreciation of slavery, racism, systematic persecution, abandonment, and the continuation of denial. Slavery and disappearance appeared to be the wretched twins of a god that had long abandoned its people and left them on merciless shores. What was this denial if not the starting point for thinking about disappearance, which could include the denial of dignity, the denial of language and culture, the denial of freedom, and the denial of a claim to live in this world without fear and daily violence? Today, the problem of disappearance remains very prevalent in Canada, which is coming to terms with its own Indigenous questions, including its history of policies that led to the systematic eradication of entire tribes of peoples, the new discovery of mass graves of young Indigenous children on sites of former residential schools, where widespread policies of cultural genocide were also enacted, as well as the continued disappearance and murder of Indigenous women and girls, as emotionally captured in Jessica McDiarmid's *Highway of Tears*.[4]

Whereas Brad's encounter with disappearance – or what a late confidant, the renowned Zapatista commentator and activist John Ross, once termed "the war against oblivion"[5] – was admittedly driven by academic concerns and came at a time when he was not yet sensitized to the problem in any explicit way, Chantal's encounter with disappearance was more personal and intimate. Like most Mexicans who grew up during a period marked by the drug wars and the inexorable growth in power, influence, and violence of the narco-trafficking cartels, she experienced disappearance as a part of everyday life. She remembers growing up with images of missing people's faces on streetposts, on television, and in newspapers. These people were "extraviado" or simply "lost" within a society that always had excuses. But it was not until early 2017 that the situation personally hit her. Back then, her country was once more on fire; now she sees it as more like ashes. As she recalled in a lecture at Harvard University in 2021 when explaining the project,

> Life took me through a stapedius climb that still today lives within me. After what happened in 2017, I lived in my own flesh, confronting the horrors of the state, looking upon broken pieces of lives that tried to make sense of forced disappearance. Nothing of these I could ever put into words, though I have many stories to tell that remain engraved in my heart and never leave my memory. Not even the seventy-four pieces I have created will ever be enough to express what I have lived in my close proximity with a world that seems to be part of another planet. Even if I won't be able to name the people that were part of this process, even if I won't be able to tell what I have experienced, even if I cannot do justice to the immensity of the terror, I felt that each of us in our own way can and must confront the unbearable.[6]

For Chantal, this confrontation with the unbearable weight of absence demanded an artistic response that led her to dedicate four years of her life to producing the artworks featured in this volume.

Before starting this project, we had already engaged in many conversations on the ways that art is linked to politics, violence, and abstraction. We had discussed how Chantal's earlier artworks revealed a certain darkness that gestured toward personal pain and suffering. However, it was through this encounter with denial that the violence in her work became all too explicit, even if the layers and textures appeared less certain and defined. Blacks and reds notably started to dominate the palette, and the ferocity of the carved lines literally tore into the canvas or sheets of paper. Many of the works did not "survive" but were discarded like the bodies of so many who are wilfully thrown away. But even here the lines are admittedly never so determinable. Appearance and disappearance, as we both learned, are not always strategically opposed. They can often be reinforcing. But what exactly was being painted here? And did it have any value or any meaning? Certainly, the work did not claim to be some kind of confession or a baring of the artist's inner-most soul on the canvas. Its creation was not about trying to project the truth of disappearance or an attempt to impose some dogmatic disposition on a problem that by definition defies neat categorizations and epistemic certainties. Besides, the problem of disappearance is far too complex to be reduced to some contrived condition of vulnerability that neatly connects to the in-vogue theories of affect so common in academia. If there was a truth to be found in the work, it was uncertain, and if the work was of critical value, it was not simply critical in an academic sense but was part of a different and necessary conversation – a different dialogue that was not about some confession of the flesh or about a collapse back into moral, let alone forensic, verification.

Organically conceived, this project was subsequently born of many conversations on the artwork as it developed in response to the states of terror that disappearance induces, with the project originally titled Estado de Terror. Indeed, as the conversations developed, it became more apparent that both of us were really grappling with the same intellectual and artistic concerns, albeit using different vocabularies and forms of expression. How could we do justice to a shattering absence? How could we bring our own grammatical tools to bear on a problem that took us beyond the threshold of intelligibility? What could political philosophy say when confronting the limits of language? And what could art say when all presence was being denied? We initially sought to respond to these questions by writing more about the art in journals and by publishing a conversation in the *Los Angeles Review of Books* titled "The Intimate Witness: Art and the Disappeared of

History."[7] This dialogue soon became instructive, as we recognized that the project demanded a much wider conversation with other critical thinkers and writers, a transdisciplinary approach in which the art needed to play a central role. The journey into the violence of disappearance was not one that we wanted to take alone. Indeed, this was not a journey that we could or should take alone. The disappeared are severed from all known social bonds and from the ethical concerns of others. Countering their forceful and violent abandonment demands reinscribing the most basic of traits – human connection. We do not mean connection here in a technologically banal or meaningless way. That kind of connection, too – as we return to in the book's Conclusion – can be complicit in the evisceration of life. Nor do we simply mean bringing together people who neatly act and think in concert, producing a school of thought that may authenticate the true meaning of forced disappearances throughout history. Nobody can ever claim to speak authentically to the deadening and deafening silence of those who have disappeared. The connections that we have in mind are born of an open trust, take time to come to fruition, require an agreement to respectfully see the issue and appreciate the world from many different perspectives, require considered reflection, challenge dogmatism and blind obedience, require knowing when to remain silent, and above all, require accepting that a project worth doing does not happen overnight.

Appreciating the importance of time, we also now look back upon this project as though it were a collaborative experiment. There were errors and mistakes, bad judgments, and many lessons to learn. Mindful of this reality, for those interested in conducting further research into the problem of disappearance or indeed for artists and cultural producers interested in learning from our experiences, we felt that it would be of value at this stage to map out a brief aesthetic and intellectual roadmap that could both prove informative and provide a different point of departure. Whereas Brad arrived at the project with a solid grounding in theories on violence, which became the basis for numerous books and articles that dealt with the spectacle of violence,[8] Chantal's early artistic experiments were inspired by resources of a more investigative-journalistic kind. It was confronting the empirical realities of violence in Mexico, including the documented stories and testimonies as well as the daily attempts to uncover the truth, that led to a search for deeper meaning.

Of notable importance was the courageous essay by Alejandra Guillén, Mago Torres, and Marcela Turati "El país de las 2 mil fosas" ("The Country of 2,000 Mass Graves"),[9] a special investigation that won three of the most important journalism awards in Latin America, as well as the project A dónde van los desaparecidos (Where Do the Disappeared Go?), a unique platform where a large group of courageous journalists have compiled all their investigations around disappeared people in the country, making it an indispensable place to go when case study research is required.[10] (Most of these journalists' lives are under constant threat, as Mexico is one of the deadliest countries in which to practise journalism, with an average of seven killings a year.) The books and public life experience of Lydia Cacho would also be at the forefront of more detailed insight. A woman who had served the country with twenty-three years of investigative journalism and human rights activism, Cacho exposed the corruption between businessmen and the Mexican government with books such as *Esclavas del poder* (published in English as *Slavery Inc.*) and *Los demonios del Edén* (*The Demons of Eden*).[11] Another equally important resource that reveals the horrors of disappearance while providing an intimate understanding of how narco-trafficking continues to shape Mexican society is the work of journalist Anabel Hernández, whose books *La verdadera noche de Iguala* (published in English as *A Massacre in Mexico*) and *Los señores del narco* (published in English as *Narcoland*)[12] accentuate the idea of a narco-state and show us how Mexican cartels work to a planetary scale.

Another writer concerned with the ways that these intricate threads are woven together is Ana Lilia Perez, whose books include *Mares de cocaína* (*Seas of Cocaine*), *Pemex RIP*, and *Verdugos* (*Executioners*).[13] Through these precise investigations, Perez explains not only how a political system was failing to protect its citizens with dysfunctional institutions but also how it was helping to spread corruption throughout its population. With a brutal killing, like so many other such killings, the life of journalist Javier Valdez ended at midday on 15 May 2017. As reported in *El País*,

> Valdez put the newspaper down at noon. He got into his red Corolla and went two streets and turned left. One street later he turned again … The car advanced another 100 metres until a white car blocked its way. The assassins spoke with the victim "for a minute or two," according to testimonies included in the investigation by the Sinaloa Prosecutor's Office and collected by the newspaper *La Jornada* … He was on his knees, with his hands on his thighs and a hat on his head. Valdez later received twelve bullets. That was the last image of one of the best chroniclers of drug trafficking in Mexico.[14]

When Valdez received international recognition for his work by the Committee to Protect Journalists in New York, he stated, "Where I work, Culiacán, in the state of Sinaloa, Mexico, it is dangerous to be alive, and doing journalism is walking an invisible line drawn by the bad guys – who are in drug trafficking and in the government – in a field strewn with explosives." He then went on to say, "This is what most of the country lives with. You have to protect yourself from everything and everyone, and there seem to be no options or salvation, and often there is no one to turn to."[15] Valdez had the courage to write the stories of a population living under a tyrannical power. His book *Huérfanos del narco* (*Narco's Orphans*)[16] showed us how you can detect a country's sick heart once its children have been co-opted and destroyed by the thoughtless neglect of those who should be providing for them. These orphans have become not only the victims but also the hapless perpetrators and apprentices of some of the most brutal practices of violence one could ever think of.

One of the first people to document cases of disappearance in Mexico was the Italian journalist Federico Mastrogiovanni. With his book *Ni vivos ni muertos* (*Neither Alive nor Dead*), he gave us a poignant analysis of the limbo in which families are left when confronting the tragic phenomenon of forced disappearance.[17] In the words of Pino Cacucci,

> An unmistakable style runs through Federico Mastrogiovanni's writing: a style that emerges from his ability to establish a confidential relationship with the people who are the protagonists of his books and reportage. The author's sensibilities not only illustrate aspects of reality but also capture and transmit the feelings of the human beings with whom he speaks. The rigour of the choral narrative distinguishes him, but this rigour in itself never verges on the detached cynicism of those who are strangers to what is happening. Involvement, indeed, makes his style unique.[18]

Today, there is a long list of not only journalists – who evidently comprise a courageous group – but also human rights defenders and local activists who have revealed how very little within Mexican society is untouched by the violence of organized crime. The illegal extraction of petroleum, the abduction of girls into prostitution, the sale of drugs and other contraband, the extortion of money from businesses, and the hanging of bodies from bridges are all part of the same fabric. Disappearance, in turn, is inseparable from this shadow economy of violence, often in fact being deployed in ways that create the climate of fear needed to suppress any local resistance. Films such as Patricio Guzmán's *Nostalgia for the Light* and Everardo González's *La libertad del diablo* (*The Devil's Freedom*) also provided a further visual impetus in the early stages of the project's development, disturbingly capturing how disappearance had arrived like a phantom in the night, slowly seducing and then torturing and persecuting people in pueblos whose suffering was all too familiar and impossible to ignore. Although these cultural outputs should be applauded and become necessary viewing for anybody trying to deal with this issue, they give us only a very figurative response, which as González's production shows, renders them faceless even in the presence of witnesses. Moreover, we also needed to account for the ways that such programs make even the viewer feel terrified and impotent in the face of a nihilistic form of violence that is truly the sum of all fears. What was it that truly haunted us about the witnessing of such testimonies of absence?

When we had arrived at this point, it became apparent that our position of entry needed to interrogate what we would elect to call the *phenomenology of disappearance*. We wanted to document a phenomenon that worked by denying the very traces and marks that determined the meaning or denial of a life. Our position of entry needed to attend to the deep structures of the experiences produced by this phenomenon. Instead of collapsing the personal into the political, it needed to give rise to an explosive creative energy that truly puts itself on the side of life in the face of its annihilation. We saw that a new opening in the conversation could link the critical power of art to political and philosophical enquiry so that we might ask more searching questions about a problem that seemingly evades comprehension and that even seeks, in its final act, to short-circuit consciousness itself by denying a meaningful death. We understood the possibility of rethinking and reimagining important resources from history in order to bring art and theory together in a life-affirming conversation. Looking back now, we can see that it was perhaps no coincidence that many of our early discussions, in turn, centred on the artistic relevance of Francisco de Goya and Friedrich Nietzsche.[19] What brings both of these tremendous figures into the fray is precisely their desire to bear witness to and account for the emergence of nihilism at the threshold of our political modernity. Indeed, if there is a singular outcome of their collective efforts and enduring influence, it has been to bring to light and concentrate our attentions on what can be referred to as the "aesthetics of disappearance." Such nihilism, understood as the will to nothing, is inseparable from the phenomenology of disappearance in their respective paintings and writings, for both Goya and Nietzsche appreciated how the gravitational pull of nihilism works by ultimately sucking everything into the abyss. And both consciously faced the need to operate within this deep shadow, which every subsequent artist and critical writer, we believe, has been trying to come to terms in one way or another. So, if there is a demand made, it is precisely that we must confront this intolerable condition by venturing into the void so that the human may be rescued from its obliteration.

This starting point provided us with a clearer set of coordinates, which opened up a discursive inventory of artworks notably framed by this aesthetics of disappearance, an attribution sometimes contested between us.

This inventory extends from Goya and the violence of secularism to the emergence of abstract expressionism and the infamous degenerate art exhibition held by the Nazi's in Berlin. It includes the postwar mindscapes of Mark Rothko and the violent screams of Francis Bacon, who we maintain were the first to properly deal with the ontology of the void as both destructively and creatively conceived; the ecologically attuned photography of Ana Mendieta, who took the disappeared body as a witness and ended up appearing rather prophetic when we consider her own violently tragic demise; and the poetic words of Paul Celan, which would later inspire the monumental and devastatingly inspiring work of Anselm Kiefer, whose project we see as an attempt to memorialize incommensurable ruptures. The inventory also encompasses those who have dealt with the harrowing atrocities of annihilations, such as 9/11, notably the outstanding Gerhard Richter, who managed to reveal something deeper from within the cloud formations that sought to deny us the right to live with an affirmative justice and who also gestured toward a more learned critical genealogy of thinking on the violence of disappearance.

With good reason, it is certainly the case that historical concerns with disappearance have been dominated by attempts to make sense of the Holocaust. Although there are countless critical examples of essential reading for any person interested in studying the annihilation tendencies of the Third Reich, the following critical volumes proved most instructive for us:

- Hannah Arendt's *Origins of Totalitarianism* and *Eichmann in Jerusalem*, which together insist upon a wider colonial reading of the Holocaust and explain why such violence can occur only if there is a war waged upon the imagination as it is colonized by the triumph of technical thinking;[20]
- Theodor Adorno's *Minima Moralia*, which asks more searching questions about the role of survival;[21]
- Primo Levi's *If This Is a Man*,[22] which as Gilles Deleuze and Félix Guattari have rightly noted, forces us to confront the "shame of being human,"[23] while tragically also forcing us to come face to face with the haunting reality that sometimes there is no surviving survival;
- Walter Benjamin's tragically poignant essay "Critique of Violence," which reveals how modern violence continues to draw upon themes that are all too theological, along with his reading of Paul Klee's 1920 print *Angelus Novus* (*Angel of History*) in the posthumously published essay "Theses on the Philosophy of History," which demands that we look upon the replenishing debris of history to reveal the hidden violence of progress;[24]

- Zygmunt Bauman's *Modernity and the Holocaust*, which shows how mass killing is not just some failure of modernity but also one of its surprising capacities, an observation that he later extends in his analysis of plight in *Wasted Lives*;[25]
- Giorgio Agamben's *Remnants of Auschwitz* and *Homo Sacer*, which make the very idea of the threshold – especially the threshold of (in) visibility – central to all concerns with violence, law, and biopolitics, an orientation that in turn demands a more poetic form of remembrance;[26]
- Griselda Pollock and Max Silverman's idea of the "concentrationary imaginary," notably inspired by Alain Resnais's essential 1956 film *Night and Fog*, an idea that provides a conceptual means and framework for excavating a more purposeful reading of history, especially as it appears in cinema and cultural memory studies;
- Jacques Rancière's incisive work on aesthetics, notably *Figures of History*, which counters the pessimism of Theodor Adorno and features an essential chapter titled "In the Face of Disappearance," where Rancière stresses the relevance of the aesthetic question in the most explicit and urgent of ways;[27] and
- Vasily Grossman's *Life and Fate* and Mathias Enard's *Zone*,[28] two works of literary mastery that bring to life in the most captivating yet unsettling fashion the horrors of the twentieth century to reaffirm the importance of what Michael Shapiro has termed "literary justice."

Inevitably, the conversations that we had around these works eventually brought us back to a wider body of (post)colonial literatures as we sought to redress how disappearance was not some random act of violence but relied upon sustained organization and effort that put into motion the nihilistic machine of forced absence – a process that we now recognized as inseparable from the historical processes bound up with the history of the political economy of capitalist development. Invariably, our attentions returned here to the following important work:

- Eduardo Galeano's *Open Veins of Latin America*, which meticulously documents the tragic fate that has continually befallen an entire continent that appears on maps like an ailing heart;[29]
- Frantz Fanon's *The Wretched of the Earth*, which deals with the brutal legacies of colonization that underwrite a system of racial hierarchy and denial on an epic planetary scale;[30]
- Edward Said's *Orientalism* and *Culture and Imperialism*, which together powerfully illustrate the relationship between aesthetic regimes of visibility and their conscious appropriation and destruction;[31]

- Gayatri Chakravarti Spivak's still resonant essay "Can the Subaltern Speak?" – which firmly places the question of language at the centre any concern with absence;[32] and
- Anne Laura Stoler's *Race and the Education of Desire*, which provides an important cultural corrective to Michel Foucault's biopolitical concern with racism.[33]

We also found renewed meaning in Jean Franco's incisive work *Cruel Modernity*,[34] which highlights the real challenge of aesthetically recalling the violence of disappearance, further inspiring a return to Achille Mbembe's work on "necro-politics"[35] in order to ask what memory of death means when memory is also eviscerated. Furthermore, ever mindful that in challenging such violence, one must recognize the importance of the poetic – understood as the irreducibly aesthetic qualities that define a life – we also continued to find critical purchase in Ngũgĩ wa Thiong'o's *Decolonising the Mind*, James Baldwin's *The Fire Next Time*, and Édouard Glissant's *Poetics of Relation*,[36] as well as in the many published fables of Rafael Sebastián Guillén Vicente (a.k.a. Subcommandate Marcos), which all once again affirmed for us that since the violence that seeks to deny an existence works by suffocating the imagination, resistance necessarily requires a creative process. After all, how does one counter the obliteration of life if not through an expressive response that has the audacity and vision to steer history in a less fateful direction?

What we take from each of these authors is that if we merely framed the problem of disappearance within the conventional area of genocide studies, we would fail to properly grasp the complexities and terrifying depths of disappearance as a lived experience and as a phenomenology of warfare and violence. Although important, genocide studies insist that we focus on seemingly exceptional acts of human slaughter, and they ferociously police what actually constitutes an act of political violence. This policing becomes especially acute when we are dealing with the politics of disappearance. Returning to Mexico, we see that the femicides that captured media attention in the late 1990s in the border town of Ciudad Juárez showed the politics at work in the decision to name something a political act of violence as opposed to a random act of abduction and killing for mere sexual pleasure. Or to put it another way, although individual acts, however frequent in occurrence, can be easily separated from wider social and political dynamics, the alternative of placing these acts in their political context turns the seemingly opportunistic into a problem that is also an imperative insofar as it speaks to and demands a political framing and solution. That the systematic policy of femicide in Juárez occurred in the immediate aftermath of the signing of NAFTA, which was seen as the first truly global treaty for neoliberalism, and that it coincided with the expansion of the maquiladora industry should have been the first dynamic that politicians and investigators considered. Invariably, the constant demands from the mothers of Juárez, who were assisted by groups such as Nuestras Hijas de Regreso a Casa (Our Daughters Back Home) in their efforts to locate the bodies of their loved ones, brought back memories of the mothers of the Plaza de Mayo in Argentina, who have been campaigning since 30 April 1977 to recover the bodies of their disappeared children, taken during the dictatorship. Children often include young boys, too, as we were reminded in 2014 by the disappeared students of Ayotzinapa, a district in the municipality of Tixtla de Guerrero. These cases would return us to insights in the theoretical work undertaken by Susan Sontag in *Regarding the Pain of Others*, Judith Butler in *Precarious Life* and *Frames of War*, Adriana Cavarero in *Horrorism*, Simona Forti in *New Demons*, Sayak Valencia in *Gore Capitalism*, Sergio González Rodríguez in *The Femicide Machine*, Fernanda Melchor in *Tiempo de huracanes*, and Lydiette Carrion in *La fosa de agua*,[37] all of which ask pressing questions about the relationship between vulnerability and the normalization of violence, especially how this normalization disrupts clear explanations of machineries of death and how the positionality of the body, especially in its forced absence, is so telling. Maybe it is worth adding here that we do not necessarily agree with the positions held by each of the authors discussed above – nor indeed with those taken by each of the authors in this volume – let alone accept some of the explanations that are offered for the causes of the violence and some of the ideas that are put forth regarding how the annihilation of the body should be conceived. We do however recognize the merits of their contributions and the critical questions that their work has raised.

Fully appreciative of the need for such a questioning voice, we instigated this collective response in firm recognition of how disappearance can quite easily be seen as a problem at the extreme ends of human denial. It is tempting and perhaps even reassuring to see it in this way, as doing so upholds the principle of sovereignty and deludes us into believing that disappearance is a mere aberration or represents a failure of liberal modernity. Of course, the limits to intelligibility remain important. But not all limits are external. This is increasingly the case in a world that no longer recognizes any outside and is merely policing its internal divisions. Besides, the exponential rise in disappearance in Mexico has coincided with its effective democratization – institutionally understood in the most familiar and reductive sense. Hence, without contradiction, we also recognized that disappearance does not occupy or live and breathe in some extrajuridical space, lurking beyond the margins to exist in some exceptional vacuum. It can be extremely normal. Its absences can be terrifyingly apparent, its unknowability defining. So, although we agreed that there is no greater terror than to be forcibly vanished without a trace, we still had many questions that demanded more sustained reflection, not least what do we actually mean by the term "disappearance," and how might it expose the limits of our political, philosophical, and aesthetic understanding? We know that individual peoples and entire groups can be forcibly removed from the planet. And we also know that human lives are sometimes rendered so absent from any universe of obligation that they are denied any right to a dignified existence. But do we need to rethink the terms of engagement? How, for instance, might we better respond to such a terrifying state of denial – the absence of presence – in an effort not only to overcome the manipulation of a truth and the denial of justice but also to raise serious questions about the hidden order of violence and its effective normalization?

Mindful of these questions, we set about to broaden the conversation by inviting participants both to critically reflect on the artwork and to use this starting point as a way to deal with the phenomenology of disappearance as it relates to multiple fields of concern. We consciously invited authors who, while being ever mindful of the need for critical and artistic integrity, would push forward and indeed transgress conventional thinking with their interrogations of the many contested ways that disappearance occurs in society. Although disappearance is undoubtedly terrifying for its victims and families, we maintained from the outset that there was a need to reimagine the term "disappearance" itself within a more considered, questioning, and intimate frame. It was necessary to account for the terror that lives on in the minds of everybody it touches, not only as a way to focus attention on the absence of bodies but also as a means to consider broader issues like the roles between perpetrators, victims, and witnesses as well as how this terror forces a fundamental rupture in the logics of space and time. Indeed, we felt that only by addressing it on these terms might we be able to ask serious questions about what role art and critical thinking may have when confronting this devastating problem, which by its very definition exceeds the limits of aesthetic and philosophical engagement on account of its absence and denials. Given these challenges, we remain truly humbled by the trust in us that others showed as they engaged with this project. We see this book as a collaborative response to the problem of human denial. In bringing together critical theory and contemporary art, the ambition has been to address the many ways that disappearance occurs and in the process to ask about the importance or limits of the arts, humanities, and critical enquiry when it comes to responding to the problem of violence in the world today. We hope that this inquiry will lead to some meaningful discussion about what it means to be human and will encourage us to confront more sensitively what freedom in the face of its total annihilation means in the twenty-first century.

In the opening chapter, Bret W. Davis provides us with a purposeful entry into this enquiry by foregrounding the question of art. Mapping out the significance of recognizing the nonlinguistic and earthly basis of our linguistically intelligible worlds, Davis examines the insightful as well as fraught dimensions of Heideggerian thinking about the originating power of artworks. This critical discussion of Heidegger leads Davis to articulate what he calls "postfigurative and prefigurative art," artforms that he argues are not properly conceptualized in terms of abstract art. Davis impresses upon us that the purpose of such art is to intimately address the concrete realities of ruination – the debris of history – while allowing us to reimagine better futures. Echoing the words of the poet Paul Celan, Davis stresses the importance of carrying the memories of victims of violence, especially since nothing less than *the world* has been violently torn asunder in each case of violent disappearance. This undertaking demands, as he argues, rethinking both the impossibility and the necessity of art after horrifying events such as the Holocaust. But if art is able to carry the worlds that are lost with the violent disappearance of others, it must do so by intrepidly gazing into the abyss. This confrontation is something that Davis detects in Chantal's paintings, which he deems to be exemplary of the post- and prefigurative art that he discusses. Indeed, if such works have power, it resides in the fact that they are more than merely affecting and thus demand a new understanding of the possible worlds that we may create in the wake of violent loss by means of a more avowedly cooperative alliance between philosophy and art. They require that we learn to speak together with multiple grammars, especially ones that can expose the role that even our good intentions can inadvertently play in the nihilistic voiding of existence. This cooperative exchange between philosophy and post- and prefigurative art will necessitate, among other things, taking much more seriously the multivalent nature of the void or nothingness into which the disappeared are thrown and out of which we must somehow manage to both faithfully and creatively carry forth their lost worlds.

Mangalika de Silva in chapter 2 turns our attention to the reality of lost worlds by introducing the lived reality of disappearance through the devastating story of M. Here, we encounter what it means to live with disappearance and with the continued return of the violence in the quest for justice. Having set out the haunting testimony of M, de Silva brings us to the Greek concept of aphanisis in order to consider the Lacanian notion of making disappear. Working through the complex interplay between lack and desire, she takes us back to the violence of disappearance and forms of desubjectification. The psychic structuring of such violence, she notes, manifests experiences where we witness the fading of subjects as an integral part of the state's dramaturgy. Given that the forced disappearance of young children is coupled here with the demands for a forced disavowal by loved ones and family members of their very existence, the evisceration of memory doubles the experience of violence through "the loss of loss." Such a doubling constitutes a form of "symbolic abortion," which severs the natal bonds so necessary to the formation of viable civic communities. In turn, the doubling of disappearance is rendered as a form of blindfolding necessary to the sovereign order. This insight provides a novel opening into the abstract as a means for excavating a new kind of history, wherein the disappeared can be revealed not only as always and already abstracted but also, in a more poetic guise, as occupying a space that allows for an intensive potentiality for change. This discussion invokes a deep concern with blind witnessing in the very act of remembrance.

Henry A. Giroux keeps the focus on memory by delivering a stark warning from history in chapter 3. Central to Giroux's concern is the recurring beast of fascism, which continues to be allied in the United States with more ferocious and uncompromising ideas concerning white supremacy. For Giroux, the resultant victory of Donald Trump in the 2016 presidential election proved to be a deeply significant moment of historical reckoning, which not only showed that the United States continued to be blinded to its history of racial persecution but also demonstrated that this blindness was matched by a failure to recognize the historic memory of fascism. This assault on the lived memory of abduction, mass killing, human denial, and disappearance amounted to what Giroux terms "the violence of organized forgetting." These insights demand that we recognize the lines leading to contemporary racialized American fascism if we are to be properly attentive to the devastating interplay at work in the present moment between novel forces of disappearance and spectacles of violence. We must recognize how discourse and aesthetics can be vocally and visibly complicit in producing both a celebrated and a hidden order of violence that works by orchestrating an outright assault on the body politic. With fascism no longer reduced to a mere apparition of the past, we must resist the disimagination machines of human oppression with a counter-memory that places pedagogical concerns at the centre of any viable claim to civic responsibility and one's rightful place to exist in any society. As Giroux reminds us, to be forcibly rendered absent of memory is to be absent of hope.

Ana Lucia Araujo also demonstrates a commitment to retelling the past in chapter 4, where she reminds us of violent histories of disappearance that are all too real. Addressing the legacy of slavery, Araujo looks directly into the processes of dehumanization and into the complex dynamics between planetary forms of abduction and the mediation of our gaze as we investigate the chains of history. Beginning with an account of the slave ships, or "floating tombs," that were witness to untold suffering by the wretched and the damned, she asks about the ways that disappearance was apparent in every stage of human slavery as the chattel economy of forced denial took hold. The task for historians facing such atrocities, she maintains, is to excavate the material traces of such brutal deniability, to dig deeper into the rubble that politically covers the violence of the past, to bring back into our perceptions the concealed memories of the systematic terror that was integral to the birth of so many nations. Of key importance here is that we focus on forgotten burial grounds, such as at the Valongo Wharf in Brazil, into which countless slaves were unceremoniously discarded. This undertaking demands a more sobering look at the final stage in the continuation of human disappearance, namely the denial of any dignity and recognition in death, which also contributes to the denial of all memory of the trade's truly devastating impact over centuries. This work represents nothing short of a rewriting of history that accounts for the disappeared, such that the afterlife of slavery – the fragments of a catastrophe – can be better pieced together. It demands that we mediate more intently on the refusal of life, learning to see how absent traces can easily condition the present by haunting landscapes and habituating loss, so that ultimately disappearance is never forgotten.

In chapter 5, Michael J. Shapiro maintains this concern with the historical, or the history of the present, in respect to the United States. Extending his earlier work on literary and aesthetic justice, Shapiro offers a powerful excavation of another concept of the sublime that reveals America's "dark vanishings." Concerned with the extraordinary violence necessary to bring about the whitening of a continent, this contribution demands a thorough critique of the role that culture plays in establishing forms of artistic and literary legitimation in the denial of entire peoples' right to exist. At the forefront of Shapiro's concerns is the plight of Native American populations, whose suffering can be properly explained only by attending to forms of appearance and eradication. Such an approach is not only historically resonant but also provides devastating insights into the fabric of American life today. Shapiro reminds us that it is the role of the critical cartographer to reimagine the geographies of disappearance while being ever attentive to the subtle forms of everyday resistance that seek to challenge the naturalized continuation of historical persecution. The role of cinema here becomes important, as it allows us to concentrate more intently on the slow violence of human and cultural eradication while reimagining what a more considered sense of justice and apprehension may mean for Indigenous peoples in the twenty-first century.

Nuala Finnegan in chapter 6 takes hold of this concern with justice to bring our attention back to where the project began for us: the ongoing tragic story of femicide and disappearance in Mexico. Observing the temporal collapse of those who are left to wait in abeyance while holding the memory of the disappeared, Finnegan is drawn to the images that continue to haunt once the absence becomes the rule. Central to her concerns is the role that the face plays in memorialization, notably the desire to move beyond mere empathy so that one may look to the potential within art to bring about societal transformation. It is through recognizing both the importance of the spectre of faces in the mothering of ghosts and the horror of the denial in the systems marked by the violence of disappearance that Finnegan finds a new opening. Such an opening appears as a deep reflection that looks beyond mere forms of representation and into the unintelligible pain of violence. It is here that she senses a counter-response that provides an alternative to the political economy of the face, whose complex lines allow us to uncouple the ghost from the specific, transforming the face into something that gestures toward a shared humanity. Within the horror, there is something to be rescued. What appears, then, are precisely ghostly apparitions that refuse to be condemned to a doubtful reading of history, which simply casts them aside on the shores of forgetting. We must strive to go deeper, Finnegan reminds us, confronting the intolerable in our memory of the faces that are concealed but whose traces may just appear if we have the courage to look.

At the book's in-between point, we provide a meditation on what we term *the theatre of the disappeared*. The problem of disappearance, as we see it in phenomenological terms, is both timely and timeless. It demands a critique that is open to a poetic style of engagement, not least since the shift toward rationalism, universality, and the technologization of life has increased the possibility for life to simply disappear exponentially. Here, we consider the various chapters in the history of human disappearance, connecting the written word with the artworks that feature in this volume and are part of the wider project, and we further consider both the violence of our own political animality and the effective weaponization of the elements of life, which reveals something more sinister about a natural history of violence. This discussion is not an attempt to resolve or to offer legal and policy guidelines when it comes disappearance. Nor is it a demand to heighten surveillance and to strengthen the power of the gaze in order to ensure that nothing is left unknown. If presence and absence can actually work to uphold regimes of enforced disappearance, it is important to recognize the multiple ways that disappearance occurs, especially when things can vanish in plain sight and when forces of denial can work to truly annihilate what makes us human. The theatre of the disappeared that we therefore imagine is not about staging or performativity but about the drama of existence, a drama where art can excavate the terrors of the world, forcing us to come face to face with obscure beasts, to listen to the silent screams of the apparitions that haunt every landscape, to look deeper into the abyss and the mirrored voids of existence, and to witness the fragments of our worldly catastrophes while considering what happens at the level of consciousness when a technologized account of being is all that remains. Our aim, in the end, is to do ethical justice to the violence of the past while being attentive to the slow and steady processes of disappearance and annihilation that are already in the making.

In chapter 7, David Theo Goldberg also focuses on the potential for forms of annihilation and total devastation to emerge in the present moment, addressing the multiple vanishing points to which biospherical life is subjected. Narrating how we are now continually witness to the violent disappearance of our ecology right before our very eyes, Goldberg portrays our impending apocalypse and the arrested developments that are now visiting us as previous forms of refuge are being fully denied. As the immediate is being vaporized and the future appears increasingly hopeless, also troubling is the accelerating technologization of life and the advent of what Goldberg has termed "tracking-capitalism." With ecological crisis and devastation seen as a condition of possibility for a new global economic arrangement, the techno-fetishization of the times means that the search for required ethical solutions is past over to the actors and entities that produced the problems in the first instance. "The 'angel of history,'" Goldberg reminds us, "is of our own making." Indeed, if the immanent ecological disaster had already forced us to confront the disappearance of ways of living, the Covid-19 pandemic accelerated these forces beyond all previously conceivable measure. The result has been a dangerous appropriation of earlier ethical sensibilities and concerns, now warped by a digital recoupment of tracking power capable of augmenting new divisions and authoritarian practices. Disappearance as such is not an end state. It is a process that continually (un)makes the world.

Adrian Parr maintains this concern with the biospherical in chapter 8, where she offers an emotive and poetic meditation on the role of witnessing. Parr's evocative poetry brings us face to face with the image of disappearance. It is a linguistic testimony to the language of lost worlds, empty shores, bodies ripped apart by the forces of history. Taking us on a journey into the unbearable, where language itself often encounters its limits, Parr confronts many questions. What does it truly mean to witness? What are we witnessing? Whose suffering are we really gazing upon? Do we not have a certain privilege or responsibility as we assume the role of this witness to history, whether it is forced or not? Certainly, the burdens of such witnessing can be overwhelming, Parr maintains. After all, who wants to consider that ferocious darkness? Yet, for Parr, there is still room to imagine a world that is better than the one where so much of life is now being forcibly disappeared and replaced by monstrous deformations. The spirit of John Lennon lives on in these words, which evince the desire for a world beyond every kind of tyranny and blind fundamentalism, a world whose eyes are open to the disappearances that wilfully condemn others to the dustbin of history, a world where, when the darkness falls silent, we awake to a future that is never forsaken.

Samuel Weber in chapter 9 turns our attention more explicitly to the role and functioning of the state itself. Returning to the work of Walter Benjamin, Weber asks us to reconsider the relationship between the exception and sovereign power, to ask whether the state itself has been subjected to its own disappearance? What concerns Weber is how dynamic processes can reveal an unstable stasis, where the state does not necessarily disappear but its functioning and where purpose can be transformed in unimagined ways. To ask questions of disappearance, we must first attend to the logics of an entity's appearance, Weber maintains. It is only by apprehending a phenomenon that we are able to trace its vanishing. This is not about things being in and of themselves but a conception of appearance/disappearance that is always a matter of perspective and part of our ways of seeing and relating to the world. But perspective alone is only part of the story, for all disappearing acts are also highly mediated by aesthetic and linguistic regimes for power. The complexities of such concerns, Weber shows, became all the more apparent with the advent of the global Covid-19 pandemic in 2020. Not only did this historical moment reveal most fully how the realms of (in)visibility are continually subjected to dynamic processes – which can seemingly render the state both visible and absent in the very same moment, showing in fact how something can appear in the act of its very disappearing – but it also demanded far more vigilance in terms of what was actually being revealed and literally masked from the world.

Santiago Zabala turns the catastrophic event around in chapter 10 to consider the veritable disappearance of emergency, compelling us to ask why we do not truly consider the threats that humanity faces. Rather than focusing on the pressing need to counter our possible extinction, what we overlook today is the absence of emergencies when we consider how things really work at the level of power. This has everything to do with attempts to preserve dogmatic orders and capitalistic control instead of taking seriously the existential threat – the threat of complete annihilation – to humanity. Countering the universal rationalism at the root of our own ruination, Zabala turns to the power of art as the only thing that can possibly save us from ourselves. Art is precisely the means through which emergencies can be properly revealed, as it overcomes the problem of distance, a problem that necessitates more considered action in response to a worldly death. It is artists who are closer to the emergency as they jolt us into it accepting its very presence and suffering. And so, if there is an absent violence about emergency that needs to be countered, what we need to reimagine are those creative responses to tragedy that have also disappeared from discussion.

In chapter 11, Julian Reid provokes an alternative account by asking whether disappearing is not a form of strategic emancipation. Reid depicts a fragmentary account of his life by connecting his experiences to the Greek concept of aphanisis. How we imagine the subject disappearing, he notes, is a question that haunts the political subject. Indeed, it is presented to us as an act of wilful neglect or a nihilistic retreat into absence. Considering instead the difference between forced disappearance and the desire to simply leave this world behind – a disappearance that provides escape and the freedom to reimagine the subject – Reid detects within disappearance itself a more intimate calling that runs counter to the superficiality of a world so fixated on digitalized connections and the need to be ever present. This is not some sexual or paternal yearning but instead points to a deep psychological awakening that wards off the need to be ever performative in the public eye, ever affected by a world that only looks in order to condemn. Reid forces us not simply to consider the idea of vanishing as a person from whatever public standing one holds but also to ask whether true liberation means embracing the vanishing of thought itself. We must ask whether we have the courage to leave behind all petty judgments. Can we meaningfully lose ourselves in the unknown vortexes of the mind, away from any hyper-moralizing gaze? To lose oneself within oneself is to allow a subject to be birthed anew. Or to put it in more pressing terms, magically disappearing from this world is maybe all that we have left.

Gil Anidjar is also concerned with the intensive and poetic interplay between appearance and the vanishing of life in the performative act, as discussed in chapter 12, where he literally moves us to consider the indeterminable space between disappearance and dance. Recalling the importance of movement in all artistic production, Anidjar addresses the visibility and fading of performance/existence, including the apprehension of the apparition. However, what begins here in an artistic sense soon turns into the drama of the political, which demands a new reading of the concept of stasis as it connects to the logics of forgetting and repression. The art of dance thus returns here, reminding us of the way that it, too, disappears from politics and the choreographed movements of the body politic. Can the political dance, or can we dance politics? Can we reimagine the pure movements of dance just as we learn to detect traces on a canvas of life? By foregrounding the disappearance of the dance in this way, Anidjar asks us to come to terms not only with the mystery of the political but also with the techniques through which a body in formation may become visible and may also fall from sight. This undertaking insists on a more nuanced theory of human traces in order to confront the desolation of stasis, a confrontation that reignites a discordant imagination in which the torments of the dance reveal to us something of the secret through the demonic, something that can be creatively returned from the domestication of stasis, something that resists oblivion through a dance that takes place in the centre of the void.

We conclude this volume by asking what shape and form disappearance is beginning to take in the emerging world. As we have come to see it, this project is bookended by two very specific and interrelated concerns, namely how the still-pressing problem of insisting on an ethically just "aesthetics of disappearance" is also being challenged and in many ways upended by the "disappearance of the aesthetic." Our intention was always to interrogate the multiple ways that disappearance occurs and respond to it through the combined efforts of art and theory. And as this volume testifies, the problem is multiple and complex, and it takes many different forms. If there is however a singularity to the violence of disappearance, it is manifest through the triumph of the technological will to rule, for it is such a triumph that permits the very kinds of organization and intention necessary to properly eviscerate a life and to remove all trace from the earth of its ever being present. The monstrosity of disappearance cannot be understood by merely attending to the act of abduction and the subsequent loss of a person whose rightful claim to walk the terrestrial plane is denied. What we have learned by attending to the phenomenology of disappearance is precisely how the violence of annihilation can materialize the immaterial only through a monstrous effort that takes meticulous planning and calculation. Part of the most horrifying of strategic plans, disappearance wages a total war upon the body, upon history, upon subjectivity, upon memory, upon the future, upon the imagination. To that end, it is no coincidence to find that art remains one of our most potent weapons. Art openly resists the evisceration of the human, for it is within art that the human itself as a free entity is most purposefully expressed. And for this reason, we feel today that we are living in a truly decisive moment. As the power of technological thinking assumes a position of unrivalled dominance, it is not only creating utter technological dependency but also colonizing every claim to creativity, originality, and meaning within a technologically enabled frame, putting the very idea of the human in question. So writing of the disappearance of the aesthetic not only provides a warning about the potential death of the arts, which are so central to a transgressive witnessing of history, but also points to the annihilation of humanity while we still breathe. Confronting this circumstance, we propose, is now the most urgent task that we face.

NOTES

1 On the politics of disposability, see Brad Evans and Henry A. Giroux, *Disposable Futures: The Seduction of Violence in the Age of Spectacle* (San Francisco: Citylights, 2015).

2 Hannah Arendt, *The Origins of Totalitarianism* (New York: Harcourt, 1976).

3 See Brad Evans, "Life Resistance: Towards a Different Concept of the Political," *Deleuze Studies* 4, no. 3 (2010): 142–62; Brad Evans, "Revolution without Violence," *Peace Review* 21, no. 1 (2009): 85–94; and Brad Evans, "The Zapatista Insurgency: Bringing the Political Back into Conflict Analysis," *New Political Science* 30, no. 4 (2008): 497–520.

4 Jessica McDiarmid, *Highway of Tears: A True Story of Racism, Indifference, and the Pursuit of Justice for Missing and Murdered Indigenous Women and Girls* (New York: Atria Books, 2019).

5 John Ross, *The War against Oblivion: The Zapatista Chronicles, 1994–2000* (Philadelphia: Common Courage, 2000).

6 Brad Evans and Chantal Meza, "The Disappeared of History," paper presented at the Mahindra Humanities Centre, Harvard University, 11 April 2022, https://www.youtube.com/watch?v=VMdTQ4NlMqo.

7 Brad Evans, "The Intimate Witness: Art and the Disappeared of History," interview with Chantal Meza, *Los Angeles Review of Books*, 22 October 2018, https://lareviewofbooks.org/article/histories-of-violence-when-art-confronts-the-denial-of-life.

8 For example, see especially Brad Evans, *Liberal Terror* (Cambridge, UK: Polity, 2013); and Evans and Giroux, *Disposable Futures*.

9 Alejandra Guillén, Mago Torres, and Marcela Turati, "El país de las 2 mil fosas," *Quinto Elemento Lab*, 12 November 2018, https://quintoelab.org/project/el-pais-de-las-2-mil-fosas.

10 For the project's website, see https://adondevanlosdesaparecidos.org.

11 Lydia Cacho, *Slavery Inc.: The Untold Story of International Sex Trafficking* (Berkeley, CA: Soft Skull, 2014); Lydia Cacho, *Los demonios del Edén* (Barcelona: Debolsillo, 2015).

12 Anabel Hernández, *A Massacre in Mexico: The True Story behind the Missing Forty-Three Students* (London: Verso, 2018); Anabel Hernández, *Narcoland: The Mexican Drug Lords and Their Godfathers* (London: Verso, 2013).

13 Ana Lilia Perez, *Mares de cocaína: Las rutas náuticas del narcotráfico* (Barcelona: Grijalbo, 2014); Ana Lilia Perez, *Pemex RIP* (Barcelona: Grijalbo, 2013); Ana Lilia Perez, *Verdugos: Asesinatos brutales y otras historias secretas de militares* (New York: Penguin Random House, 2016).

14 "Javier Valdez fue ejecutado de rodillas y con 12 disparos," *El País*, 21 May 2017, our translation.

15 Juan Paullier, "Matan a tiros en Sinaloa a Javier Valdez, el periodista que cubrió como nadie el narco mexicano," *BBC Mundo, Ciudad de México*, 15 May 2017, our translation.

16 Javier Valdez, *Huérfanos del narco: Los olvidados de la guerra del narcotrafic* (Toronto: Aguilar, 2015).

17 Federico Mastrogiovanni, *Ni vivos ni muertos: La desaparición forzada en México como estrategia de terror* (Barcelona: Grijalbo, 2016).

18 Cited at the website of the author's literary agent: https://mertinwitt-litag.de/portfolio-items/federico-mastrogiovanni.

19 These discussions also became instructive in the development of another book project. See Brad Evans, *Ecce Humanitas: Beholding the Pain of Humanity* (New York: Columbia University Press, 2020).

20 Arendt, *Origins of Totalitarianism*; Hannah Arendt, *Eichmann in Jerusalem: A Report on the Banality of Evil* (London: Penguin Classics, 2006).

21 Theodor Adorno, *Minima Moralia: Reflections on Damaged Life* (New York: Verso, 2005).

22 Primo Levi, *If This Is a Man* (London: Abacus, 1991).

23 On this idea, see Brad Evans, "The Shame of Being Human," *Frame: Journal of Literary Studies* 33, no. 2 (2020): 53–71.

24 Walter Benjamin, "Critique of Violence," in *Reflections: Essays, Aphorisms, Autobiographical Writings*, 277–300 (New York: Shocken Books, 1986); Walter Benjamin, "Theses on the Philosophy of History," in *Illuminations: Essays and Reflections*, 253–64 (New York: Shocken Books, 1969).

25 Zygmunt Bauman, *Modernity and the Holocaust* (Cambridge, UK: Polity, 1991); Zygmunt Bauman, *Wasted Lives: Modernity and Its Outcasts* (Cambridge, UK: Polity, 2003).

26 Giorgio Agamben, *Remnants of Auschwitz: The Witness and the Archive*

(New York: Zone, 2002); Giorgio Agamben, *Homo Sacer: Sovereign Power and Bare Life* (Stanford, CA: Stanford University Press, 1998).

27 Jacques Rancière, *Figures of History* (Cambridge, UK: Polity, 2014).

28 Vasily Grossman, *Life and Fate* (London: Vintage Books, 2006); Mathias Enard, *Zone* (London: Fitzcarraldo, 2014).

29 Eduardo Galeano, *Open Veins of Latin America: Five Centuries of the Pillage of a Continent* (New York: Monthly Review, 1996).

30 Frantz Fanon, *The Wretched of the Earth* (London: Penguin, 2001).

31 Edward Said, *Orientalism* (London: Penguin Classics, 2019); Edward Said, *Culture and Imperialism* (London: Vintage Books, 1994).

32 Gayatri Chakravorty Spivak, "Can the Subaltern Speak?" *Die Philosophin* 14, no. 27 (1988): 42–58.

33 Anne Laura Stoler, *Race and the Education of Desire: Foucault's History of Sexuality and the Colonial Order of Things* (Durham, NC: Duke University Press, 1995).

34 Jean Franco, *Cruel Modernity* (Durham, NC: Duke University Press, 2013).

35 Achille Mbembe, "Necro-Politics," *Public Culture* 15, no. 1 (2003): 11–40.

36 Ngũgĩ wa Thiong'o, *Decolonising the Mind: The Politics of Language in African Literature* (London: James Currey, 1986); James Baldwin, *The Fire Next Time* (London: Penguin Classics, 1990); Édouard Glissant, *Poetics of Relation* (Michigan: University of Michigan Press, 1997).

37 Susan Sontag, *Regarding the Pain of Others* (London: Penguin, 2004); Judith Butler, *Precarious Life: The Powers of Mourning and Violence* (New York: Verso, 2006); Judith Butler, *Frames of War: When Is Life Grievable?* (New York: Verso, 2010); Adriana Cavarero, *Horrorism: Naming Contemporary Violence* (New York: Columbia University Press, 2007); Simona Forti, *New Demons: Rethinking Power and Evil Today* (Stanford, CA: Stanford University Press, 2014); Sayak Valencia, *Gore Capitalism* (Cambridge, UK: Semiotext(e), 2017); Sergio González Rodríguez, *The Femicide Machine* (Cambridge, UK: Semiotext(e), 2012); Fernanda Melchor, *Tiempo de huracanes* (New York: Random House, 2017); Lydiette Carrion, *La fosa de agua: Desapariciones y feminicidios en el río de los Remedios* (Madrid: Debate, 2018).

1

Postfigurative Im/memorial Art: For the Sake of Carrying Disappeared Worlds

Bret W. Davis

How can we memorialize what has been erased from memory? What are we to do when the voices of victims have been silenced, and when not only all meaningful speech but also any artistic figuration would say or show too much, misrepresenting the violent disappearance that has taken place in its very effort to represent it? How can we face the meaningless void that remains without either turning away or papering over it with sense-making sounds and shapes? There are certain images – including the powerful paintings by Chantal Meza displayed in this volume – that I venture to call "postfigurative im/memorial art." In order to explain what is meant by this term, and why it is called for, let me begin by recalling the vital roles played by language and art in the formation of our meaningful worlds.

ART AS THE GARDEN OF BEING

"Kein ding sei wo das wort gebricht" (Where word breaks off no thing may be), writes the poet Stefan George.[1] The "linguistic turn" in twentieth-century philosophy has impressed upon us the fact that our meaningful worlds are constructed mainly out of words. "*The limits of my language* mean the limits of my world," writes Ludwig Wittgenstein.[2] "Only where there is language, is there world," declares Martin Heidegger.[3] "Being that can be understood is language," concurs Hans-Georg Gadamer.[4]

Yet is being, the appearance of "what is," always something that is already linguistically meaningful? What about being that resists understanding? What about being that cannot yet, can no longer, or even cannot ever be fully articulated within a given system of linguistic signs?

"Language is the house of being," Heidegger famously remarks.[5] Language, as it were, domesticates being for us; it makes it intelligible and

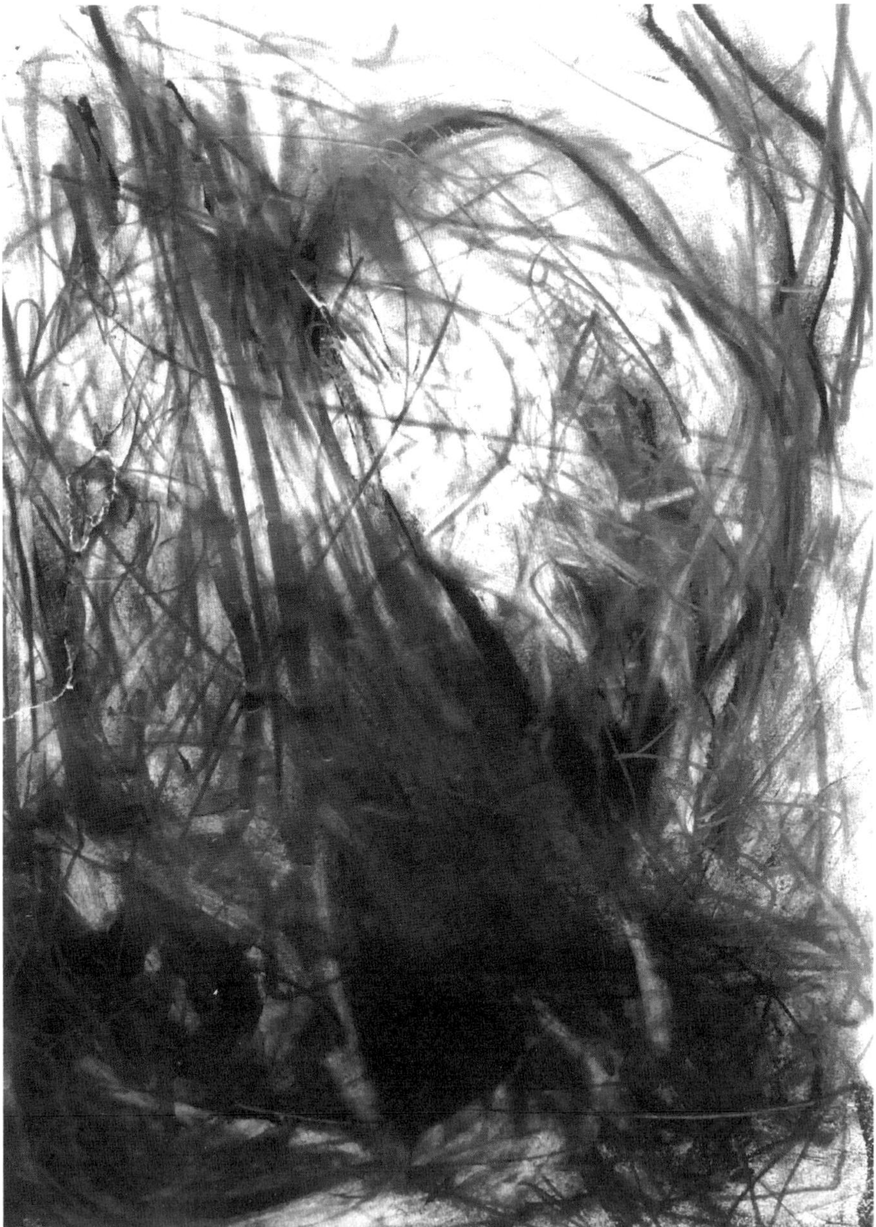

Chantal Meza, *The Void IV*, 2019, graphite and charcoal on paper, 29.5 x 42 cm

thus livable. Yet a house is a home, responds the Zen philosopher Ueda Shizuteru, only in the process of leaving and returning to it; otherwise, it is a bird cage or a prison house.[6] Outside our linguistically meaningful houses of being lies what Maurice Merleau-Ponty calls the "la région sauvage" (the wild region),[7] the undomesticated field of being that has not yet been ordered by our always culturally specific language and concepts. In between the linguistic domicile and the wild region lies the garden of art.

THE ARTWORK: MEDIATING EARTH AND WORLD

We can relate the wild region to what Heidegger calls the "earth," which both undergirds and undercuts, shelters and shatters, our linguistically – and more broadly artistically – formed worlds of meaning. It is the work of art to expose and reconnect our wordy worlds to the earthly elements that underlie them. "To be a work [of art]," writes Heidegger, "means to set up a world."[8] Yet the world of an artwork is set up and preserved only by remaining in an "essential strife" with the earth that supports it at the same time as it withdraws from its open space of meaning.

In "The Origin of the Work of Art," Heidegger writes of the artwork as the site of this essential strife between world and earth:

> The world is the self-opening openness of the broad paths of the simple and essential decisions in the destiny of a historical people. The earth is the spontaneous forthcoming of that which is continually self-secluding and to that extent sheltering and concealing ... The world grounds itself on the earth, and earth juts through world ... The world, in resting upon the earth, strives to surmount it. As self-opening it cannot endure anything closed. The earth, however, as sheltering and concealing, tends always to draw the world into itself and keep it there.[9]

It may well be an exaggeration – and a politically dangerous one at that – to imply that a single artwork could set up a communal world for an entire "historical people." It would be more appropriate to think of a historical people as a world of worlds, a more or less cohesive gathering of the overlapping and only partially encasing worlds of singular individuals, families, communities, and so forth. And it is hardly ever, if ever, the case that a single work of art is solely responsible for setting up any of these worlds. Nevertheless, it is not an exaggeration to say that every genuine artwork, more or less, shapes or reshapes our life-worlds. As the concluding line of Rainer Maria Rilke's poem "Archaic Torso of Apollo" puts it, every genuine artwork addresses us with an imperative: "You must change your life."[10] When we confront artworks, they confront us; and they often have the power to change the courses of our lives, the shapes of our worlds – and to remind us of the rootedness of our life-worlds in the bodily and earthly dimensions of existence.

Although Heidegger tends to stress the "reliability" and "sheltering" qualities of the earth in "The Origin of the Work of Art," and later its supportive and nourishing qualities in essays such as "The Thing" and "Building Dwelling Thinking,"[11] we should also bear in mind the violent aspects and episodes of what he initially calls the "shattering" manner in which it "juts through world."[12] For world to be grounded on earth also means, after all, for it to be subjected at times to earthquakes, to tsunamis, and to pandemics. In the wake of such earth-shaking and world-shattering events, we have to rebuild, again relying on the earth to inspire and sustain the artistic and linguistic construction of our worlds, even as it refuses to be ever entirely consumed or owned by them.

POSTLINGUISTIC AND PRELINGUISTIC ART

Since Aristotle, philosophers have often characterized human being as the animal with linguistically articulated reason (*zōon logon ekhon*) and as the political animal (*zōon politikon*), whose social structures are shaped by literary stories and secured with linguistically articulated laws.[13] Yet the artistic formation of our meaningful – or at least partly meaningful – worlds is not limited to linguistic artforms; poiesis is not limited to poetry. To be sure, meaningful human worlds require words. Yet what about things that are in the process of slipping away from, or still in the process of emerging into, being linguistically meaningful? What about things that are meaningless, or only half-meaningful? What about things that maintain only a trace of the meaning that they once had or things that are still groping their way into meaning but have not yet found their place in a linguistically articulated world?

Art is often a pre- or postlinguistic medium through which our meaningful worlds are shown in the process of coming into or going out of being.

However groundbreaking Heidegger's "The Origin of the Work of Art" was, and despite the fact that the examples of art on which it focuses are a Greek temple and a painting by Vincent van Gogh, he still ends up privileging the linguistic art of poetry. Toward the end of the essay, he writes, "All art, as the letting happen of the advent of the truth of beings, is as such, *in essence, poetry* [*Dichtung*] ... Nevertheless, the linguistic work, poetry in the narrower sense, has a privileged position in the domain of the arts ... [for]

language alone brings beings as beings into the open for the first time."[14] Thus even Heidegger, who would later announce "the end of philosophy," repeats here what Dennis Schmidt calls philosophy's "special difficulty in confronting the image, since philosophy lives in and is oriented to and by the *logos*, by words."[15] Schmidt credits Gadamer with going a step beyond Heidegger in this regard, insofar as he is one of a few major Continental philosophers – others include Theodor Adorno, Maurice Merleau-Ponty, and John Sallis – who have recognized that art "is not bound by concepts that are given, but points beyond the realm of the concept, and hence beyond the realm of the understanding."[16] Schmidt compellingly interprets artistic "gestures" as a "language of the lived body," "a language 'prior' to language" as verbal speech. "Gesture is how the human being, the being of *logos*, responds to what is otherwise inexpressible." Gesture is thus, "in a sense, prior to, more elemental than, the spoken word" and "remains closer to the limits of what can be said at all." At the same time, this unspoken "language" of gesture "opens a space of signification, or sense, out of which spoken language can emerge."[17]

Of special concern in the present essay is the kind of post- and prefigurative gestures that are embodied in artworks that display the violent disappearances and/or creative refigurations of our linguistically and emotionally meaningful worlds.

I do not wish to make overgeneralizing statements about "art." Art can mean many things. And it can do many things. I am suspicious of our tendency to dehistoricize and universalize our modern Western high-culture conception of art as the kind of objects that have no utility other than as commodities for us to buy and sell at galleries or to "ooh" and "aah" at in museums. There have been significant shifts in the historical development of the Western terms for and concepts of "art" (*technē*, *ars*, *Kunst*, etc.) on the way to the modern conception of "fine art" as what we ceremoniously pay homage to in museums and pay money for in galleries, setting it over and against what we condescendingly categorize as "primitive art," "religious or ceremonial art," and "craft art."[18]

Hence, I do not wish to speak of "art in general" since I am not sure that there is such a thing. But I do want to talk about certain kinds of art – in some ways, the most important kinds. These kinds of art are not merely representational. They do not simply reproduce, with clay or paint, something already preformed. "Art does not reproduce the visible but makes visible," writes Paul Klee.[19] The art that he is speaking of allows us to see things in a certain way for the first time; it allows things to show themselves in a particular, more or less meaningful, manner. This kind of art co-creates meaning; it is a human cooperation with the self-showing of things that allows us to coexist with them in a concretely meaningful world – or at least a half-meaningful world since it is the excess of meaning, the earthly remainder, after all, that grounds, and always potentially ungrounds, a world.

This kind of originary art first delimits the horizons, sketches the contours, of a world that is still on the way to becoming meaningful. Such artworks allow the world to become meaningful by telling us where to look – and how to look. They divide and connect, juxtapose and correlate. If living without language would be like watching a movie with the volume muted, living without artistic organization of any kind would be like staring into the unfiltered light of a film projector. Art, in this broadest and deepest sense, co-creates the perspectives, contours, and horizons of our more or less meaningful life-worlds.

Such art does not just decorate or celebrate the already constituted world. It often aims, and sometimes succeeds, in showing the experienced world as it is still in the process of constituting itself. Chinese "mountain-and-water" (*shan shui*) landscape paintings display – and respirationally participate in – the interplay of *yin* and *yang*, the elemental energies of the psychophysical breath-energy (*qi*) that forms and animates the dynamically interconnected cosmos.[20] The eleventh-century painter Guo Xi's masterpiece *Early Spring* is exemplary in this regard. Following the deaths and hibernations of winter, it reveals a world of mountains and waters coming back to life, a natural world in which human civilization plays a diminished and decentred, yet still significant, part.

IM/MEMORIAL ART

Art can also bear witness to the disappearance of worlds, whether by natural catastrophes, such as floods and famines, or by human atrocities, such as dirty wars and ethnic cleansings. One thinks of Pablo Picasso's *Guernica* (1937), painted in the wake of the first indiscriminate carpet bombing of a city; or of Takeda Shinpei's *Antimonument* (2015), a three-room installation that memorializes, in more and also less linguistically intelligible forms, the second atomic bombing of a city.[21]

In *Being with the Dead: Burial, Ancestral Politics, and the Roots of Historical Consciousness* – a book of phenomenological philosophy that also draws on work in the sociology and anthropology of mortuary culture as well as on burial archaeology and cultural memory studies – Hans Ruin acknowledges the merit of Emanuel Levinas's and Jacques Derrida's critiques that "the experience of mourning and the 'ghost' of the dead other are largely absent in Heidegger."[22] Even though it was Heidegger who coined the expression "being with the dead" (*Mitsein mit dem Toten*),[23] he did so "only in passing and in a context [i.e., in a passage in *Being and Time*] intent on downplaying its significance." Nevertheless, the dead "continue to inhabit the argument [of *Being and Time*] and the overriding question of *Dasein*'s [human existence's] temporality and historicity."[24] Indeed, as Ruin compellingly argues, our human being-in-the-world always entails a being-with-the-dead. This is an integral and inexorable part of our existential-ontological constitution as communal and historical human beings. We can disguise and distort it, but we cannot escape the fact that we always and inevitably memorialize the worlds of our predecessors. Even after we bury or burn their bodies, we carry the spirits of the dead with us – and they continue to accompany or haunt us – wherever we go. Herein lies the importance of memorial art, with which we attempt to acknowledge our being-with-the-dead and to consciously carry our ancestors and neighbours, and perhaps also, if all too seldom, even strangers and enemies.[25]

When I visited Bhutan in 2014, I was duly impressed by the country's widely celebrated attempt to focus on the well-rounded well-being of its people rather than merely on their economic prosperity, even while I found this Gross National Happiness project not only to be riddled with quandaries about how to weigh apples and oranges but also to exist in disturbing tension with the country's also widely censured treatment of its substantial Nepalese migrant population.[26] In any case, one of the things that I found to be most impressive was something that I was told by a temple official about the war memorial at Dochula, a mountain pass overlooking the Himalayas on the road from Thimphu to Punaka. The memorial consists of 108 *chortens* (stupas), which are dome-shaped Buddhist memorial shrines. What struck me was being told that the *chortens* memorialize *all* who died in the war, including not only Bhutanese soldiers and civilians but also the insurgents of the National Democratic Front of Boroland, against whom they were fighting.[27] Although I have not been able to confirm this account,[28] this idea and ideal left a lasting impression on me: a memorial for *all* who died in a war, regardless of which side – or sidelines – they were on. I thought of the otherwise subtly and magnetically moving Vietnam War Memorial in Washington, DC, and for the first time, I wondered why only the names of American soldiers were inscribed there.

Although it may be emotionally and nationalistically challenging, it does seem possible to memorialize all sides of a bloody conflict, if only we could summon the political will, which would entail suspending Carl Schmitt's claim that all politics is based on the friend-enemy distinction.[29] If Simone Weil is right, the first Western work of literature, Homer's *Iliad*, is not a triumphant origin story about a great conflict that united the Greeks by pitting them against a wicked common enemy; rather, it is a remorseful account that laments the great tragedy of the Trojan War. She writes, "Greek history began with an atrocious crime: the destruction of Troy. Far from deriving glory for itself from this crime as nations ordinarily do, the Greeks were haunted by the memory of it; that is, by remorse. From this, they derived a sense of human misery."[30] In the *Iliad*, Weil proclaims, "the destitution and misery of all men is shown without dissimulation or disdain, no man is held either above or below the common level of all men, and whatever is destroyed is regretted … The extraordinary equity which inspires the Iliad may have had other examples unknown to us; it has had no imitators. One is hardly made to feel that the poet is a Greek and not a Trojan."[31]

Although Weil can be criticized for being overly eager at times to discover "intimations of Christianity among the early Greeks," not only does her extraordinary interpretation of the *Iliad* shed new light on this foundational text of the Western tradition – whereas that other foundational text, the Bible, alas, usually paints a far less empathetic picture of the enemies of God's chosen people – but it also casts a critical shadow on all of our modern triumphally nationalistic origin stories. Rereading the *Iliad* through her lens allows it to intimate another, more honest, and in the end, more salutary way of retelling our own tragic origin stories. To be sure, the conservative political backlash that such attempts will inevitably trigger can be witnessed today in the Republican uproar over *The 1619 Project*, a series of articles conceived by Nikole Hannah-Jones and writers at the *New York Times* that treat the aftermath of slavery and the contributions of black Americans to the country's history.[32]

Yet there are still more difficult, if not impossible, demands made on memorial art. How could we ever adequately memorialize lives that have been systematically annihilated? How can we remember those subjected to the most brutal psychological as well as physical violence when the violators have sought to erase even the traces of their existence? How can we "never forget" not only the violence but also the violated, the singular lives that were mercilessly interrupted, the shared lives that were suddenly sundered? How can we not merely mark mass grave sites but also revive memories of those who were unceremoniously and anonymously buried? How can we memorialize the immemorial, including those whose lives have been intentionally immemorialized, buried far down beneath the graveyard of retrievable artifacts and recollectable stories? We can safeguard manuscripts in a museum, but how could we preserve books that have been burned? How can we never forget what we have been rendered incapable of remembering?

Giorgio Agamben ponders the paradox that the only people truly capable of bearing witness to the most extreme forms of violence are those who have been rendered speechless, having been reduced either to a lifeless corpse or to "bare life" – that is, to a human being who is still biologically subsisting yet who has been utterly dehumanized internally as well as externally. He concludes that it is only those who have somehow survived the experience of – or at least intimate exposure to – such utter dehumanization who can bear witness to the kind of extreme violence that was perpetrated by the Nazis in their concentration camps.[33] Yet, even given the paradoxical possibility of survivors somehow speaking of the unspeakable, the question remains: Are we capable of truly hearing their testimony?

Agamben endeavours to relate the haunting shame reported by survivors of the Holocaust to a kind of shame that he argues is a universal trait of being a human subject, namely the shame of being inescapably exposed to bodily and linguistic desubjectification.[34] Yet, whatever one makes of his generalizing theory, the specific shame that I feel upon being exposed to testimonies of murderous and dehumanizing violence concerns rather an incapacity to adequately hear and respond. I feel shame regarding the limits of my capacity for empathetic understanding and compassionate response. Moreover, in addition to this shameful personal incapacity, I wonder how we as a society could ever properly memorialize such testimony? How could we create sites – monuments or, perhaps more appropriately, "counter-monuments"[35] – where we could at least challenge the limits of our capacities for hearing and responding? And, with so many forms and travesties of political violence,[36] where to begin and what to prioritize?[37]

As a citizen of the United States, let me at least start by acknowledging some shameful episodes from the past and present of this country. How could Americans ever adequately address the unprecedented mass killing of civilians in Hiroshima and Nagasaki – and let us not forget the firebombings of Tokyo and Dresden[38] – as well as all the killings thereafter of noncombatant civilians in places like Vietnam, Iraq, and Afghanistan, all the elderly men, young mothers, baby boys, and schoolgirls whose corpses we have coldly calculated in terms of "collateral damage" in our "theatres of war"? Have we lost all respect for the lives and memories of our slain enemies, whom we only ever encountered in the first place as ant-like figures disappearing under the smoke of our bombs or, from an increasingly safe and disengaged distance, as blips on a target screen for our unmanned drones? And, to begin with, how could we ever adequately address the generations of physical, psychological, cultural, and political violence – the genocidal persecution and forced assimilation of Native American peoples[39] as well as the inhumane brutalities of chattel slavery and subsequent unequal segregation and socio-economic suppression of African Americans[40] – upon which our country was built, a country where white supremacy still simmers just under the surface, recently boiling over and bellowing forth from the White House itself, a country where white privilege still stubbornly reigns above ground, a country where black and brown bodies are still incarcerated and victimized by police brutality at alarmingly disproportionate rates?

One particularly powerful postfigurative memorial, which opened just a few years ago, is the National Memorial for Peace and Justice in Montgomery, Alabama. It is dedicated to the 4,400 victims of lynching and other atrocious legacies of white supremacy in the United States. An article in the *New York Times* describes the installation at the centre of the memorial:

> At the center is a grim cloister, a walkway with 800 weathered steel columns, all hanging from a roof. Etched on each column is the name of an American county and the people who were lynched there, most listed by name, many simply as "unknown." The columns meet you first at eye level, like the headstones that lynching victims were rarely given. But as you walk, the floor steadily descends; by the end, the columns are all dangling above, leaving you in the position of the callous spectators in old photographs of public lynchings.[41]

HEIDEGGER'S WORDS BREAK OFF AT THE HOLOCAUST

For all of his writings on nihilism as the abandonment of being, and even though his favourite poet, Friedrich Hölderlin, sombrely sang of the flight of the old gods and the refusal of new ones to arrive, Heidegger was more adept at explaining how art is an origin, how it gives birth to worlds, than he was at explaining how art can also mourn the demise of worlds. When Heidegger thinks of the ruins of a Greek temple, for example, he tends to speak of them as traces of the *birth* and *life* – rather than the *decay* and *loss* – of the ancient Greek world. In "The Origin of the Work of Art," Heidegger is mainly concerned with artworks that inaugurate or renew the meaningful world of a historical people rather than with artworks that memorialize or mourn the loss of an individual or communal life-world.[42]

"The Origin of the Work of Art" reached its final form in 1936. In that essay, Heidegger mentions in passing other ways that the truth of a historical world is established, including "the act that founds a political state."[43] This is a chilling statement, insofar as just a few years earlier Heidegger had committed himself to supporting Adolf Hitler's establishment of the Third Reich.[44] It is no coincidence that after Heidegger's failed year as the first National Socialist rector of Freiburg University (1933–34), he stepped away from a direct engagement in politics and into a prolonged dialogue with art, especially poetry, as the proper vehicle for the founding of a meaningful world. It is also not surprising that this shift from politics to art and poetry eventually led him to turn away from thinking, in 1935, about the basic trait of human existence (*Dasein*) in terms of a "violence-doing" (*das Gewaltbrauchen*) against the overpowering sway of being (*Sein*), understood as "the violent, the overwhelming" (*das Gewaltige, das Überwältigende*),[45] and toward thinking, in 1945, about the proper comportment of human being as that of "releasement" (*Gelassenheit*) from all wilful violence-doing into a nonwilful relation of waitful correspondence to the letting-be (*Seinlassen*) of being.[46]

However, Heidegger never did come to terms with what he reportedly came to call the "grosse Dummheit" – great stupidity, blunder, or blindness – of his official involvement with National Socialism in its early years.[47] Although starting in the mid-1930s he did become increasingly and even severely critical of Nazism in his unpublished writings, Heidegger did not publicly denounce the Nazi regime until after it lost the war. Moreover, he remained inexplicably – and, for many, inexcusably – reticent about the horrific culmination of that regime in the systematic ("technological") mass murder of millions of Jews and other human beings who were deemed unfit to live in the world of Hitler's Third Reich.

Much has been said of Heidegger's silence, his inability or refusal to acknowledge and apologize for his complicity with an ultimately genocidal regime. Derrida generously suggests that his silence can be understood as a kind of speechless confession of being incapable of speaking about the Holocaust.[48] Although Heidegger could speak sorrowfully and bitterly about the "annihilation of freedom" experienced by German prisoners of war,[49] the only thing that he managed to say about the "production of corpses in the gas chambers and the extermination camps" – where millions of irreplaceable life-worlds were unceremoniously erased with the ice-cold efficiency of a disassembly line – was that it was "in essence the same" as the "mechanized food industry" of modern agriculture.[50] Whereas Heidegger presumably meant to impress upon his readers the nihilistic nature of technology as a "way of revealing" that flattens everything out into homogenous resources, we are more likely to be shocked by his failure to reveal an "essential" difference between mechanically harvesting crops and mercilessly gassing human beings.

THE IMPOSSIBILITY, YET NECESSITY, OF ART AFTER AUSCHWITZ

Are we capable of speaking of, thinking about, or artistically memorializing what happened in the concentration camps? It seems that we must at least begin by recognizing *both* our inadequacy *and* our unending responsibility to try to do so. There is no excusable escape from dealing with this dilemma. Yet can any form of art succeed in memorializing the Holocaust without appearing to be a cruelly insensitive type of kitsch? If not, then Adorno was right to say, "Writing poetry after Auschwitz is barbaric."[51] Nevertheless, Adorno later wrote, "Suffering has as much right to be expressed as a martyr has to cry out. So it may have been false to say that writing poetry after Auschwitz is impossible." And he wrote that "because the world has outlived its own demise it needs art as its unconscious chronicle."[52] Indeed, perhaps it is the case that nothing is possible after Auschwitz *without* poetry and other forms of art. Perhaps, for anything more than fleeing into a phony Disneyworld to be possible after Auschwitz, we must tarry with the dilemma and somehow find a way to memorialize at least the very impossibility of its memorialization.

When I visited Auschwitz some years ago, I was struck by the way that the ruins of this concentration camp, including its gas chambers – partially demolished by the Nazis at the end of the war in an attempt to destroy evidence and now in the process of slowly being reclaimed by the nonhuman life-forces of nature – have been largely allowed to speak for themselves, or rather, to expose us to their ghastly silence.

More recently, I spent a day of solitary reflection at the Holocaust Memorial and at the Jewish Museum in Berlin. The Holocaust Memorial, designed by Peter Eisenman and Buro Happold and officially named Denkmal für die ermordeten Juden Europas (Memorial to the Murdered Jews of Europe), is a massive and hauntingly postfigurative installation, consisting of 2,711 concrete rectangular slabs, or stelae, spread out in an eerily uneven grid pattern across an open-air site of 19,000 square metres in the heart of a reunified Germany's capital. As one wanders into the memorial, its uneven ground lures one ever deeper into an almost inaudibly murmuring maze until, utterly disoriented and as if by chance, one comes across a "Place of Information" that contains the names of approximately 3 million Jewish victims of the Shoah.

The Jewish Museum of Berlin includes a new building designed by Daniel Liebeskind, a Jewish American architect influenced by both Paul Celan's poetry and Heidegger's philosophy.[53] This new building is laid out in a disorienting zigzag pattern, and the floor plan consists of three intersecting hallways, or "axes." As the museum's website explains, "Libeskind designed the floor plan based on two lines: the building's visible zigzagging line and an invisible straight line. At the points where the two lines intersect are the 'voids,' empty spaces that cut through the building from the basement to the roof ... Libeskind uses the voids to address the physical emptiness that resulted from the expulsion, destruction, and annihilation of Jewish life in the Shoah, which cannot be refilled after the fact."[54]

As one walks down each of the three hallways – the Axis of Exile, Axis of the Holocaust, and Axis of Continuity – one finds small displays of objects that tell the always singular stories of persecuted, exiled, and murdered Jews.

The museum's website states, "The Axis of the Holocaust ends in the 'Voided Void,' or Holocaust Tower, an isolated building splinter whose sole connection to the Libeskind building is underground. Daylight penetrates the tower only through a narrow slit in the unheated concrete silo and any exterior sounds are heavily muffled by the walls. Many visitors experience a feeling of oppression or anxiety inside the Holocaust Tower."[55]

Indeed, after a few minutes of suffocating silence in the Holocaust Tower, I found myself groping in the dark for the door.

The Axis of Continuity leads to a staircase that takes one up into the light of the second-floor exhibition space. Among the exhibitions in the Liebeskind building of the Jewish Museum of Berlin is one placed in the Memory Void, a powerfully postfigurative installation by Menashe Kadishman entitled *Shalekhet* (*Fallen Leaves*). It consists of thousands of individually designed iron faces with open mouths covering the floor, which clang when one walks over them – as if jarringly beckoning us to never forget either their irreplaceable lives or their unconscionable deaths. In fact, Kadishman dedicated *Shalekhet* not only to the Jewish victims of the Shoah but also to all victims of violence and war.

The Axis of Exile leads to the Garden of Exile, which consists of forty-nine tall concrete stelae laid out on sloping ground. The experience of walking in the Garden of Exile is somewhat similar to that of wandering in the deepest areas of the Berlin Holocaust Memorial, except that in this case atop the stelae are planted wild olive bushes. Although the thriving bushes are said to be a "symbol of hope," I found that their out-of-reach greenery, together with the lively cacophony of chirping birds, actually enhanced the sense of being exiled – of somehow being saved from live burial in the graveyard of a disordered dystopia yet still being abandoned to wander about through its unmarked gravestones, unable to find a ladder or a staircase on which to ascend to the obliviously happy life of a new land, which, in any case, is populated by another species whose cheerful chatter remains as unintelligible as it is unreachable.

The day that I spent at the Holocaust Memorial and the Jewish Museum of Berlin was deeply moving. These admirable attempts to say what can never adequately be said, to show what is no longer visible, allow us to at least test the limits of our empathetic imagination and ability to remember and carry forth the world of another.

I have also been brought to a standstill and beckoned to bow down and read the many name plates of Jewish and other persecuted and murdered individuals and families that one stumbles across – indeed, they are called *Stolpersteine* (stumbling blocks)[56] – on sidewalks across Germany. Such plates include those in front of the Liefmann-Haus, where I lived for a time in

Freiburg while translating a text that Heidegger wrote at the end of the war, a text in which he bemoans the Nazi's "blinded leading-astray of our own people."[57] During my time there, I also frequently paid my respects at the grave of Edmund Husserl, Heidegger's teacher, whom he did nothing to shield from the purge of Jewish professors from Freiburg University.[58]

CARRYING THE WORLD OF ANOTHER

Heidegger greatly admired the poetry of Paul Celan, who he said "stands further forward than anyone else and keeps more back than anyone."[59] For his part, Celan, a Holocaust survivor, struggled to reconcile his profound admiration for Heidegger's thought, and their budding friendship in the last few years before Celan took his life in 1970, with his revulsion at Heidegger's political past, particularly Heidegger's silence regarding the Holocaust. Celan evidently waited in vain for what he called – first in a comment left in the visitor's book of Heidegger's mountain hut and later in a poem – "a coming word in the heart."[60]

Celan ended one of his hauntingly cryptic poems with the line "Die Welt ist fort, ich muß dich tragen" (The world is gone, I must carry you). It is striking, and revealing, that Celan does not write "*Eine* Welt ist fort (*A* world is gone), but rather "*Die* Welt ist fort (*The* world is gone). Each singular and irreplaceable life is not just *a* world; it is *the* world. Commenting on this line, Derrida writes,

> For each time, and each time singularly, each time irreplaceably, each time infinitely, death is nothing less than an end of *the* world. Not *only one* end among others, the end of someone or of something *in the world*, the end of a life or of a living being. Death puts an end neither to someone in the world nor to *one* world among others. Death marks each time, each time in defiance of arithmetic, the absolute end of the one and only world, the end of the unique world … The survivor then remains alone … he feels solely responsible, assigned to carry both the other and *his* world, the other and the world that have disappeared, responsible without world (*weltlos*), without the ground of any world, thenceforth, in a world without world, as if without earth beyond the end of the world.[61]

You cannot tell parents who have lost *their* child to one of our horrific school shootings that it was just *a* child. That child meant the world to them, we say – and we mean it. When a loved one dies, the world disappears with them. We who remain can either accompany our loved ones in death as we did in life – and some do – or somehow we can keep going. But the only way to keep going, to keep the world going, is if we figure out how to carry them. We must recreate the world, a world in which both the *presence of their past* and the *absence of their presence* have a place.

This "carrying" of the lost world of the Other is, as Derrida says, a matter of "carrying without appropriating to oneself." It is a matter of letting oneself and one's world not simply be one's own. It is a matter of allowing an "absolute transcendence in the very inside of me."[62] A half-century earlier on the other side of the planet, the Japanese philosopher Kitarō Nishida wrote that we encounter an opening to the alterity of the Other in the very depths of the self, such that – as the successor to Nishida's successor in the Kyoto School, Shizuteru Ueda, formulates it – I am myself only insofar as I am not myself.[63] Harbouring the memory of the world of the Other, my world is no longer merely mine. Our worlds must somehow make room for and carry the worlds lost with the disappearance of each and every Other, even if only as irretrievably lost worlds.

POSTFIGURATIVE AND PREFIGURATIVE ART

Art can play a pivotal role in this carrying. Again, there are many kinds of art, and there are many roles that art can play. But the pivotal kind of art that I have in mind here operates beyond the limits of speech, beyond the meaningful or even half-meaningful words that constitute the intelligibility of our worlds, yet its post- or prefigurations nevertheless hover over the abyss of sheer meaninglessness. This kind of art is in fact two kinds, insofar as it pivots between tracing the final terrors of disappearance and sketching the first tremors of reappearance. I call these pivotal kinds of art *postfigurative* and *prefigurative* art.

Neither post- nor prefigurative art is "abstract art," even though they are most likely to be called that in today's artworld, even by the artists themselves. Since the nineteenth century, the artworld has spawned a great variety of schools and styles of abstract art, and the adjective "abstract" means something a little (or a lot) different in each case. Abstract art is usually contrasted with what is called "figurative art" or "representational art." The post- and prefigurative artworks that I have in mind are also non-representational, in the sense that they do not re-present something that pre-exists. Rather, they are "presentational" in the sense that they participate in the presentation of something no longer, or not yet, wholly meaningful or completely configured. That something might be a felt absence, a slipping-away of sense and significance, a trace of disappearance. Or it may be an anticipatory beckoning-into-birth of a novel or reconfigured sense and significance. But in neither case are these artworks "abstract" in the literal sense of "drawing out" some essential traits from something fully constituted and concretely present.

"Abstract expressionism" was, perhaps, a misnomer. What Jackson Pollock and others were doing might have been better termed "prefigurative expressionism." They did not start with a fully present and fully formed emotion or thought and then try to paint the abstract essence of it. Rather, their acts of painting were themselves prefiguratively presentational and concretely expressive.

In any case, to call the pivotal kinds of post- and prefigurative art that I have in mind here "abstract" is to misconstrue both what they are confronting and how they are responding. These artforms neither represent nor abstract from a meaningful and completely configured world. Rather, they are utterly concrete responses to a world that is in the process of either disappearing or newly arising. They are as concrete as any artform could possibly be that exposes itself to the murky mess of a reality stripped of the fabricating filters that make sense of things by means of distorting simplification. It is, after all, representational art that is abstract. Representational art always selectively simplifies – drawing, for example, clear and distinct lines between separate and static objects, where in reality there are only dynamically intermingling processes.

CHANTAL MEZA'S POSTFIGURATIVE PAINTING

The paintings of Chantal Meza are exemplary of what I am calling postfigurative art. In interviews, she is frequently asked, in one way or another, why she creates abstract paintings in response to witnessing the horrific disappearances of victims of political violence in her native Mexico and elsewhere. She usually responds by saying, in effect, that because the realities of our experiences – our perceptions as well as our feelings – are often unclear, confused, without distinct shape, this artform seems to her to be the most appropriate artistic response to such experiences. In other words, in her so-called "abstract paintings," she is being as true as possible to the concrete realities of experience.

In one interview, Meza says that "while [her] work might be abstract it is not abstracting."[64] It is as if the artworld has put a label on her work that she senses is not really appropriate. She goes on to say, "Just because something appears abstract doesn't mean to say it's not real or doesn't connect in a meaningful way to people's everyday lives. It is messy, complicated, and disrupting, because life is messy, complicated, and disrupting, especially once we factor in our emotions … Art is about showing empathy for the suffering of the world."

In response to the suffering not just of those who have been abruptly kidnapped, brutally murdered, and covertly buried but also of those who have been left behind to live in the wake of these traumatic disappearances, Meza – sometimes painting with her bare hands and working with the raw materials of the earth – offers herself, body and soul, as a vehicle for the expression of the close-up facts and raw feelings of that physical and psychological suffering.

Her paintings do not pretend to be intelligible. They barely speak. If they were audible, they would sometimes gasp and groan, sometimes mutter and murmur, and often scream and howl. They expose us to the concrete and brutal realities from which we coldly distance ourselves – not the least through our often all too abstract talking and writing about violence.

Meza's statements and writings about her art are revealing, and her collaborations with the philosopher Brad Evans – including in this volume – are insightful and thought-provoking. Plato complained that, although artists may be capable of creating inspired and inspirational works, they are unable to explain their work and especially unable to judge whether what they say is true.[65] Meza, however, is adept at talking about her work, as are many artists these days. Indeed, artists today are trained and expected to be able to interpret as well as produce their work. In our logocentric world, in which it is assumed that to be is to be linguistically meaningful, all artists are, in effect, required to be conceptual artists. An artist cannot just show her paintings; in today's artworld, she is also obligated to tell us what they mean.

The interviews and talks that Meza and other artists give often do enable us to more fully appreciate their works. Yet there is a danger here – the danger of looking away from their works as we listen to their words, and then looking back at their works only through the lenses of their words. We often do that not just with the artist's own words but also with the words of art critics and philosophers of art – words such as the ones that you are now reading. Unawares, we are apt to mistakenly come to believe that art is the practical application or concrete expression of an abstract theory.

At times, we become aware of this problem and try to counter it by saying, "We must let the artwork speak for itself!" Yet it cannot speak for itself because its medium is not language. After all, together with artists, we need art critics, philosophers of art, and artists who can reflectively interpret their own work. But we also need to be clear about what we are doing so as not to confuse these roles or expect one of them to do something that it is not intending or able to do. If the task of the artist is to show what cannot be said, I understand the task of the philosopher writing about art to be twofold. On the one hand, it is to turn the reader's attention back to the artwork in a manner that lets the artwork show itself from itself. This task is often deconstructive rather than constructive; in this case, for example, it involves dismantling the assumptions that we make when we look at Meza's work as "abstract art."

On the other hand, the task of the philosopher is to allow what the artwork *shows* to *speak*. This is an inevitably, and often fruitfully, interpretive endeavour. Many years ago, I saw a work in the Metropolitan Museum of Art that consisted of the painted letters of a saying attributed to Adorno: "Art says what philosophy cannot, by not saying it." The intentional irony of this artistic echo of Adorno's philosophical statement about art was certainly clever and thought-provoking. Yet we could also say – albeit with artless redundancy rather than artistic irony – that philosophy says what art cannot, by saying it. Philosophy is needed to say what art can only show. In view of Meza's paintings, and given the clues from her own statements about her work, the task is to write in response to the visceral visuals of her paintings, which bear witness to violent disappearance.

Meza's paintings are mainly postfigurative. They convey to us a sense of the ghastly and ghostly remains of life-worlds in the process of violent disappearance. They do not preach, and they do not plan. They are not "propaganda," she insists. And she warns us not to rush to make sense of things: "I don't try to deal with this reasonably or rationally. Such coldness is often the cause of so much cruelty, anguish, and human devastation on this planet."[66] The road to hellish violence is paved with good ideological intentions. Of course, we need political projects – demonstrations, petitions, campaigns, legislation, governance – but that is not the role of Meza's postfigurative art. Rather, her paintings expose us to the artificial limits of our well-organized worlds and to the bloody soil on which we obliviously walk to this or that predetermined destination in our busy lives. Their arresting aesthetic causes us to pause, rendering us unable to turn away too quickly from unbearable cruelty and suffering and back into blissful ignorance and amnesia. They show us that, in each case, nothing less than the world has disappeared – violently, viciously, senselessly – and that we must somehow find a way to carry this pain and this loss without either letting its memory be destroyed or letting it destroy us.

Pivoting from Postfigurative to Prefigurative Art

At least some of Meza's works – perhaps, in part, all of them – are also prefigurative. They do not just show the dissolution of the meaningful configurations of the world but also begin to gesture toward the world's reconfiguration. The large gallery installation *Mirroring the Void* and the series *The Void* are particularly noteworthy in this polysemic regard.[67] The void is, on the one hand, said to be a "mirrored sight of anguish and madness." The mirrors of art tolerate no "violating optimism," they permit "no tale of redemption or salvation" but rather coldly reflect back to us a "landscape of human devastation."[68]

Yet the void in which the hopes and dreams of countless victims are drowned is not an absolute void. An absolute void would be a complete disappearance of sense. In an absolute void, it would seem, there would no longer be even the slightest trace of sensible form, much less intelligible meaning. However, as Nishida and subsequent Kyoto School philosophers have taught us, perhaps it is better to call such sheer privation of sense and significance a "relative nothingness" since it is still defined by what it is not. Perhaps, following their lead, we should reserve the expression "absolute nothingness" for the "place" that encompasses even the opposition of determinative being and privative nothingness.[69] In any case, Daoist and Zen philosophers have long taught, and East Asian artists have long shown, that the original void is not an inert vacuity.[70] An inert void is an abstract idea. It exists neither in physics nor in experience. The concrete void is chaotic, to be sure, and to be unwillingly caste into its vortex is certainly violent. Yet the void can also be experienced as creative; its emptiness is also an amorphous field of formative energies, a plenum of possibilities.

Meza remarks in an interview that artistic creation is also, in a sense, violent; yet this artistic violence is different from the political violence to which her art responds.[71] We might recall that the Hindu god Shiva and his especially violent female consort Kali represent the divine powers of destruction – the kind of destruction that is needed for creative transformation and revitalization. It is the destruction carried out by farmers who burn their own fields in order to fertilize them, not that of invaders who burn the fields of their enemies in order to starve them.

In releasing herself voluntarily into the void, the artist may end up eventually finding herself participating in the first stirrings – in Meza's case, we might say, the first swirlings and scratchings – of the reconfiguration of the world. As predominantly postfigurative, Meza's paintings confront us with the violence of disappearance, and they commemorate the untold lives lost. Furthermore, out of the depths of the abyssal void into which her paintings compel us to peer or even to plunge arises the first prefigurative stirrings – still somewhat chaotic yet already also rhythmic swirlings and scratchings – of a new world to come, one that is capable of carrying a disappeared yet unforgotten past into an unknown yet avowed future.

Thousands upon thousands of worlds – each one *the* world – have been unceremoniously interred in unmarked graves. They lay almost entirely concealed under the blood-soaked earth on which we obliviously walk and obnoxiously talk. We must find a way to be silent and allow the living as well as the dying voices of those brutally buried worlds to be heard. And we must find a way to carry them with us as we somehow still speak, create, and make sense of the world.

Reflecting on what she has shown, Meza says, "I want to convey the thunderous cry, which echoes the devastation many are feeling, and try to awaken others with its call. This is where I truly believe art can do something positive. For what is art if not an ethically and empathetically considered testimony to the idea that we are born as collective individuals, who, forced to confront the pain of existence, still retain something magical in how we make sense of the world."[72]

NOTES

1 See Martin Heidegger's commentary on this poem in Martin Heidegger, *On the Way to Language*, trans. Peter D. Hertz (New York: HarperOne, 1971), 140–56.

2 Ludwig Wittgenstein, *Tractatus Logico-Philosophicus*, trans. D.F. Pears and B.F. McGuinness (London: Routledge and Kegan Paul, 1964), 56, original emphasis.

3 Martin Heidegger, *Elucidations of Hölderlin's Poetry*, trans. by Keith Hoeller (New York: Humanity Books, 2000), 56.

4 Hans-Georg Gadamer, *Truth and Method*, 2nd ed., trans. Joel Weinsheimer and Donald G. Marshall (New York: Continuum, 2004), 470.

5 Martin Heidegger, *Basic Writings*, 2nd ed., ed. David Farrell Krell (New York: HarperCollins, 1993), 217.

6 Ueda Shizuteru, *Zen: Kongen-teki ningen* [Zen: Original human being], *Ueda Shizuteru shū* [Collected writings of Ueda Shizuteru], vol. 4 (Tokyo: Iwanami, 2001), 387. On Ueda's understanding of human existence as an irreducible and ceaseless process of "exiting language and exiting into language," see Bret W. Davis, "Expressing Experience: Language in Ueda Shizuteru's Philosophy of Zen," in *The Dao Companion to Japanese Buddhist Philosophy*, ed. Gereon Kopf (New York: Springer, 2019), 713–38.

7 Maurice Merleau-Ponty, *Signs*, trans. Richard C. McCleary (Evanston, IL: Northwestern University Press, 1964), 120, translation modified.

8 Heidegger, *Basic Writings*, 170.

9 Ibid., 174.

10 See John Lysaker, *You Must Change Your Life: Poetry, Philosophy, and the Birth of Sense* (University Park, PA: Penn State University Press, 2002).

11 Martin Heidegger, *Bremen and Freiburg Lectures*, trans. Andrew J. Mitchell (Bloomington: Indiana University Press, 2012), 16; Heidegger, *Basic Writings*, 351.
12 Heidegger, *Basic Writings*, 172–4.
13 See Aristotle, *Nicomachean Ethics*, bk 1, ch. 7, 1098, sec. a; and Aristotle, *Politics*, bk 1, ch. 2, 1253, sec. a.
14 Heidegger, *Basic Writings*, 197–8, original emphasis.
15 Dennis J. Schmidt, *Between Word and Image: Heidegger, Klee, and Gadamer on Gesture and Image* (Bloomington: Indiana University Press, 2013), 12.
16 Hans-Georg Gadamer, *Gesammelte Werke*, vol. 8 (Tübingen: J.C.B. Mohr, 1993), 197, quoted in Schmidt, *Between Image and Word*, 5.
17 Schmidt, *Between Image and Word*, 132–3.
18 See Larry Shiner, *The Invention of Art: A Cultural History* (Chicago: University of Chicago Press, 2003).
19 Paul Klee, *Kunst-Lehre* (Leipzig: Reclam, 1987), 60, quoted in John Sallis, *Transfigurements: On the True Sense of Art* (Chicago: University of Chicago Press, 2008), 19.
20 For insightful and provocative philosophical interpretations of this artform, see François Jullien, *The Great Image Has No Form, or On the Nonobject through Painting*, trans. Jane Marie Todd (Chicago: University of Chicago Press, 2009); and François Jullien, *Living Off Landscape, or The Unthought-of in Reason*, trans. Pedro Rodriguez (Lanham, MD: Rowman and Littlefield, 2018).
21 See Ari M. Beser, "In Nagasaki, New Art Exhibit 'Antimonument' Rethinks the Bomb," *National Geographic*, 20 August 2015, https://blog.nationalgeographic.org/2015/08/20/in-nagasaki-new-art-exhibit-antimonument-rethinks-the-bomb.
22 Hans Ruin, *Being with the Dead: Burial, Ancestral Practices, and the Roots of Historical Consciousness* (Stanford, CA: Stanford University Press, 2018), 24.
23 Martin Heidegger, *Sein und Zeit*, 17th ed. (Tübingen: Max Niemeyer Verlag, 1993), 238–9, adopting Hans Ruin's translation.
24 Ruin, *Being with the Dead*, 29.
25 For a landmark anthology on memorial art among other forms of cultural memory, see *A Companion to Cultural Memory Studies*, ed. Asrtid Erll and Ansgar Nünning (Berlin and New York: De Gruyter, 2010). In his introduction to the volume, Erll stresses the necessarily interdisciplinary character of cultural memory studies, given that it is "concerned with social, medial, *and* cognitive processes, and their ceaseless interplay" (6, original emphasis). The present essay focuses on some enigmatic philosophical issues at stake in that interplay.

26 I further discuss the issues facing Bhutan in Bret W. Davis, "Cultural Identity and the End of Happiness: Two Dilemmas and Other Lessons from Bhutan," forthcoming.

27 The National Democratic Front of Boroland was an Indian separatist group whose members had built camps in Bhutanese territory from which they were conducting raids on the government of their native Indian state of Assam. Unsurprisingly, the official Bhutanese account of this battle is contested; for example, see Kaustubh Deka, "Preserved in Bhutan's 108 Chortens: A Saga of Blood and Bonhomie," *East Mojo*, 12 November 2018, https://www.eastmojo.com/news/2018/11/12/preserved-in-bhutans-108-chortens-a-saga-of-blood-and-bonhomie.

28 The 2014 guidebook *Bhutan*, published by Lonely Planet, does report that the *chortens* were "built in 2005 as atonement for the loss of life caused by the flushing out of the Assamese militants" (94). Yet tourist reports on the Internet generally correspond to the statement on Wikipedia that the chortens "were built as a memorial in honour of the Bhutanese soldiers who were killed in the December 2003 battle against Assamese insurgents from India." Does this interpretation reflect a confirmation bias on the part of tourists, who may tend to assume that countries memorialize their own dead?

29 Carl Schmitt, *The Concept of the Political*, trans. G. Schwab (Chicago: University of Chicago Press, 2007), 26.

30 Simone Weil, *Intimations of Christianity among the Ancient Greeks* (New York: Routledge, 1957), 74–5.

31 Ibid., 48, 51.

32 See Nikole Hannah-Jones, Caitlin Roper, Ilena Silverman, and Jake Silverstein, eds, *The 1619 Project: A New Origin Story* (New York: One World, 2021).

33 Giorgio Agamben, *Remnants of Auschwitz: The Witness and the Archive*, trans. Daniel Heller-Roazen (New York: Zone Books, 2002).

34 Ibid., ch. 3.

35 James E. Young writes the following with regard to the motives of the artists who have produced "counter-monuments" to the Holocaust: "Instead of searing memory into public consciousness, they fear, conventional memorials seal memory off from awareness altogether; instead of embodying memory, they find that memorials may only displace memory. These artists fear rightly that to the extent that we encourage monuments to do our memory-work for us, we become that much more forgetful. They believe, in effect, that the initial impulse to memorialize events like the Holocaust may actually spring from an opposite and equal desire to forget them." James E. Young, "The Texture of Memory: Holocaust Memorials in History," in

A Companion to Cultural Memory Studies, ed. Asrtid Erll and Ansgar Nünning, 357–65 (Berlin and New York: De Gruyter, 2010), 360.

36 For a variety of approaches to various forms of political violence, see Brad Evans and Terrell Carver, eds, *Histories of Violence: Post-War Critical Thought* (London: Zed Books, 2017); Brad Evans and Natasha Lennard, eds, *Violence: Humans in Dark Times* (San Francisco: City Lights Publishers, 2018); and Brad Evans and Adrian Parr, eds, *Conversations on Violence: An Anthology* (London: Pluto, 2021).

37 On the need to avoid a zero-sum competition between efforts to memorialize the various atrocities of genocide and colonialism, see Michael Rothberg, *Multidirectional Memory: Remembering the Holocaust in the Age of Decolonialization* (Stanford, CA: Stanford University Press, 2009).

38 As someone who lived for many years in Japan and who still speaks Japanese at home, I also feel compelled to add that Japanese society as a whole has largely failed to address its colonializing past and the atrocities that Japanese soldiers committed in Nanjing and elsewhere during the Second Sino-Japanese War.

39 See David E. Stannard, *American Holocaust: Columbus and the Conquest of the New World* (New York: Oxford University Press, 1992); and Tzvetan Todorov, *The Conquest of America: The Question of the Other*, trans. Richard Howard (Norman: University of Oklahoma Press, 1999). For a philosophical study of the loss of world that the Crow Nation experienced when its people lost their way of life, see Jonathan Lear, *Radical Hope: Ethics in the Face of Cultural Devastation* (Cambridge, MA: Harvard University Press, 2006). For a more in-depth treatment of the displaced and suppressed, yet never entirely destroyed, worldviews of Native Americans, see Vine Deloria Jr, *God Is Red: A Native View of Religion*, 30th ed. (Golden, CO: Fulcrum, 2003). And let us not forget the legacies of colonial and political violence in Latin American countries – violence in which the United States has often played a significant role.

In an online seminar held on 21 April 2021, María del Rosario Acosta López, as the Chaire internationale de philosophie contemporaine de l'Université Paris 8, insightfully lectured on the work of the Colombian artist Clemencia Echeverri and then led an illuminating discussion with Echeverri, whose powerful postfigural work *Duelos* was the inaugural installation at the "countermonument" and exhibition space Fragmentos: Espacio de Arte y Memoria, designed by Doris Salcedo and built around the ruins of a colonial house in the historic centre of Bogotá. The uneven floor of the Fragmentos space is made from weapons surrendered by the guerrillas of the Fuerzas Armadas Revolucionarias de Colombia after the peace agreement of

2017. The weapons were melted down and poured into moulds hammered out by victims of sexual violence during the decades of conflict. See José Roca, "And When Do the Disappeared Return? Each Time We Think of Them," *Universe in Universe Magazine*, November 2019, https://universes.art/en/magazine/articles/2019/duelos.

40 On the traumatically disorienting "afterlives of slavery," see Saidiya Hartman, *Lose Your Mother: A Journey along the Atlantic Slave Route* (New York: Farrar, Straus and Giroux, 2007); and Christina Sharpe, *In the Wake: On Blackness and Being* (Durham, NC: Duke University Press, 2016). On the ongoing history of racism against African Americans and their resilience in confronting it, see Ibram X. Kendi, *Stamped from the Beginning: The Definitive History of Racist Ideas in America* (New York: Nation Books, 2016); and Isabel Wilkerson, *Caste: The Origins of Our Discontents* (New York: Random House, 2020).

41 Campbell Robertson, "A Lynching Memorial Is Opening: The Country Has Never Seen Anything Like It," *New York Times*, 25 April 2018, https://www.nytimes.com/2018/04/25/us/lynching-memorial-alabama.html.

42 Heidegger, *Basic Writings*, 174, 202.

43 Ibid., 186.

44 The literature on Heidegger's complicity with Nazism is extensive. A good place to start is the concise account given by Charles Bambach, "Heidegger, National Socialism, and the German People," in *Martin Heidegger: Key Concepts*, ed. Bret W. Davis, 102–15 (Durham, UK: Acumen, 2010). For my own attempts to understand the abhorrently aberrant episode of Heidegger's embrace of National Socialism in the context of the development of his path of thought as a whole, see Bret W. Davis, *Heidegger and the Will: On the Way to Gelassenheit* (Evanston, IL: Northwestern University Press, 2007), especially ch. 3; and Bret W. Davis, "Heidegger on the Way from Onto-Historical Ethnocentrism to East-West Dialogue," *Gatherings: The Heidegger Circle Annual* 6 (2016): 130–56.

45 See Martin Heidegger, *Introduction to Metaphysics*, 2nd ed., trans. Gregory Fried and Richard Polt (New Haven, CT: Yale University Press, 2014), 166–7.

46 See Martin Heidegger, *Country Path Conversations*, trans. Bret W. Davis (Bloomington: Indiana University Press, 2016), 37–42, 48–50, 67–71, 79, 92–101, 143. For an in-depth study of this pivotal turn in Heidegger's thought, see Davis, *Heidegger and the Will*; and for a sketch, see Bret W. Davis, "Will and Gelassenheit," in Davis, *Martin Heidegger*, 168–82.

47 See Pierre Bourdieu, "Back to History: An Interview," in *The Heidegger Controversy*, ed. Richard Wolin, 264–71 (Cambridge, MA: MIT Press, 1993), 267.

48 Jacques Derrida, "Heidegger's Silence," in *Martin Heidegger and National Socialism*, ed. Günter Neske and Emil Kettering, 145–8 (New York: Paragon House, 1990), 148.

49 Martin Heidegger, *Was heißt denken?* 4th ed. (Tübingen: Max Niemeyer Verlag), 159, my translation. This passage is not included in the English translation.

50 Heidegger, *Bremen and Freiburg Lectures*, 27.

51 Theodor Adorno, *Can One Live after Auschwitz? A Philosophical Reader*, ed. Rolf Tiedemann (Stanford, CA: Stanford University Press, 2003), xv.

52 Ibid., xvi.

53 See Martin Woessner, *Heidegger in America* (Cambridge, UK: Cambridge University Press, 2011), 253–62.

54 "The Libeskind Building: Architecture Retells German-Jewish History," Jewish Museum Berlin, n.d., https://www.jmberlin.de/en/libeskind-building.

55 Ibid.

56 "The idea was first conceived by artist Gunter Demning in Cologne in 1992 as part of an initiative commemorating Roma and Sinti victims of the Holocaust." Since then, Demning has personally laid more than 70,000 *Stolpersteine* all across Europe and Russia, and in 2005 he began to rely on the craftsman Michael Friedrichs-Friedländer to engrave each one by hand. Eliza Apperly, "'Stumbling Stones': A Different Vision of Holocaust Remembrance," *Guardian* (London), 18 February 2019, https://www.theguardian.com/cities/2019/feb/18/stumbling-stones-a-different-vision-of-holocaust-remembrance.

57 Heidegger, *Country Path Conversations*, 133.

58 See Hugo Ott, *Martin Heidegger: A Political Life*, trans. Allan Blunden (New York: HarperCollins, 1993), 172–86.

59 Rüdiger Safranski, *Martin Heidegger: Between Good and Evil*, trans. Ewald Osers (Cambridge, MA: Harvard University Press, 1998), 422.

60 Cited in ibid., 423.

61 Jacques Derrida, *Sovereignties in Question: The Poetics of Paul Celan*, ed. Thomas Dutoit and Outi Pasanen (New York: Fordham University Press, 2005), 140, original emphasis.

62 Ibid., 161.

63 See Bret W. Davis, "Ethical and Religious Alterity: Nishida after Levinas," in *Kitarō Nishida in der Philosophie des 20. Jahrhunderts*, ed. Rolf Elberfeld and Yōko Arisaka, 313–41 (Freiburg and Munich: Alber Verlag, 2014).

64 In Brad Evans, "The Intimate Witness: Art and the Disappeared of History," interview with Chantal Meza, *Los Angeles Review of Books*, 22 October 2018, https://lareviewofbooks.org/article/histories-of-violence-when-art-confronts-the-denial-of-life.

65 Plato, *Laws*, bk 4, 719c–d. Elsewhere, Plato stresses that artworks are not merely representational but also mimetic, imitations of particulars, which are in turn imitations of forms. They are thus twice removed from true reality. See Plato *Republic*, bk 10.

66 In Evans, "Intimate Witness."

67 See Chantal Meza, *Mirroring the Void*, https://www.chantal-meza.com/mirroringthevoid; and Chantal Meza, *The Void*, https://www.chantal-meza.com/stateofdisappearance.

68 Brad Evans, "Mirrors of the Void," n.d., https://www.chantal-meza.com/_files/ugd/dde864_8d4c7cbb48284998a83a3bf9b0370aed.pdf.

69 See John C. Maraldo, "Nishida Kitarō's Philosophy: Self, World, and the Nothingness Underlying Distinctions," in *The Oxford Handbook of Japanese Philosophy*, ed. Bret W. Davis, 417–30 (New York: Oxford University Press, 2020); and Bret W. Davis, "The Kyoto School," section 3, in *Stanford Encyclopedia of Philosophy Archive*, Summer 2019 ed., ed. Edward N. Zalta, http://plato.stanford.edu/archives/sum2019/entries/kyoto-school/.

70 See Jeeloo Liu and Douglas L. Berger, eds, *Nothingness in Asian Philosophy* (New York: Routledge, 2014); Jullien, *Great Image Has No Form*; Bret W. Davis, "Forms of Emptiness in Zen," in *A Companion to Buddhist Philosophy*, ed. Steven Emmanuel, 190–213 (West Sussex: Wiley-Blackwell, 2013); and Bret W. Davis, *Zen Pathways: An Introduction to the Philosophy and Practice of Zen Buddhism* (New York: Oxford University Press, 2022), ch. 19.

71 Chantal Meza in the video interview with Brad Evans at https://www.chantal-meza.com/stateofdisappearance.

72 In Evans, "Intimate Witness."

2

A Murder of Possibilities: The Altricidal State as a Robinsonade

Mangalika de Silva

> Surviving – that is the other name of a mourning whose possibility is never to be awaited.
>
> Jacques Derrida

> For the signifier is a unit in its very uniqueness, being by nature symbol only of an absence.
>
> Jacques Lacan

CAPTURED BY CATASTROPHE

In 2009, M was in the midst of a raging war in northern Sri Lanka – a war against witnessing disapparition. Since 2008, she, her husband, and their five children had been refugees on the move as they fled on foot from the precipice of uninhabitable "free fire zones" instigated by security forces in a dizzying coda to South Asia's longest war. They lived in improvised underground bunkers hastily assembled from sarees, sandbags, trees, and mangled furniture retrieved from charred houses. When shelled, they abandoned their precarious refuge, running from ruin to ruin. In March 2009, M witnessed the shelling of a hut that killed the blind adults and children sheltering within. As she searched for relatives of the deceased to assist in burial, an army truck (painted white) suddenly pulled up, and state security forces began rounding up children, who scattered out of fear of the notorious white vans associated with political abductions. In the pandemonium, M witnessed her daughter being whisked into the white van, and she rushed to grab the child despite being beaten repeatedly. Mother and daughter were driven away. The truck screeched to a halt at a desolate intersection,

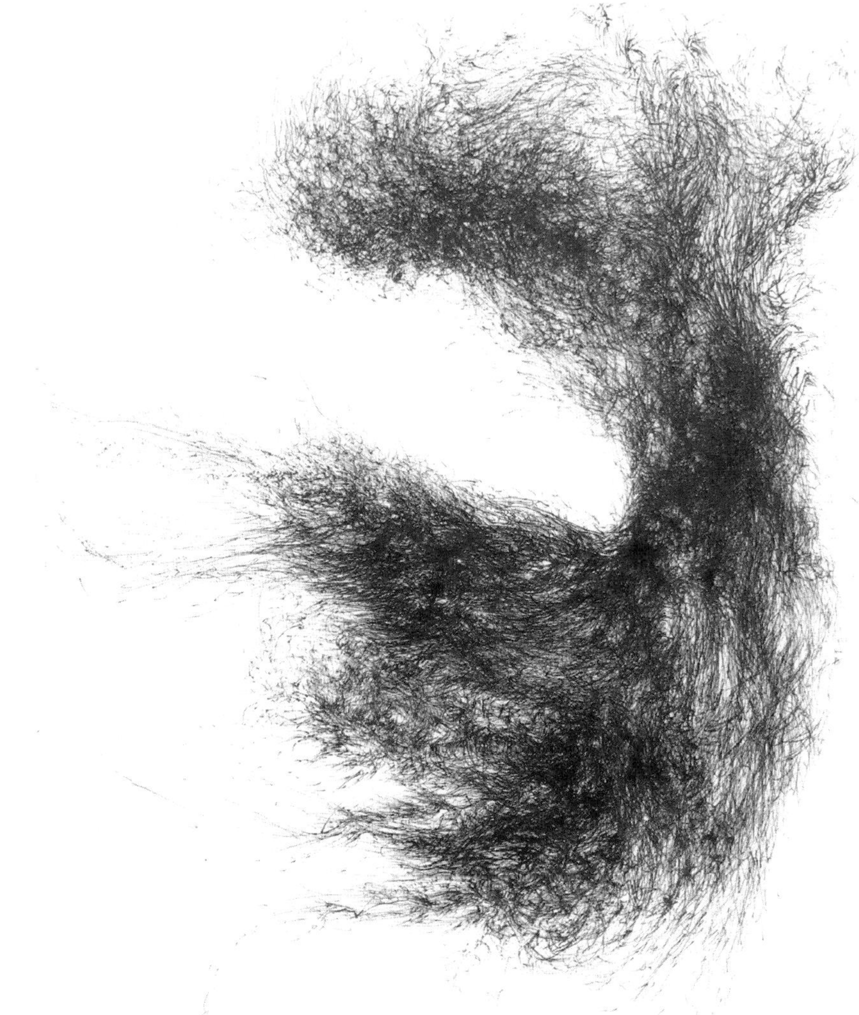

Chantal Meza, *Apparitions IX*, 2017, ink on paper, 35 x 27 cm

where the soldiers assaulted M and threw her on the roadside. She was later reunited with her remaining family members and escaped the advancing troops. The family were apprehended in May 2009 and interned just before the war ended. After extensive mandatory security screenings, they were released six months later.

Upon returning to her village, M petitioned government agencies in search of her daughter. In 2014, the district office of military intelligence summoned her to ask whether she still believed her daughter to be alive. She reminded the officer of the army's repeated assurance that her child was in state custody, at which point the officer countered, "Thousands of children have disappeared during the war … Your daughter is most likely dead." M retorted, "You took my child away and now you say she is not in your custody … If my child is no more, then why do you keep dragging me to your office?"

The state, as a will to truth, demanded an avowal of her daughter's death as an indemnifying confirmation of wartime impunity and postwar normalization. M disdained the hegemonic postwar periodization and immunized her abjection and loss from this falsified historiography. The sovereign command for an avowal of her daughter's death inflicted testimonial inequity wherein the police, as an entrenched epistemic power, pre-empted what could be known and said – and by whom – concerning the war and its repercussions.

In 2015, a propaganda vehicle appeared in M's village distributing campaign leaflets for Maithripala Sirisena, former wartime Cabinet minister turned presidential candidate. This manifesto printed in Tamil targeted the occupied population, declaring, "Sirisena's vision: Let us cultivate, let us develop the nation … to enhance its agriculture. Truly, this will help farmers to become kings in their field." Complementing its rhetoric of pastoral guidance, the leaflet foregrounded a photograph of Sirisena as a paternal-sovereign figure hovering over a group of girls in school uniforms. M's children brought these pamphlets home and arranged them on the floor out of sheer curiosity. They silently identified their missing sister among the bevy of photographed girls. On election day in January 2015, M happened to take a cursory glance at the leaflet but quickly spurned it. After Sirisena won a resounding electoral victory, M was forced to contend with the incredulous and gathered her neighbours to authenticate her missing child in the photo. Other missing children in the photograph were identified by the neighbours.

M met with President Sirisena in August 2015, urging his personal intervention. He denied any responsibility for her tragedy, saying her daughter had disappeared under his predecessor's regime, although he promised help if evidence of her abduction was produced. She placed the leaflet in his hands, drawing his attention to her daughter and three other girls in the photo identified by their kin as disappeared. M claimed the photo was taken after her child's disappearance in 2009 and that after the war the girls were kept in a secret location and raised "in the habits and customs" of the Sinhala Buddhist majority. The uniform, tie, and badge worn by her daughter in the photo conformed to Buddhist school dress codes and insignia. The president was visibly shaken.

The newly elected Sirisena regime pledged that those still held in detention without charge would be released and that the National Security Council would make public lists of detainees, political prisoners, and persons who surrendered to the army in the final phase of warfare. Sirisena himself denied any knowledge of "secret detention camps." When mothers insisted on their existence, he offered them a chance to break the deadlock: if they could identify any place, he would authorize the police to accompany them to such camps and to search for the missing. This offer, however, did not include organized and funded searches and excavations by forensic experts for clandestine mass burial grounds. Nor did it involve investigations of orphanages and their records of children adopted by surrogate Sinhalese parents. Rather, Sirisena instituted an Office of Missing Persons to issue "Certificates of Absence" and to pay compensation to families who could document missing relatives whose deaths they could not certify. In early 2017, Prime Minister Ranil Wickremesinghe of the Sirisena government informed the families that their children were presumed to be dead.

When a team of presidential investigators visited M's hometown, they were keen to ascertain not the child's disappearance but documentary proof of the child's birth and existence, despite being shown her state identification card, dated 2008. Linked to the commodification of disappearance through promised reparations, state forensics shifted from abduction to natality. Enforced disappearance denies the right to cohabitation but also the right to natality (*natio*) within the nation-state. The police's charge of "natal falsification" indicated the extent to which forensics of the disappeared could effectively be transformed into a disciplinary apparatus, a coercive technology of memory wherein certain forms of witnessing and its supportive artifacts became inadmissible. To fabricate a nonexistent daughter and her nonexistent abduction was an intolerable ekphrastic crime of making the inexistent real. Such a prerogative could only be a monopoly of a state ideologically invested both in the virtualizing power of disappearance and in the refutation of any past accountability. The state's injunction to forget placed the emphasis less on amnesia and more on the recall and avowal of a hyperbolic fixed memory of the war.

DELETION DOUBLED: THE LOSS OF LOSS

Despite the school administration's authentication of the girl's photograph and thus the truth of her existence prior to 2009, the military intelligence was intransigent and fanatically invested in ridding the land of regressive terrorism, including the "fabrications" and mourning ceremonies of Tamil women. The daughter's National Identification Card assumed a contaminated metonymy with the mother since through the card, M established herself as a conduit of the absent, who resisted being harmonized, pacified, curbed, or disappeared and who obtruded into the maw of statist auto-indemnification. M fell under police surveillance and was routinely summoned by intelligence services for serial cross-examination. She was accused of a crime she did not commit – of not giving birth. Her daughter was twice disappeared through a symbolic abortion: she was kidnapped and subsequently disincarnated and stripped of natality, citizenship, and law to render M's case nonactionable. It was as though M was advocating for an illegal immigrant, not for a Sri Lankan citizen, which recalls the treacherous legacy of anti-Tamil epistemologies. M assumed ontological ground and the demand for location, which impelled her to complain, "My child matters! … Where is my daughter?" The assumptive logic of military intelligence perversely turned the girl into a phantasm of the defeated. M's plea exacerbated the core conundrum of postwar periodization – the contradiction between Tamilness and ontology as personified in the nonbeing of M's daughter.

This mise en scène of institutional doubt and indemnity attests to how the event of disappearance recursively rescripts the civil biography of both the disappeared and the survivor. The regime of disapparition analeptically takes recourse to the falsification of the pre-disappearance past, thereby submitting victims to a recursive time axis in order to proleptically arrive at a desired outcome that invalidates those who possess the power of ekphrastic evocation/invocation. The women of the postwar polity, replete with their absentees – the dead, the disappeared, the missing, the exiled, the deported, and the detained – demand an absence *from* historical absence. Sri Lanka's forensically disqualified survivors are pre-emptively denied the right to earth as the right to a portentous natality that conjoins potential, potency, and portent as defining future political interlocutors. This Arendtian focus on natal cohabitation on the surface of the earth is resonant with, yet more fundamental than, Carl Schmitt's concept of the nomos of the earth. Hannah Arendt identifies the visual logic of genocide as an aphanisis that withholds the right of certain populations to appear on the earth; genocide and campaigns of enforced disappearance fuse the withholding of a right to cohabitation with the refusal of natality (*natio*) within the territorial unit of the nation-state. Arendt foregrounds the co-originarity of earth and cohabitation as the condition of possibility of all law. Being denied the possibility of earthly ontology is part and parcel of being denied law's possibility. For Arendt, the right to the earth and cohabitation originates the *right to rights* as the locus of inceptual natality before all states and their laws, including, but exceeding, birth certificates and legal entitlements.

EKPHRASIS/APHANISIS

Quintilian emplaces the aesthetic operations of *phantazein* (*visiones* in Latin) within forensics, arguing that *phantasia* (φαντασία) is integral to *ekphrasis* as the discursive faculty of representing absent things with convincing vividness (*evidentia in narratione*), which relates the effect of beholding (*graphike enargheia*) through speech and writing what is historically or perceptually withdrawn from the immediacy of the present – a testimonial condition undergone by the survivors of the disappeared. The Greek *phantazein* (φαντάζειν) means "to make visible," and *phanein* (*φαίνειν*) is "to show." *Phantasma* derives from *phainesthai* (to shine forth). Aristotle uses *emphasis* (ἔμφασις), derived from *phainesthai*, to refer to the visual effect of *anaklasis* as a "break *within*" or an obstacle to vision.[1]

Phantazein cannot be detached from *aphanisis* (disapparition). For Jacques Lacan, aphanisis occurs as a disappearance of the subject constitutive of that subject: "Aphanisis is to be situated in a more radical way at the level at which the subject manifests itself in this movement of disappearance, the fading of the subject."[2] Subjectivation originates not with apparition but in disapparition.[3] Subjectifying aphanisis is the splitting of the subject-in-lack by desire, which detaches the subject from a field of previous, positivizing psychic investments. Lacanian aphanisis is processual – *aphanisios* (to make disappear) – rather than a passive and instantaneous disappearance. Lacan does not deploy the abrupt binary of presence/absence but implicitly stresses an interval – temporal, spatial, affective, and sensorial – between disappearance and aphanisis. This elongation of absence into emergent apparition infers that aphanisis does not abrogate subject formation but galvanizes a becoming that subsumes prior subject positions.

Although Lacan is focused on the Cartesian subject, we can ask what ultimately counts as the subject here and where the ordering of lack and desire is to be located. Lacanian aphanisis intersects with late-modern notions of the subject in literature and cinema as riven by biographical discontinuity, ellipses, gaps, and *contretemps* that desubjectify by foreclosing memory, intentionality, and action. The modern subject – once presumed to be invested with full presence by Enlightenment schema of self-determination, autonomy, rights, and individuated sovereignty – is here reconfigured as the ekphrastic screen of absence and discontinuity marred by liminality and lacunae. The modern aphanisic subject cannot be easily detached from the particular modernity inaugurated by racial capitalism and by settler colonial terror as aphanisis writ large; nor can this eclipsed subject be divorced from the struggle of the ekphrastic witness to escape the ruins of a history not well lived.

Aphanisis as statist power confers desubjectivation as a prerequisite of resubjectivation and conjures ekphrastic supplementation as fantasy, imputation, and political program. Disappearance instigates ekphrastic outcomes by fantasizing culpability in the sheer act of being disappeared. The psychic infrastructure of Lacanian aphanisis inflects political regimes of vanishment under which the chosen deportee undergoes an erasure, fading, and ellipses that resubjectify and interpellate the latter in accordance to a master predicate and transcendental signifiers, be they "Black," "Muslim," "terrorist," "immigrant," or "minority." Aphanisis as reapparition is an extraordinary rendition that returns a surplus of proxy culpable alterities. Statist aphanisis is the needful deletion of those who impinge on terrestrial habitus and completes its fantasy by making them reappear as transgressive alterity ex post facto. Ekphrastic disappearance often invokes the racialized and autochthonous purity of a past without Arendtian cohabitation – that is, without heterotopic difference. Through ostracization and denial, it disappears the prior existence of the disappeared by rescripting and remediating a contaminated contemporaneity as a purified past made present and future.

Disappearance solidifies state fantasy but equally drives the ekphrastic imaginings of the stranded survivors of the disappeared. The latter experience vanishment in accordance with Aristotle's concept of *emphasis* and *anaklasis* as a break in perception and memory that accelerates compensating fantasy – an imaginary of the absentee and deportee that compels the ekphrastic tactics of survivors to publicly make what is absent present as they seek the return or redress of what and who has been stolen. Aphanisis is aligned with a transgression that splinters the symbolic community to which the lapsed subjecthood of victim and survivor once belonged. In this schema, the politically disappeared subsist at the extremity of the social order, its political and historical precipice, where these floating bodies form Jacques Derrida's border of the border. Their formation as societal lack delineates a perceptual crisis at the thresholds of a polity that signals the end of what has been convened as postwar periodization as a political consensus. Derrida writes, "But let me be clear – the experience of an absence of horizon is not one that has no horizon at all; it is where the horizon is, in a sense, 'punctured' by the other. With the coming of the other, there is a non-horizon."[4] In being utterly alienated through disavowal, disinformation, and therapeutically enforced amnesia, the disappeared personify a mnemic frontier that ignites ekphrastic evocation by survivors. Derrida writes of a broken threshold of invasive alterity that originates in aphanisis: "Each time the decision concerns the choice between the relation to another who is *its* other (that is to say, an other that can be opposed in a couple) and the relations to a *wholly, non-opposable, other*, that is, an other that is no longer *its* other. What is at stake in the first place is therefore not the crossing of a given border. Rather, at stake is the *double concept of the border*, from which this aporia comes to be determined."[5]

For Slavoj Žižek, aphanisis opens up a terrain where the political unconscious becomes a tool of sovereign power that disfigures the core ensembles of everyday life.[6] Disappearance not only abstracts the vanished fraction of the population from itself but also abstracts and alienates a now entirely inoperative polity from itself. This incision obstructs ekphrastic recuperation of the missing in public and private spheres. The political unconscious inculcated by state aphanisis is the spreading of the unspoken threat against illicit avowal by those who demand a right to know and by those communities left bereft by the subtracted. Intimidated survivors respond to their own possible *hetero*-aphanisis from without by performing an *auto*-aphanisis from within as self-censorship. Civil subjects, in observing a self-enforced silence about disappearances, relinquish their symbolic citizenship by virtually vanishing from the public sphere in order to forestall their anticipated material disappearance from the polity in toto and, in so doing, find themselves exiled to the unpolitical.

Aphanisis – whether threatened, collectively endured, or witnessed – generates an irreducible discordance whose effect is such that the instituted narratives that sustain selfhood no longer make sense. This dissonance is equated with the loss of a self to make sense of and sense with. As Arendt suggests, as the withdrawal of a right to the terrestrial surface, political aphanisis disrupts quotidian experience by dissolving concepts of space and time that sustain selfhood and inflicts a social death upon those who anticipate internal deportation but have yet to disappear.[7] The oscillation of the survivor-subject between social presence and absence, whether inflicted from without or within, is irrevocably entwined with the collapse of individual and collective narratives that support subject positions, however previously precarious. To name the disappeared, to search for the missing, is to risk self-defacement. Auto-aphanisis begins when desiring survivors are constrained by cognitive segregation from contributing to the stock of shared knowledge and meanings – the pool of concepts and tropes at work in a society gripped by programmed forgetting and disavowal. The witness is silenced through testimonial pre-emption, a logocentric aphanisis inflicted by a subjugating speech economy. Conversely, in persisting to speak of the disavowed, survivors commit to auto-ekphrasis in fantasizing their now elapsed epistemic and linguistic citizenship. This mutilation of the epistemic economy is akin to W.J.T. Mitchell's ekphrastic indifference, defined as that which has been erased, secreted, classified, destroyed as evidence, and otherwise historically foreclosed and whose disfigurement cannot be recuperated.[8] This foreclosure of speech, of the public exercise of the right to know, indexes the cognitive power of a testimonial injustice, defined as the injurious pre-emption of what can be known and said, and by whom, in afflicted societies. Prohibiting interlocution forecloses testimonial avowal that disrupts the *dejà-dit*, the already said. Justice seekers are wronged in their very capacity to make knowledge claims, to exercise a right to ekphrasis as the witnessing of the vanished by a political order founded on criminal impunity.[9]

BLINDNESS AND WITNESSING

The state's lack of a relation to visual evidence constitutes an "opthalmo-pathology" concerning the very birth and abduction of M's child.[10] The anguished mother is treated as doubly blinded in envisaging the disappearance of an "unborn" child twice rendered inexistent by the state. The child disappears from her birth and then from her own disappearance and possible death – *the absence of absence.* The mother must now demonstrate "proof of life," a burden customarily borne by abductors, before the state will allow M's demand for habeas corpus or certify "proofs of absence." Derrida's opthalmo-pathology is a chronic condition that anticipates the demise of the witness: "The staring eye always resembles an eye of the blind, sometimes the eye of the dead at that precise moment when mourning begins; it is still open, a pious hand should soon come to close it; it would recall a portrait of the dying."[11]

Post-atrocity witnessing emerges from two blinding traumas: the survivors' unassimilable experience of the event and the inadmissibility of evidentiary testimony for institutional memory. Derrida assigns the trope of blindness to the errancy of the dislocated witness, an errancy metaphorized as the blindness of one who, although devoid of perceptual immediacy and thus retinal veridiction, has access to absence:

> Subject to being mistaken, the blind man is also the subject of punishment. As soon as it is assigned a meaning, the blow that makes one lose one's sight inscribes sacrifice into the economic representation of a kind of justice. This fatality is all the more intractable in that it follows a law of retribution or compensation, of exchange and equivalence. The logic of punishment overlaps and recovers the logic of acquittal or repayment … Turning into martyrdom, and thus into witnessing, blindness is often the price to pay for anyone who must finally open some eyes, his own or another's, in order to recover a natural sight or gain access to a spiritual light. The paradox stems from the fact that the blind man thus becomes the best witness, a chosen witness. In fact, a witness,

> as such, is always blind. Witnessing substitutes narration for perception. The witness cannot see, show, and speak at the same time, and the interest of the attestation, like that of the testament, stems from this dissociation. No authentification can show in the present what the most reliable of witnesses sees, or rather, has seen and now keeps in memory – provided that he has not been borne away by fire. (And as for the witnesses of Auschwitz, like those of all extermination camps, there is here an abominable resource for all "revisionist" denials.)[12]

The blind witness subverts law's commensuration of blindness and impartiality. In its penalized persona and civic disability, the juridical personality of the blinded witness incarnates a theatre of sacrifice and punition all at once. The blind witness becomes the uncanny interlocutor from the outside, the shunned seer and alien diviner in the polis whose troubling difference is amplified in an interminable adherence to witnessing the unwitnessable that contests omnivoyant state power. The blind witness bears the pollution, the scandal, and the miasma that the polity can only disavow and deface. The witness to war crimes, rendered juridically and perceptually disabled, politically inconvenient, and discursively impertinent, is a sacrificial surrogate (the original sacrifice being the dead and the disappeared) whose amputation from historiography, cultural sensibility, and the evidentiary sutures a community of denial and impunity from the wounding contamination of war. Their invalidation is not marginal but axial to the postwar pathway to the surplus dividends of "peace."

A POSTCARD FROM THE EDGE

The image in the election brochure is a triangulated composition of optical governmentality. The presidential candidate occupies the vertical apex around which the children orbit. According to Jean-Luc Nancy, "the sovereign is at the height because the height separates the top from the bottom and frees the former from the humility of the latter: from the humus … and from extended things in general."[13] These figures dramatize the optics of pastoral power, where an executive power – God, pastor, the king – guides the "flock" toward well-being and maintains them on the "right path."[14] The sovereign's apparition in the photo amidst unnamed and perhaps unnameable (Tamil) children establishes his circumdomination over them – a dominion in which the sovereign, like Robinson Crusoe on his island, exercises the right to name and to individuate and therefore to unname and to disappear all the denizens of his encircling realm.[15] This right to name and unname as the bestowal and refusal of rights is dramatized by Sirisena's disavowing muteness in response to M's identification of her child and other lost children in the photo.

The political sadism of disappearance instigates the insularity, solitude, and solipsism of an islanded autochthony – a Robinsonade, which is to say, a world without the other that is the imperative of genocide. Gilles Deleuze contends that the perversion of the sadist lies in making the other suffer not because he desires the spectacle of suffering but because the sadist's violence deprives the other of the "quality of otherness."[16] The sadist makes a world where "the other-structure is lacking."[17] As Deleuze writes, "The world of the pervert is a world without other and thereby a world without possibility. The other is what possibilizes ... All perversion is *autruicide*, altricide, a murder of possibilities. But *altricide* is not committed by perverse behavior, it is presupposed in the perverse structure."[18] The sadism of the Robinsonade, to which the disappearance of difference belongs, posits a deficient anti-world lacking an other-structure. If, as Deleuze claims, all perversion is a murder of possibilities, what possibilizes here is the gaze of the mothers intruding on the pastoral perversion of Sri Lanka, with its falsified and coercive reconciliation of victors and vanquished. Pastoral power that seeks to isolate the body politic from exterior peril and to master internal difference is perverse since it aligns its constitutive subject with the evacuation of any extimate subject who harbours an other-structure of possibility.

There is a lacerating aphanisis at the core of the image; the sovereign figure posed as the shepherd of the children was part of the regime that engineered Tamil genocide and incarcerated thousands within an apparatus of disappearance and secretive, anonymized mass burials. The image encrypts the negativity of cynegetic (predatory) power as the precondition of its pastoral iconography. Gregor Chamayou remarks that "cynegetic power is exercised over prey, living beings that escape and flee."[19] He observes that whereas the shepherd walks in front of his flock to guide them, the predator pursues from behind to ensnare and consume. These two postures encapsulate the performative front space and dehistoricized backspace of the pastoral phantasmagoria of the leaflet.

The mothers' disruptive gaze detaches the missing daughters from their saccharine encirclement in the photo by exposing its political scaffolding in the predatory culling of historical possibilities for the abducted and anonymized. M performs optical surgery on the campaign photo, "an eye graft, the grafting of one point of view onto the other."[20] If the recognized girls are abducted, disappeared, and murdered Tamils, then the image, which poses the sovereign-shepherd in front of the flock, is a *dissimulation* founded upon the occlusion of pursuit and capture lurking beneath the surface. Here, the political theology of pastoral power has its elasticity and possibility in the microphysics of cynegetic seizure. The pastoral gaze, intolerant of any residue of invisibility, hiddenness, and secrecy, effectively resides in the aphanisis of the citizen rendered an *infans* deprived of voice, language, agency, and testimony. The silent and unnamed children of the pamphlet are avatars of all disenfranchised Tamils, adults or otherwise. The sovereign's denial of any knowledge of abduction confesses the vigilance of the good shepherd: his custodial gaze is predicated by an unscathable sovereign *unseeing*. Very little penetrates the sovereign's generative blindness, which screens the children through aphanisis, wherein they appear in the pamphlet only to disappear elsewhere. This photo-immunization of pastoral power disappears disappearance. The pastoral *dispositif* is founded on an abyss: the visual securing of subjugated subjects is precipitated by the actuality of appearing under erasure.

Unlike pastoral power centred on individualization, this tableau requires anonymization, in which children play cinematic extras without notable qualities. They are backgrounded as identificatory props for the pacified triumphalist postwar order promising security from out of the carnage for the assaulted and occupied Tamils. Positioned around a petrified sovereign pristine in his all-white apparel, the children transmogrify into a tantalizing collation of lost faces and names. In this drama of pastoral fantasy, the recognizable children are a phantasmagoric assembly, posed as neither corpus nor corpse but rather as a "non habeas corpus;" an interstitial being dispossessed of a living and deceased body. The survivors claim and commemorate the body, neither dead nor alive, that they no longer have:

> The dead person no longer has the corpse at his or her disposal, there is no longer any habeas corpus. Habeas corpus, at least, is not a habeas corpse, supposing there ever were such a thing. Habeas corpus concerns the living body and not the corpse. Supposing, I repeat, that there ever were a habeas corpus for the living body. Because you can guess that I believe that this habeas corpus never existed and that its legal emergence, however important it may be, designates merely a way of taking into account or managing the effects of heteronomy and an irreducible non habeas corpus. And the non habeas corpse, at the moment of death, shows up the truth of this non habeas corpus during the lifetime of said corpus.[21]

If habeas infers having a living body, Derrida's non habeas invokes the dispossession and aphanisis of a subject neither living nor deceased but a spectre – *sous vivant* and *revenant* – someone who survives below categorical life and death as a proof of absence:

> Survivance in a sense of survival that is neither life nor death pure and simple, a sense that is not thinkable on the basis of the opposition between life and death … a survival that is not more alive, nor indeed less alive than life or more or less dead than death, a sur-vivance that lends itself to neither comparative nor superlative, a survivance … without superiority, without height, altitude or highness, and thus without supremacy or sovereignty … The survivance I am speaking of is something other than life death, but a groundless ground … *It* [Ça] begins with survival. And that is where there is some other that has me at its disposal; that is where any self is defenseless. That is what the self is, that is what I am, what the *I* is, whether I am there or not.[22]

The photo is sundered by the artificed blindness of the sovereign and the dystopian wish image of the bereft women. Their gaze does not belong to *vita contemplativa* but to *vita activa* in being a disclosive action in which the public act of ekphrastic seeing, of witnessing from out of state-mandated blindness, is as important as what is seen. In probing the epistemic power that is the image and its promissory manifesto, women have departed from the political closure of the self-evident that the pamphlet simulates – the aphorisms and axioms of victory, reconciliation, majoritarian largesse, and therapeutic forgetting. The mothers question the self-evidence of the self-evident. Their traumatropology recovers the fissure in the evidentiary, now profiled against the shadowy zone and errancy of its own hypocrisy. In reclaiming epistemic power, women affirm a *dis-communitas* of the incommunicable and the excommunicated. This inoperative community rests on the disarticulation of the staged school children and their unrepresentable abduction; their mode of current exposure is enabled by prior disposure. In dissecting the visual continuity and idea of progress of the utopian nation fostered by the manifesto, women extricate their absent children from a discarded past and profanely insert them into the present Robinsonade of islanded and sutured sovereignty. Opthalmo-pathology disrupts the sovereign's projection as a man of the present and the future with no murky historical entanglements. The mothers disassociate the iconic sovereign from the adulation of children and imbricate the purity of his white-washed present in a detained and disavowed past held hostage. Here, historical inoperability bears the hallmarks of what Giorgio Agamben calls *destituent* power: "Defined only by an absence of representation … where a relation is rendered destitute and interrupted, its elements are in this sense in contact, because the absence of every relation is exhibited between them … At the point where a destituent potential exhibits the nullity of the bond that pretended to hold them together, bare life and sovereign power, anomie and nomos, constituent power and constituted power are shown to be in contact without any relation … in order to allow a different use of them."[23]

If the photograph is a representation of a sovereign *arkhe*, its destituency is due to the mothers' deactivating optical excision of what actually animates and informs the photo – the theft of children. The women's gaze exposes a relation of a nonrelation in which pastoral power undergoes a scattering by an intrinsic, uncontainable and piercing punctum. Inoperability here means that the identity of pastoral power "can only determine or delimit itself through differential relations to other elements and … hence bears the mark of this difference."[24] The women's decisive optico-epistemic power rescripts the photo's projection of a faux harmonious polity effectively predicated upon predation. Their gaze as "the solidarity of the shaken" liberates this new content. Jan Patočka writes of war-time triumphalism, "The means by which this state is overcome is the solidarity of the shaken; the solidarity of those who are capable of understanding what life and death are all about, and so what history is about. That history is the conflict of mere life, barren and chained by fear, with life at the peak, life that does not plan for the ordinary days of a future but sees clearly that the everyday, its life and its 'peace,' have an end. Only one who is able to grasp this … is capable of conversion, of metanoia."[25] The mothers' gaze points to a traumatizing missed encounter with the historical real that enables their optical grafting of the repressed past onto the amnesiac present. This intrusive vision unfolds the disidentity of sovereignty with itself, the polity over which it rules, and the sterilized history that the polity fantasizes as an imagined community. The political and juridical pre-emption of the survivors as a witnessing assembly claiming epistemic right stifles their capacity to unfix and overcome the "factical tyranny" of the present.[26] The mothers' dystopian gaze surrogates the pastoral dream of the war machine with the nowhere (*u-topos*) of hoped-for reclaimable children – an ekphrastic *anticipatory topology* of possibility. Of such a place-to-come, Reiner Schürmann writes, "It deals with a possible historial locus, one already given, yet still to be occupied; thus, it is a locus spaced out from within. Its description is first of all negative since topos here no longer signifies any region of beings whose relations can be maximized to produce some archic referent."[27] Gendered dystopian incursion advances the children to the photo-political foreground as historical actors and silent accusers who no longer serve as fashion accessories to the sovereign. His phallic image, summarily emptied of its appellate power, illuminates the political ruin and wreckage through which the lost children haunt the nation-state as its dangerous supplement.

EPILOGUE: ANARCHIC FORENSIC ABSTRACTION

Art is a lie that tells the truth.

Pablo Picasso

The imaginal in Chantal Meza's art pulverizes the gaze and conscripts the viewer in its call, which addresses those who look and those who refuse to look – as another type of (un)seeing. Her own conversion to witnessing was not accidental. She visited Chiapas in Mexico in 2017 and met with the Zapatistas and related communities affected by systematic disappearances committed by the federal government. The subject matter is critical to Meza's aesthetic choices – the tension between painterly abstraction and the figuring of disfiguration. As Gustave Flaubert asserts, with pure art, the subject is irrelevant, "style in itself being an absolute manner of seeing things."[28] Meza articulates the psycho-poetics that gestures toward the co-originarity of earthly existence and the cohabitation of alters. The politically disappeared who have been axed from earthly coexistence are the unacknowledged forgotten (*amnestos*) whose lives have been placed under erasure (*sous rature*). The sovereign decision about who counts as a presence and who does not prescribes the foundational abstraction to install the disappeared as valueless deindividualized magma. As such, the disappeared delimit figuration as aporetic in being disfigured by seizure and erasure. There is a doubling of erasure; following the act of seizure is the surreptitious hand of impunity, eliminating any trace of obliteration. Erasure thus assumes the envelope of form(lessness) as the silhouette implicating the real with the abstract. Art, however, is irreducible to signification and discursivity, as always leaking out and resisting the latter's interception. Meza animates the haze of amnesia – that shadowless shadow – trying to pierce through the enigmatic unfathomability of the hauntological.

The performance of disappearance is the becoming of the absentee. The unmournable are a half-way house between presence and absence; their hauntology precedes and shadows a lost ontology. Necromantic disappearance administrates disimagination and spectralization as the injustice of deworlding. Disappearance's crime against humanity is to install an abstractive and extractive deontology of ghosting constitutive of world unmaking. Abstraction in Meza's series *Apparitions* poses the *sensing* of disappearance as the advent of an indemnifying right to be without right – for what rights are there for the ghostly multitude who are and are not?[29] Her art serves as a minimalist meditation upon the material disappearance of the very materiality of the other's disapparition. The disappearance of disappearance – the nonappearing appearance of appearance, to invoke Derrida – evokes a radical, irreparable, and absolute groundlessness of subsisting in the occluding blink (*Augenblick*) of a rupturing historical event in the Kierkegaardian sense of distraught absence.

Derrida elaborates,

> If I am getting ready to speak at length about ghosts, inheritance, and generations, generations of ghosts, which is to say about certain others who are not present, nor presently living, either to us, in us, or outside us, it is in the name of justice. Of justice where it is not yet, not yet there, where it is no longer, let us understand where it is no longer present, and where it will never be, no more than the law, reducible to laws or rights. It is necessary to speak of the ghost, indeed to the ghost and with it, from the moment that no ethics, no politics, whether revolutionary or not, seems possible and thinkable and just that does not recognize in its principle the respect for those others who are no longer or for those others who are not yet there, presently living, whether they are already dead or not yet born. No justice – let us not say no law and once again we are not speaking here of laws – seems possible or thinkable without the principle of some responsibility, beyond all living present, within that which disjoins the living present, before the ghosts of those who are not yet born or who are already dead, be they victims of wars, political or other kinds of violence, nationalist, racist, colonialist, sexist, or other kinds of exterminations, victims of the oppressions of capitalist imperialism or any of the forms of totalitarianism. Without this non-contemporaneity with itself of the living present, without that which secretly unhinges it, without this responsibility and this respect for justice concerning those who are not there, of those who are no longer or who are not yet present and living, what sense would there be to ask the question "where?" "where tomorrow?" "whither?"[30]

What do we actually see, feel, or know about disappearance when gazing into a nonfigurative work of art? Critical race theorist Leigh Raiford examines the juridical and political category of abstracted personhood associated with the techniques of abstraction that simultaneously deploy epidermalized chromatic exclusion of Blacks in order to foreground whiteness (construed in terms of the Kantian notion of the sublime) *as* the foundation of universal law that adjudicates questions of value and worth from the vantage of a propertied right that configures the human.[31] For Louis Althusser, legal abstraction is an inheritance of Roman law whose language exerts the arbitrary abstraction residing in the material force of surplus signifiers.[32]

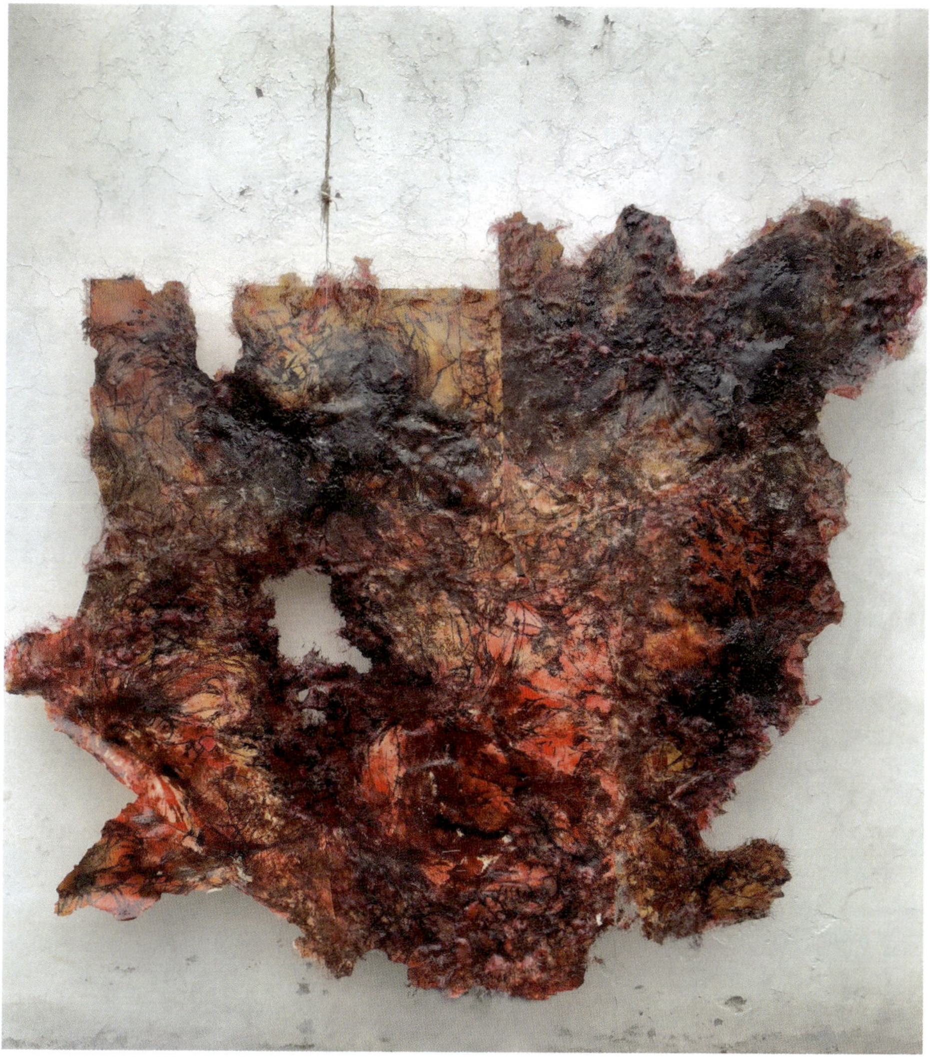

Since the Beginning, 2019, mixed media on paper, 200 x 200 cm

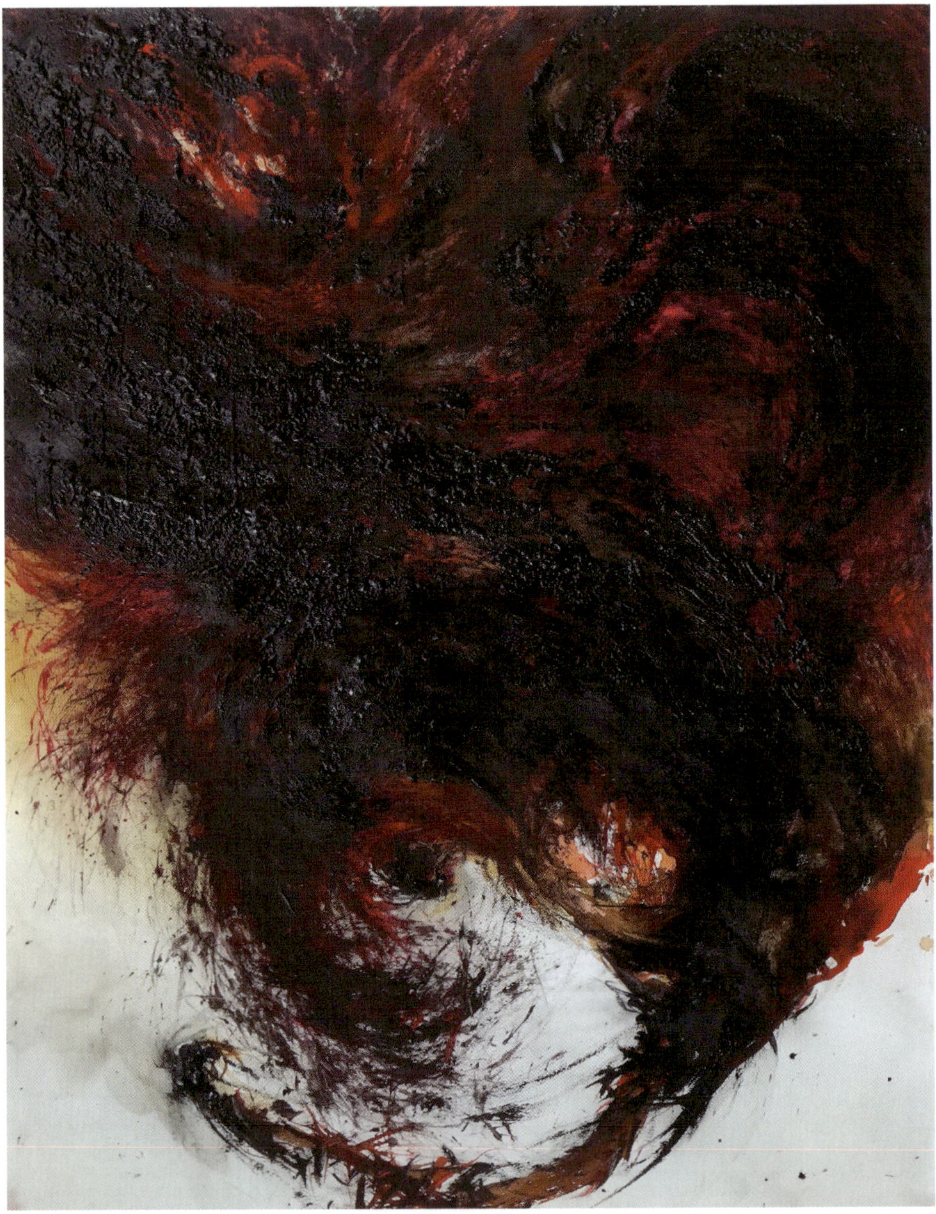

Obscure Beasts V, 2018, mixed media on paper, 115 x 96 cm

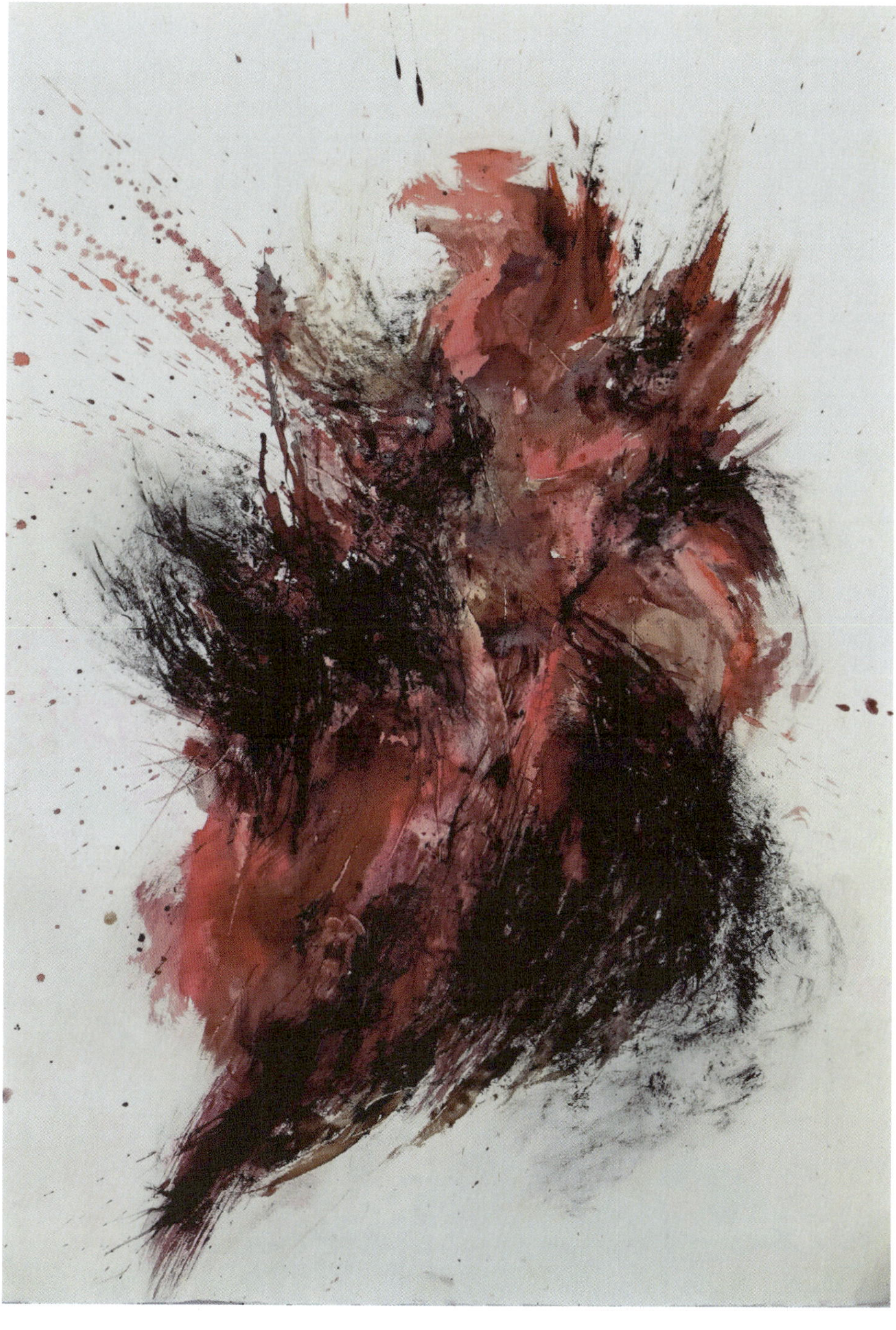

Obscure Beasts IX, 2018, mixed media on paper, 100 x 76 cm

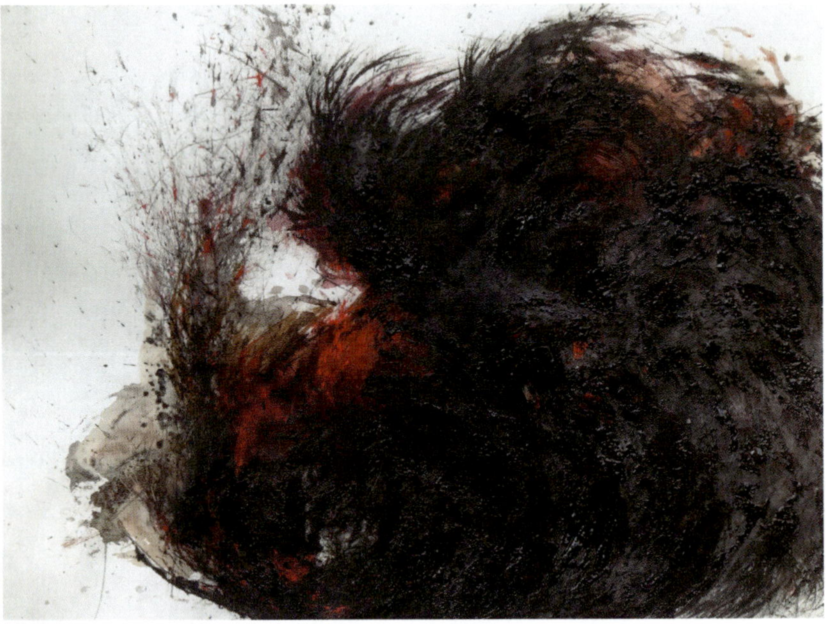

Obscure Beasts II, 2018, mixed media on paper, 115 x 96 cm

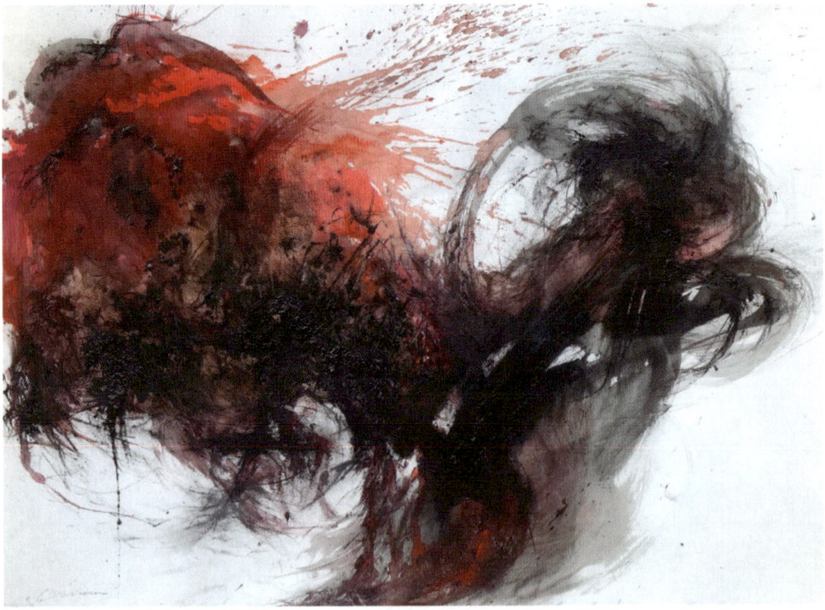

Obscure Beasts III, 2018, mixed media on paper, 115 x 96 cm

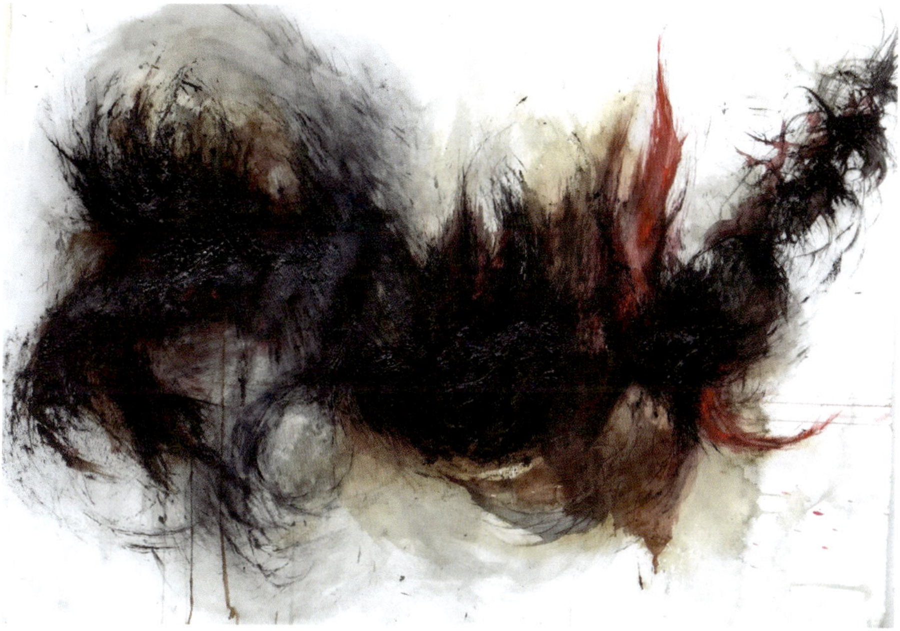

Obscure Beasts IV, 2018, mixed media on paper, 115 x 96 cm

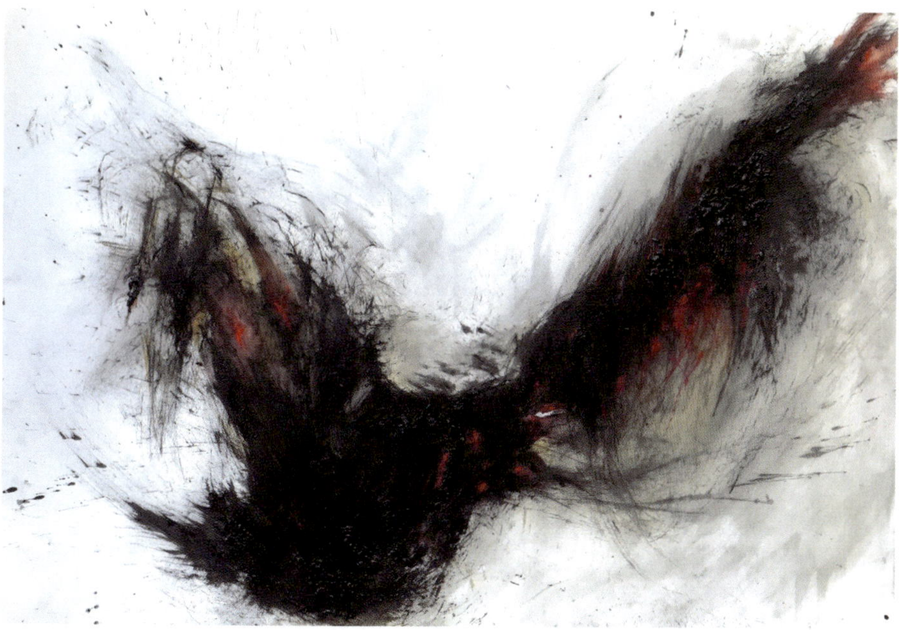

Obscure Beasts VI, 2018, mixed media on paper, 115 x 96 cm

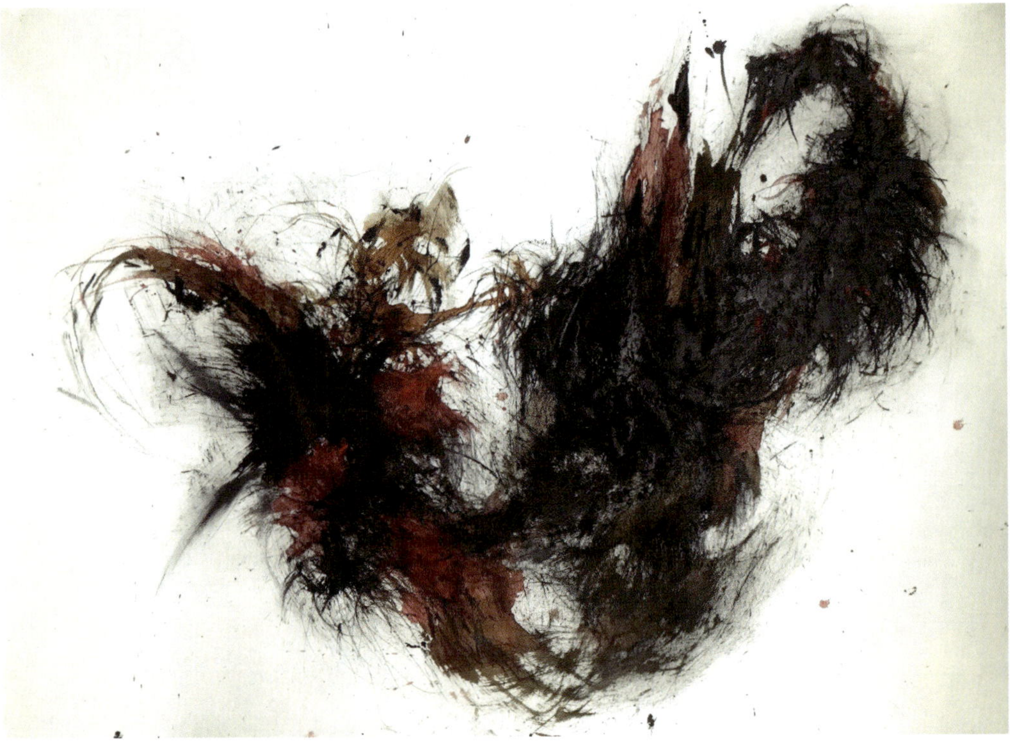

Obscure Beasts VII, 2018, mixed media on paper, 115 x 96 cm

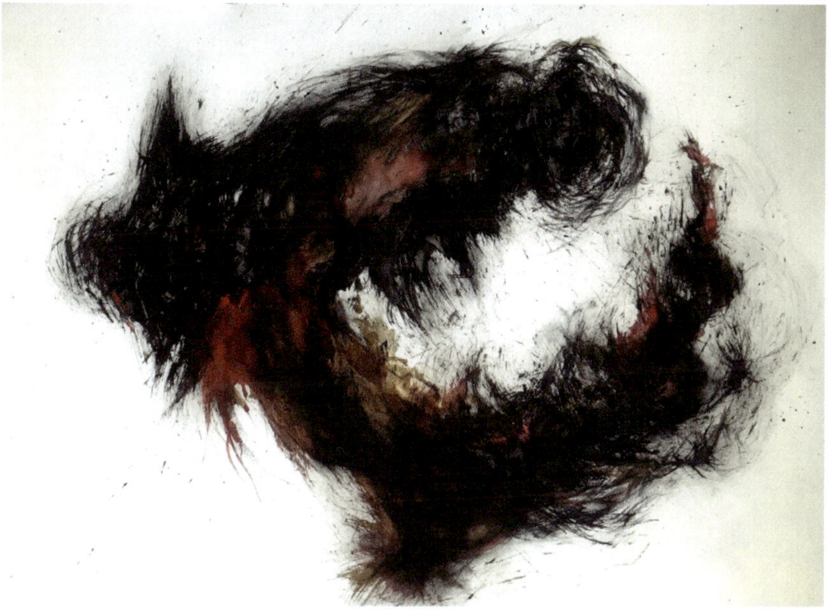

Obscure Beasts VIII, 2018, mixed media on paper, 115 x 96 cm

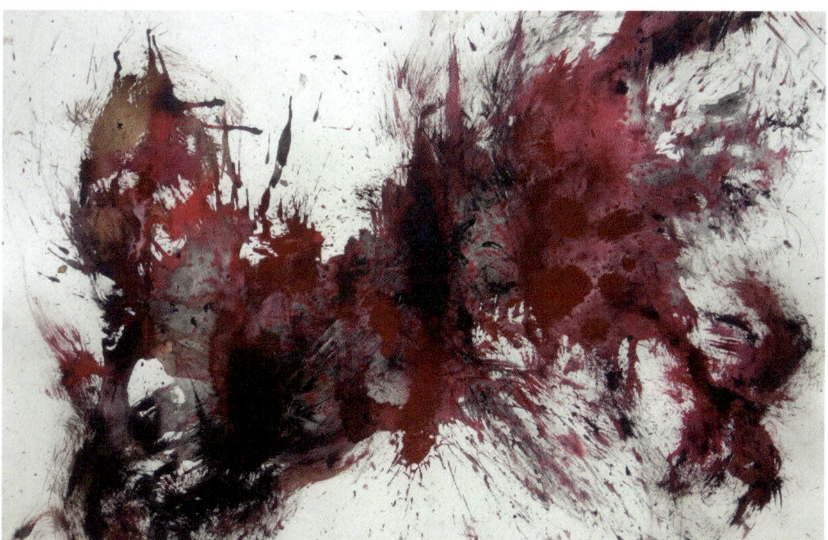

Obscure Beasts X, 2018, mixed media on paper, 100 x 76 cm

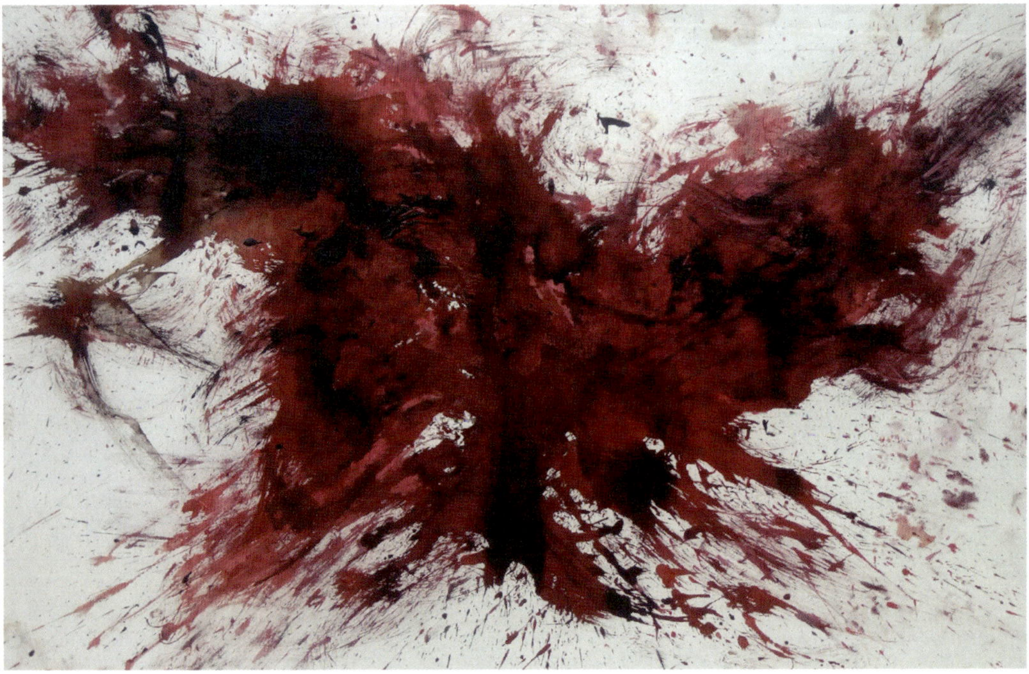

Obscure Beasts XI, 2018, mixed media on paper, 100 x 76 cm

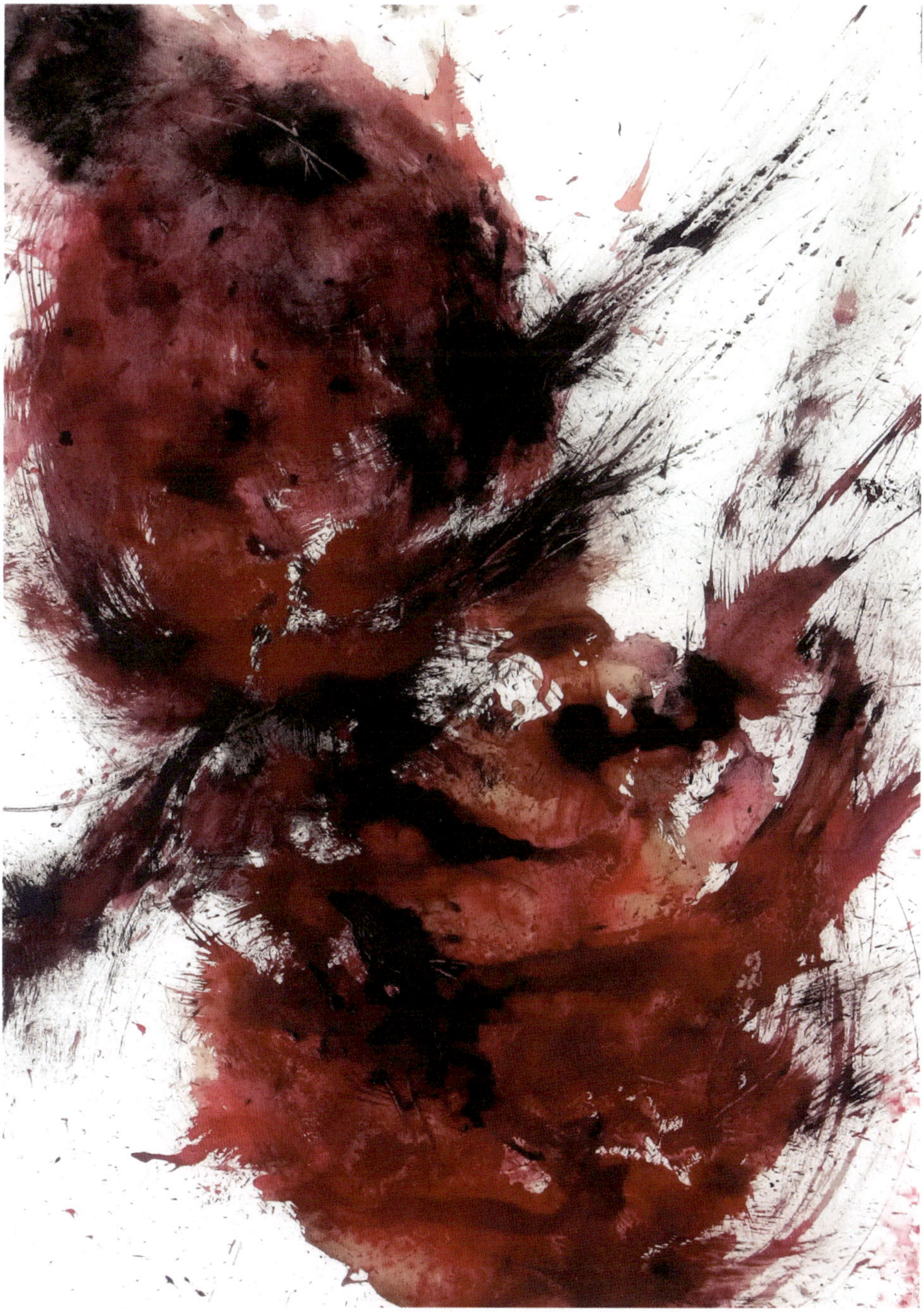

Obscure Beasts XII, 2018, mixed media on paper, 100 x 76 cm

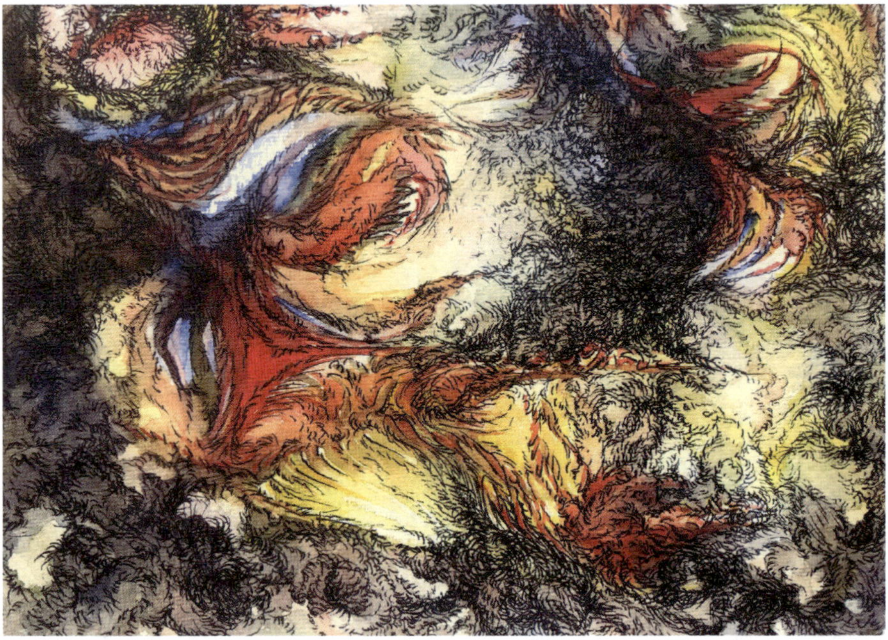

Fragments of a Catastrophe I, 2018, mixed media on paper, 25 x 20 cm

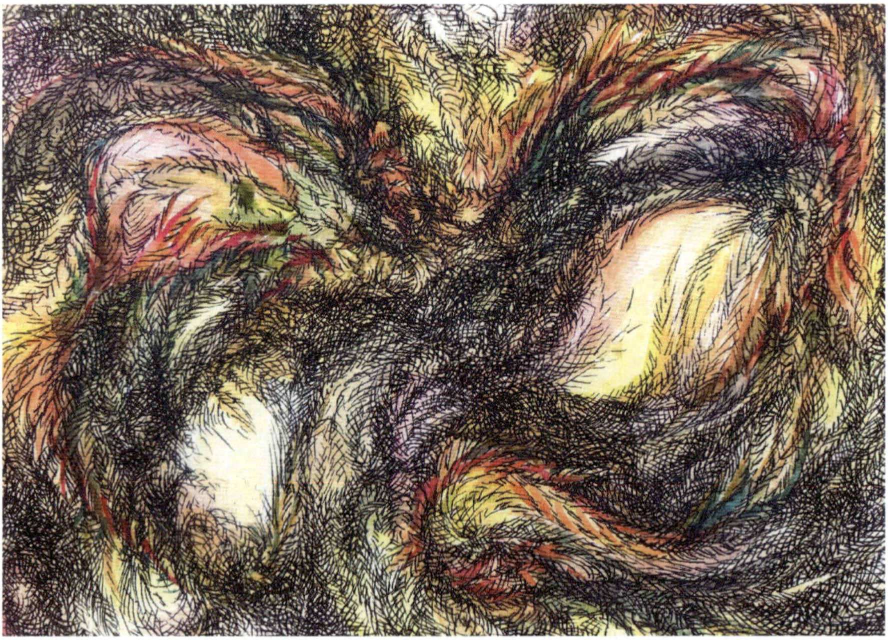

Fragments of a Catastrophe II, 2018, mixed media on paper, 25 x 20 cm

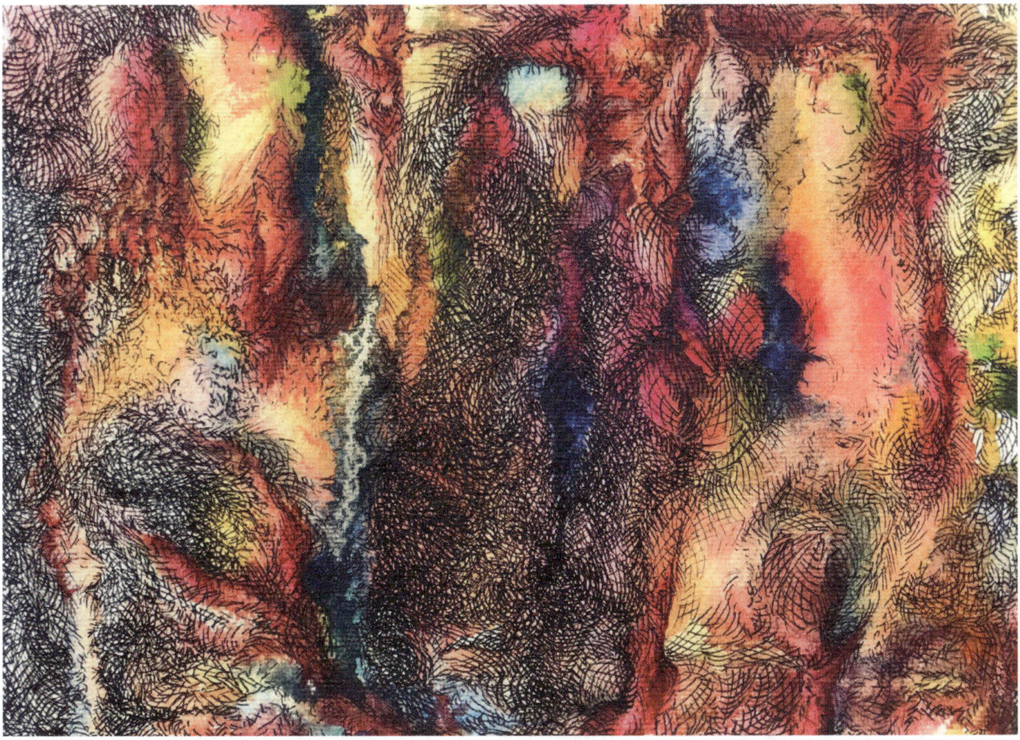

Fragments of a Catastrophe VII, 2018, mixed media on paper, 25 x 20 cm

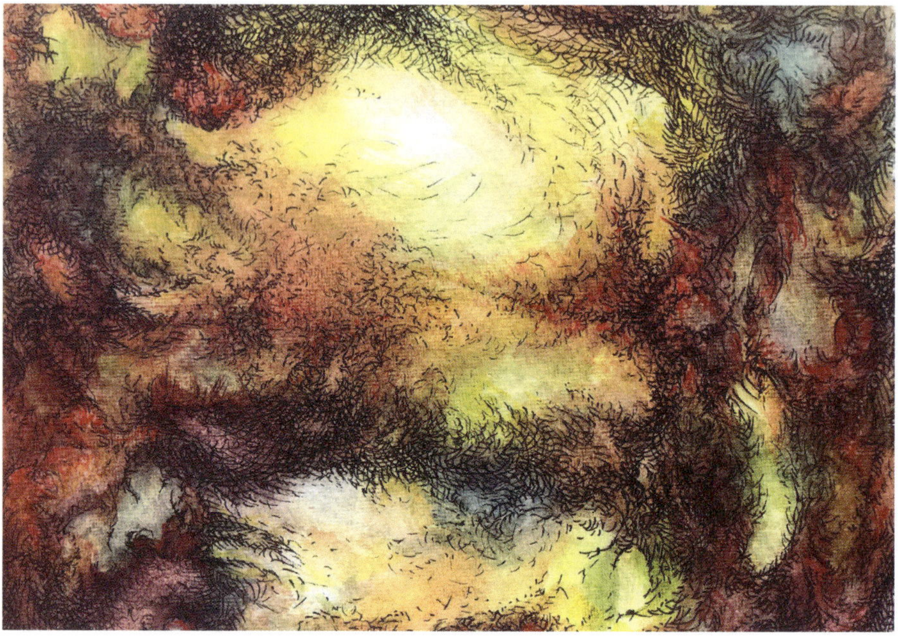

Fragments of a Catastrophe V, 2018, mixed media on paper, 25 x 20 cm

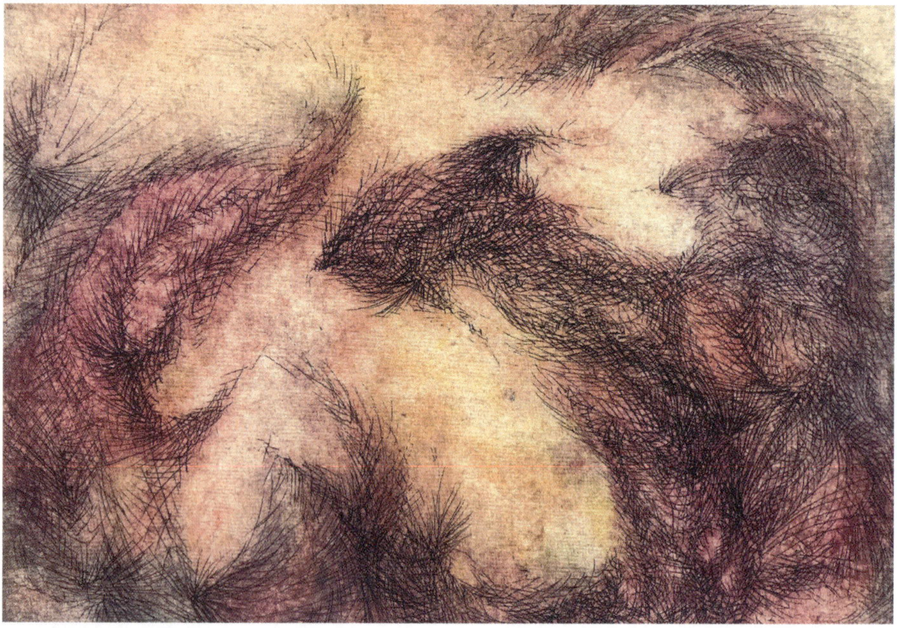

Fragments of a Catastrophe XV, 2018, mixed media on paper, 25 x 20 cm

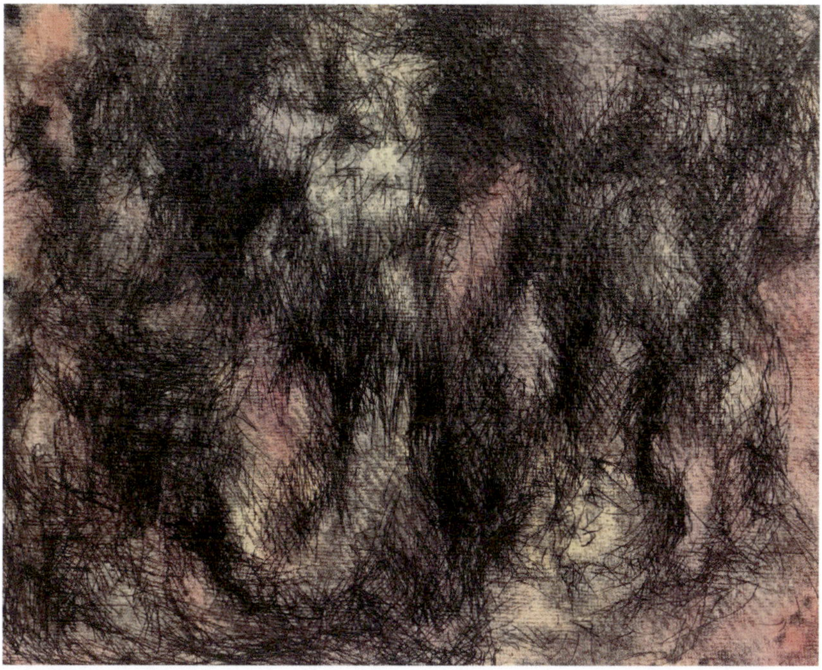

Fragments of a Catastrophe XIII, 2018, mixed media on paper, 25 x 20 cm

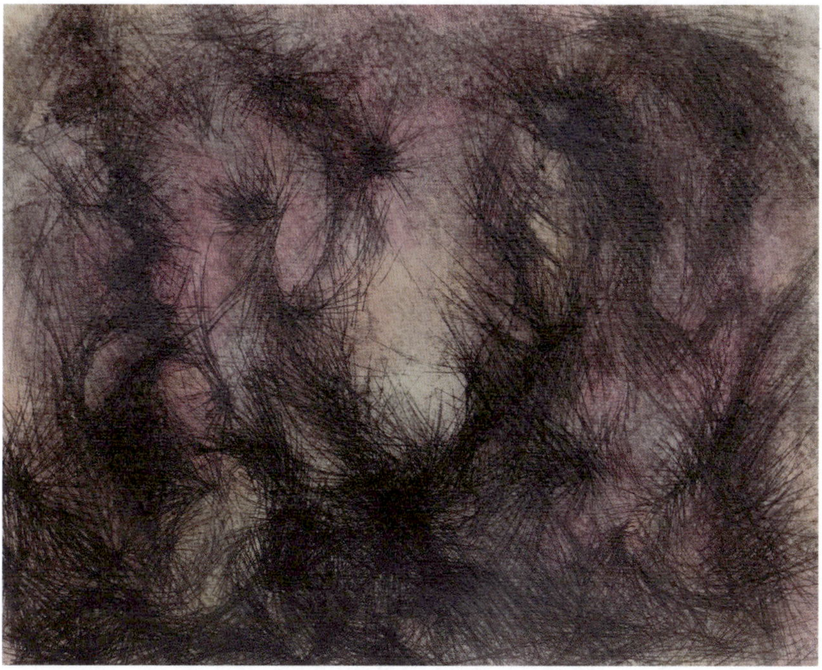

Fragments of a Catastrophe XIV, 2018, mixed media on paper, 25 x 20 cm

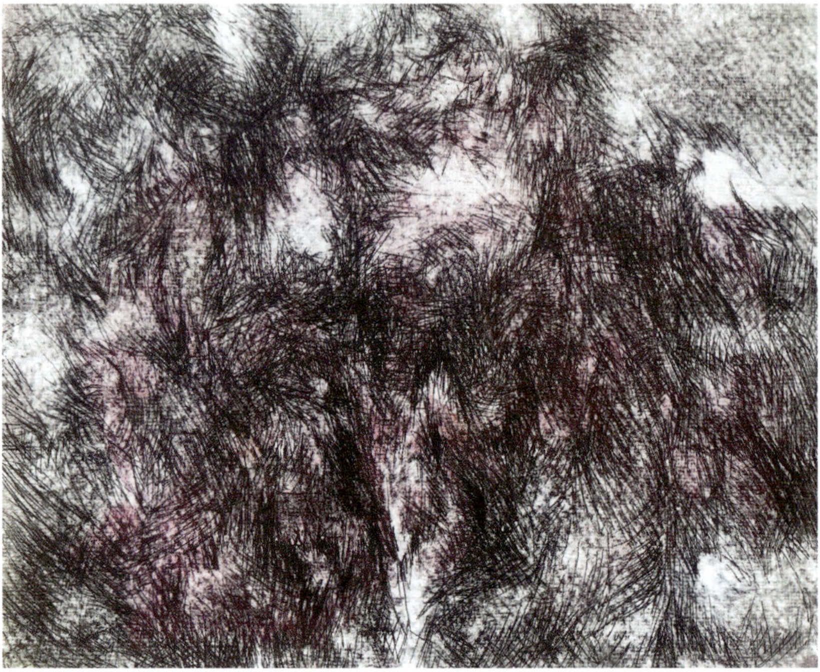

Fragments of a Catastrophe XX, 2018, mixed media on paper, 25 x 20 cm

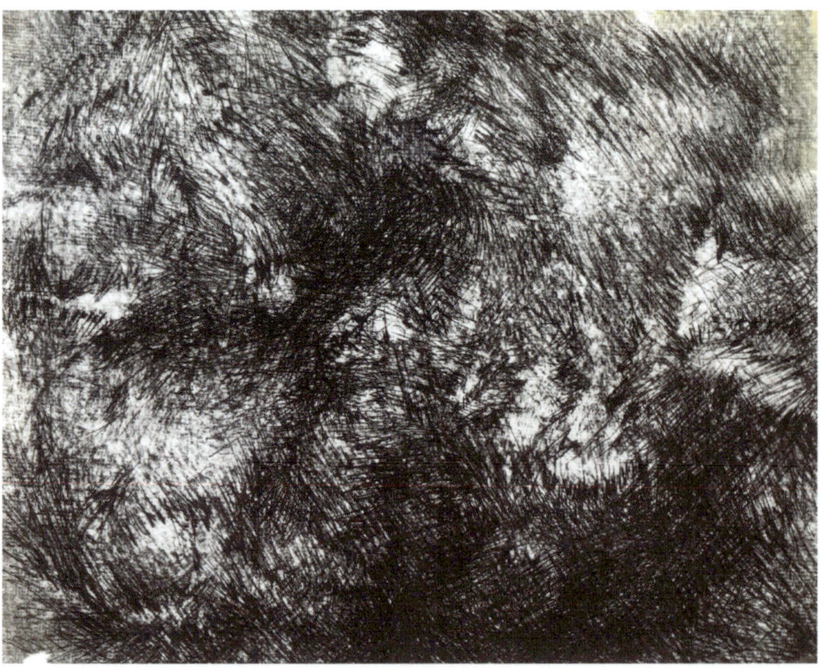

Fragments of a Catastrophe XXII, 2018, mixed media on paper, 25 x 20 cm

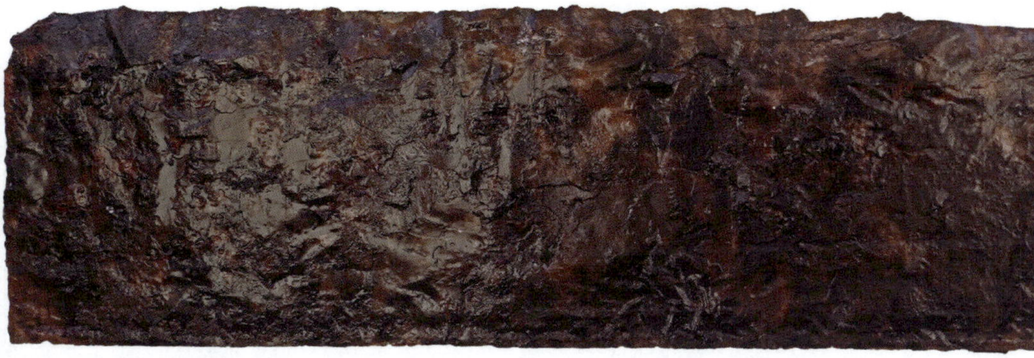

Collapse of Consciousness, 2020, resin, ink, charcoal, fiberglass, pastel, and acrylic on paper, 3.28 x 1.10 m

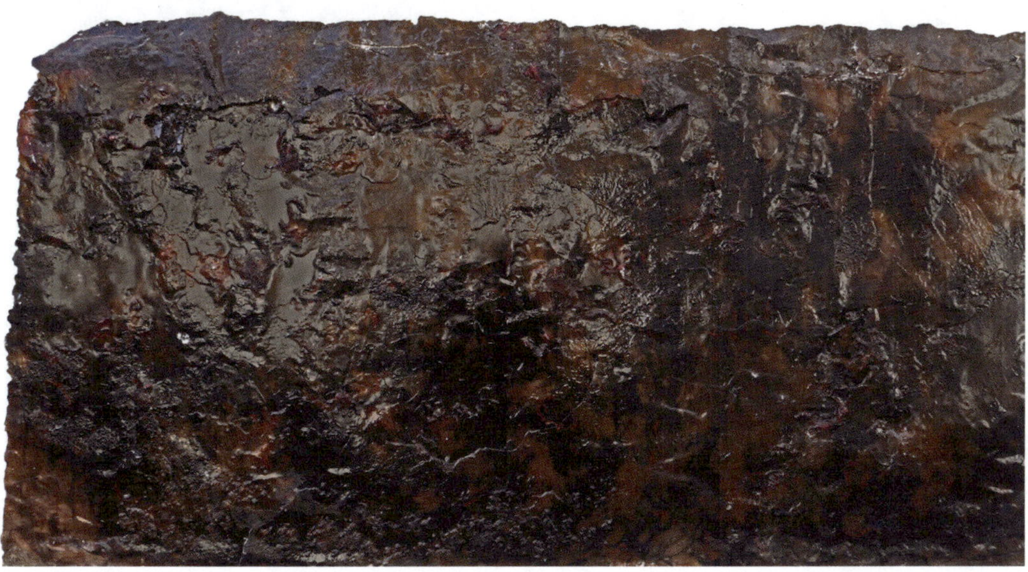

Detail, *Collapse of Consciousness*, 2020

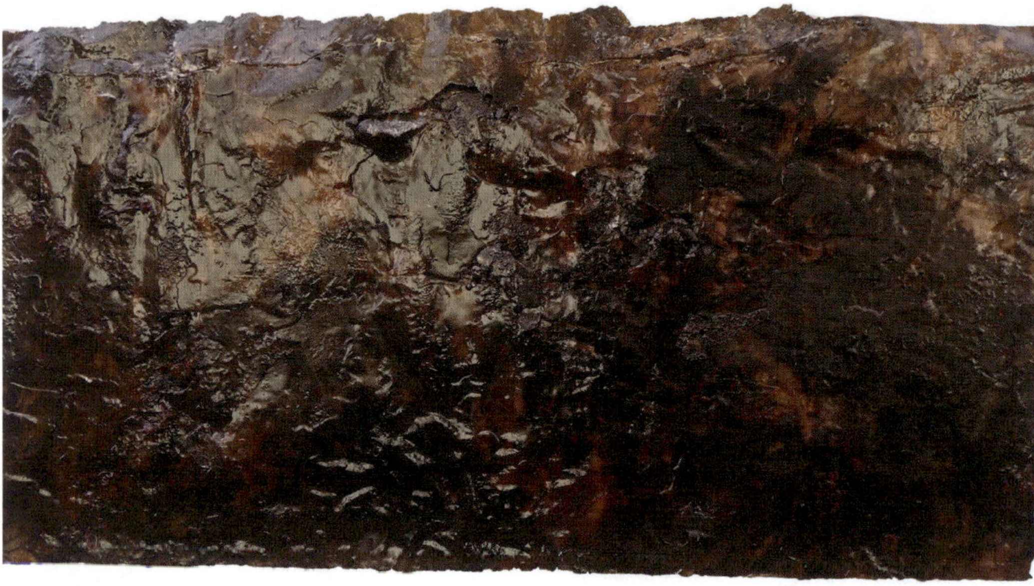

Detail, Collapse of Consciousness, 2020

To juridically abstract is to detach the lived reality of Blackness and the category of the "disappeared" as forms of abstruse absence.[33] Black specificity as that which is subject to abstraction is subtended by other machines of abstraction, namely slavocracy and post-slavocratic racial capitalism. The political denegation of the disappeared is a haptic abstraction inclusive of race, class, caste, religion, and gender; the signifying creature uneasily dwells in this *immundus* of sub-slimed nonbeing. Positioned as an already innumerable anonymity, the disappeared do not provide access to the real. They *are* the real, defined by Lacan as that which absolutely resists representation as an abstraction. With abduction, all singularities are annihilated. Conventionalized and admissible abstractions therefore may not even survive the absolutist sovereignty of esoteric disappearance. Humanitarian enumeration as the sacrificial substitution of flesh and blood bodies is an abstractive/extractive regime serving as a surrogate of inoperable justice. Foundational colonial technologies of forensic accounting and cartography reduce embodied singularities to the calculable, rendering persons as *always already* abstracted.

Meza's art featured in this volume promises not so much the extensity of readability as a Deleuzean "affective-intensive" as an asignifying register.[34] Affect names the intensive quality of life – the movement from passive indifference to truthful restlessness, the becoming tangible of the unaccountable ghosts around us. The affective-intensive shifts from rupture to a lived disjunctive conjuncture. Nietzschean philosophy anticipates Deleuze when he asks how to view art from the perspective of life. The world of disappeared alterity – that is, disappearance as radical incommensurability – may not be thinkable or imaginable, but for Deleuzean theory, it can be delineated as a mythopoetics irreducibly as real as the synesthesia of the vital and material that exceeds intelligible reference. For Hegelian thought, abstraction is a sign of a nonphilosophical attitude. Only philosophical thought assumes the form of the truly concrete. Hegelian logic precipitates a movement from the abstract to the concrete. Contra Hegel, Deleuze sets into motion a different relation, structure, and logic: the abstract in opposition to the discrete not as poles of any hierarchy but as perceptual semiotics.[35] Deleuzean abstraction evokes the intensive as the potentiality of alterity. When taken as a limit or empty form, time ceases to be a unit of measure and is "filled up" by intensive magnitudes, or differently put, "degrees of the real"; lived experience is an intensive haptics that overflows time. For Deleuze, intensity is what constitutes the abstract: the truly lived experience – *le vécu* – is an absolutely abstract thing that is no-thing but lived experience itself: "Le véritable vécu c'est absolument de l'abstrait. L'abstrait c'est le vécu" (True experience is absolutely abstract. The abstract is the lived).[36] With lived experience, one has reached the "most fully living core of the abstract … Lived experience represents nothing. And you can live nothing but the abstract and nobody has ever lived anything else but the abstract. I don't live representation in my heart, I live a temporal line which is completely abstract. What is more abstract than a rhythm?"[37] Life is informed by the rhythms and the velocities of abstractive intensity. Deleuze's play on the meaning of abstract is derivative of the notion of abstract art not because it is insufficiently or incompletely concrete but because it does not traffic in discrete representations and fetishized realisms.[38] From a Deleuzean perspective, abstract art produces not representations but affects that cannot be discreticized. Discreticization – linguistic, alpha-numeric, iconographic, and algorithmic – is a compressive intervention that impoverishes intensity, chromatic or otherwise. The intensity of affect engenders alterities, from alertness or vigilance to flight from peril. Affective intensity refracts signs of life without delimitation and outline. In *What Is Philosophy?* Deleuze and Guattari advance a more general argument about painting, whose task is not to reveal the ontogenesis of the actual and the lived but to extract the virtual and to embody it as a feverish archive of the event: "Every work of art is a monument, but here the monument is not something commemorating a past, it is a bloc of present sensations that owe their preservation only to themselves."[39] The virtual seized by Meza's colours eludes actualization and exceeds any determination of the human to exist in itself as percept instead of perception, affect rather than affection – an existence without iconostasis. Meza labours to reveal neither the virtually visible nor any transition from the virtual to the actual but rather to extract a bloc(age) of sensations. For Deleuze and Guattari, "The aim of art is to wrest the percept from perceptions of objects and the states of a perceiving subject, to wrest the affect from affections as the transition from one state to another: to extract a bloc of sensations, a pure being of sensations."[40] The absence of existence – disappearance as the haptic intensity of negation or nihilism – delineates an aborted unbecoming in an infinite dissolution.

The genre of the splash in Meza is a fecund conjuration, a ghostly presence of absence, the spectre of miscarried futures of the past. Aborted futures forebodingly leap over into sensations, refusing enforced slumber or oblivion. Her manifold canvas allegorizes botched futurity – the failure of any arrival for those precariously positioned on the edge of annihilation as ambushed lives begin to fade, smothered by the political unconscious of collective disavowal. A hermeneutic frustration subtends the art's revealability (*offenbarkeit*), a desire for the (im)possible figuring-out of the historical violence, and exposes the *abgrund* (abyss) of worlding for the living.

Alberto Toscano theorizes the materialism of absence without any reference to matter that presumes a shapeless demateriality. Matter is assumed to be coterminous with the visibility and intelligibility, or perceptibility, of forms; what is invisible to the naked eye is abstract and frustrates the desire to make things tangible or palpable. Laterality, indirection, and anamorphosis allow one to picture a structuring absence or presenting invisibility. Abstraction can be thought of as a critical evacuation or emptying-out of reified social content.[41] Maurice Merleau-Ponty conceives of art as bringing truth into being. Abstraction signifies the unfinished and the incomplete, the quest for the illusory or the fictive – for the missing corpus as the intact truth of appearance.

The intensities of Meza's brush dangle etching tones and tinges, shades and twinges in dispersion to form stark unrecognizable edges and trails – a cascade of amorphous yet seditious colours casting multiplying shadows in motion that curdle morphing hues of black and red against the white surface as they glide past synesthetic, swirling hurricanes of shapelessness that yield bare and abstracted glyphs. The expressive mountains of colours overlap freely without delimitation, exerting their inner necessity and the immediacy of sensorial difference and dematerialized violence without sublimation. Penetrated by discolouration, shadows at times appear to move in a frenetic dancing style, evoking fear and trembling. Other angles merge into an arresting mosaic of volcanic fire, erupting into the destitute ecosystem. Like the final chord of a symphony, colours are pushed to extremity, amplifying their vibrational frequencies in an apocalyptic movement of biographical nullity that ends with a fortissimo coda. It lays bare the abject(ed) human condition and its entrapment in the encircling world, capturing the *stimmung* (mood) of terror and pain as a refusal of amnesia and anesthesia. This refusal exposes the modern state's affliction with anosognosia, an existential-epistemic disorder indifferent to crime of epidemic proportions. The disappeared are the phantom limb of "postwar" society's refusal to mourn and be held accountable for the loss and privation of being-in-the-world and being-with (*Mitsein*). According to Merleau-Ponty, "The phantom limb is thus, like a repressed experience, a previous present that cannot commit to becoming past."[42] The punitive-retributive postwar culture's pareidolia refuses to acknowledge the erasure of the social world for the survivors who are denied being-with those present and absent.[43] An emasculating fear parasitically takes hold of the state in a repetition compulsion to pre-emptively thwart its own amputation in auto-immunizing acts of violence and in the denial and dismissal of consequent irredressible wounds rendered invisible. The state proactively reinvents its own power of abstraction through its alienating remediation of law to sustain its right to be without right.

Meza's prodding and prompting brush strokes summon into her consciousness what was narrated by survivors, shared and circulated in fragmentary, disjointed sequences interrupted by the inarticulate and the ungraspable.[44] Her chromatic weaving creates a sinuous web to guide us through the *gestalt* of aphanisis as she finds herself immersed in disappropriating synesthesia. If the body is our anchorage in the world, with disappearance, the disembodying world is thrown (*geworfen*) into the blot, becoming blur. To invoke Lacan, the symbolic here precedes its object and does not encounter reality except when it precedes it into the imaginary.

Franz Marc (for whom abstraction was a strategy of enchantment) "insisted on the dualism of essence and appearance and charged the artist with the task of penetrating to the 'essence of the world,' what he regarded as the purpose of abstraction, affirming that '[e]ach thing in the world has its form, its formula, which we cannot touch with our coarse hands, but which we can embrace intuitively in the degree that we are artistically gifted.'"[45] Marc defined "das Abstrakte" as "natural sight, as primary, intuitive vision," in contrast to "das Sentimentale," the "hysterical sickness and reduction of our spiritual capacity to see."[46] In his view, abstraction points to a transcendence that, in abiding by its effaced subject, contours an invisible reality to behold. Abstraction performs evocation, an ideological transfiguration of the world through art.[47] For Derrida, one condition of possibility of figuration is the aphanisis of blindness, even its unique characteristic. Ekphrastic witnessing as a form of blind witnessing attests to what is not there: a forced absence. If Meza's art is about bearing witness, it bears witness to losing sight of those who have vanished – a sight in the midst of blindness – to losing sight of the vanished who are being lost from sight. It bears witness to this lack, privation, and ruin without restitution or compensation.

In adopting a distinctive splash style without contours that is akin to the Pollockian aesthetic, Meza opts for the absence of any distinct points of emphasis or identifiable parts within the canvas. The splash's lack of dimensions evokes a precipice (*abîme*, *abgrund*) with the capacity to conscript the viewer into the state of chromatic evaporation and leakage. The *abgrund* of disapparition leaves a trail of flotsam and jetsam, the ruins of once inhabited but now annihilated worlds, that institutes the uninhabitable for those left behind. They must live in fear of the same fate that predatorily pursues them as the unrelenting search comes up against state fabulation – whose law is the obligation to ignorance – turning its victims into society's phantoms, into phantasmagoria. Here, if I may slightly twist the insight advanced by Nicolas Abraham and Maria Torok in *The Shell and the Kernel* in order to emphasize the ethico-political and philosophical implications of living with, accounting for, and normalizing egregious state violence, what haunts are not the dead (or the disappeared) but the gaps left within institutional structures and cultures by state secrecy and silence – its cryptonomy.[48] The apparatus of disapparition works resolutely to purge any trace of encrypting effacement, making it impossible to psychically and somatically metabolize the catastrophic trauma of disappearance, the moment of seizure, torture, captivity, invisibility, and oblivion, the no-man's land and blind zones of a clandestine encounter, which even as a cognitive map or mental picture, only break, fragment, and dissolve like melancholic splashes of memory in disarray.

Sigmund Freud contends that there are no beautiful surfaces without a terrible depth. The possible readability of the art with language is a result of a "consummated experience" (to invoke Mark Rothko's insight) in the active sense of affecting and being affected.[49] We seize in the act of perception something that outruns perception itself. Meza's nonlinear avalanche of colours is a dramaturgy of the tragic, engulfing the spectator in scale and intricacy. The splash's indeterminacy intertwines with Derrida's theorem that since justice is heterogeneous to law, it *demands* the event of a decision taken in a moment of madness, hence the splash of the spontaneous brush stroke.[50]

The insensible begins to sink in, and communities fathom the unfathomable in broken signs, symbols, and grief-stricken idioms. Without speech, Freud argues, the subject cannot symbolize trauma. Meza's response is to haltingly map the dynamic between the psyche and the imperceptible; her art performs an anachronic void in absenting objects, places, times, and moments that repel consumption. Rather than sustaining *relations* that bind objects, places, and times, as in Leonardo Cremonini's abstract art, Meza's work hollows out the social tie decimated by state violence in its acceleration of the alienation between things, time, and *human* relationality. Her canvas depicts not relations but the intolerable quaking and quivering atmospherics without a resting place that ensue when life is abstracted from all sociality and potentiality. For Meza, abstraction is the raw turbulence that is ever present and never absent but always imperceptible, visible yet invisible to the perceptive eye as it waits and yearns to be felt, touched, and sensed. The artwork presented here, encompassed under the rubric "state of disappearance," heightens the tangibility and intangibility of a life form as it compels the gaze to imagine the unimaginable: the technologies of annihilation. We are seized by an unaccountable caesura that envisions the chaotic destruction of a world and the destruction of its destruction. Meza stages a visually visceral confrontation not with the centrality of the body – missed and missing – but with a necessary noncentrality as absent referent. Here, abstract sensibility assumes an opacity of unknowable disembodiment made tactile. The disorientating dusk and blinding murkiness as an event (*Ereignis*) of colours conjure up the thematic of ekphrastic evocation as a form of blind witnessing that dialectically unravels the phantasmatic work – a seeing of the unseen and an unseeing of the seen that are fiercely engaged by survivors in their search for the erased absentees, a vocation that the artist dramatizes as an anarchic crossing.

There are no images or icons that cathect around the vast expanse of Meza's tortuously layered patches of atmospheric colour – a sensorium of the nullification of the cathected. The Freudian cathexis (*Libidobesetzung*), etymologically derived from the Greek *kathexis* (retention), presupposes a proximity of zones of incorporation or introjection. With the series *Apparitions*, there is a proximity to a distance that awaits the impossibility of its arrival. The act of "with-drawing" abstraction, what Derrida calls "retrait," is a retreat or remotion that speaks of an origin point that never takes place.[51] Meza's staging of agon, with unintelligibility bursting out of the borders of the canvas in upheaval, derails and annuls referential language. Yet the descent into the nebulous night of disappearance is a necessary passage toward attesting to the legacies of the politically uninheritable – as an ethical imperative and chilling alibi – in the face of – destruction and forgetfulness.

NOTES

1 Aristotle, *De Anima*, trans. R.D. Hicks (Cambridge, UK: Cambridge University Press, 1907).

2 Jacques Lacan, *The Four Fundamental Concepts of Psychoanalysis*, trans. Alan Sheridan (New York: Norton, 1981), 207–8.

3 Jacques Lacan, "The Subject and the Other: Aphanisis," in *The Seminar of Jacques Lacan*, book 11, *The Four Fundamental Concepts of Psychoanalysis*, trans. Alan Sheridan, ed. Jacques Alain Miller, 216–32 (New York: Norton, 1981).

4 Jacques Derrida and Richard Beardsworth, "Nietzsche and the Machine," *Journal of Nietzsche Studies*, no. 7 (1994): 7–66 at 51.

5 Jacques Derrida, *Aporias*, trans. Thomas Dutoit (Stanford, CA: Stanford University Press, 1993), 18, original emphasis.

6 Slavoj Žižek, "Melancholy and the Act," *Critical Inquiry* 26, no. 4 (2000): 657–81.

7 Hannah Arendt, *Eichmann in Jerusalem: A Report on the Banality of Evil* (New York: Penguin, 2006).

8 W.J.T. Mitchell, *Picture Theory: Essays on Verbal and Visual Representation* (Chicago: University of Chicago Press, 1994).

9 See Miranda Fricker, *Epistemic Injustice: Power and the Ethics of Knowing* (Oxford: Clarendon, 2007).

10 See Jacques Derrida, *Memoirs of the Blind: The Self-Portrait and Other Ruins*, trans. Pascale-Anne Brault and Michael Naas (Chicago: University of Chicago Press, 1993).
11 Ibid., 57.
12 Ibid., 102–4.
13 Jean-Luc Nancy, *The Creation of the World or Globalization*, trans. Raffoul François (Albany, NY: SUNY Press, 2007), 96–7.
14 Michel Foucault, *Security, Territory, Population: Lectures at the College de France 1977–1978*, trans. Graham Burchell (New York: Picador, 2009).
15 Jacques Derrida, *The Beast and the Sovereign*, vol. 2, trans. Geoffrey Bennington (Chicago: University of Chicago Press, 2011), 27.
16 Gilles Deleuze, *The Logic of Sense*, trans. Mark Lester and Charles Stivale (New York: Columbia University Press, 2001), 320.
17 Derrida, *Beast and the Sovereign*, vol. 2, 55.
18 Deleuze, *Logic of Sense*, 320, original emphasis.
19 Gregor Chamayou, *Manhunts: A Philosophical History* (Princeton, NJ: Princeton University Press, 2012), 15.
20 Derrida, *Memoirs of the Blind*, 87.
21 Derrida, *Beast and the Sovereign*, vol. 2, 144.
22 Ibid., 130–1, original emphasis.
23 Giorgio Agamben, *The Use of Bodies*, trans. Adam Kotsko (Stanford, CA: Stanford University Press, 2016), 272.
24 Jacques Derrida, *Limited Inc*, trans. Jeffrey Mehlman and Samuel Weber (Evanston, IL: Northwestern University Press, 1988), 53.
25 Jan Patočka, *Heretical Essays in the Philosophy of History*, trans. Erazim Kohák (Chicago and La Salle, IL: Open Court, 1996), 135.
26 Francis Barker, *Culture and Violence: Essays on Tragedy and History* (Chicago: University of Chicago Press, 1993).
27 Reiner Schürmann, *Broken Hegemonies*, trans. Reginald Lilly (Bloomington: Indiana University Press, 2003), 234.
28 Quoted in Nicole L. Brownfield, "Style as a '[M]anner of Seeing': The Poetics of Gustave Flaubert" (MA thesis, Liberty University, 2010).
29 Chantal Meza, *Apparitions*, https://www.chantal-meza.com/stateofdisappearance.
30 Jacques Derrida, *Specters of Marx: The State of the Debt, the Work of Mourning and the New International*, trans. Peggy Kamuf (New York: Routledge, 1994), xviii.
31 Leigh Raiford, "Burning All Illusion: Abstraction, Black Life and the Unmaking of White Supremacy," *Art Journal* 79, no. 4 (2020): 76–91.

32 Ibid., 71.

33 Alberto Toscano, "The Detour of Abstraction," *Diacritics* 43, no. 2 (2015): 68–90 at 70.

34 Simon O' Sullivan, "From Aesthetics to the Abstract Machine: Deleuze, Guattari and Contemporary Art Practice," in *Deleuze and Contemporary Art*, ed. Stephen Zepke and Simon O' Sullivan (Edinburgh: Edinburgh University Press, 2010), 200.

35 Brent Adkins, "Who Thinks Abstractly?" *Journal of Speculative Philosophy* 30, no. 3 (2016): 352–60.

36 Cited in ibid., 359.

37 Cited in ibid., 355.

38 Ibid., 357.

39 Gilles Deleuze and Félix Guattari, *What Is Philosophy?* (New York: Columbia University Press, 1991), 167.

40 Ibid.

41 Alberto Toscano, "Towards a Realism of the Abstract," *Foreign Objekti*, 9 March 2021, https://www.foreignobjekt.com/post/alberto-toscano-towards-a-realism-of-the-abstract-1.

42 Maurice Merleau-Ponty, *Phenomenology of Perception*, trans. Donald A. Landes (New York: Routledge, 2013), 88.

43 The term "pareidolia" is derived from the Greek words *para* (faulty, wrong, instead of) and *eidōlon* (image, form, or shape). Matteo Pasquinelli examines the history of the phantom limb syndrome as mediated through the link (identified by Kurt Goldstein) between abnormality and abstraction. I have shifted Goldstein's theory away from individual pathologies and toward the pathological dynamics of the state, whose power (of abstraction), I claim, repeatedly alienates it from that which gives the state its own singular, sovereign screen or skin, namely the law, which renders it scathable (*tuché* in Lacan). Matteo Pasquinelli, "The Alien Hand of the Technosphere: Kurt Goldstein and the Trauma of Intelligent Machines," *Technosphere Magazine*, 15 November 2016, https://technosphere-magazine.hkw.de/p/The-Alien-Hand-of-the-Technosphere-Kurt-Goldstein-and-the-Trauma-of-Intelligent-Machines-nae2PUYQ2kK3v8AHYnmCcs.

44 Chantal Meza in the video interview with Brad Evans at https://www.chantal-meza.com/stateofdisappearance.

45 David Morgan, "The Enchantment of Art: Abstraction and Empathy from German Romanticism to Expressionism," *Journal of the History of Ideas* 57, no. 2 (1996): 317–40 at 334, citing Franz Marc, *Schriften*, ed. Klaus Lankheit (Cologne: DuMont Buchverlag, 1978).

46 Cited in ibid., 336.

47 Ibid., 337.

48 Nicolas Abraham and Maria Torok, *The Shell and the Kernel* (Chicago: University of Chicago Press, 1994).

49 Adolf Gottlieb and Mark Rothko, with Barnett Newman, "Statement," published in art critic Edward Alden Jewell's column, *New York Times*, 13 June 1943.

50 Jacques Derrida, "Force of Law: The 'Mystical Foundation of Authority,'" in *Deconstruction and the Possibility of Justice*, ed. Drucilla Cornell, Michel Rosenfeld, and David Carlson, 3–67 (New York: Routledge, 1992), 26.

51 Jacques Derrida, "Le retrait de la métaphore," in *The Phenomenology of Man and of the Human Condition*, ed. Anna-Teresa Tymieniecka, 273–300 (Dordrecht: Springer, 1983).

3

The Violence of Organized Forgetting

Henry A. Giroux

> People who remember court madness through pain, the pain of the perpetually recurring death of their innocence; people who forget court another kind of madness, the madness of the denial of pain and the hatred of innocence.
>
> James Baldwin

In January 2020, more than two hundred survivors of Auschwitz, the notorious Nazi death camp in Poland, gathered to commemorate the seventy-fifth anniversary of liberation from the camp. They testified to the brutalities of the Nazi state-sanctioned killing machine – to which, at the time of the war, the rest of the world had appeared indifferent. More than 1.1 million Jews – along with thousands of Roma, dissidents, and others considered "enemies of the state" – were murdered at the camp while the international community looked away. Calls to never let such crimes happen again were mixed with impassioned indignation and a warning against the complicity, apathy, and demagoguery that paved the way to the mass slaughter of about 11 million people. This was an instance of state-sanctioned disappearance on a truly epic scale. Several of the survivors spoke not only of the terrifying criminal nightmare and systemic ethnic cleansing undertaken at Auschwitz but also of the conditions that made the camp possible, warning that the lessons there have not been learned by existing generations. A number of the survivors also expressed alarm at our current moment in history, when authoritarianism is on the rise again. They argued that indifference and the failure to hold power accountable provide the moral abyss and political foundation that make mass murder possible. Ninety-one-year-old Elza Baker warned, "There are signs to look out for. If you don't watch out one day you wake up and it's too late."[1]

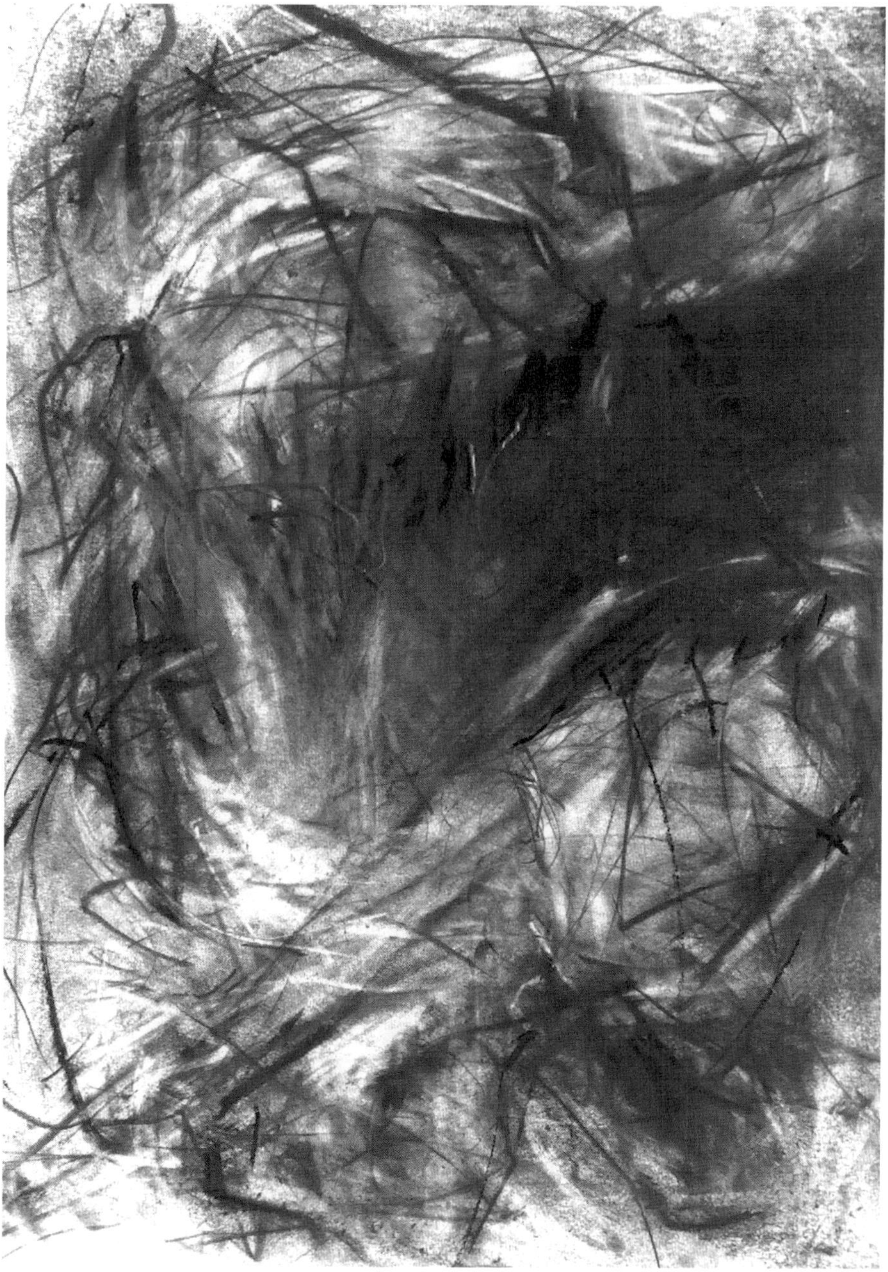

Chantal Meza, *The Void III*, 2019, graphite and charcoal on paper, 29.5 x 42 cm

The toxic shadow of Auschwitz and the collective repulsion against bigotry, discrimination, racism, and racial purity appear to have been forgotten, subjected to their own disappearance, as fascist forces long kept at bay on the margins of society have moved again to the centre of power. Such events suggest with great urgency the danger that collective indifference poses to democracy and echo the words of Marian Turski, a survivor of Auschwitz, who warned that "when you see that the past is stretched to fit the current political needs … do not be indifferent, otherwise you should not be surprised when another Auschwitz crashes down on us."[2] David Marks, another survivor, echoed Turski's admonition with a warning perfectly suited for the contemporary era: "A dictator doesn't come up from one day to the other … [but in] micro steps."[3]

Although we are not in an era of full-blown fascism marked by genocidal mass killing, fascism's microsteps are increasing, aided by a growing number of governments across the globe. What is more, as we see in countries such as Mexico and elsewhere, the forces of systematic disappearance are alive and well, although the logical connections with historical atrocities such as Auschwitz are underplayed, and all the while a toxic mix of militarism, state violence, and a politics of disposability becomes normalized in the white heat of an emerging rise of fascist politics globally. What is shared here is a distinct relationship to neoliberal capitalism, which thrives on the violence of organized forgetting. This is a system that has normalized disappearance, such that its real sources are denied. Where there is disappearance, there is always the denial – always the violence – especially against cultures of resistance and the political imagination.

Repressive apparatuses associated with fascist politics have been further normalized through a culture of fear and a language of demonization, depravity, and racism long associated with fascist ideas and culture. For example, in the United States, there have been well documented mainstream appeals to the racist sentiments of neo-Nazis, ultranationalists, white Christian fundamentalists, and white supremacists. Ignorance, then, has become a form of weaponized refusal to acknowledge the violence of the past and now revels in a culture of media spectacles where public concerns are translated into private obsessions, unchecked consumerism, and fatuous entertainment. As James Baldwin rightly warns, "Ignorance, allied with power, is the most ferocious enemy justice can have."[4] The warning signs from history are all too clear. Failure to learn from the history of state-sanctioned disappearance has disastrous political consequences. Such ignorance is not simply about the absence of information but also has its own political and pedagogical categories whose formative cultures threaten both critical agency and democracy itself. What I call the violence of organized forgetting signals how, in contemporary politics, emotion triumphs over reason, spectacle over truth, and self-help over collective resistance, thereby erasing history by producing an endless flow of fragmented, privatized, and disingenuous knowledge. Once ignorance is weaponized, the habits of critical citizenship are denounced, the space for enabling the grammar of political and moral imagination withers, and violence seems to be a tragic inevitability.

Ignorance is not innocent, especially when it both legitimates white supremacists and right-wing extremist groups and enables the violence at the heart of their ideology. The regime of former US president Donald Trump offers a case study in the merging of historical amnesia, the savagery of neoliberalism, and the rise of white nationalism and white supremacy. For instance, in an almost unprecedented and equally dangerous move, Trump's White House became a monument to white nationalism. Consider Trump's defence of Confederate monuments and his support for racial sorting, his characterization of the suburbs as white public spheres, his attempt to pass laws that denied citizenship to particular groups, and his definition of cities as dark enclaves of criminality, all of which echoed earlier forms of fascist politics.

In his first presidential debate with future president Joe Biden during the 2020 election, Trump refused to denounce white supremacy while signalling his support for members of the right-wing extremist group Proud Boys, stating that they should "stand back and stand by" – as though they were his personal militia waiting to be called into service. His inflammatory remarks not only revealed a tribute to white supremacy and his willingness to stoke racial fears but also his support for the continued use of violence by right-wing extremist groups to promote social change. His incitement to violence among his followers culminated in their unprecedented murderous assault on the Capitol on 6 January 2021, in which 140 people were injured and 5 people eventually died. Trump made it clear that he was a candidate for aggrieved white Americans and that he was more than willing to fan the flames of hatred and bigotry. His racist remarks revealed the degree to which he turned democracy into ashes.

A viable civic culture requires that we be present. And being present requires the ability to be recognized – to rightfully appear without fear of reprisals. We live in an age of relentless crisis marked by the collapse of civic ideals, ethical values, and democratic institutions that serve the public good. Language now operates in the service of violence, and ignorance has become the prevailing ideal that informs contemporary politics.[5] Religious fundamentalism, white supremacy, and economic tyranny now inform each other, giving rise to an updated recurrence of fascist politics, with its own novel forms of forgetting and violence.[6] How else explain the massive voter suppression campaign taking place in the United States, supported by almost the entirety of the Republican Party, Conservative evangelicals, and powerful organs of the right-wing media such as Fox News, Newsmax, and Sinclair Broadcast Group.[7] Fascist ideology is no longer on the margins of society but now constitutes a totality that has produced a cult-like following where economics, politics, and the discourse of hate and violence merge.

This is an age when apocalyptic prophecies replace thoughtfulness and sustained acts of social responsibility. In this age of crisis, where every nihilistic prophecy is liberated, right-wing populist regimes continue to fuel conspiracy theories, normalize lying as a way to degrade public discourse, and elevate emotion over reason as a way to legitimate a culture of cruelty, and society experiences its own pleasure through the need for vengeance and the imposition of brutality and injury upon those minorities considered disposable. Indeed, although we may even look upon these events, they are also forgotten too quickly. If fear diminishes our intellectual vitality and undercuts our civic imagination, language degenerates into clichés, allowing the world to become smaller, flat, and devoid of hope. Language now becomes thinner, detached from history except as a force for denial, while undermining viable democratic social spheres and spaces where people can be brought together as collective agents and critically engaged citizens. What disappears under such circumstances is a world that refuses to be read through the categories of bigotry, hatred, racism, and ultranationalism.

A culture of withdrawal, privatization, and immediacy reinforces an indifference to public life, the suffering of others, and what Hannah Arendt calls "the ruin of our categories of thought and standards of judgment."[8] The space of traditional politics and a media-driven society are marked by an ongoing culture of diversion and disappearance. Such spaces no longer provide the language for understanding the totality of the crisis rooted in the absence of a comprehensive politics capable of defining the related parts and threads that point to a society in crisis. Violence, especially as relates to the joining of a predatory neoliberalism and a fascist politics of white supremacy, has become the regulative principle of everyday life. As Nancy Fraser points out, "these forces have been grinding away at our social order for quite some time" and constitute not only a highly visible crisis of politics and economics but also a not so visible crisis of ideas.[9]

But there is no disappearance without the spectacle to cover the organization of its forgetting and the evisceration of ethical consciousness. States of disappearance today are now matched by a mainstream and corporate-controlled digital media and screen culture that produces political theatre, heightens ignorance, fractures narratives, and abides racial hysteria.[10] The spectacle becomes a workstation for a politics of disappearance, covering over the lawless policies aimed at those considered unworthy, unthinkable, and unknowable. We can be seduced by the spectacle so that other forms of violence remain hidden in plain sight, producing states of disappearance of a more arbitrary yet no less sinister kind. Hence, without contradiction, contemporary states of disappearance authorize and produce a culture of sensationalism designed to increase attention and the pleasure quotient at the expense of truth, justice, and reason, thereby undermining a complex rendering of the related nature of social problems and fostering the suppression of a culture of dissent and informed judgments.

Politics is now laden with bombast, words strung together to shock, to numb the mind, and images overwrought with a self-serving sense of riotousness and anger, which prove to be far more than petty distractions. Particularly distinct about this historical period is what Susan Sontag calls a form of aesthetic fascism, with its contempt of "all that is reflective, critical, and pluralistic."[11] We can make sense of this through both the hard and soft disimagination machines of contemporary politics. Whereas the hard disimagination machines function as overt and unapologetic propaganda machines that trade in nativism, misrepresentations, and racist hysteria, all wrapped in the cloak of a regressive view of patriotism, the soft disimagination machines function largely to cater to the digital and technical universe, celebrity culture, and the cutthroat, "survival of the fittest" ethos of the market, all the while isolating social issues, individualizing social problems, and making the workings of power only superficially visible in order to conjure up an illusion of the appearance of value. As the realm of the social is refigured in the shadow and legacy of a fascist past, economic activity is removed from social costs, America forgets its civic lessons, and the disimagination machines work overtime to produce a public that lacks any understanding of how neoliberal fascism infantilizes them politically while undermining the conditions that enable them to connect private issues to larger social considerations, engage in collective resistance, and refuse to be trapped in the fog of fear, manufactured ignorance, and unparalleled cruelty and greed.

A politics of the spectacle saturates the senses with noise, cheap melodrama, lies, and buffoonery. Election results are denied, science is disparaged, and informed judgment is viewed as a liability. This is not to suggest that the spectacle that now shapes politics as pure theatre is meant merely to entertain while distracting us from the more mundane realities of life. On the contrary, the current spectacle functions largely to separate the past from a politics that in its current form has turned deadly in its attack on the values and institutions crucial to a functioning democracy. In the age of Trumpism, for a large part of the population both in the United States and globally, the politics of disappearance thrives when democracy is in crisis and the public denied. Again, without contradiction, it is the echoes of a fascist past that in this instance remain hidden, their traces unseen. Such fascist lines appear before us like the harrowing depths of Chantal Meza's series *The Void*, which although difficult to determine slowly reveal the most monstrous, brutal, and devastating of faces. The brilliance of Meza's work is to show how the violent traces of the past tear into the present, as in the series *Fragments of a Catastrophe*, revealing like Paul Klee the disasters that layer history.[12] But for memory to be effective, as Meza shows, it is not enough for historical memory to be merely stated or acknowledged. It also needs to be imaginative, equipped with a resistive defiance in the face of those forces that continue to annihilate humanity and our courage to express the truth.

Meza's work suggests a language beyond the power of words, especially words that cannot grasp the loss of historical consciousness or the way that it can be maligned, mangled, and ruthlessly reconceived in the interest of domination. Her series *Since the Beginning* and *Obscure Beasts* engage senses that in authoritarian times have become atrophied, reduced to the pornographic politics of immediacy.[13] The vibrancy of the colours and the way that the paintings merge the power of colour with the shapes of an aesthetic in search of memory and redemption push at the frontiers of the aesthetic as a political form while expanding the frontiers of the moral and political imagination. There are alarming echoes of the past here, a danger bursting forth in images with no boundaries, only the depth of learning to see differently, hopefully, and politically. Her work repudiates the spectacle by refusing to allow it to be consumed by its own aura. The politics of disappearance is no longer the handmaiden of fascism and capitalism but a signpost for mediating, the power of seeing more, refusing to look away – art in search of the socialist imagination. Her work is created for the Others – the disposable, the excess, the forgotten – only to remind us how much work art can do as a form of memory for those of us still here. Her brilliant *The Void* takes everyday experience and reminds us of how the smallest details can be used to bear witness, that memory work can emerge from and challenge the hegemonically induced desire to forget. All of Meza's work refuses Max Horkheimer and Theodor W. Adorno's insistence that "all reification is forgetting,"[14] and in doing so, it offers us a powerful visual pedagogical register regarding how we see, remember, and hopefully act differently. Meza's art is cultural and pedagogical work at its best and offers us a new map of meanings, desire, and hope with which to think, fight back, and inhabit difference as a source of solidarity and community.

A flair for the overly dramatic, where the spectacle triumphs over the poetic and the ethical, eliminates the distinction between fact and fiction, lies and the truth. Under such circumstances, the spectacle functions as part of a culture of evisceration, division, and fragmentation, all the while refusing to confront fascist aesthetics and even denying its very existence. It is no coincidence to see political theatre in its current form embracing elements of a fascist past. In doing so, it creates a form of self-sabotage among a public that largely refuses to "pose the question why Hitler and Nazi Germany continue to exert such a grip on modern life"[15] and that regards Nazism instead as the standard against which all contemporary forms of fascism can be continually denied. If it is not a death camp, then it is not fascism. This is a proposition that in itself ignores the very brutal processes of experimentation that preceded the ghastly attempts at the final solution of absolute disappearance. Any reference to fascism is now taken to be a direct comparison and dismissed as an overreach. There is no sense here of treating fascism as a political and ideological force that mutates, travels, and appears in different and often updated forms, all the while refusing to be interred in the past as though it were a museum piece. The historian Timothy Snyder is right in stating, "My own view is that greater knowledge of the past, fascist or otherwise, allows us to notice and conceptualize elements of the present that we might otherwise disregard and to think more broadly about future possibilities ... This is not because the present repeats the past, but because the past enlightens the present."[16]

Historical memory informed by a rigorous engagement with the past is thus crucial not only if we are to learn important lessons from the past but also if we are to recognize what has been *unlearned* and what has been purposely forgotten or rewritten to camouflage and hide the emergence of twenty-first-century fascism. Both memory and civic education are in crises when politics is reduced to daily pageants of menace, amplified by Twitter storms, and normalized by a mainstream media attentive to a culture of shock and immediacy. Again, like the brutal layers of history drawn in Meza's work, historical consciousness and civic education become mere shadows of the past, caught up in a frenzied assault whose lines and lessons are difficult to decipher. Under such conditions, historical memory and moral witnessing get in the way because they either are too dangerous to recall or are reduced to a tool for spreading falsehoods, lies, and elements of a fascist politics. Collective ignorance reproduced in a culture of consumerism with the compliance of profit-driven media is crucial to undermining the ability of people to make sense of history while also being attentive to the truth offered by the past.

To be absent of memory is to be absent of hope. And to be absent of hope is to be removed from any sense of critical agency. Another lesson to be learned from the absence of history is not only how ignorance gets normalized but also how the absence of critical thought allows us to forget that we are moral subjects capable of changing the world around us. Educators, writers, poets, and artists are crucial if we are to counter the grammar of violence and the pedagogical cultures of disappearance. Critical history and its grammars of appearance that confront intolerable conditions, so vividly painted in the brutal landscapes of Meza's art, offer a model that can be used to learn something from earlier turns toward authoritarianism, making it more difficult to assume that fascism is merely a symbolic and degenerate relic of the past. Contemporary forms of disappearance enabled through a theatre of cruelty renders life disposable, all the while producing a fog of ignorance that gives contemporary credence to Arendt's claim in *The Origins of Totalitarianism* that "the ideal subject of totalitarian rule is not the convinced Nazi or the convinced Communist, but people for whom the distinction between fact and fiction (i.e., the reality of experience) and the distinction between true and false (i.e., the standards of thought) no longer exist."[17]

The horrors that we are witnessing under demagogues across the globe should be connected to a past that reminds us of the suffering, misery, and violence endemic to a fascist politics and demonstrates how in its updated forms fascism can be challenged individually and collectively. As some of the survivors of Auschwitz made clear, memory in this instance allows us to reconsider the entire project of politics with an urgency necessary to enable us to think our way through to a future where we can view both history and the world through the democratic and moral lens of redemption, justice, and hope.

History shows that fascist politics and its annihilating impulses must be interrogated as a source of possibility, critique, and resistance. The horrors that we are witnessing across the globe should be connected to a past that reminds us of the suffering, misery, and violence endemic to a fascist politics and how, in its updated forms, it can be challenged individually and collectively in creative ways. But this undertaking cannot be comforting. Looking upon Meza's series *Obscure Beasts*, we are reminded that the worst we can do is look away. Politics in the absence of dangerous memories enables fascism to colonize our dreams, shut down the power of imagination, and foreclose critiques of neoliberalism's carceral regimes of social atomization, privatization, and savage discipline. Let us not forget that for the violence of organized forgetting to operate on a grand scale, it must be shaped by the language, rituals, and invocations of war and machineries of terminal exclusion and death. We have seen this conduct on full display in America in the past few years, reinforced by some academics who decry any mention of fascism in the contemporary context, making them more complicit than informative in these troubling times.

Fascism is not merely an apparition of the past. Nor can its re-emergence in a different and obscure form be dismissed as a kind of ideological paranoia.

State violence, with the multiple forms of disappearance that it produces, is not an abstraction but a visceral reality. It kills people, ruins their lives, takes away their loved ones, and does so by waging war against those populations deemed to be disposable. It operates through a grammar of impunity and mobilizes hateful desires, such that appearance is inseparable from disappearance, wealth from disposability, spectacle from annihilation, truth from falsehood, and greed from the evisceration of all ethical coordinates. Arrogant in power and unaccountable for its defence of bigotry, racism, and hatred, fascist language thrives on legitimated lawlessness while fanning the flames of violence in the name of order and greatness. It is as though we have learned nothing from Zygmunt Bauman, ignorant that violence has again become a project of dehumanization and disposability and a warning to those marked for terminal abandonment.[18]

We should also remember that disappearance is not just about the suppression of ideas but also about bodies, about lives, and that some lives, some bodies are more disposable than others. Contemporary forms of fascist violence are undeniably rooted in the historical legacy of lynching, mass murder, and sordid appeals to eugenics, which appropriates elements of a fascist politics, colonialism, and the genocide politics aimed at Indigenous populations. Such violence is normalized through the haze of political performativity, entertainment as a fantasy machine, and updated forms of fascist aesthetics that play out in the lies and circuses on display every evening in the mainstream news cycles. It is a form of blinding fascism marked not only by an extraordinary capacity for denial about the haunting legacy of slavery – the first systematic mastery of disappearance for profit on a truly global scale – but also by the self-perpetuating fantasies of political exceptionalism and supremacy.[19] Violence on this scale is what should be addressed, and it should be analyzed not through the lens of moral righteousness and regressive notions of indignation but by means of political insights and convictions that couple moral outrage with imaginative responses. For example, calling out the destruction of property or the pulling-down of symbols of institutional racism while ignoring state violence is not commentary but an act of cowardice.

The history of disappearance points explicitly to a history of racial injustice, which is maintained by replacing historical consciousness with a form of historical amnesia and the blinding of people to truth. Attempts to recover a history of slavery for public school students through undertakings like *The 1619 Project*, a series of *New York Times* articles,[20] were attacked by Trump and his reactionary clones as un-American and at odds with what Trump labelled as "patriotic education."[21] Such a purging of history is endemic to all authoritarian regimes. Yet history in these dark times is once again being written in the interests of tyrants and oppressive groups who do everything that they can to cleanse it of its alleged impurities, elements of resistance, and what Arendt terms "instants of truth."[22] The attempts to rewrite history by labelling forms of education that address racial injustices as dangerous have been happening at a historical moment when ignorance has lost its innocence, as Baldwin warned, aligning itself with the forces of bigotry, which marches with the ghosts of the monsters of the past. Malicious in their disdain of criticism, these unapologetic pedagogical assaults are an attempt to undermine the value of historical consciousness by disappearing critical historical gains and by rendering invisible modes of historical understanding and social issues that lie on the side of political and economic justice. It is worth repeating that disappearance is not then just about the disappearance of bodies but also about the dangerous memories, values, knowledges, and dreams that those bodies carried and breathed into the world. When the calls and struggles for racial justice are labelled as unpatriotic or are dismissed, the abyss of fascist politics is not far away. To misread history is to misread power while denigrating those who have fought the battles of the past and risked their lives for the promises of a substantive democracy.

Historical amnesia is often used as a weapon of (mis)education, politics, and power. At stake here is the erasure of struggles by those who fought for justice in the past because they offer dangerous memories and lessons to those protesters marching in the streets today. The notion that the emancipatory elements of the past must be erased is a centrepiece of all authoritarian societies, as it causes public memory to wither and the threads of authoritarianism to become normalized. When history is weaponized, it is often accompanied by a broader attack on critical education, civic literacy, oppositional journalists, and a free media. Although some critics have recently eschewed comparisons with contemporary populist leaders and historical authoritarian regimes, it is crucial to recognize the alarming signs that echo the horrors of a fascist past. Once again, rejecting any possible comparison makes it easier to believe that we have nothing to learn from history and to take comfort in the assumption that a fascist politics cannot surface once again. No democracy can survive without an informed and educated citizenry. Historical amnesia provides the conditions for the truth to disappear, conspiracy theories to proliferate, and education to be stripped of its critical function. What every global citizen should learn from the manipulation of racist fears as a political strategy is that no democracy can survive this assault if it goes unchallenged. We have seen this outcome before under the dictatorships of Adolf Hitler, Augusto Pinochet in Chile, and others.

None of this history can be divorced from the economic dimensions of human disposability and its evisceration of life. That was as true for Nazi Germany as it was for Pinochet. Following the late 1970s, inspired by the Chilean model, there was a notable intensification of neoliberal modes of governance, ideology, and policies in the United States, Canada, the United Kingdom, and other European countries – a historical period when the foundations for democratic public spheres were dismantled. Schools, public radio, the media, and other critical cultural apparatuses were under siege, viewed as dangerous to a market-driven society that considers critical thought, dialogue, and civic engagement to be a threat to its basic values and structures of power. In this historical era, the discourse of democracy and the common good came crashing to the ground, its promise buried within the ruins. Prime Minister Margaret Thatcher in Britain and soon after President Ronald Reagan in the United States – both hard-line advocates of market fundamentalism – announced that there was no such thing as society and that government was the problem, not the solution.

Democracy and the political process were sacrificed to the unseen power of corporations and the emerging financial service industries, just as hope was appropriated as an advertisement for a whitewashed world in which the capacity of culture to critique oppressive social practices was greatly diminished. Large social movements fragmented into isolated pockets of resistance, mostly organized around a form of identity politics that largely ignored a much-needed conversation about the broader issues affecting society, such as the growing inequality in wealth, power, and income. Against this backdrop, particularly new is the way that young people have been increasingly denied a significant place in an already weakened social contract and the degree to which they are absent from how many countries now define the future. The future itself has become a terrain of disposability. Youth are no longer the place where society reveals its dreams. Instead, youth are becoming the site of society's nightmares. Within neoliberal narratives, youth are mostly defined as a consumer market, a drain on the economy, or an indicator of trouble. Young people increasingly have become subject to an oppressive disciplinary machine that teaches them to define citizenship through the exchange practices of the market and to follow orders and toe the line in the face of oppressive forms of authority. They are caught in a society where almost every aspect of their lives is shaped by the dual forces of the market and a growing police state. The message is clear: buy and sell or be punished. Appear as we want you to or vanish into insignificance. Mostly out of step, young people, especially poor minorities and low-income whites, are increasingly inscribed within a machinery of dead knowledge, social relations, and values in which there is an attempt to render them voiceless and invisible.

How young people are represented betrays a great deal about what is increasingly new about the economic, social, cultural, and political constitution of fading liberal societies and their growing disinvestment in young people, the social state, and democracy itself. The structures of neoliberal violence have put the vocabulary of democracy on life support, and one consequence is that subjectivity and education are no longer the lifelines of critical forms of individual and social agency. The promises of modernity regarding progress, freedom, and hope have not been eliminated but reconfigured, stripped of their emancipatory potential, and relegated to the logic of a savage market instrumentality – a logic that absorbs as much as it casts aside. Modernity on these terms has reneged on its promise to young people to provide social mobility, stability, and collective security. Long-term planning and the institutional structures that support them are now relegated to the imperatives of privatization, deregulation, flexibility, and short-term profits. Social bonds have given way under the collapse of social protections and the attack on the welfare state. Moreover, all solutions to socially produced problems are now relegated to the mantra of individual pathologies. Collectives are after-all much more difficult to eradicate than a solitary life.

The structures of neoliberal modernity not only disinvest in young people and commodify them but also transform the protected space of childhood into a zone of disciplinary exclusion and cruelty, especially for those young people further marginalized by race and class, who now inhabit a social landscape where they are increasingly disparaged as flawed consumers or pathologized others. With no adequate role to play as consumers, many are now considered disposable, forced to inhabit zones of social abandonment extending from homeless shelters and bad schools to bulging detention centres and prisons. Amid the rise of the punishing state, the circuits of state repression, surveillance, and disposability increasingly link the fate of blacks, Latinos, Native Americans, poor whites, and Asian Americans, who are now caught in governing through a crime-youth complex, which increasingly serves as a default solution to major social problems. Young people live in a society where every institution becomes an "inspection regime" – recording, watching, gathering information, and storing data. Complementing these regimes is the shadow of the prison, which is no longer separated from society as an institution of total surveillance. As Michel Foucault notes, "The prison begins well before its doors. It begins as soon as you leave your house – and even before."[23] Total surveillance is increasingly the general condition of society as a whole. Moreover, the shadow of the prison is only one register of what has been called the imprisonment binge. Angela Y. Davis sums it up well: "Instead of building housing for the homeless, throw them in prison. Instead of developing the educational system, throw the illiterate in prison. Throw people in prison who lose jobs as the result of de-industrialization, globalization of capital, and the dismantling of the welfare state. Get rid of all of them. Remove these dispensable populations from society. According to this logic the prison becomes a way of disappearing people in the false hope of disappearing the underlying social problems they represent."[24]

All of this would be exacerbated in 2020 with the arrival of the Covid-19 virus, which inaugurated a new chapter in the history of disposability and human disappearance. A darkness spread across the globe driven by a pandemic pestilence that exhibited a dystopian presence at odds with any just, prudent, and equitable notion of the future. The world was in lockdown, and America more than anywhere else was in a state of crisis. The racial, economic, and educational nature of this crisis touched every aspect of public life. We were also in a period when the old was in the midst of a legitimation crisis and the new was trying to be reborn. Out of this period of uncertainty, new forces for change appeared evident in the presence of millions across the globe protesting racial injustice and state violence. Police violence against black people no longer disappeared into the fog of an indifferent, if not complacent, media chamber. Millions marched across the globe in the wake of the murders of George Floyd and Breonna Taylor, among others, using their collective bodies to demonstrate against the brute police violence promoting the plague of racial terrorism. Such resistance is a form of refusal against the forces of annihilation. The plague, however, produced an age of uncertainty, fragmentation, despair, and a dire foreboding about what was to come. Certainties were replaced by shared fears. More troubling was the apprehension that the crisis had an air of longevity about it, constituting a turning point in history as such. Now, the stark choice of what the future might look like appears to hang between the forces of despotism and democracy, disappearances and a fading hope. Yet, as real as this foreboding appears, history is open, and how it will unfold remains in the balance.

The pandemic was a crisis that cannot be allowed to foment a catastrophe in which all hope is lost. On the contrary, having threatened democracy's ability to breathe, the pandemic also offers up the possibility to rethink politics and the habits of critical education, human agency, values, and what life would be like in a caring society. Amid the corpses produced by neoliberal capitalism and Covid-19, there are also flashes of optimism, a chance to move beyond a contemporary resurgence of authoritarianism and to reappear in a more radically considered way. This outcome requires rejecting the normalizing ideologies of a poisonous cynicism and the paralyzing conformity endemic to neoliberal capitalism. It also points to the need to reclaim a vision of a radical democracy that is more compassionate, equitable, just, and inclusive.

Within a new wave of resistance and rebellion, anti-democratic principles that had been normalized, weakening society's democratic defences, are being questioned with an inspiring sense of collective urgency. This is especially true among blacks and others who have for so long suffered disappearance while bearing the heavy burden of economic and political colonialism as the historical victims of abduction and slavery. The contemporary horrors of inequality, compulsory austerity, the defunding of public health systems, and the collapse of the economy in 2008 produced by four decades of neoliberalism, which destroyed communities of colour, have revealed forces that are finally being acknowledged as the fundamental plague behind the injustices in evidence during the Covid-19 pandemic. This is a plague marked by egregious degrees of exploitation, unchecked militarism, and a racialized politics of disposability and terminal exclusion that views human beings as the embodiment of human waste, a politics reinforced, if not propelled, by an ethos of white nationalist supremacy. This long residue of unbridled capitalism is inseparable from its deep-rooted institutionalized racism and from a pestilence of disposability, updated as a form of fascism today. Fascist principles, derived from one version of what I call a pandemic pedagogy of fascist politics, now operate at so many levels of everyday society that it is difficult to recognize them, especially as they have the imprimatur of power at the highest levels of government. Fascist pedagogical ideas, practices, and desires work through diverse social media platforms and mainstream and right-wing cultural apparatuses in multiple ways. This is the space of a pandemic pedagogy that is produced in the cultural apparatuses that function ideologically and politically to objectify people, promote spectacles of violence, endorse consumerism as the only viable way of life, and legitimate a murderous nationalism.

Pandemic pedagogy now unashamedly makes ignorance a fundamental principle of politics and in doing so tends to function so as "to erase everything that matters."[25] Shaped in the discourse of common sense, pandemic pedagogy works subconsciously through the discourse of common sense as an affective mode of self-sabotage. It legitimates the discourse of hate in everyday exchanges, degrades people of colour, and promotes thoughtlessness through the ubiquity of a culture that produces an endless array of authoritarian pedagogical practices that serve to exploit, dominate, and depoliticize us. In the pandemic fog of historical amnesia, where the violence of forgetting is more brutal than ever, moral boundaries also disappear, just as people become more accepting of extreme acts of cruelty and willingly submit to propaganda machines that disdain notions of truth and view any viable critique of power as "fake news," all the while disconnecting language and policies from their social costs.

But this dark plague of neoliberal fascism is just one invisible yet traceable pestilence among many. This is a pestilence that has now fully engulfed American society as memories of caged children disappear into a vaporized culture of immediacy, the killing of journalists is forgotten, and the lynching of black bodies is buried beneath the discourse of a post-racial society. In addition, the terror of a fascist politics evaporates in the affective modalities of pleasure and fear that mark a rampant culture of political theatre and spectacles. As the underside of fascist politics, pandemic pedagogy closes down the space of translation and thrives on a machinery of inscriptions that erases the notion that human beings are not only moral and political agents but also historical subjects capable of both understanding and changing the world. This depoliticizing practice is not only a political and ethical issue but also an educational issue that connects the power of critical understanding to the capacity for action, empowerment, and transformation. If pandemic pedagogy functions to bury what Foucault calls "the dramaturgy of the real,"[26] critical pedagogy works to establish a symbolic relationship with the world whereby politics becomes educative and functions to change the way that people see things and how they resist those ideas and institutions that thrive on the energies of the political zombies who fuel the multiple pandemics that accelerate the deaths of the unwanted and make social death a self-generated practice.

The greatest pandemic we face in the world today is the pandemic of ignorance, white supremacy, white nationalism, militarism, and the willingness to surrender power as individual and social agents to those who write the past and present in the scripts of domination. Pedagogy has never been more valuable as a political tool that can offer the resources to challenge the ideological, educational, and militant practices deployed by emerging right-wing and fascist groups. Pedagogy is crucial for understanding how power shapes and is reinvented with respect to questions of culture, sexuality, history, and political agency. As a political project, pedagogy is the struggle over those public and private spaces where people's everyday lives are aligned with particular narratives, identities, cultural practices, and political values. As such, pedagogy is the essential scaffolding of social interaction and the foundation of the public sphere. It is a crucial political practice because it takes seriously what it means to understand the relationship between how we learn and how we act as individual and social agents; that is, it is concerned not only with how individuals learn to think critically but also with how they come to grips with a sense of individual and social responsibility. It is the essential component in the realm of visibility, the realm of appearance, the realm of acknowledgment. At issue here, then, is the crucial political question of what it means to be responsible for one's actions as part of a broader attempt to be an engaged citizen who can expand and deepen the possibilities of democratic public life instead of condemning life to the unknown chapters of disposability. Human agency is inseparable from the formative cultures and pedagogical practices that create the possibility of a mobilized citizenry and radical change.

The violence of disappearance surrounds us today. It is a prison with and without cells; it is the pit where the dead bodies of journalists and poets are buried; it is the police who come in the night to arrest dissidents; it is the deep grammar of a social system at war with democracy. The ghosts of resistance, like the figures intimated in Meza's series *Apparitions*, are everywhere. They wait for memory to come alive, for moral witnessing to hold power accountable and to give voice to the dead, whose presence is a reminder that one can never look way in the face of barbarism. They move in the menacing shadows of the present and serve as an early warning system for illuminating the darkest moments of history. We are in the midst of a crisis where it is crucial for individuals and social movements to learn anew how to take responsibility, to learn how to listen, to act with vigilance against the forces of annihilation, and to have the courage to reimagine better worlds. The pandemics of injustice that are ushering in massive degrees of poverty, exclusion, suffering, and death must be resisted with a new understanding of politics and agency. Moreover, the move away from extending the capacities for individual agency must be countered by a notion of social agency imbued with a sense of collective resistance. In the current historical moment, this imperative points to the necessity to create an international social movement from all walks of life for the defence of public goods and the principles of a democratic socialist society. If the radical political horizons of a future society are to be brought into being, it is crucial to engage those everyday pedagogical spaces where identities are produced, modes of recognition come into play, and critical points of view can be redeemed by bringing their value to light. The energies of fascism have become less intense and more fragile, opening them to challenge as the limits of right-wing and updated fascist populist movements become more visible. As the virus of fascism spreads, the merchants of misery and hate have no language to explain or address "the ubiquity of death" across the planet.[27] Theirs is the nihilistic language of disappearance. Ours has to be a visible politics of hope – a language that embraces the grammar of social justice, a passion for equality, and the struggle for a socialist democracy.

NOTES

1 Cited in Kate Connolly, "Survivors Call for End to World Indifference at Auschwitz Memorial," *Guardian* (London), 27 January 2020, https://www.theguardian.com/world/2020/jan/27/auschwitz-survivors-75th-anniversary-commemoration.

2 Cited in ibid.

3 Cited in Ishaan Tharoor, "75 Years after Auschwitz's Liberation, the Ghosts of the Past Loom Large," *Washington Post*, 28 January 2020, https://www.washingtonpost.com/world/2020/01/28/75-years-after-auschwitzs-liberation-ghosts-past-loom-large.

4 James Baldwin, *No Name in the Street* (New York: Vintage Books, 2007), 149.

5 Ruth Ben-Ghiat, "Beware of President Trump's Nefarious Language Games," *Washington Post*, 21 December 2017, https://www.washingtonpost.com/news/democracy-post/wp/2017/12/21/beware-of-president-trumps-nefarious-language-games. See also Naomi Fry, "The Year in Stupidity," *New Yorker*, 13 December 2019, https://www.newyorker.com/culture/2019-in-review/the-year-in-stupidity.

6 Timothy Snyder, *On Tyranny: Twenty Lessons from the Twentieth Century* (London: Polity, 2017); Jason Stanley, *How Fascism Works* (New York: Random House, 2018).

7 Brendan Fischer and Ed Pilkington, "Rightwing Group Pours Millions in 'Dark Money' into US Voter Suppression Bid," *Guardian* (London), 13 January 2023, https://www.theguardian.com/us-news/2023/jan/13/heritage-foundation-voter-suppression-lobbying-election-action-plan; Jay Michaelson, "Republicans Want to Stop You from Voting: Here's How to Fight Back," *Rolling Stone*, 29 October 2022, https://www.rollingstone.com/politics/political-commentary/republican-voter-suppression-midterm-elections-1234620519; Annika Brockschmidt, "The US Christian Right Groups Actively Involved in Voter Suppression," *Open Democracy*, 3 November 2022, https://www.opendemocracy.net/en/5050/midterms-election-christian-right-voter-fraud; Igor Derysh, "Conservative Groups Are Writing GOP Voter Suppression Bills – and Spending Millions to Pass Them," *Salon*, 27 March 2021, https://www.salon.com/2021/03/27/conservative-groups-are-writing-gop-voter-suppression-bills---and-spending-millions-to-pass-them.

8 Hannah Arendt, *The Last Interview and Other Conversations* (Brooklyn, NY: Melville House, 2013), 33.

9 Nancy Fraser, *The Old Is Dying and the New Cannot Be Born* (London: Verso, 2019), 9.

10 On the issue of screen culture, see Richard Butsch, *Screen Culture: A Global History* (London: Polity, 2019).

11 Susan Sontag, "Fascinating Fascism," *New York Review of Books*, 6 February 1975, https://www.nybooks.com/articles/1975/02/06/fascinating-fascism.

12 Chantal Meza, *The Void* and *Fragments of a Catastrophe*, https://www.chantal-meza.com/stateofdisappearance.

13 Chantal Meza, *Since the Beginning* and *Obscure Beasts*, https://www.chantal-meza.com/stateofdisappearance.

14 Max Horkheimer and Theodor W. Adorno, *Dialectic of Enlightenment: Philosophical Fragments*, trans. Edmund Jephcott (Stanford, CA: Stanford University Press, 2002), 191.

15 Richard Brody, "When Bad Nazis Happen to Good Directors: Terrence Malick's 'A Hidden Life,'" *New Yorker*, 16 December 2019, https://www.newyorker.com/culture/the-front-row/when-bad-nazis-happen-to-good-directors-terrence-malicks-a-hidden-life.

16 Timothy Snyder, "The American Abyss," *New York Times Magazine*, 9 January 2021, https://www.nytimes.com/2021/01/09/magazine/trump-coup.html.

17 Hannah Arendt, *The Origins of Totalitarianism* (New York: Harvest Books, 1973), 474.

18 Zygmunt Bauman, *Modernity and the Holocaust* (Cambridge, UK: Polity, 1991); Zygmunt Bauman, *Wasted Lives: Modernity and Its Outcasts* (Cambridge, UK: Polity, 2003).

19 Raoul Peck, "James Baldwin Was Right All Along," *Atlantic*, 3 July 2020, https://www.theatlantic.com/culture/archive/2020/07/raoul-peck-james-baldwin-i-am-not-your-negro/613708.

20 See Nikole Hannah-Jones, Caitlin Roper, Ilena Silverman, and Jake Silverstein, eds, *The 1619 Project: A New Origin Story* (New York: One World, 2021).

21 Cited in Valerie Strauss, "Trump's 'Patriotic Education' Report Excuses Founding Fathers for Owning Slaves and Likens Progressives to Mussolini," *Washington Post*, 19 January 2021, https://www.washingtonpost.com/education/2021/01/19/trump-patriotic-education-report-slavery-fascists.

22 Hannah Arendt, *Nach Auschwitz: Essays und Kommentare I* (Berlin: Bitterman, 1989), 135.

23 Cited in Michael Hardt and Antonio Negri, *Declaration* (New York: Argo-Navis Author Services, 2012), 20.

24 Angela Y. Davis, *Abolition Democracy: Beyond Empire, Prisons, and Torture* (New York: Seven Stories Press, 2005), 40–1.

25 Ibid., 90–1.

26 Michel Foucault, "Lives of Infamous Men," in *Power: Essential Works of Foucault, 1954–1984*, vol. 3, ed. James D. Faubion, 157–75 (New York: New Press, 2000), 160.

27 John Keane, "Democracy and the Great Pestilence," Geneva Graduate Institute, 14 April 2020, https://www.graduateinstitute.ch/communications/news/democracy-and-great-pestilence.

4

Slavery, Death, and Disappearance

Ana Lucia Araujo

The Atlantic slave trade forcibly displaced enslaved Africans within the African continent and across the Atlantic Ocean between the late fifteenth century and the middle of the nineteenth century. The history of this human tragedy is one of exploitation but also of survival and resistance. In theory and in practical terms, the ultimate goal of transporting captive Africans to the Americas was to extract their labour, not to annihilate them. At least not immediately. The state of disappearance of enslaved African bodies therefore emerged as a by-product of the inhuman trade. Disappearance operated through various stages and superposed layers that corresponded to the actual death of enslaved persons, who were either directly assassinated or who died from indirect causes at some point between the moment that they were captured in Africa, transported to the coast, shipped across the Atlantic Ocean, sold in slave markets, and held in plantation or urban settings in the Americas.

Historians have been grappling to find the traces of enslaved men and women who very often remained nameless and invisible in the historical record.[1] Like historians, artists who address the human condition in their works have also hunted the ghosts of the men and women who disappeared. In her work, artist Chantal Meza hunts the disappeared. But her work is also haunted by the disappeared. In the series *Since the Beginning*, Meza plays with thick layers of paint, texture, and material.[2] This accumulation of black, red, and grey matter evokes body fluids, blood, and hair. This mass evokes remains of beings who have been there, who are no longer there, but who resist disappearance – reminding us of the work of West Central African ritual practitioners and carvers who create objects of power incorporating human remains such as hair, bones, and teeth. Like them, Meza's brush, hands, and gestures bring these disappeared beings back to life.

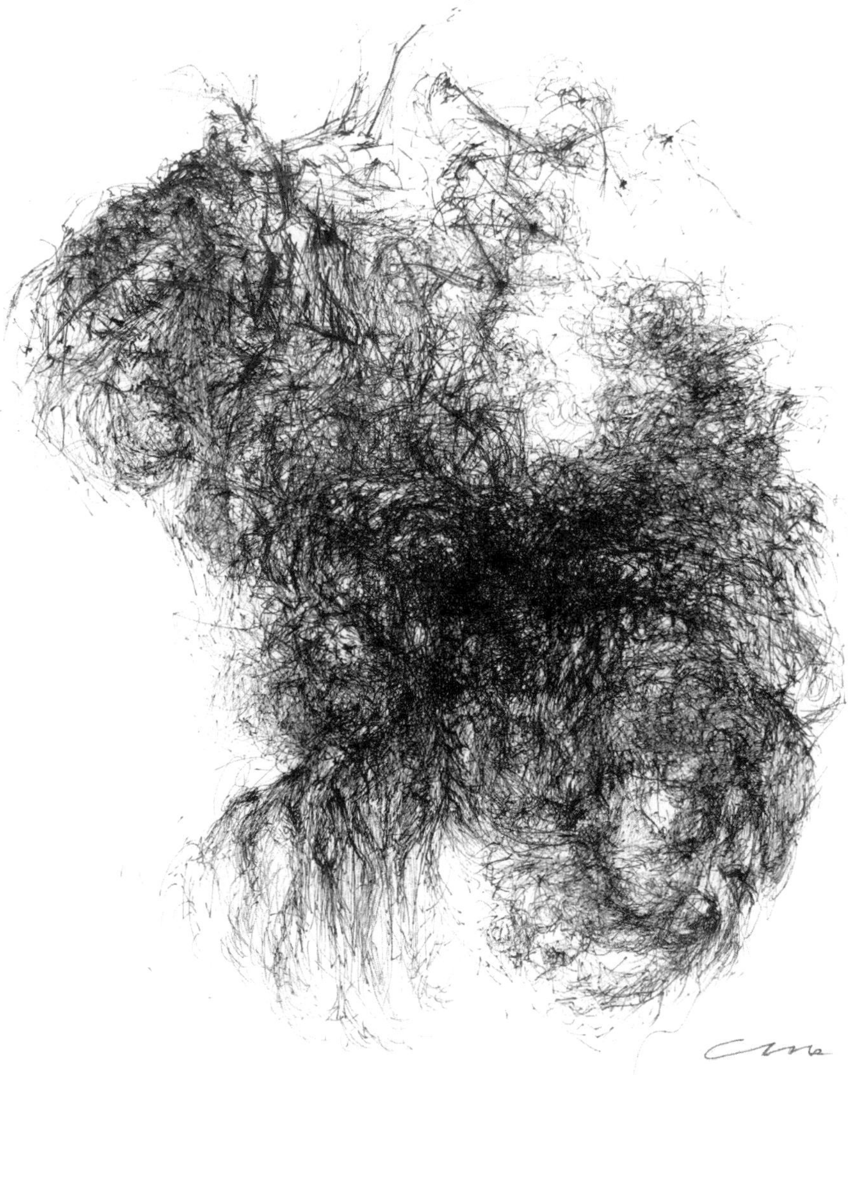

Chantal Meza, *Apparitions II*, 2017, ink on paper, 35 x 27 cm

Disappearance in the context of the Atlantic slave trade and slavery is not a metaphor; it was a deadly reality. But even for the men, women, and children who survived all the stages of these atrocities, disappearance was a ghost that followed them throughout their lives. During the process of forced displacement, their families and dear ones disappeared. The names that they had received from their parents were stripped away from them. Virtually disappearing, these names continued to resonate only in their thoughts, memories, and dreams. The languages and the religions of their mother countries were also under threat of fading away and eventually disappearing. Because their bodies and minds were dehumanized, the traces of their existence were predestined to disappear. Although the Atlantic slave trade and slavery remained in force for several centuries, the past existence of enslaved people was also doomed to be erased, concealed, and disappear. Yet in the context of the history and memory of slavery and the inhuman trade, the state of disappearance has never reached the status of permanence but has constantly been threatened by the state of reappearance.

For many captives, the long journey from the interior to the coast ended quickly, while they were still in Africa. Men, women, and children, their names, faces, and stories now forgotten, were killed during the long journeys that displaced them from the interior of the continent to the coast. Others saw the face of death before being boarded on slave ships while they were being confined in the improvised barracoons, dungeons, and slave depots on the shores of African ports. Then followed the horrors of the Middle Passage. Death came in the rhythm of the waves. Ship captains and crew members packed African men, women, and children in the hold of slave ships, far often too small to accommodate increasingly larger cargoes of human living flesh.[3] Chained in the darkness – naked, hungry, and thirsty, asphyxiated by the odour of urine and feces – these enslaved persons shared their body fluids during several weeks.[4] The Portuguese were probably the ones to employ the most accurate name for these vessels: *tumbeiros* (floating tombs).[5] Disease spread fast under these horrible conditions of transportation, killing already weakened bodies and transforming these slave voyages into a living nightmare.

In many regions of the Americas where these Africans disembarked, they replaced the Native American populations who prior to them were enslaved and killed. Meza's series *The Void* reminds us of the ambiguous nature of these spaces that were destroyed and whose peoples were dispossessed. Spaces that were new to enslaved Africans but not at all empty for the Indigenous populations who had been in the Americas for thousands of years. Colourless, the drawings in *The Void* evoke what these new spaces were and what they would become. Gradually, the series *Apparitions* takes shape from the vacant black and white networks of blurry lines to become a mass of detailed round shapes. Hair. Heads. Pubic hair. Movement. A new life is possible. But one that is not free of blood and violence.[6]

The experience of the Middle Passage was the first stage in the process of disappearance of African bodies. Many captives did not survive this long voyage of death. Then crew members threw their perished bodies overboard. Other enslaved people were simply put to death when they were ill. This was the tragedy of the infamous slave ship *Zong*. In August 1781, the overcrowded ship left the Gold Coast in West Africa on its way to Jamaica with 442 enslaved persons.[7] But a navigation mistake extended the voyage by three weeks. By then, a viral dysentery was already ravaging the ship. On 29 November 1781, the ship captain (and former surgeon) Luke Collingwood ordered the crew to throw overboard one-third of the enslaved cargo.[8] The captain justified the mass murder as a measure to save the remaining African captives, but the real motivation was securing insurance compensation for the loss of human property.

The *Zong* massacre inspired the British painter William Turner to produce what is probably his most famous painting, *The Slave Ship* (1840). In the background, a slave vessel is lost in a dramatic rendering of clouds and waves. The foreground shows a turbulent sea swallowing the bodies of enslaved Africans thrown overboard. Representing an atrocity that is ultimately irrepresentable, *The Slave Ship* can only tragically render the state of disappearance of enslaved bodies drowned in the darkness of the Atlantic Ocean. The sounds and colours of the *Zong* tragedy and the echoes of Turner's *The Slave Ship* can be sensed in Chantal Meza's series of artworks *Obscure Beasts*.[9] Darkness is rendered through the accumulation of brushstrokes that form intertwined thick textures. Meza's bodily gestures produce these dramatic brushstrokes, evoking this deep ocean and monstruous trade. The red colour of the blood of those who perished in the sea remains imprinted on the paper. In Meza's work, the layers of red colour behind the black brushstrokes conjure the blood stains created by the annihilation of African bodies. They document disappearance. But forgetting and memory are two sides of history's obscure beast. The bloody red, the evidence of the crime, eternally seeks to resurface.

For those who outlived the tragic days of confinement in the hold of slave ships, the torment experienced during the Middle Passage did not end upon arrival on American shores. Weak and ill, a number of enslaved Africans died a few days after disembarking in ports such as Cap-Français in the French colony of Saint-Domingue, in Kingston in the British colony of Jamaica, or in Rio de Janeiro in Brazil, the largest slave port of the Americas. Here, the dehumanization of these newly arrived Africans led to a second layer in the process of disappearance.

The material traces of slavery and the Atlantic slave trade were erased from public view in several former slave-trading ports of the United States. Charleston in South Carolina was the largest such port of arrival in the territory of the United States, and nearly 150,000 enslaved Africans had disembarked there by 1808, when the international slave trade was prohibited in the country. But until the 1990s, Gadsden's Wharf – today's Liberty Square – was not highlighted as the place where enslaved Africans disembarked. In more recent years, a series of panels telling the history of the wharf included one indicating that Liberty Square was once the wharf where enslaved Africans disembarked in Charleston after spending time in quarantine on Sullivan's Island.

Over the past fifteen years, a few projects memorializing slavery have emerged on the island as well. In 2006, the late Toni Morrison through her Toni Morrison Foundation created the Bench by the Road Project to memorialize sites associated with the history of the African diaspora. Through this initiative, the foundation placed one of its iconic benches on Sullivan's Island. Each bench is an invitation to meditate on past atrocities and on the history of enslaved people and their descendants in the Atlantic world. But these public spaces remain disputed sites of public memory. In 2013, when Charleston still had no monument or memorial honouring the victims of the Atlantic slave trade, a large memorial dedicated to the city's Irish immigrants was unveiled next to Gadsden's Wharf. More than erasing Charleston's central role in the Atlantic slave trade, this addition reinforced the process that made enslaved Africans invisible in the city's public space. In 2023, after years of debate, the International African American Museum will finally open in the area covering Gadsden's Wharf. Once unveiled, the museum will be an important step toward opposing the longstanding attempts to erase the memory of slavery from Charleston's public space.

Like in Charleston, the wilful disappearance of material traces of the Atlantic slave trade remained in progress in other slave-trading ports nearly two centuries after the end of the nefarious human trade from Africa to the United States. And this process was not limited to the southern states but was also active in several northern states, where slavery remained alive at least throughout the first three decades of the nineteenth century. For instance, New York City was an important slave port, even if the 8,500 enslaved Africans who disembarked on its shores numbered far fewer than the enslaved Africans who arrived in the many other slave ports in the Americas, including not only Charleston but also Rio de Janeiro and Salvador in Brazil.

After slavery was abolished in the state of New York in 1827, the two-century presence of Africans and their descendants in New York City – which was first a Dutch colony and then, starting in 1664, a British colony – was largely forgotten. Historian Leslie M. Harris calls our attention to this process of disappearance, which had been taking shape since the seventeenth century, noting that with "each movement of black people out of an area, new residents erased their history there, sometimes deliberately, other times incidentally."[10] Like in other urban areas of the Americas where slavery existed, enslaved people performed all kinds of activities in New York City. And burying their dear ones was an important dimension of their lives. Africans and their descendants organized funeral processions with drumming and chanting, as men and women did in West Africa and West Central Africa. Slave owners put to rest a few enslaved individuals in the yard of the Anglican church. But the city's Black community buried their deceased members in the "Negro Burial Ground."[11] The origins of the Black graveyard date back to 1712 and perhaps to the end of the seventeenth century.[12] This cemetery, which contained the remains of nearly 15,000 individuals of African descent, born both in Africa and North America, remained in function until its closure in 1790. Henceforth, its existence was gradually erased from the public landscape through several construction projects.

But the burial ground was not sentenced to the state of disappearance. In 1991, hundreds of bone remains emerged during the excavation to construct a federal building in Manhattan. As the work stopped, researchers concluded that they had rediscovered the old "Negro Burial Ground." Henceforth known as the African Burial Ground, the site became the largest of its kind in the Americas. Its recovery brought to light New York City's neglected history of slavery. As researchers examined the remains and uncovered precious information about the men, women, and children interred there, activists and organizations discussed the future of the burial ground. Eventually, the different groups involved decided to construct a memorial on top of the burial site. In 2006, the African Burial Ground was proclaimed a national monument, and the memorial was eventually dedicated in 2007. Three years later, a visitor centre housing a permanent exhibition was also unveiled in the federal building constructed adjacent to the memorial. The site where Africans and their descendants were put to rest in New York City, which had disappeared for nearly two centuries, eventually re-emerged and gained recognition in the city's public landscape.

Brazil experienced at least one similar case. Until the middle of the eighteenth century, enslaved Africans who arrived in Rio de Janeiro disembarked at the wharf near Largo do Paço, present-day Praça XV (Square XV), where numerous public buildings, including the Customs House and the Royal Palace, were located. From there, organized in lines, the captives were walked to the city to be sold in the dozens of shops located along

Rua Direita (Right Street), present-day Rua 1 de Março (1 March Street). But the long lines of naked newly arrived enslaved Africans entering the city remained a disturbing spectacle and raised fears about the spread of disease. Therefore, in 1758, colonial authorities transferred the slave market to the Valongo neighbourhood, located in the city's northeastern zone near the waterfront at the present-day intersection of Avenidas Barão de Tefé and Perimetral. Starting in 1774, enslaved Africans brought by force to Rio de Janeiro could disembark in Valongo. Therefore, between 1758 and 1831, and especially after 1811 when the wharf's construction was completed, about 1 million enslaved Africans landed at the Valongo Wharf, located in the same region as the city's slave market. But starting in 1831, with the legal ban on the slave trade from Africa to Brazil, slave merchants who continued to illegally bring enslaved Africans to Brazil had to seek hidden and distant shores to discreetly perpetrate their criminal activities. Consequently, Valongo became inactive, as it was no longer possible to disembark human cargo at such a visible wharf.

After 1831, the Valongo Wharf gradually disappeared from Rio de Janeiro's urban space. In 1843, the wharf underwent major work to receive the Empress Teresa Cristina, who arrived in Brazil that same year to marry the Brazilian emperor Dom Pedro II. The site was then covered with granite blocks and renamed Cais da Imperatriz (Empress Wharf). As Brazilian historian Jaime Rodrigues emphasizes, the renewal work and the new name were intended to erase the slave-trading past of the site where so many Africans had disembarked. Henceforth, the place incorporated a commemorative memory of the Brazilian monarchy.[13]

Several other construction works concealed the Valongo Wharf. In 1871, the site was the venue of the ceremony that inaugurated the Dom Pedro II Dock, the first one to be built in Brazil. Then it was transformed into the Praça Municipal, the first of Rio Janeiro's monumental squares. The last layers that suppressed the old slave wharf were added in the early twentieth century. Mayor Francisco Pereira Passos led a major urban reform in Rio de Janeiro that covered the wharf with a landfill. Eventually, the construction of Avenida Barão de Tefé at last buried the old wharf. As part of this erasure, the traces of the Atlantic slave trade also disappeared from the entire neighbourhood. During the twentieth century, the old port zone of Rio de Janeiro, close to the downtown area, remained neglected. Public authorities totally ignored the underprivileged Black population still residing in the port zone. Likewise, the buildings and heritage sites located in the area entered an advanced state of decay.

Several newly arrived Africans died before they could be sold in the Americas. In Rio de Janeiro, these men, women, and children were interred without the performance of any rites associated with their original African religions. Although many of them had already been baptized, they were buried as anonymous individuals without the observance of any Catholic sacraments in a common grave known by then as the Cemitério dos Pretos Novos (Cemetery of New Blacks).[14] The burial ground remained active until approximately 1830, but in the second half of the nineteenth century and during the twentieth century (as had occurred with the Valongo Wharf), the site was gradually erased from Rio de Janeiro's public space.

Following the legal prohibition of the Atlantic slave trade to Brazil in 1831 (even though the illegal trade continued until 1850) and with the abolition of slavery in 1888, the sites where slave-trading activities were held and where slavery existed, such as wharfs, markets, and plantations, were gradually destroyed. Modern urban development launched new constructions, therefore adding an unplanned and deliberate third layer to the process of disappearance of enslaved African bodies. Still, despite the several attempts to annihilate Black bodies and the heritage of African peoples brought by force to the Americas, African cultures and traditions as well as the heritage and memory of slavery obviously survived and transformed themselves in Brazil.

In a city like Rio de Janeiro, African cultures continued to live through the activities of its large population of African descent, whose music, religious practices, dance styles, and foodways were incorporated into the city's fabric. Yet, by creating whitening policies, the Brazilian state added a fourth layer to the process of disappearance imposed on the country's Black population. Through the promotion of European immigration, Brazilian society engaged in erasing African cultures by constructing an ideology of racial democracy that emphasized the country's racial mixture while denying the existence of racism. In the United States, comparable (but unsuccessful) attempts to annihilate Black cultures operated through different mechanisms that made racism and white supremacy overt ideologies that kept African Americans segregated and without access to basic civil rights. But as the civil rights movement emerged after the Second World War, Black citizens started demanding in much more explicit ways that the heritage of slavery be made visible in the public space of cities and former plantations.

Despite the similarities between Brazil and the United States, Rio de Janeiro was different from New York City. Perceived as a Black city, references to its past associated with slavery were abundant in written documents and visual representations. Slavery was a central element in Rio de Janeiro's daily life until the end of the nineteenth century. So it was not a big surprise when, in 1996, similar to what occurred in New York City, an archaeological excavation on a private property owned by the Guimarães family at 36 Rua Pedro

Ernesto (formerly Rua do Cemitério) in the Gamboa neighbourhood revealed a burial ground containing bone fragments of dozens of enslaved African men, women, and children. The site was identified as the Cemetery of New Blacks. Between 1824 and 1830, after continuous complaints from the residents and because of the official ban on the Brazilian slave trade, the cemetery was closed. Scholars estimate that more than 6,000 newly arrived Africans were buried at the site.

Despite this unprecedented discovery, the cemetery and the port region remained abandoned for a long time. Unlike the African Burial Ground in New York City, the site where the bone remains were recovered was not located on land soon to be occupied by a federal building but was on private property. Thus the Brazilian federal government had no authority on the site, whose preservation was the responsibility of City Hall. Although the couple who owned the property where the cemetery was uncovered decided to embrace the cause of protecting the site and received great support from activists in Rio de Janeiro's Black movement, they barely received any public or official assistance. Still, in 2001, the municipal secretary of culture organized a symposium to discuss the archaeological findings and in 2002 proposed several measures to highlight the African heritage in the port area. Among the proposals was a plan to establish several markers indicating the significant sites of memory associated with the African presence in the region. At this point, the site of the former burial ground was opened for public visitation, but due to the persistent lack of public support, the Guimarães family gradually transformed it into the location of a nongovernmental organization called the Instituto de Pesquisa e Memória Pretos Novos (New Blacks Institute of Research and Memory). The space was created with the intention to bring to light the history and the memory of the enslaved Africans and their descendants buried in the Black cemetery.

This new valorization of African heritage re-emerged in the context of Brazil's redemocratization following a two-decade civil-military dictatorship, during which Afro-Brazilians activists were silenced. The new context also coincided with the election of President Luiz Inácio Lula da Silva in 2002. His two terms as president of Brazil were marked by the emergence of numerous official projects promoting Afro-Brazilian history in the country. In the next years, the space of the institute was expanded with the creation of modest exhibitions and a small library. Yet this situation drastically changed in March 2011 when drainage work started in the Rio de Janeiro port region as part of the project Rio de Janeiro: Porto Maravilha (Wonderful Port), aimed at recuperating the city's old port in view of the 2014 FIFA World Cup and the 2016 Olympic Games. During the work, the ruins of the Valongo Wharf were eventually rediscovered. The excavations also recovered numerous African artifacts, including ceramic pipes and cowries employed in religious practices and buttons made of animal bones.[15] Celebrated by public authorities in various newspapers around the world, Valongo Wharf was gradually appropriated in numerous ways by the neighbourhood's Black communities and by Rio de Janeiro's Black citizens, who organized capoeira circles, religious ceremonies, and Black history tours led by local historians and members of the Black community. After long efforts to create proper signage telling the story of the Valongo Wharf, academics and activists sought the wharf's inclusion on the UNESCO World Heritage List. In 2017, the site was declared a World Heritage Site. Although not located in a very touristic area of the city, and despite the continuing neglect by public authorities, thousands of international, national, and local tourists visit the Valongo Wharf annually. No longer invisible, Rio de Janeiro's slave-trading past, as materialized in these two important sites, is now publicly recognized.

In the United States, African Americans have led historical efforts to preserve the sites where their ancestors were enslaved, especially the cemeteries, where the bodies of bondspeople were often buried in common unmarked graves. For example, approximately three hundred enslaved men, women, and children lived and worked at Mount Vernon, the plantation owned by the president and founding father of the United States, George Washington, in the state of Virginia, about seventeen miles from the country's capital of Washington, DC. Like on other plantations, enslaved persons were buried in the unmarked graves of a separate cemetery located on the plantation grounds. After Washington's death, the plantation remained among successive members of the family.

The property was finally purchased by the Mount Vernon Ladies' Association in 1859. Until the eve of the Civil War, enslaved people continued working at Mount Vernon. Yet, with the end of the war and the abolition of slavery in 1865, former enslaved people who for several decades had interpreted the site for the numerous visitors, were gradually replaced. By 1920, most of the workers at Mount Vernon were white individuals. Gradually, the traces of slavery on the former plantation were concealed from public view. During the twentieth century, a few initiatives were created to memorialize the presence of enslaved men, women, and children on Washington's plantation. But several sections of the plantation were deteriorating.

In 1928, during the annual meeting of the Mount Vernon Ladies' Association, the chairwoman of the Tomb Committee, Frances C. Maxey, warned the board that in Mount Vernon's slave cemetery, the remnants of the unmarked graves of possibly more than a hundred enslaved persons were disappearing. She then recommended the creation of a gravestone to mark the slaves' graveyard, and another member of the association offered to contribute funds to purchase the memorial stone.

Eventually unveiled in 1929, the tombstone is inscribed, "In memory of the many faithful colored servants of the Washington family buried at Mount Vernon from 1760 to 1860. Their unidentified graves surround this spot." Acknowledging the existence of the burial ground, the association avoided using the term "slave." The tricky reference to enslaved people as "colored servants" implies that the workers buried in the cemetery were free individuals. Therefore, despite preserving the heritage of enslaved workers at Mount Vernon, these early initiatives helped not only to obscure the existence of slavery on the plantation but also to promote the paternalistic myth of slavery as a benign institution.[16]

Four decades later, Mount Vernon renewed one building that had housed the slave quarters of craftsmen and house servants. But overall, the presence of enslaved people and slavery continued to be ignored at Mount Vernon, an erasure that led to growing pushback from the professional Black communities of the Washington, DC, area. In 1982, during Black History Month, Dorothy Butler Gilliam, an African American journalist, published an article in the *Washington Post* denouncing the slave burial ground's state of decay and calling attention to how the public interpretation of Mount Vernon simply ignored the existence of the cemetery: "It seems not to matter that these men and women provided the free labor on which the plantation operated."[17]

After reading Gilliam's article, a group of African Americans started pressuring political officials to enforce the preservation of the slave cemetery. At the time, the Mount Vernon Ladies' Association had plans to open two tax-exempt restaurants at Mount Vernon. Fairfax County supervisor James Scott saw it as an opportunity to negotiate the cemetery's preservation. Scott contacted Frank Matthews, the legal counsel to the Fairfax County National Association for the Advancement of Colored People. Backed by a national organization representing a huge number of members defending Black rights, Matthews attended the Board of Supervisors meeting that would decide on the request. He then opposed it, arguing that the association could not get its restaurants the tax-exempt status until memorialization of the slave burial ground was implemented. The answer to these objections was fast. Not only did the association clear the site and open it to tourists, but its members also met with a working group of African American leaders to discuss the creation of a memorial.

The memorial project was eventually assigned to a group of students in the School of Architecture at historically Black Howard University in

Washington, DC. Still, the Mount Vernon Ladies' Association insisted that the memorial should exclude images of degradation and should underscore the "courage and strength of a people." Dedicated on 21 September 1983, the memorial consists of a three-step circular platform, each one respectively engraved with the words "faith," "hope," and "love." A granite column at the centre of the third step in the middle of the circle is engraved, "In memory of the Afro Americans who served as slaves at Mount Vernon." In contrast to the tombstone unveiled in 1929, which refers to "colored servants," the language of the new memorial no longer erases the legal status of enslaved men and women. The deceased members of Mount Vernon's slave community are no longer invisible, even though the memorial still goes unnoticed by most ordinary visitors to the plantation, who only stop by at the tomb of George Washington, which is not very far from the location of the slave burial ground.

The institution of slavery was central to the development of several societies in the Americas. From birth to death, enslaved bodies were exemplary of the incessant fight against annihilation. The persistent existence of enslaved Africans and their descendants continuously defied the state of disappearance imposed on them. As the memory of slavery has resurfaced in recent decades, descendants of enslaved people have increasingly claimed the sites associated with the history of their enslavement by leading initiatives to recover their visibility and in some instances to create memorials naming enslaved individuals who lived and worked in particular places.

New forms of oppression emerged after the end of slavery. As Achille Mbembe puts it, "[R]acism is the driver of the necropolitical principle insofar as it stands for organized destruction, for a sacrificial economy, the functioning of which requires, on the one hand, a generalized cheapening of the price of life and, on the other, a habituation to loss."[18] The afterlives of slavery and the Atlantic slave trade continue to haunt societies in Europe, Africa, and the Americas. But like in Meza's series *Fragments of a Catastrophe*, they take new forms.[19] Now, their lines and colours are more defined, giving us fragments of hope that disappearance is also a transitional state and that new life can also emerge from annihilation. These paintings, like the long deadly history of slavery and the inhuman trade, lead us to meditate, to consider that despite the increasing deadly violence imposed on the Black populations of countries like Brazil and the United States, Black men, women, and children continue to successfully resist, becoming exemplary fighters against the state of disappearance.

NOTES

1 Several historians have problematized these absences and silences. See Marisa J. Fuentes, *Dispossessed Lives: Enslaved Women, Violence, and the Archive* (Philadelphia: University of Pennsylvania Press, 2018); Jessica Marie Johnson, *Wicked Flesh: Black Women Intimacy and Freedom in the Atlantic World* (Philadelphia: University of Pennsylvania Press, 2020); and Jennifer L. Morgan, *Reckoning with Slavery: Gender, Kinship, and Capitalism in the Early Black Atlantic* (Durham, NC: Duke University Press 2021).

2 Chantal Meza, *Since the Beginning*, https://www.chantal-meza.com/stateofdisappearance.

3 Marcus Rediker, *The Slave Ship: A Human History* (New York: Viking, 2007).

4 Sowande Mustakeem, *Slavery at Sea: Terror, Sex, and Sickness in the Middle Passage* (Champaign: University of Illinois Press, 2016).

5 Joseph C. Miller, *Way of Death: Merchant Capitalism and the Angolan Slave Trade, 1730–1830* (Madison: University of Wisconsin Madison, 1988), 314.

6 Chantal Meza, *The Void* and *Apparitions*, https://www.chantal-meza.com/stateofdisappearance.

7 James Walvin, *The Zong: A Massacre, the Law and the End of Slavery* (New Haven, CT: Yale University Press, 2011).

8 See Jeremy Krikler, "A Chain of Murder in the Slave Trade: A Wider Context of the *Zong* Massacre," *International Review of Social History*, 57, no. 3 (2012): 393–415.

9 Chantal Meza, *Obscure Beasts*, https://www.chantal-meza.com/stateofdisappearance.

10 Leslie M. Harris, *In the Shadow of Slavery: African Americans in New York City, 1626–1863* (Chicago: University of Chicago Press, 2004), 2.

11 Ibid., 41.

12 Cheryl J. LaRoche, "Beads from the African Burial Ground, New York City: A Preliminary Assessment," *BEADS: Journal of the Society of Bead Researchers* 6 (1994), 3–20.

13 Jaime Rodrigues, *De Costa a Costa: Escravos, marinheiros e intermediários do tráfico negreiro de Angola ao Rio de Janeiro (1780–1860)* (São Paulo: Companhia das Letras, 2005), 298.

14 On the cemetery, see Júlio César Medeiros da Silva Pereira. *À flor da terra: O cemitério dos pretos novos no Rio de Janeiro* (Rio de Janeiro: Garamond, Instituto do Patrimônio Histórico e Artístico Nacional, 2007).

15 See Tania Andrade Lima, "Valongo: An Uncomfortable Legacy," *Current Anthropology* 61, suppl. 22 (2020): 317–27.

16 I further discuss the disappearance of the traces of slavery in Mount Vernon in Ana Lucia Araujo, *Slavery in the Age of Memory: Engaging the Past* (London: Bloomsbury Academic, 2020).

17 Dorothy Butler Gilliam, "Remembrance," *Washington Post*, 6 February 1982.

18 Achille Mbembe, *Necropolitics*, trans. Steven Corcoran (Durham, NC: Duke University Press, 2019), 38.

19 Chantal Meza, *Fragments of a Catastrophe*, https://www.chantal-meza.com/stateofdisappearance.

5

Disappearances

Michael J. Shapiro

PRELUDE

In June 2004, I attended a cultural studies conference in Beja, Portugal. I was initially disappointed with the venue. Beja, a roughly two-hour train ride from Lisbon, seemed to have nothing distinctive to explore – even though the Crazy Tourist website advertises the "15 Best Things to Do in Beja."[1] However, throughout the town, there were posters advertising an exhibition of drawings entitled *Los Desaparecidos* (*The Disappeared*). The exhibition, which featured political activists who had been "disappeared" in many global venues – many in Latin America but also elsewhere, such as Turkey – was hard to find. It was in a very small, one-room gallery on a narrow street in a residential neighbourhood. The gallery lacked a prominent sign, and as I wandered around looking for it with my wife, Hannah Tavares, as well as my former student Jorge Fernandes,[2] we stopped at a house where three teenage boys were hanging out on the front steps. With the help of Jorge, who had been born and raised in Cape Verde and spoke fluent Portuguese, we asked them whether they knew where the gallery was, but they had no idea. It turned out to be right next door. The irony was stunning: an exhibition on historically hidden atrocities was in a nearly hidden venue. Disappearance was continuing to haunt the victims.

At the time, I was not planning to write an essay about my encounters with both finding and viewing a broad range of disappearances. However, the experience must have kept incubating because it sprang up again in response to two new and related encounters: Brad Evans's invitation to write about disappearance and Chantal Meza's accompanying images, which provide a provocative aesthetic framing. Inasmuch as my task was to reflect on how to make a mute reality speak again, I was struck by Meza's series *Fragments of a Catastrophe*,[3] which accords with Theodor Adorno's

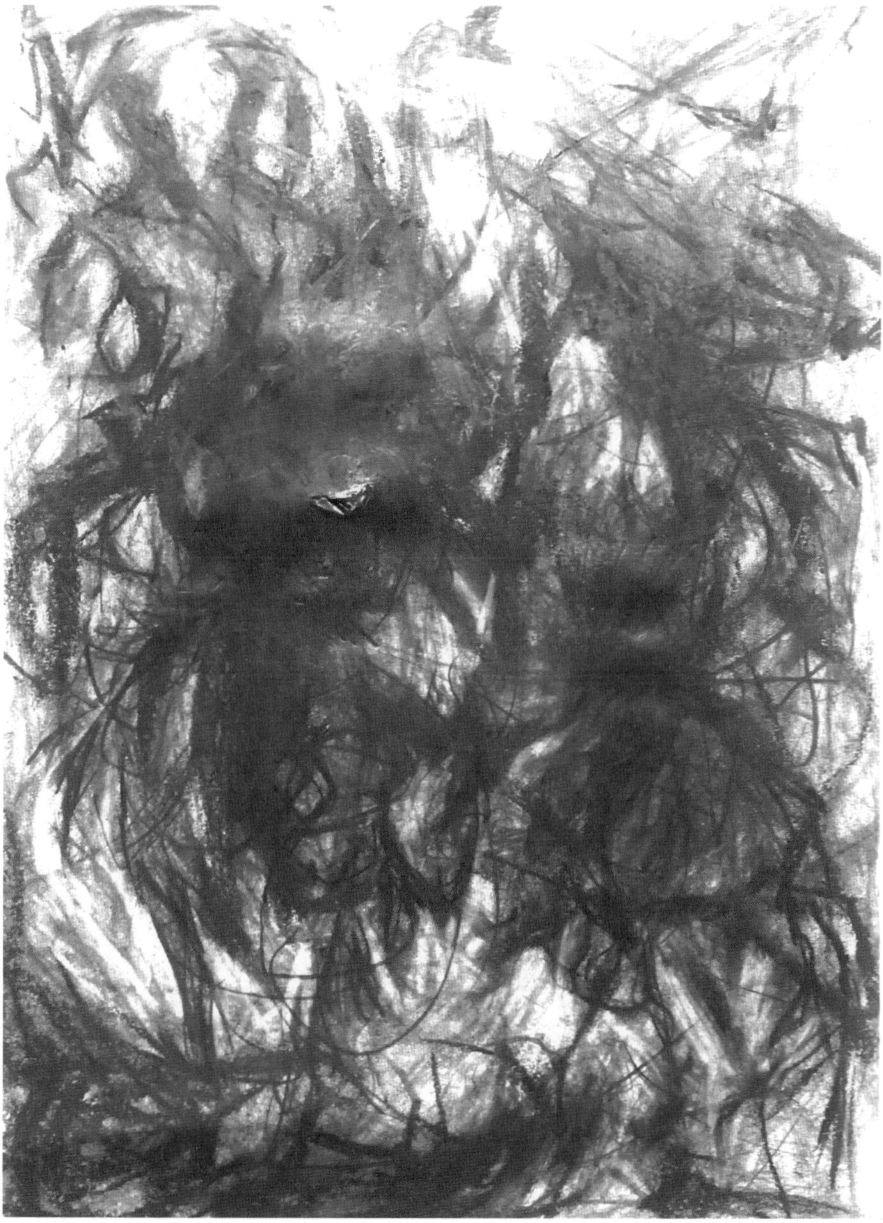

Chantal Meza, *The Void VIII*, 2019, graphite and charcoal on paper, 29.5 x 42 cm

famous characterization of modern art as an "explosion," which is one of its "invariable traits."[4] I was reminded that the task of modern art is homologous with the task that I faced as a writer, that of turning what has passed into silence into a loquacious explosion. In this essay, I introduce concepts that expand the bandwidth of my experience conceptually and historically.

THE MEDIA/TEMPORALITY OF PRESENCE

I don't know how broadly the *Desparicitos* exhibition travelled. Doubtless, it did not enjoy the degree of circulation of Fernando Botero's famous paintings of the torture scenes in the American-run Abu Ghraib prison in Iraq. Whereas atrocities that make the daily news are soon forgotten, those documented in exhibitions invite deeper contemplations.

I offer a comparison prompted by my reading of Milan Kundera's novel *Slowness*, which opens with a married couple's vacation scenario.[5] At one point, the husband/narrator provides a commentary on images of suffering in the daily media, remarking that their stay in a chateau "coincides with the period when, every day for two weeks," the television news media "showed the children of an African nation, whose name is already forgotten, ravaged by war." Those children appear "thin, exhausted, without the strength to wave away the flies walking about on their faces."[6] Later in the novel, when the images are no longer being carried by the television networks, the narrator remarks that "the situations history stages are floodlit only for the first few minutes" and that "no event remains news over its whole duration, merely for a quite brief span of time, at the very beginning."[7] However, as I have noted elsewhere, "while the momentarily timely images carried by news media may be ephemeral, the genre of the exhibition, which yields an accompanying and enduring catalogue/text, is one in which what becomes effaced as a news event is restored, reflected on, and made publicly available for extended ethical and political negotiation."[8]

Nevertheless, although the media play a major role in the "now you see it, now you don't" game of human presences, the phenomenology of inattention is also implicated. Bruce Robbins captures this effect in a reflection on what he calls "the sweatshop sublime": "One morning, while getting dressed, you either do or do not examine the label of your shirt. If you do, you either do or do not realize the conditions of life under which this shirt was, or perhaps was not, produced: the pitifully inadequate wages, not to speak of the locked fire exits, the arbitrary harassments and firings, the refusal of genuine union representation, and so on."[9]

In what follows, I elaborate Robbins's use of the sublime to pursue American disappearances.

ANOTHER SUBLIME: AMERICA'S "DARK VANISHINGS"

Chandos Michael Brown points out that the "first American sublime" was a legacy of elements of the European thought-world, noting that "intellectuals on the far side of the world" – Thomas Jefferson and others involved in creating the "American Revolution" – "looked eagerly to English and continental savants to help them make sense of their place, even as they inhabited a landscape that few across the Atlantic could imagine."[10] However, the forces involved in Euro-America's imperial expansion needed additional ideational support, much of which cast an earlier "civic entity" – as Thomas Pynchon puts it in his novel *Mason & Dixon* – as part of vanishing nature.[11] There is no better representation of this effect than Frances Palmer's lithograph *Across the Continent: "Westward the Course of Empire Takes Its Way"* (1868).

As the westward-moving train is leaving, the white residents of the town gather on one side of the tracks, and two Native Americans on horseback appear on the other side, partially obscured by the smoke from the train's stack.[12] Along with other nineteenth-century landscape paintings, this work participates in the motivated evacuation of the Indigenous presence in the Americas. These efforts were part of what I have called "the first American sublime"[13] – the imagination of an empty continent – which, when put into violent practice, manifests what William Boelhower calls the Euro-American "ethnogenesis," or the whitening of the continent.[14]

However, along with imagistic practices were texts involved in what Larzer Ziff identifies as the "literary annihilation" of Indianness.[15] However, whereas Ziff examines texts by Thomas Jefferson, Timothy Dwight, and Nicholas Biddle, I want to focus on the role of James Fenimore Cooper, whose literary corpus serves as a eulogy to a "vanishing race."

Influenced by the style of Sir Walter Scott's approach to historical fiction, notably in his Waverley novels, James Fenimore Cooper wrote fiction that mimicked Scott's literary form as well as the political ideology that it delivered, providing a literary legitimation for the consolidation of diverse peoples into a (mythic) national people (or what is euphemistically called "nation building" in political science texts). However, there is a radical difference in the nation-building appreciations of the two writers. Whereas Scott was erasing anthropological borders in order to symbolically consolidate the United Kingdom, Cooper was erasing an ethnos in order to invent a Euro-dominant nation. His elegiac Leatherstocking novels participated in what Patrick Brantlinger calls a "dark vanishing." "Cooper, like Scott," he writes, "offers a future-oriented history or prophecy by hindsight, according to which the past of the new nation-state of American lies all in the future – in contrast to the Mohicans who have no history."[16]

Cooper repeated his view that the Indians are outside of history in a chapter that he contributed to a coffee-table book featuring "picturesque" landscapes. Saying that his contribution is meant to "serve those who, unable to travel in the American continent, must depend on the pen, the pencil, and the graver" for their information,[17] he contrasts the "American landscape," which has "an air of freshness, youthfulness, and in many instances ... rawness,"[18] with the landscapes of Europe, "on which are impressed the teeming history of the past."[19] His evacuation of the national and cultural Native American presence from the landscape in his contribution to an anthology on American scenery follows his novelistic evacuation of them from America's future. It was an evacuation that Theodore Roosevelt was to repeat in his famous *The Winning of the West*, where he describes Native American territories as "waste spaces" occasionally visited by a few "savages."[20] By the time Cooper published his scenery reflections, he had already helped to legitimate the disqualification of Native Americans' entitlement to their lands. For example, his 1823 novel *The Pioneers* addresses and endorses an answer to the question "Who has the right to own and govern the land originally possessed by Indians and inherited through the Revolution?"[21] His answer is the European conquerors.

Whereas it is visual technologies that evacuate the presence of Native Americans in Cooper's evocation of the picturesque in his American scenery, it is the narrative that extinguishes their presence on the land in *The Pioneers*. With a turn to a different technology – the legal instrument – Cooper supports an assertion of Euro-American sovereignty that "rested upon the rights of conquest" and the "Doctrine of Discovery," specifically evidence of "direct ties of political kinship and inheritance between the United States and England," since such evidence was required if one wanted to assert these rights.[22] Accordingly, Chief Justice John Marshall, in his opinion in *Johnson v. McIntosh* (1763) – although conflicted because of misgivings about what natural law would indicate to be an injustice – used the principle of conquest and the continuity of the Euro-community to assert civil law, which allowed him to turn "the Indian inhabitants" from owners into "occupants to be protected."[23]

Cooper's *The Pioneers* is complicit with Marshall's tortured reasoning. His aesthetic subject/protagonist, Natty Bumppo, because of his commitment to natural law, challenges the legal weapons used against Indians, inadvertently becoming one who "fulfills a strategic function of Cooper's management of the conflict between natural and civil law as it intersects with the problem of race."[24] By assembling a hybrid "family" residing in

Natty's hut, one of whom is an adopted son of the Indian Chingachgook, Cooper invented an "inheritance through an unbroken family lineage," thereby enacting the same justification for seizing Native American land as the one to which Marshall turned.[25] As is well known, the legal erasure of Native Americans' legitimate rights to space was followed by more violent forms of erasure, direct military assaults aided by weapons technologies, and the encroachments of predatory commercial enterprises aided by steel manufacturing, which provided the tracks and trains that enabled the establishment of markets and thus the movement of capital and settlers westward.

A contemporary technology is associated with another more recent erasure of Native American (historical) presence: robot-created semiconductor circuits. From 1965 to 1975, the Fairchild Corporation, "the largest private employer of indigenous workers in the US," manufactured the circuits in its semiconductor divisions using mostly female Navajo workers. "Because of their weaving skill (part of the 'traditional' Navajo arts), Navajo women were represented as 'naturally' suited to the detailed labor involved in building the circuits." Now replaced by circuit-printing technology, "Native American women have been all but erased from official histories of the microchip."[26] Whereas large corporations do not write romantic elegies to the people erased from their milieu, Cooper did just that with *The Last of the Mohicans*. Although a bloody account of genocidal battles, which constructs Indians as vicious killers decimating each other as well as threatening settlers, this novel is also a romantically inclined elegy to their disappearance. Rather than wondering what might have become of Indigenous peoples if the continent had been shared in the form of a negotiated structure of co-governance – the subjunctive mood rarely entered Cooper's literary musings – he begins the novel with a eulogy: "The Mohicans were the possessors of the country first occupied by the Europeans in this [the eastern] portion of the continent. They were, consequently, the first dispossessed; and the seemingly inevitable fate of all these people, who disappear before the advances ... of civilization, as the verdure of their native forests falls before the nipping frost, is represented as having already befallen them."[27]

Cooper's Natty Bumppo, whom he sends into the midst of Indian country, expresses this view – a combination of sympathy and a sense of civilizational superiority, of admiration on the one hand and contempt on the other. However, while symbolically evacuating the landscape of an Indian presence, Cooper, unlike Jefferson, envisioned the Euro-American dominance as maritime rather than agricultural: "The tide of emigration, which has long been flowing westward, must have its reflux ... The great outlet to the rest of the world, the path of adventure, and the only, at least the principal, theatre for military achievements open to the people of this country, is on the ocean."[28]

Cooper nevertheless shared a patrimony with Thomas Jefferson, whose father was a surveyor. In the "Introduction" to *The Pioneers*, Cooper identifies his father's real estate accumulation and the surveying vocation with which it was abetted: "In 1785, the author's father, who had an interest in extensive tracts of land in this wilderness, arrived with a party of surveyors." And his character Judge Temple sees what Cooper imagines his father saw when "the scene met his eye"[29]: the same opportunity to possess the emptiness that Jefferson presumed as he gazed outward from his estate. As attested by the literary geography of his Leatherstocking novels, Cooper inherited from his father a commitment to what Joseph Conrad calls "imperial geography." More attuned than Cooper to "the representational violence intrinsic to geographic imaginaries," Conrad "proposed a chronology of geographic perspectives that accompanied and legitimated various stages in the process of European colonization," from "'geography fabulous,' based on myths of the new world, through 'geography militant,' coinciding with 'invasions,' to 'geography triumphant,' expressed in the subsequent cartographic representations of the European settlements."[30]

Cooper's geographic imaginary and his narrative legitimation of the law of conquest amount to a literary historiographic realization of what Michel Foucault mapped out elaborately in his 1975–76 lectures at the Collège de France: a history of invasion that supplants the mythic contact-history model attributed to the origin of the state. State building, Foucault shows, is owed to a "war-repression," rather than a "contrast-oppression," model of power.[31] Cooper's Leatherstocking novels offer a post hoc legitimation of exterminism on the American continent, and they draw on many canonical texts in doing so. For example, at one point, while articulating his legal tropes through his protagonist, Natty Bumppo, he resorts to a classical defence of natural law in order to justify turning land in its pristine state – what he calls "wilderness," which is not owned by anyone – into property. Here, he adopts John Locke's labour theory of value, where mixing one's labour with land, such as by farming, translates into ownership.[32] He accomplishes this Lockean justification for possession with his usual literary form, using the Indian character Chingachgook as his aesthetic vehicle. Early in *The Pioneers*, he describes Chingachgook's appearance, noting his frail arms: "His shoulders, and body to his waist, were entirely bare, with the exception of a silver medallion of Washington, that was suspended from his neck by a thong of buckskin, and rested on his high chest, amid many scars. His shoulders were rather broad and full; but the arms, though straight and graceful, wanted the muscular appearance *that labor gives to a race of men*."[33] Through the invention of a disability in Chingachgook's body, Cooper disqualifies Native Americans as property holders because of their inability to engage in the kind of labour that, within the Lockean version of natural law, justifies ownership.

I have suggested elsewhere that Thomas Pynchon's novel *Mason & Dixon* is an anti-Jeffersonian text.[34] Here, I want to add that it is also an anti-Cooper text. Whereas Cooper's elegy for the American continent's Indians is located in a romantic adventure novel whose protagonist, without irony, affirms his political affirmation of an inevitable Euro-American dominance, Pynchon's novel is a parody rather than an elegy. Whereas the aesthetic ideology in Cooper's elegy celebrates conquest even as it delivers some sympathy for the conquered, Pynchon's "counter-song" (the Greek meaning of "parody"), sung in the subjunctive, constructs the Mason-Dixon Line's westward movement while representing "European Mobility" as a historic *mis*adventure that turned "Possibilities into Simplicities that serve the ends of Government."[35] Nevertheless, although Cooper's legitimation of Euro-American imperialism in his Leatherstocking novels contrasts with the anti-imperial force of Pynchon's epics, there is a significant figurative convergence among their works. For both Cooper and Pynchon, the land speaks, albeit with different resonances. Whereas Cooper invents a Gothic mood in *The Last of the Mohican*s, where he has the landscape mimic an Indian menace – "When the [Euro-American] characters approach Glen Falls to secrete themselves for the night in its caves, the ominous landscape adds to the Gothic mood" by casting up shadows that appear like hidden enemies[36] – Pynchon's "Warrior Path" with a "sub-audible hum" testifies to the unheeded civic life of the Indians.[37]

Pynchon's parody operates within the literary genre that Linda Hutcheon famously refers to as historiographic metafiction, which "works to situate itself within historical discourse without surrendering its autonomy as fiction … it is a kind of seriously ironic parody that effects both aims: the intertexts of history and fiction take on parallel (though not equal) status in the parodic reworking of the textual past of both the 'world' and literature."[38] In his film *Dead Man* (1995), Jim Jarmusch accomplishes this parody cinematically as his story parodies both the Western film genre and the heroic "winning of the West" story incorporated into mainstream Euro-American history.

This genre is exemplified by director John Ford, whose cinematic landscape imagery and tendency to view Indians from a distance accord with Theodore Roosevelt's influential rendering of the western landscape in his monumental *The Winning of the West*, which simultaneously celebrates Euro-American cultural and territorial expansion and evacuates the Native

American presence.[39] Within a variety of media genres, this "winning" has been the dominant figuration and story of the American West, from the three aesthetic genres of legendary history, painting, and fiction – as represented by Theodore Roosevelt, Frederick Remington, and Owen Wister respectively – to the classic Western films of at least part of John Ford's film corpus.

Roosevelt's view of the superiority of the English "race" was popularized in much of his friend Owen Wister's fiction. For example, in his story "The Evolution of the Cowpuncher," Wister features an English nobleman who, after ending up in Texas, adapts rapidly because of his superior horsemanship and marksmanship.[40] And the painter Frederick Remington, a friend of both Roosevelt and Wister, supported their biopolitical conceits by depicting their invention of the cowboy as a legacy of the English aristocracy. Among the paintings with which he lent visual support to their narrative of the Anglo legacy is *Last Cavalier* (1895), which shows a cowboy against a background that consists of "a faded panorama of historical horsemen, of which the most prominent are generations of English knights."[41] In addition, Remington did the illustrations for many of Wister's stories in *Colliers* magazine, which represented the West as an evolving (and whitening) social order.

CINEMATIC RESTORATIONS

Cinema provides a critical response to the historical erasures because, as a medium, it tends to restore what other media have evacuated – for example, the destructive effects of steel manufacture. Jarmusch's film *Dead Man* is explicit about the role of steel in the demise of the Native American ethnoscape and landscape. The film features a naive character named William Blake who is headed to the Far West for a job as an accountant at the Dickinson steel mill in the town of Machine (perhaps a reference to Leo Marx's famous imagery of "the machine in the garden").[42] Along the way, the plaid-suited and bowler-hatted protagonist is warned that although he has a letter confirming his employment, the job may not be available. The train's stoker (a white man with a blackened face, making him a stand-in for nonwhites) warns him before they arrive to "trust no words written down on no piece of paper written by Dickinson out in Machine," doubtless referring not only to the fragility of the work contract but also to the broken treaties with Native American nations during the Euro-American westward expansion.

The oblivious William Blake – who, after finding no job and being mortally wounded, is led through a wilderness toward a Native American village by an Indian named Nobody – consistently fails to comprehend Native American culture. Every time Nobody asks him if he has any tobacco, inquiring in effect if he is able to establish a bond through an exchange, he responds to the effect that he does not smoke. Without going into all the details of a complicated treatment of the destruction of Native America – for example, as the train reaches the Far West, white men in the garb of hunters shoot buffalo from the train's windows – I want to mention two scenes where architecture is prominent. In the first, Blake alights from the train in the town of Machine and walks slowly down the town's main street toward the Dickinson steel mill, which turns out to be a huge building full of industrial workers, office staff, and the mill's owner, the homicidal maniac Dickinson, who chases Blake away with a shotgun.

The second scene clearly refers to the first. At the end of the film, as William Blake nears the place where Nobody is taking him to fulfill his destiny as a dead man (like his namesake, the deceased eighteenth-century poet), he again walks slowly down a long street. In this case, it is the main thoroughfare of an Indian village filled with destitute Native Americans (in contrast with the revellers Blake passes on his walk toward the Dickinson steel mill). At the end of his walk, he enters a large ceremonial building where he is ushered inside by a Native American shaman. The building is a "cosmic house," looking quite like the "large plank houses of Northwest Coast Indians,"[43] such as the Haida, whose dwellings were constructed to be located symbolically at the centre of the universe, between the forest and beach, and with a verticality that represented three worldly zones: the sky world, the earth world, and the underworld.

It would be too facile to simply assert that the juxtaposition of Blake's two walks – toward the steel mill and toward the Haida spiritual house – reflect the displacement of Native American spirituality by a Euro-American predatory commercial life. Certainly, the Euro-American conception of investment property differs markedly from many Native American tendencies to spiritualize landscapes, but the architecture of the American city, which has become the dominant feature of the modern landscape, is not wholly isolated from spiritual practices. Although, as Lewis Mumford points out, the city "through its concentration of physical and cultural power" played a major role in the commercialization of life, "heighten[ing] the tempo of human intercourse and translat[ing] products into forms that could be stored and reproduced," it also played a role similar to that of the Native American ceremonial house: "By means of its storage facilities (buildings, vaults, archives, monuments, tablets, books), the city became capable of transmitting a complex culture from generation to generation."[44] In short, the city's buildings are also sites of historical memory. To underscore the homology between the city and Haida house (a "cosmic house" as Peter Nabokov and Robert Easton describe it),[45] it should be noted that Mumford refers to the "cosmo-city," arguing that the modern city, which is organized around central buildings, evolved from architectural forms that were seen as replicas of the universe, most notably the "royal citadel."[46] The commerce-facilitating city thus contains not only a utilitarian architecture of circulation but also a ritual architecture of cultural memory.

Certainly, Jarmusch's film alerts us to a process of violent destruction and appropriation. And, in Foucault's sense, to recognize that violence is to become open to a counter-history that impugns the traditional sovereignty-oriented social-contract narrative. But my aim in emphasizing the juxtaposition is to note that inasmuch as there are alternative architectural thought-worlds, there are also alternative "public histories" – in Dolores Hayden's terms[47] – or alternative architectural thought-worlds that embody varying relationships between architecture and memory. Yet my concern is not merely to point to difference but also to frame a diversity-welcoming, nonclosural politics of American architecture. What, then, are the remaining signs of Native America? I draw once again on cinema to explore this question.

SEAN PENN'S *THE PLEDGE*

If we were attentive only to the plot of Sean Penn's film *The Pledge* (2001), we would be following a story based on a Friedrich Dürrenmatt novel whose protagonist, the police detective Jerry Black (Jack Nicolson), defers his retirement to try to solve a series of murders of young girls after promising the mother of one of the victims that he will find the perpetrator. The film narrative focuses on an ambiguity. It is never clear if the clues that Black is following point to a serial killer or if they are a manifestation of his pledge-driven obsession with solving the case. However, if we heed the film's aesthetic objects – the film's treatment of its land- and ethnoscapes, which are disconnected from its narrative – we can observe a challenge to the sublime that I want to emphasize in my reading of the film, one that has played into a "peculiarly American status quo of domination and blindness … an unconscious enterprise that asserts the present as the only temporal dimension: a depthless phenomenological now where awe and entertainment encircle one another."[48]

The spatial setting of the film is the Reno area of the state of Nevada, which from the point of view of the film's narrative is irrelevant. It is merely the space where the action takes place – the discovery of a murdered seven-year-old girl, the interruption of Black's retirement party with the report of the crime, the decision of the police to blame the killing on a Native America, and Black's subsequent search for the actual perpetrator after he watches the Indian's confession being coerced and promising the girl's mother that he will solve the case. However, *The Pledge* is a film where aspects of the land- and ethnoscapes are "*freed from the eventhood*"[49] – in this case, from the events of the crime and from the events associated with Black's search for clues. The camera's exploration of the land- and ethnoscapes recovers a history of encounter and atrocity that the phenomenology of everyday life in the West – a "status quo of domination and blindness" and a "depthless phenomenological now" – has evacuated.

As I note in an earlier analysis of the film, "surrounding one man's drama is an institutionalized space, a western venue with a significant temporal trajectory." Reno and the surrounding area, a consolidated and recently white-dominated part of the West, "exist in both ethnic and geopolitical time."[50] This surrounding milieu – the land- and ethnoscapes, explored by the camera with zooms, pans, depth of focus, and close-ups – stands apart from the film's narrative portrayal of Black's investigation. To manage the dramatic narrative, much of the camera's attention is on Black's face. These shots, constituting what Gilles Deleuze calls "affection-images," carry the burden of the film's treatment of the psychic intensity of Black's quest to fulfill his pledge. As Deleuze points out, affection-images, which are "abstracted from spatio-temporal co-ordinates," have the effect of "undoing space."[51] However, there is a disjunctive story that is revealed as the film narrative proceeds, and what is evacuated with face shots returns as landscape shots. To put it simply, the story is about the historical whitening of the West as the space is incorporated into Euro-American nation building, the virtual effacement of the Native American population, and the discrediting of those who remain.

Here, I want to point to several scenes that tell this parallel story. Whereas the close-ups and the tracking shots articulate Jerry Black's investigatory story, depicting respectively his psychic and clue gathering experiences, the close-ups, the long takes, and the depth of focus shots tell the spatio-temporal story of the Euro-American ethnogenesis. In the context of the two sublimes that I have elaborated, this story implies that Euro-America, both in its westward movement in the nineteenth century and in its uranium mining, nuclear testing, and waste dumping in the twentieth, was heedless of the value of Native American life-worlds.

As is well known, before nuclear radiation poisoning afflicted the health and longevity of Native Americans in the West, alcohol did part of that job. Two close-up long takes early in the film refer obliquely to this aspect of the destructive result of the encounter between Native Americans and Europeans. In an early scene where Black is ice fishing on a frozen lake, the camera enters his small hut and lingers with a long take of a bottle of Glenfiddich scotch on a shelf. In a later scene at Black's retirement party, the camera gives us long takes of alcoholic drinks being carried on a tray and of a drink in the hand of one of the police officers dancing.

The alcohol shots would be inconsequential if not for later scenes that refer subtly both to the degradation of the Native American population of the area and to white hegemony. As the retirement party proceeds, there is a cut to a snowfield where a plump white teenager is snowmobiling, followed by long takes of his face, which is so white that pink patches show on his flush cheeks. When his snowmobile breaks down and he climbs off, he is shown to be virtually unable to manage on foot in the deep snow. The camera then cuts to a Native American who, more physically attuned to the snowscape, is shown running gracefully through deep snow to his truck with his animal traps in hand. After the snowboarder discovers the body of the murdered seven year old and later identifies the Native American whom he saw departing from the murder scene, the Indian Toby Jay Wadenah (Benicio del Toro) is interrogated and coaxed into admitting the crime. The camera cuts to a police detective who has drawn a degrading caricature of an Indian while watching the interrogation on closed-circuit television.

If those scenes seem inadequate to support an interpretation of the film's parallel story of the violent Euro-American ethnogenesis, a scene later in the film – after Black has bought a gas station with a convenience store near the scene of several murders in order to locate himself near clues – makes the case unambiguously. A Native American stops for gas at Black's store, and a (doubtless allegorical) Indian-white interaction takes place. After Black fills the tank of the Indian customer's car, he has difficulty getting the credit card machine to record the Indian's American Express card. As he botches the transaction several times, having difficulty making the slide mechanism on the recording machine work, the two men stare awkwardly at each other. An ex-policeman (on unfamiliar commercial ground) is failing to process smoothly the credit card of a person whose people have been historically discredited (on their former ground), calling to mind a history of fraught Anglo-Indian transactions and negotiations.

Adding to the "image facts"[52] that point to the Euro-American takeover of the territory, late in the film, as Black, his girlfriend, and her daughter (whom Black ultimately uses as a decoy to lure the murderer) are watching a Fourth of July parade, the plump white boy from the earlier snowmobile scene goes by with his vehicle atop a float. Accompanying shots of the sparse Native American portion of Nevada's ethnoscape – where the Indian population had dropped from roughly 50 per cent in the early 1860s to slightly more than 1 per cent by 2004[53] – are landscape shots that often juxtapose Euro-American settlement with a natural world that looks unsettled. For example, early in the film, a tracking shot of Black's car travelling from the lake, through a tunnel, and into the city of Reno cuts to an unsettled landscape that interrupts the crime narrative, all suggesting that the context of the drama has a violent historical trajectory that precedes it. In *The Pledge*, the landscape shots make oblique reference to the slow violence through which Native America was violently evacuated as the landscape became a product of a white territorial imaginary. Cinematic landscape shots perform many functions. In *The Pledge*, the "extreme long shots, long shots, and deep focus shots, using a bird's-eye view or high angle camera setup,"[54] serve as a way of "looking back."[55] This essay is also a way of looking back, which, Adorno suggests, is characteristic of "the essay as form."[56]

NOTES

1 See "15 Best Things to Do in Beja (Portugal)," Crazy Tourist, https://www.thecrazytourist.com/15-best-things-beja-portugal.

2 Our dear friend Jorge lost his life in a car accident while attending a wedding in Pennsylvania two months after the conference. Jorge enriched the lives of everyone with whom he came in contact and was launching an impressive scholarly career while a faculty member at Bowling Green University at the time of his death. See his posthumously published book Jorge Fernandes, *Challenging Euro-America's Politics of Identity* (London: Routledge, 2008).

3 Chantal Meza, *Fragments of a Catastrophe*, https://www.chantal-meza.com/stateofdisappearance.

4 Theodor Adorno, *Aesthetic Theory*, trans. C. Lenhardt (New York: Routledge and Kegan Paul, 1984), 34.

5 Milan Kundera, *Slowness*, trans. Linda Asher (London: Faber and Faber, 1996), 12. I discuss that passage in an earlier review essay; see Michael J. Shapiro, "Slow Looking: The Ethics and Politics of Aesthetics," *Millennium* 37, no. 1 (2008), 181–97.

6 Kundera *Slowness*, 12.

7 Ibid., 79.

8 Shapiro, "Slow Looking," 182.

9 Bruce Robbins, "The Sweatshop Sublime," PMLA 117, no. 1 (2002): 84–97 at 85.

10 Chandos Michael Brown, "First American Sublime," in *The Sublime: From Antiquity to the Present*, ed. Timothy M. Costelloe, 147–70 (Cambridge, UK: Cambridge University Press, 2012), 147.

11 Thomas Pynchon, *Mason & Dixon* (New York: Henry Holt, 1997), 650.

12 See my treatment of the painting in Michael J. Shapiro, *Methods and Nations: Cultural Governance and the Indigenous Subject* (New York: Routledge, 2004), 129.

13 See Michael J. Shapiro, *The Political Sublime* (Durham, NC: Duke University Press, 2018), 147.

14 See William Boelhower, *Through a Glass Darkly: Ethnic Semiosis in American Literature* (New York: Oxford University Press, 1987).

15 Larzer Ziff, *Writing in the New Nation* (New Haven, CT: Yale University Press, 1991), 172.

16 Patrick Brantlinger, *Dark Vanishings: Discourse on the Extinction of Primitive Races, 1800–1930* (Ithica, NY: Cornell University Press, 2003), 62.

17 James Fenimore Cooper, "American and European Scenery Compared," in *The Home Book of the Picturesque, or American Scenery, Art, and Literature*, facsimile reproduction by Motley E. Deakins, 51–69 (Gainesville, FL: Scholars Facsimiles and Reprints, 1952), 51.

18 Ibid., 68.

19 Ibid., 52.

20 Theodore Roosevelt, *The Winning of the West* (New York: G.P. Putnam's Sons, 1889), 189.

21 Susan Scheckel, *The Insistence of the Indian: Race and Nationalism in Nineteenth-Century American Culture* (Princeton, NJ: Princeton University Press, 1998), 17.

22 Ibid., 17–18.

23 Ibid., 18.

24 Ibid., 30–1.

25 Ibid., 34.

26 Neda Atanasoski and Kalindi Vora, *Surrogate Humanity: Race, Robots, and the Politics of Technological Fuures* (Durham, NC: Duke University Press, 2019), 92–3.

27 James Fenimore Cooper, *The Last of the Mohicans* (Oxford: Oxford World's Classics, 1990), 6–7.

28 James Fenimore Cooper, *Notions of the Americans: Picked Up by a Travelling Bachelor*, vol. 2 (Philadelphia: Carey, Lea & Blanchard, 1838), 86, quoted in Thomas Filbrick, *James Fenimore Cooper and the Development of American Sea Fiction* (Cambridge, MA: Harvard University Press, 1961), 49.

29 James Fenimore Cooper, *The Pioneers, or The Sources of the Susquehanna: A Descriptive Tale* (1823; reprint, London: Heritage Illustrated, 2014), 4.

30 Michael J. Shapiro, "The Events of Discourse and the Ethics of Global Hospitality," in *Ethics and International Relations*, ed. Hakan Seckinelgin and Hideaki Shinoda, 110–31 (London: Palgrave, 2001), 112, citing Joseph Conrad, "Geography and Some Explorers," in *Last Essays*, 1–31 (New York: J.M. Dent & Sons, 1926), 8, 13.

31 Michel Foucault, *Society Must Be Defended*, trans. David Macey (New York: Picador, 2003), 17.

32 See John Locke, *Second Treatise of Government*, ch. 2, sec. 6, in *Two Treatises of Government* (Cambridge, UK: Cambridge University Press, 1988).
33 Cooper, *Pioneers*, 59, emphasis added.
34 Michael J. Shapiro, *Writing Politics: Studies in Compositional Method* (New York: Routledge, 2021).
35 Pynchon, *Mason & Dixon*, 345.
36 Donald A. Ringe, "Mode and Meaning in *The Last of the Mohicans*," in *James Fenimore Cooper: New Historical and Literary Contexts*, ed. W.M. Verhoeven, 109–24 (Amsterdam and Atlanta, GA: Editions Rodopi, 1993), 111.
37 Pynchon, *Mason & Dixon*, 651.
38 Linda Hutcheon, *A Poetics of Postmodernism: History, Theory, Fiction* (New York: Routledge, 1988), 124.
39 See Roosevelt, *Winning of the West.*
40 Ibid., 188.
41 Ibid., 189.
42 Leo Marx, *The Machine in the Garden: Technology and the Pastoral Ideal in America* (London: Oxford University Press, 1964).
43 Peter Nabokov and Robert Easton, *Native American Architecture* (New York: Oxford University Press, 1989), 39.
44 Lewis Mumford, *The City in History* (New York: Harcourt Brace Jovanovich, 1961), 569.
45 Nabokov and Easton, *Native American Architecture*, 39.
46 Mumford, *City in History*, 49.
47 Dolores Hayden, *The Power of Place: Urban Landscapes as Public History* (Cambridge, MA: MIT Press, 1997).
48 Robert Morris, "From a Chomskian Couch: The Imperialistic Unconscious," *Critical Inquiry* 29, no. 4 (2003): 678–94 at 685.
49 Martin Lefebvre, "Between Setting and Landscape in the Cinema," in *Landscape and Film*, ed. Martin Lefebvre, 19–60 (New York: AFI/Routledge, 2006), 22, original emphasis.
50 Michael J. Shapiro, *Deforming American Political Thought: Ethnicity, Facticity, and Genre* (Lexington: University Press of Kentucky, 2006), 71.
51 Gilles Deleuze, *Cinema 1: The Movement-Image* (1986; reprint, London: Bloomsbury, 2013), 136.
52 I analyze film theorist André Bazin's concept of "image facts" in Michael J. Shapiro, *Cinematic Geopolitics* (New York: Routledge, 2009), 154.
53 Nevada State Library, Archives, and Public Records, https://nsla.nv.gov/home.
54 Chris Lukinbeal, "Cinematic Landscapes," *Journal of Cultural Geography* 23, no. 1 (2005): 3–22 at 8.

55 Gillian Rose, "Afterwords: Gazes, Glances and Shadows," in *Studying Cultural Landscapes*, ed. Iain Robertson and Penny Richards, 165–69 (London: Arnold, 2003), 167. Rose states that a landscape's "visuality is seen as looking back … and having an effect itself."

56 Theodor Adorno, "The Essay as Form," in *Notes to Literature*, vol. 1, trans. Shierry Weber Nicholson, 3–14 (New York: Columbia University Press, 1991).

6

Art and the Disappeared: Beyond the Face

Nuala Finnegan

Our Mother Who Art Missing[1]

And then quietly, she disappeared again. With strange smiles in
  our eyes,
we searched and searched for her between the washing lines,
all the slap and flap of her skirts and all the empty spaces between.
She wasn't there.
We peered into the dark cave under the stairs,
then searched and searched for her between the washing lines
again. The oven, empty. In the wardrobe, blouses shrugged. Still,
she wasn't there. We peered into the dark cave under the stairs,
where her hats and shoes and coats were all empty. We waited.
Again, the oven. Empty. In the wardrobe, blouses shrugged, still.
We listened to the telephone's dull drone. We stared out windows.
  Still no sign
where her hats and shoes and coats were. All empty, we waited.
The cupboards were bare. Still, we searched and searched.
We listened to the telephone's dull drone. We stared out windows,
  still no sign
at all of the slapping flap of her skirts. All the empty spaces
  between the
cupboards were bare, still. We searched and searched

This extract from Doireann Ní Ghríofa's poem "Our Mother Who Art Missing" captures the sense of temporal collapse brought about by disappearance, for it emphasizes the time spent by the children peering, waiting, staring, and searching for their mother. The recurrent use of the word

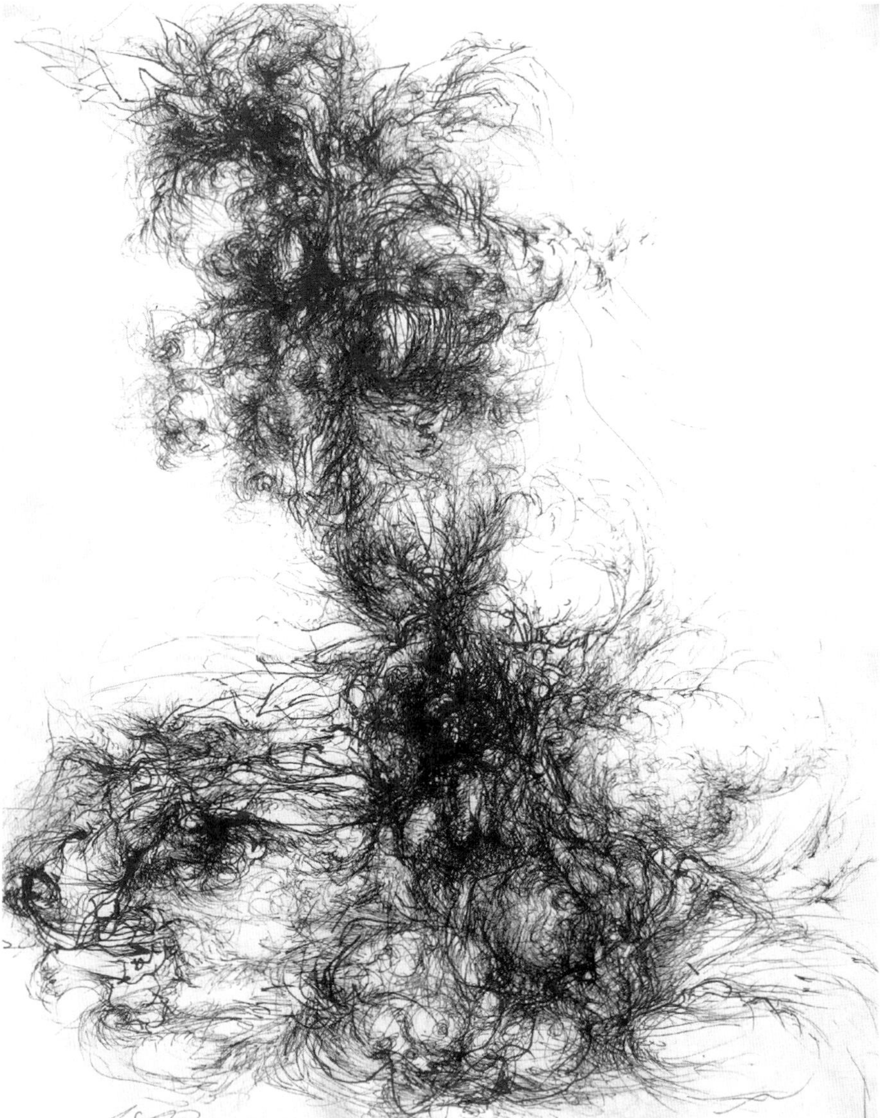

Chantal Meza, *Apparitions V*, 2017, ink on paper, 35 x 27 cm

"again" alerts us to the fact that each search registers as a counterpoint to the search that has just happened and to the one about to start since there is "still no sign." We note the temporal disjunctiveness, conveyed by the continuing reconfiguration of the same words, by the insistence on the sensory impact of disappearance through images of emptiness, and by the absence of sound, as in the line "no sign of the slapping flap of her skirts." All these elements conjoin to evoke a powerfully immersive, lived experience of disappearance. This poem has a happy ending and hints at a life lived beyond the domestic by the mother, who returns at the end: "And then, quietly she appeared again, a stranger's smile in her eyes." Such happy endings, however, those that speak of hope and return, are dismally absent from most stories of violent disappearance across the world, and the poetic resolution offered here by Ní Ghríofa is rare.

I commence this set of reflections while listening to the news that today they will search for the remains of Columba McVeigh, one of several disappeared by the Irish Republican Army (IRA) in Northern Ireland during the period of violent political upheaval called the Troubles (1968–94). The atrocities of the Troubles were the soundtrack to my childhood in the West of Ireland: Bloody Sunday, hunger strikes, distorted voices on news programs where actors did voice-overs for the spokespeople of Republicanism, residents leaving in droves for life beyond the island, the fate of the unreturned. I do not remember hearing stories about McVeigh when I was young, but I do remember Jean McConville, the mother of ten, who was abducted and disappeared by the IRA in 1972, her body found in bogland after years of searching amid dead ends and fractured hopes. Indeed, after 1999, when the IRA admitted to her murder, the image of McConville became an eerie omnipresence in the Irish mediascape, a shorthand for incomprehensible cruelty, the flouting of unwritten moral laws, the whispered question shared by many: who would take a mother of ten children?[2] We can perhaps imagine, transposing the poetic evocation of Ní Ghríofa, how those first moments of their mother's disappearance must have felt. The only recorded image available of her reveals a haunted, wasted face set beside three smiling children, an image invoking the incalculable sadness and irrevocable losses that the family had already faced.

It is often through the faces of the forcibly disappeared, like that of Jean McConville, that their stories are transmitted. We see these faces on milk cartons or bottles, on banners or posters fixed to lampposts, in artworks that seek to memorialize and mourn, and in political campaigns mounted with ferocity and anguish by family members. I have taken this detour through my own personal horizon of disappearance because it leads me directly to my research on victims of *feminicidio* (femicide) in Ciudad Juárez, Mexico.[3]

Indeed, I have stared at many of their faces on posters, T-shirts, petitions, and a host of other paraphernalia of disappearance that form part of its narrative, political, and societal arc. Starting with the poetic incantation of Ní Ghríofa – words spoken to raise the dead or absent – I aim to connect these different contexts and temporalities of disappearance in order to explore the function of artistic and poetic practice more broadly within the whirling temporal disjunctiveness that it generates. This essay, then, is about images that haunt and connect across contexts. It asks what happens when art enters this space of multiple, reiterative violence. In what follows, I consider two contrasting artistic approaches to the loss and pain of violent disappearance (and death). One has recourse to the face as a mode of transmission, and the other turns to abstraction as a way of activating the emotional register of disappearance on multiple levels.

SPECTRAL AESTHETICS

My first set of reflections leads me to the face of Erika Pérez Escobedo, whose image hangs on the wall outside my office at University z Cork, Ireland. Disappeared in 2002 in Ciudad Juárez on the Mexico-US border, her body was later found, one of the legions of disenfranchised dead in that city, which has become globally synonymous with the grisly spectacle of women's body parts. Her mother, Elia, continues to seek justice for the crime and my encounter with both Elia and her daughter's story came about through a portrait project led by Irish artist Brian Maguire and first initiated in 2009.[4] This project centred the faces of victims of *feminicidio* as part of a process of rehumanization, breathing life into a powerful counter-narrative meant to mediate societal discourses around crimes that attempt to delegitimize and dehumanize victims and their families. In an earlier analysis of my relationship with this project and its subjects,[5] I asked whether it might be possible for me to be sutured into an affective economy with Erika through a shared ethics of the face so eloquently theorised by Emanuel Levinas and developed into a hopeful vision for coalitional solidarity by Judith Butler.[6] In my daily encounter with Erika, I took comfort from those many scholars who have sought ways of going beyond empathy to seek out the lines along which productive political change might be brought about through this kind of coming together of her world and mine. Bracha Ettinger's compelling thesis about "wit(h)nessing" invites us to consider that images such as Maguire's portrait of Erika construct a "matrixial alliance."[7] Levinas's work on human sociality shows us that through the *rapport de face à face* (face-to-face relation), an ethical response is demanded of us. More specifically, he says that the human face "orders and ordains" us. "The face speaks. It speaks, it is in this that it renders possible and begins all discourse."[8] Erika's face inflects my surroundings, where femicidal violence is an everyday horror. Her death hovers in the air, set against a pale blue background with a smile frozen on her face. I am ordered and ordained by her, in Levinasian terms. In this sense, too, she is a ghost along my path. Notions of ghostliness and haunting are central to our understanding of the disappeared, those spectral presences that exist somewhere between time (the then and the now) and between space (the here and the there, or wherever *they* are). In their work on haunting, Eve Tuck and C. Ree offer an illuminating reading of the ending of Hideo Nakata's Japanese film *Dark Water* (2002). Their analysis shows how the mother figure "enters a quasi-spectral alternate realm to become the lost mother the ghost has craved all along, thereby bartering a sort of truce. Mothering the ghost becomes a way to live with ghosts."[9] I detect certain parallels between my behaviour toward Erika's portrait and that of mothers, such as making sure that her portrait hangs straight, saying "hello" to her on mornings when I am in the office, drawing people's attention to her, taking care. Indeed, drawing on this notion of care-fulness from a feminist theoretical framework enables us to see how a paradigm of mothering – akin to Ettinger's notions of the matrixial – might generate relations of solidarity and kinship, however unstable, unsatisfactory, or futile.[10]

Photographic images of faces of the disappeared frequently offer similar opportunities to mother ghosts in the way suggested by Tuck and Ree. Indeed, because of photography's rich history of recording family intimacy and because of family photography's function as a unit of ontological stability, photos of faces nudge us to frame them mentally as part of these intimate spaces, as though to say, *this could be your family photo; this could be your daughter*. The knowledge of the subject's brutal removal from family intimacy and closeness renders us helpless to the power of ghosts. It is perhaps in the context of a grim parade of the disappeared that circulates, seemingly endlessly, in a global mediascape that we feel most forcefully Tuck and Ree's observation that "haunting is the cost of subjugation."[11]

Whatever the ethical dilemmas posed to spectators of the faces of the disappeared, it is fair to state that the face and its corollary, facelessness, have become central to debates about violence and disappearance in Mexico. Whether through the horror of those whose faces have been removed literally or figuratively from public discourse or through the horror of those whose faces have been weaponized to diminish their humanity, there has emerged what Guillermo Espinosa Estrada calls "an unsettling rhetoric of the face."[12] In light of the particular atrocities of the case of forty-three disappeared students of Ayotzinapa, Guerrero, in 2014, which included the infamous case of Julio César Mondragón, whose body was found with the skin of his face removed, it is, perhaps, not surprising that the dichotomy of face/facelessness and its related dichotomy of identity/anonymity should be so terrifyingly present in cultural discourse. Mexico is in a particular moment of crisis in relation to the forced disappearance of its citizens. The announcement by the United Nations in 2022 that the numbers of forcibly disappeared in Mexico had reached 100,000[13] was a chilling riposte to those institutions of the state that had obfuscated, deflected, or ignored calls from family members and organizations of family members seeking news of their loved ones at various points since the current wave of violence took root across Mexican society in 2006.[14] Scholars consider this sustained practice of forced disappearance to be a continuity of, not a rupture with, models of *desaparición forzada* (forced disappearance) in operation since the fabled *guerra sucia* (dirty war) of the 1970s.[15] In this sense, there is a long trajectory of bodies disappearing from public space in Mexico, and what is being witnessed currently is a new tentacular system of terror that infects and intrudes on the everyday life of all of its citizens. Joaquín Barriendos, following Jacques Derrida's *Specters of Marx* (1994), reads the present situation in Mexico involving massive, forced disappearances as a sort of spectral violence inflicted on the social body as a whole. He asserts, "The legal indeterminacy of the disappeared and the biopolitical transposition of terror from absent bodies to the society can be properly characterized as the spectral condition of mass violence."[16] Rosanna Reguillo, suggesting that we think of this violence as something diffuse, writes of "that violence which is 'gaseous,' whose origin is impossible to attribute to anything other than phantasmagoric entities (narcos, terrorism), and which is almost impossible to prevent because it does not follow an intelligible pattern."[17] It is no surprise that disappearance, being noxious and omnipresent, has turned its brutal calligraphy to the face as a way to metabolize loss, reinscribe humanity, and instigate shared spaces for mourning.

But how might we move beyond this unsettling rhetoric of the face to consider other ways of framing, containing, and piercing the pain of forced disappearance? The abstract Mexican artist Chantal Meza has raised her unease about the face as a mechanism of exploration of the violence of disappearance:

> That was the first frustration I encountered really because you know, with … forced disappearance, what happens is … if something has disappeared – what is it? … Is it a person? So alright, we can help you to find this person – how does it look? – and so you have a face. Then you start seeing these faces all the time. All the time when I was a child, I already had these images in my memory. They seemed to be part of my imaginary already. As a child, I remember looking at images

on television, on the streets in newspapers, asking whether you have seen this person that has disappeared? ... Children, young people, adults, there were women, there were men ... As a child of course, I couldn't really make sense of this, but I knew it was there. It was only years later, now as an adult, I encountered this problem once again. I thought to myself, "I remember looking at all those faces." And I think, the question for me was, "How can we explore this problem through abstraction?" Because these people need this particular person – it's so specific – they need this person, and so what can you do about that?[18]

Meza's work, then, refuses the affective economy of the face that was referenced earlier, and I focus here on her monumental project *State of Disappearance* as a way of teasing out how facelessness, the nonhuman, and the abstract can help us to confront, contest, and resist the realities of forced disappearance in contemporary Mexico. Here, I continue to consider the link with the spectral through a focus not on specific ghosts but on ruptures in space and time, on the afterlife of disappearance, and on how Meza's abstract swirling shapes are an attempt to capture the chaos of disappearance, to articulate its humanity, and to share in its grief.

Writing persuasively about the spectral impact of a regime of terror inflicted through disappearance on Mexico's societal fabric, Barriendos states, "Spectral violence erodes the public right to know and blurs the terrain of the politics of truth, extending and updating the domain of governmentality. Inflicted 'from up to down,' but somatised and reproduced horizontally, spectral violence derives from the following paradox: in order to be fully spectral, this form of violence begins by mastering the materiality of the absent body."[19] Meza's work grapples with this conundrum of absence, and in the next section, I concentrate on her series *Apparitions*, part of her project *State of Disappearance*, which also features the series *Obscure Beasts*, *Fragments of a Catastrophe*, *Since the Beginning*, and *The Void*. The twenty-eight drawings in the series *Apparitions* offer explosions of ink, images that refuse any singular story, refuse any singular narrative, refuse to materialize disappearance, to show, to tell. Instead, what they offer is a world of ink and lines.[20]

If abstract art is said to imagine an interior world, one of texture, colour, and shape, then how do we interpret these shape-shifting forms as a deep, bodily response to disappearance? I suggest two lenses through which we might approach the images as somatic engagement with disappearance. The first concerns the phantasmagorical, drawing on ideas from Reguillo, referenced earlier. The second involves the tentacular dimension of the drawings, which I link to ideas of the rhizome, as theorized by Gilles Deleuze and

Félix Guattari, which help us to see how dispersal and multiplicity can be mechanisms for transformative potential. Refusing more conventional opportunities of witnessing, understood as a spectator's encounter with the face or body of a disappeared person, these images do not give us faces but instead swirling inky forms that move in and out of each other. Each of the twenty-eight images in the series has a unique shape, yet each relates to the one preceding and to the one following; these bodies of ink are non-human forms that seem to speak directly to Reguillo's conceptualization of an expressive violence. According to Reguillo, the power of expressive *violencias* lies in their infinity and inevitability, to the extent that they form a giant "necromachine."[21] In her formulation, bodies are at the service of the machine, as are its servants. Moreover, as we have already seen, she speaks of a phantamasgorical violence that is almost impossible to prevent because it does not follow an intelligible pattern. It is precisely this lack of intelligibility that is captured by the spinning shapes of Meza's drawings. These are apparitions that appear for a moment and transmogrify into something else, constantly shifting from one form to another. Thus the first three images in the series almost constitute a murmuration, a movement of shapes, difficult to make out, but a solid body of black, which moves immediately into other forms and shapes in the images that follow. Their traces of ink may not speak stories or be legible in conventional ways, but these spaces of entanglement cleave to the very essence of the ghostly that stalks the Mexican body politic. Some of the drawings appear to have barbs or sharp edges, whereas others are plays of light and shadow, a juxtaposition of density and disintegration. Shapes lead into and away from each other, such that I cease to be aware of where one edge begins and the other closes. Some of the lines appear sharp, like thorns, as in *Apparitions XIII* and *XIV*.

These forms, abstracted into graphic shapes, produce optical effects that are profoundly unsettling, as though they contain truths beyond me, bodies of light that I cannot reach. Reguillo touches on this dimension of the expressive violence currently being enacted in Mexico: "Expressive violence is without a doubt preceded by a complex system of pursuit of 'profit,' but this remains concealed, encrypted, hidden as residual elements."[22] Meza's apparitions echo this system of concealment and encryption, mirroring its methods, evoking its core. These shapes may not hold stories told in linear ways, but their encrypted ghostly presence speaks of bodies, of "vibrant matter,"[23] and most critically, of their agency.[24] As Meza reminds us, "it's not like there's no agency; someone is doing the disappearing."[25] Her disconcerting recreations of the encoded and ghostly dimension of forced disappearance, then, help us to get at and into its materiality, to live among it.

Meza centres another section of her project *State of Disappearance* around the idea of the void, that philosophical space of absence that is almost the inevitable destination of any contemplation of extreme violence. Brad Evans cautions us against any impulse to interpret the void as always absence: "For if extreme violence results in us being thrown into [the] void, which in itself is the absence which haunts and underwrites all forms of sacred meaning, this void can also be a space of pure creation, where the immensity of terror and the affirmation of life collide."[26] We can read the churning shapes of the artworks in the series *Apparitions* as exactly this articulation of pure creation, as objects and shapes that speak, that leave a trace, that bear witness to violence. In this way, Meza uses artistic practice to theorize notions of absence and forces her spectators to face disappearance full on.

THE RHIZOME: BEYOND INTELLIGIBILITY

But if Meza's shapes form a ghostly register of this particular regime of terror, we can also begin to understand how they also form patterns or networks of meanings that might be described as rhizomatic. The rhizome originates in botany, of course, but is theorized in more capacious terms in the well-known work of Deleuze and Guattari, who resist the dominant ontological model of binary thought by proposing rhizomatic structures that are both heterogenous and multiplicitous: "The rhizome is reducible neither to the One nor the multiple … It is comprised not of units but of dimensions, or rather directions in motion."[27] Considering the swirling shapes of the artworks in *Apparitions* with this in mind, we can start to see this multiplicity in action, most notably in lines that form figures, some poised as though to take flight, as in *Apparitions XIV*; others barbed and appearing, from certain angles, to pull apart; and still others seeming to dance in the air, as in *Apparitions XV*, *XVII*, and *XXII*. The fact that the first image appears to be tree-like adds weight to this idea that the series moves away from what Deleuze and Guattari identify as the dominant, binary, centralized model of the tree in order to embrace a freer, more dispersed rhizomatic sensibility that allows for the ink to spill over the frame, as in *Apparitions VIII* and *IX*. The liquid dimension of ink, a material that endlessly spills and extends, adds to this sense of the infinite as it roams indeterminately over the white paper. Thus the tree-like figures of the first three images, suggesting authority and strength, give way to more horizontal linkages, both between patterns of ink and between the images themselves. Are these the same images, endlessly reconfigured in twenty-eight different ways, a special effect, a sleight of hand? Can we see them as an assemblage in the sense discussed by Deleuze and Guattari, a gathering or grouping of colour and shape? According to Meza, *Apparitions* speaks to the notion of accumulation, the scale of loss in disappearance that the series tries to capture: "The *Apparitions* series, well drawings, were to me … lots of faces, images that were there in the collective memory. I don't have anybody who has been disappeared, so I tried to understand the way I was engaging with it and how does society receive this? For me, *Apparitions* was … another image, another image, another image, somebody else, somebody else disappeared … All these faces, all these people, they are families."[28]

However, Meza's homage to the notion of infinity – which as seen in Reguillo is a central feature of the gaseous violence that is poisoning the Mexican body politic – also incorporates series of rhizomatic crossings and contestations. Indeed, in certain images, the figures seem to reach for the air, dancing across the canvas toward each other, as in *Apparitions XV*. Ideas of accumulation, scale, and saturation – all deeply embedded in discourses around disappearance in Mexico – can be found in the dizzying mess of ink. But so, too, do we encounter the idea of cross-cutting renewal. On the one hand, the forms seem to clearly uphold Deleuze and Guattari's principles of multiplicity and heterogeneity, an ever-expanding body. However, they also evoke the impossibility of rupture, an investment in continuity, in the rhizome that cannot be broken or stopped. I see this as a sort of dialogic encounter between different lines of ink, as though in a state of dynamic interaction, where lines of absence and pain are in turn crossed by lines of life and agency. If *Apparitions XII* seems to suggest a black body at its centre – Meza reminds us of the materiality of the burned body, "the blackness, what a burned body looks like"[29] – it metamorphoses in the next image, *Apparitions XIII*, into an image that beckons outward, its diminished blackness posed with delicate lines at each corner that curve up and out.

The images embrace the edges of their frames in ways that seem to say, "Onward to the next," each one indelibly tracing a line or set of lines to their next re-creation, their next set of reimaginings. If we strain to read these artworks in emancipatory terms given the realities of extreme violence that prompted the series in the first place, it is important to recognize that the rhizomatic connectedness that contests and beckons outward sits side by side with the slashes of blackness. In this sense, the network of relations that disappearances bring into being has its ghostly dark side but also its tentacular openness, its capacity to generate directions in movement, directions that can agitate and unsettle, contest and renew. Donna Haraway thinks of tentacularity as "life lived along lines,"[30] a notion that resonates strongly with the life of these drawings, which spill over their edges and connect to one another, reaching outward. These networks contest and challenge. Operating as sites of exploration and openness, they defy linearity and authority. They are essential, then, if the aesthetic possibilities of disappearance are to be generative, allowing for hope as well as for darkness, allowing the ghosts not only to move alongside each other but also to be mothered and to be still.

CONCLUSIONS

In this rather circuitous tour through and around the philosophical and artistic challenges posed by forced disappearance, I have lingered on Irish poet Doireann Ní Ghríofa's sensory and lyrical evocation of a mother who disappeared. Linking this to a real mother, Jean McConville, and to the spectral omnipresence of her face as part of my own visual landscape, I have reflected on my personal interaction with the face of Erika Pérez Escobedo, considering the hauntological capacity of such faces and whether, to quote Tuck and Ree, "mothering the ghost, allows us to live with the ghost."[31] The faceless forms in Meza's series *Apparitions* present altogether different challenges, and through them various tensions and fissures have been revealed. I have noted how images that foreground a face that has been brutally removed through *feminicidio* or forced disappearance attempt to suture the spectator into an affective and potentially politically transformative relationship with its subject so that we may bear witness to its humanity and share its burden. How, then, can abstract art help us to frame the very desperation on which disappearance is predicated – a desperation "located beyond the threshold of intelligibility"[32] – without recourse to the face that is so central to transnational practices of witnessing? Ultimately, what is it that connects the face of Jean McConville or Erika Pérez Escobedo to the inky play of light and shadow in Meza's work?

Acclaimed journalist Marcela Turati writes of *feminicidio* that "we must strive to go deeper. Not to simply stay in the scenes of horror."[33] Her plea is for a more somatic connection with the structural patterns that sustain these violences. What we have seen in Meza's series *Apparitions* is an attempt to sketch not only the horrors that disappearances imply but also their lines of contestation and resistance, their rhizomatic connectedness across time and space. The *Oxford English Dictionary* defines "disappearance" as "an act of someone or something ceasing to be visible." Underneath this definition is the example in italics of "the sun's disappearance at night," evoking the notion of night becoming day and hinting at the sun's return. This image suggests the transformative potential of artistic practice, whether through work that foregrounds the face and therefore the human-centred nature of disappearance or through work that seeks other ways to capture its horrors and discursive power. Meza's lines of movement speak to a context that is frequently hopeless and paralyzed in Turati's multiplying scenes of horror, but perhaps her abstract approach sidesteps the ethical dilemmas presented by works that foreground the face, delving deeper into the ontological reality of disappearance to grapple with its philosophical foundations, its materiality. We need multiple ways of accessing the different nodal points in the "ecology of terror"[34] brought about by the regime of forced disappearance in Mexico. Meza's dancing lines offer us one such glimpse; we are yet to see where they may take us.

NOTES

1 This extract of a poem by Irish- and English-language poet Doireann Ní Ghríofa is from her collection *Clasp* (Dublin: Daedalus, 2015), 45.

2 For a comprehensive account of the McConville case, see Patrick Radden Keefe, *Say Nothing: A True Story of Murder and Memory in Northern Ireland* (Glasgow: William Collins, 2018).

3 *Feminicidio* in Mexico, recognized by the Federal Penal Code as a crime since 2007, is defined as the deprivation of life of a woman on the grounds of gender. Feminist scholars in the region, most notably Marcela Lagarde y de los Ríos, presented a case for using the term *feminicidio* as a more appropriate cultural translation of the English term "femicide" not only because it takes account of the crime's systemic nature but also, critically, because it suggests the responsibility and complicity of the state, whose neglect enables the crime to continue. For the purposes of this study, I follow the lead of Ríos in referring to the crime as *feminicidio* and retain the Spanish form wherever possible. As a feminist critic working in the privileged context of European academia, I recognize that it is vital to register this theoretical complexity and to continue encouraging debate on the topic in the English-speaking world. For further reading, see Rosa-Linda Fregoso and Cynthia Bejarano, *Terrorizing Women: Feminicide in the Américas* (Durham, NC: Duke University Press, 2010).

4 Maguire is by no means the only artist to work with portraits of the victims in his response to femicidal crime in Mexico. In 2001, the exhibition *Facing Faces*, curated by Belgian artist Gino d'Artali, featured 162 diptychs by eighty-three artists from thirty different countries. In 2008, artists Swoon and Tennessee Jane created an installation entitled *Portrait of Silvia Elena*, in reference to Silvia Elena Morales, a victim of *feminicidio* in Ciudad Juárez in 1998, and a mural project in the city in 2020 sought to foreground the faces of other victims. Faces also feature prominently in cultural and political responses to the disappeared of the dirty war in Argentina. For a useful discussion, see Jordana Blejmar, "Spectral Topographies: Photography

and Disappearance in Argentina," *Photography and Resistance*, https://photographyandresistance.wordpress.com/2018/12/12/jordana-blejmar-spectral-topographies-photography-and-disappearance-in-argentina.

5 Nuala Finnegan, *Cultural Representations of Feminicidio at the US-Mexico Border* (New York: Routledge, 2018).

6 For further exploration, see Emmanuel Levinas, *Entre Nous: Thinking-of-the-Other*, trans. Michael B. Smith and Barbara Harshav (New York: Columbia University Press, 1998); Judith Butler, *Frames of War: When Is Life Grievable?* (London: Verso, 2009); and Judith Butler, "Precarious Life: The Obligations of Proximity," Neale Wheeler Watson Lecture 2011, Nobel Prize Museum, Svenska Akademiens Börssal, Stockholm, 24 May 2011, https://www.youtube.com/playlist?list=PL3F0991F34D08719A.

7 Bracha Ettinger, *The Matrixial Borderspace* (Minneapolis: University of Minnesota Press, 2006).

8 Emmanuel Levinas, *Ethics and Infinity: Conversations with Philippe Nemo*, trans. Richard A. Cohen (Pittsburgh: Duquesne University Press, 1985), 87.

9 Eve Tuck and C. Ree, "A Glossary of Haunting," in *Handbook of Autoethnography*, ed. Stacy Holman Jones, Tony E. Adams, and Carolyn Ellis, 639–58 (Walnut Creek, CA: Left Coast, 2013), 646.

10 On feminism and care, see Sara Ahmed, *Living a Feminist Life* (Durham, NC: Duke University Press, 2017); and Sara Ahmed, "Selfcare as Warfare," *feministkilljoys*, 25 August 2014, http://feministkilljoys.com/2014/08/25/selfcare-as-warfare/. See also Silvia Federici, *Revolution at Point Zero: Housework, Reproduction, and Feminist Struggle* (Oakland, CA: PM Press, 2012). There is a long, rich history of mother-inflected activism central to debates about violence in the Americas more broadly and probably most associated with the Mothers of the Plaza de Mayo in Argentina. See Diana Taylor, "Making a Spectacle: The Mothers of the Plaza de Mayo," *Journal of the Motherhood Initiative for Research and Community Involvement* 3, no. 2 (2001): 97–109, https://jarm.journals.yorku.ca/index.php/jarm/article/view/2774.

11 Tuck and Ree, "Glossary of Haunting," 643.

12 Guillermo Espinosa Estrada, "Las voces de Ayotzinapa," review of John Gibler, *I Couldn't Even Imagine That They Would Kill Us: An Oral History of the Attacks against the Students of Ayotzinapa* (San Francisco, CA: City Lights, 2017), *Horizontal*, 26 July 2017, my translation.

13 United Nations, "Mexico: Dark Landmark of 100,000 Disappearances Reflects Pattern of Impunity, UN Experts Warn," 17 May 2022, https://www.ohchr.org/en/statements/2022/05/mexico-dark-landmark-100000-disappearances-reflects-pattern-impunity-un-experts.

14 The current context of forced disappearance in Mexico relates principally to

the precipitous wave of violence experienced from 2006 onward, which coincided with the election of President Felipe Calderón that year and a change of policy toward curbing so-called cartel violence. For scholarship on this topic, see Ioan Grillo, *El Narco: Inside Mexico's Criminal Insurgency* (London: Bloomsbury, 2012); Oswaldo Zavala, *Drug Cartels Do Not Exist: Narco-Trafficking and Culture in the US and Mexico*, trans. William Savinar (Nashville, TN: Vanderbilt University Press, 2022); Anabel Hernández, *Los Señores del Narco* (New York: Penguin Random House, 2012); Benjamin T. Smith, *Dope: The Real History of Mexico's Drug Trade* (London: Ebury, 2021).

15 Apart from a substantial body of cinematic work, including feature-length, documentary, and short films, as well as a a diverse array of digital media, such as podcasts, there is much scholarship on genealogy and on the *guerra sucia*. For a comprehensive overview, see Silvana Mandolessi and Katia Olalde, eds, *Disappearances in Mexico: From the 'Dirty War' to the 'War on Drugs'* (London: Routledge, 2022). See also Carolina Robledo Silvestre, "Combing History against the Grain: The Search for Truth amongst Mexico's Hidden Graves," in *Beyond the Drug War in Mexico: Human Rights, the Public Sphere and Justice*, ed. Wil G. Pansters, Benjamin T. Smith, and Peter Watt, 164–84 (London: Routledge, 2017).

16 Joaquin Barriendos, "Spectral Violence: Art and Disappearance in Post-Ayotzinapa Mexico," *Porto Arte: Revista de Artes Visuais* 24, no. 42 (2019): 1–19, https://core.ac.uk/download/pdf/327051234.pdf.

17 Rossana Reguillo, "The Narco-Machine and the Work of Violence: Notes Toward Its Decodification," trans. Margot Olavarría, *Hemisferica* 8, no. 2 (2010), https://hemisphericinstitute.org/en/emisferica-82/reguillo5.html.

18 Chantal Meza in the video interview with Brad Evans at https://www.chantal-meza.com/stateofdisappearance. My interpretation of Chantal Meza's work is based on my sustained engagement with the images that make up her project *State of Disappearance* and on my conversations with Meza when she generously gave her time to work with students at University College Cork in February 2020.

19 Barriendos, "Spectral Violence," 11–12.

20 Some of the images in the series *Apparitions* are reproduced in this volume. The full series, along with the other artworks in the project *State of Disappearance*, can be viewed at https://www.chantal-meza.com/stateofdisappearance.

21 Rossana Reguillo, *Necromáquina: Cuando morir no es suficiente* (Barcelona: Ned Ediciones, 2021).

22 Reguillo, "Narco-Machine."

23 Jane Bennett, *Vibrant Matter: A Political Ecology of Things* (Durham, NC: Duke University Press, 2010).

24 In her analysis of agency in relation to the Argentine photographer Paula Luttringer, Jordana Blejmar invokes Jane Bennett's work, cited above. See Blejmar, "Spectral Topographies."

25 Chantal Meza in the video interview with Brad Evans at https://www.chantal-meza.com/stateofdisappearance.

26 Brad Evans, *Ecce Humanitas: Beholding the Pain of Humanity* (New York: Columbia University Press, 2021), xxi.

27 Gilles Deleuze and Félix Guattari, *A Thousand Plateaus: Capitalism and Schizophrenia*, trans. Brian Massumi (London: Continuum, 1987), 23.

28 Chantal Meza in the video interview with Brad Evans at https://www.chantal-meza.com/stateofdisappearance.

29 Ibid.

30 Donna Haraway, *Staying with the Trouble: Making Kin in the Chthulucene* (Durham, NC: Duke University Press, 2016), 32.

31 Tuck and Ree, "Glossary of Haunting," 646.

32 Brad Evans in the video interview with Chantal Meza at https://www.chantal-meza.com/stateofdisappearance.

33 Cited in Frida Guerrera, *#Ni una más: El feminicidio en México: Tema urgente en la Agenda Nacional* (Mexico City: Aguilar, 2019), n.p., my translation.

34 Brad Evans in the video interview with Chantal Meza at https://www.chantal-meza.com/stateofdisappearance.

INTERMEZZO

Theatre of the Disappeared

Brad Evans and Chantal Meza

CASTING

I barely grasp the pain of my own story. They have made me confront too much darkness, too much denial, too much of the unbearable. This is not a confession. It is a drama that is filled with perpetrators, victims, and witnesses, whose fabled existence is no less real. It is my wretched life. I am the story of everybody. I am the story of nobody. We write together, yet we have always been one. I recognize now, in the void of myself, ourselves, that the world is a stage, but too many are condemned to the shadows. Some appear before us, only to vanish without a trace. Some are never cast at all. The disposable of history. They go by many forgotten names. Unknown. Unwanted. Undetermined. Unjust.

The plot that I narrate is never fully bound to the terrestrial plane. It has its moments. It has its times. It has its places. But when and where are less important than the atmospheres created by ecologies of suffering. If I write of a natural history, I write of a natural history of violence. I am concerned with the elements. I have been tormented by them. They have hidden secrets, which fleetingly appear in my terrifying dreams. Others will seek and weaponize their immersive potentials. And if I concern myself with the body, I also concern myself with its disembodiments, its ghosted presence, its mental collapses, which can be just as ruinous as the explosive destruction of the grandest of temples.

I know, too, of my own contradictions. This play of words is riddled by my own shameful compromises with power. I have also been blinded. I am Oedipus. And I am Antigone. Fated and sorrowful. Seduced by the desire to look upon other appearances. Helping to hide things in plain sight. I also write this on a machine, which is interfaced into a machine, which is interfaced into a machine, which promises to save me, make me visible, make me relevant, while denying what makes me human.

How can I begin to make sense of disappearance when society teaches me to be so doubtful? How can I find the strength to gaze upon the intolerable if I must reveal my inner most vulnerabilities? How can I account for the complex condition of absence when I am overexposed to banalities while denied my own secrets? I insist that this is not a confession. Nor does it seek legal justice. Sovereignty was always key to understanding erasure. It is however an abstract testimony. A testimony to the power of abstraction. My call for a more poetic justice. The only necessity I have. To take nothing seriously.

But what of the disappeared? Is it enough to emancipate the spectators? What is their role in this drama? Are they lost from the start? Can they ever properly return? I see them before the script is written. And I search for them once the final word has been said, once the final letter has been uttered, once the silent applause ends. They are the silences. The in-between of every word, haunting every character, encouraging me to misspell so that we may focus on the accident, faintly making scratches beneath the printed paper, disrupting the brilliance of the solitary pixel on my laptop screen.

There are times when I, too, wish to disappear. But that is my choice. My image has also been overexposed. Curated by systems that know only how to curate throwaway images, throwaway dreams. Yet still I have cast myself. Alone. Together. Cast out on wretched seas in search of ships full of phantoms. I bring only an axe. Kafka's advice. It just may break the frozen seas.[1] It just may allow us to look beyond, deeper and deeper, into the depths so that we may find the strength to look again.

ACT ONE: SINCE THE BEGINNING

Life. Nasty, short, brutish. Survival, nothing but survival, only the fittest. Fire, wilderness. Kill the barbarians. They know only destruction. But what of nature? Beautiful, deadly. The site of all betrayal. Where only wolves among men and seductresses reside. Let's tame those savage ecologies. Call it civilization. And later we will call it progress. Yet this comes at a price. Dispossession always does.

Race becomes us all. An infernal Babylon. Let's create them out of the ashes of the sacred crises. The imperial condition: invented by life. Made to live, allowed to die. And so it begins. Millions abducted. Taken from the shores of golden lands. Sold like cattle, punished as chattel. Confessions of the flesh. Lacerated by time. Later we will hang them from trees, parade them through the streets, shoot them in the grimy gutters of every metropolis, just because it remains the natural order of things.

Globalization, discovery. The world made visible. The world as picture. Cortez. Columbus. De Bry. Doré. How we suffered into truth. But only for the ancestral to perish. The circularity of denial, the rotation of power, but only for the select few. Everything returns. Slavery to Syrians. From the Atlantic pass into the depths of the Mediterranean, the Platonic shadows that gave rise to the imperial model, generation imitating generation, imitating nature, continue to dwell in imprisoning caves. Shadows that wish to dance, looking deep into a poetic flame, merely disappear with the violence of time. Yet who lit the embers? And who led them into the cave to deny them their very existence?

Their silence was never empty. Not every abyss total. Counter-history learns to hide, knowing that the unintelligible can also be life-affirming in the face of destruction. So the watchpersons refuse to let memory be a victim of this history. How many, they ask, have already been forgotten? How many consigned into the dust of history? History tells us that we remember only the brightest and the best. But whose version of history? What violence committed in the act of being remembered so that others can be so swiftly forgotten? Or is it the reverse? It doesn't matter. It's all the same. That's the real seduction. Apologists. Deniers. Those who know that the burning of books has always taken many different forms.

Still, the memory of the earth tells a different story. Real histories, the real depths of human suffering, sites of disappearance – they were never shown on ordinance maps for power. True places never are. What's needed is a different image of this landscape, hung like an animal carcass on the wall, documenting all the atrocities just like a fateful trophy to the impotence of human beings in the face of our mortality, in the face of our bestiality. The beginning tells us of this slaughterhouse that we created for ourselves – a world where the blood seeps through the flesh of the earth, where the topography is brutally torn, where the black soil appears to remind us of the shadows cast by the black sun of the void.

Who is beast?
In the dark, the admixture, the prance
In his violent act
The death in its body explodes, the ash to disappear
An image?
Beast
Bring about, the shape of your image

Beast
Dance, walk, cry
Ask me to find your trace
Your face
The blood falls
You, the one, explodes, splashes
A sea of blood
Dissolved bodies
A beast, embracing you
Lifetime
Leave your wounds exposed
They are necessary
Your memory?
A predisposed abyss
Lapses of memory
Leave a shadow

ACT TWO: OBSCURE BEASTS

What is left to imagine when the body is absent? How can we return something of the human when its very presence is denied? What can be revealed about the monstrosity of annihilation? How can we aesthetically testify to suffering without glossing over the complexities of human loss? And by what means can we expose how the lines between perpetrators, victims, and witnesses are blurred beyond all certainty? Obscure beasts emerge through the violent traces torn into the flesh of the canvas and its mutilated landscapes of historical despair. They dance with raw realities of human misery and its unnecessary deaths. From a distance, the beasts take on many different shapes, although witnesses already project what is subconsciously embedded in their archives of hope and torment! Upon closer inspection, the landscape itself is revealed to be too close yet still out of reach, confounding any attempt at forensic certainty. It is full of lines of miscommunication, whose subtly revealing tortured bodies and disfigured forms draw the viewer into the scene like some unwitting accomplice. The shame of being human takes hold. Am I not complicit? Am I still not the animal that they always said I was? So they inevitably withdraw from the intimacy. The most brutal landscapes of devastation always prove easier to view than the murder of a single wretched soul by demons who look all too familiar and all too human in their brutalizing states. But there is more at stake here. The wounds existed long before the lines were made visible for all to see and witness again.

Yet the real mask of mastery is to call all this violence abstract. To insist that one must get closer to the bodies, sleep with the corpse, so that a more affective theory of the human becomes apparent. Two visions of purity – the technical and the critical – neither of which take the abstract seriously. Still, the obscure beasts continue to defy the essence of things. They show that it was always about necessity. The framing of life as survival makes beasts of us all. Yet still they recoil at the sight of red consuming the black, swallowing the void, and haunting the likes of Mark Rothko in his grave.[2] But don't they see that the red, too, has so many meanings, seeping out of the darkest centres of the unknown earth when called upon, only to colour the primordial flames whose tales we are yet to fully decipher.

Disappear. Where?
Within the fire
Let my pain, your anger
Their fear and dementia
Burn in the flames that my body is now
Listen …
Become the fire
What does it say?
I am solemn, my tremor is intense
Savage
The sound of my flames, reaches you
You feel it, there, in the heart
The heat of my body penetrates your chest
It burns your eyes
Those eyes that do not forget
I'm there, in your hands
They are burning
Just like your feet
Yes, your feet
You want to run away, you want to burn
Because I
I am already fire
The fire that consumes
And rises with the air
The fire that burns us
Ignited ones disappear

ACT THREE: APPARITIONS

Wretched ghosts of history haunt the landscapes of the present. But often we choose not to see their appearances. Blind to the traces that they leave as warnings from the past, we erase their memory through the violence of organized forgetting, remaining silent to their screams and turning away from the violence of their demonic performances. Yet such apparitions – the guilty and the damned – refuse to leave us in peace. Their subtle and brutal lines still find a way to cut through the material surfaces of the earth, through the pages of every political declaration, inducing ephemeral states that burden the ethical spirit. They call to us on deserted streets. They cry out each time a gun is fired or a bomb explodes. They walk like an army of the condemned down every corridor of justice and peace. Yet our memory of them often serves to add more recruits to their ranks. They refuse to vanish, even though more lives are mercilessly destroyed in their names. This is the lesson that they give to us – the certainty that nothing will prevail, especially when everything is possible. Virgil, Hamlet. They saw only what was plain to see by those armed with wretched eyes.

The sites are everywhere, yet the sight is haunted by the memory of those absent. Of those vanished into the ground, left to fate alone, left to summon an excavation. Where is the justice for them now? We read out as a euphemism for evil. Maybe there is some comfort, the barest of hopes, in the notion that everything eventually finds its place – locations that memorialize the senseless, the merciless, the triumphant onslaught of calculative thinking. Wounded Knee, Guernica, Bykivia, Belsen, Auschwitz, Hiroshima, Choeung Ek, Kigali, Batajnica, Vukovar, Duraiappa, Maguindana, El Mozote, Medellin, Iguala, Palmyra. And many others. Known and unknown, waiting to be discovered, yet to be filled.

Among the debris, there is always a crack. No tomb can contain the apparitions indefinitely. Plato's prison was always an illusion. The walls were real and the shadows true, but they always retained a life of their own. And the apparitions of death certainly don't belong to the realm of mimesis. The memory of death mimics life no less than art mimics nature. It remains an excess. The haunting exceeds us. The lightness of nonbeing weighs so heavily on the living. The ephemeral past forcefully orchestrates the burdens of the future. But are we not already ghosts in the making? And do we not carry with us the ghosts of our ancestors, which the delusions of progress ask us to forget? Apparitions remind us that the weight of history comes in many different measurements. Some are quantifiable, like the violence that is incapable of answering when too much killing is enough. More and more, the technical masters and progressive visionaries cry out. More and more, until we prove it works. See, there were ghosts in the abstract machine. Or at least that was their intention. And that was the haunting schizophrenia. Remember the dead but forget the cause of death.

Disappear. Where?
In the air
Be dust in the night
Be dust in the day
Be the pain and then rise
Surround us within
Observe
Be the smoke that permeates and blurs
Becoming the shadow, in your darkness
In the midst of that darkness
We are here
You are searching
Who are you looking for?
Yes, air
Breathe
Who is it?
It's me
Wind, dance with the wind
Pour yourself into the mountains
Move the trees
Halt in there
Behold
Descend
Feel the ground I walk
Walk
Walk on my feet

ACT FOUR: MIRRORS OF THE VOID

Mirrors hang to reveal a landscape of human devastation. But these mirrors are not simply reflective. They have no concern for the passing viewer's all-too-fleeting curiosities. They know that they outlive us. Side by side, what they offer is a visual testimony to histories of persecution. Fixed in place, they immobilize us with their dark movements. Yet as we walk past, it is clear that they don't exist for our purpose or aesthetic pleasure. They speak to themselves. Assuming the right to project their truth back to each other, back into the world. Having already foreseen the extinction of all human life, they never required our narcissistic presence or self-centred validations. And they have no care at all whether humans need art. These mirrors ask whether art ever needed us?

So it commences, as always, with a misplaced sense of elation – the violating optimism. Once again, the masses are seduced by the spectacle and glory of power. Flight into the future is presented as the only solution to the curse of the past. Progress, they say. Onward they march, with an intellectual army also marching in formation. History has a way of making such things appear inevitable, certain, foreclosed. Such is the grand sweep of this uncompromising force, which has the capacity to displace all that stands before it. How they learned to desire their own oppression. This is the force of nihilism and the violence of reactive minds. And so the lines begin to appear yet are already torn. Deeper and deeper, they cut into the canvas of the earth, revealing bodies caught in the unstoppable winds of a merciless storm. Yet still they project their ambition across planes of denial, cutting into certainty, feeling their way into existence like a liberating force already cloaked in the blood of the innocent. There is no absolving the shameful destitution. This is always their intention, always their desecrating purpose. They carry life with them on their fated journey.

But the majestic lines witnessed on their destructive flight soon turn into the most intimate voids of despair. Everybody is a victim. Everybody is complicit. Our attentions therefore shift to another frame of reference and suffering. Into the abyss, we now descend. We are consumed by the primordial waters. The river Styx was always but a tributary. The pain appears to us in the hopeless depths of subjugation, taking control over every aspect of human existence. That's why the void is a mirrored sight of anguish and madness. They who stare into the depths see the Gorgon with his deep black eyes at the bottom of the icy pit looking back at them with a monstrous vision. Inner demons thus return as wretched souls of prejudice and hate. Their intimate violence provides a new chapter in the brutalizing movements and flight of men. But it's a mistake to see them as victims born of the original scene. They were already there, waiting, alongside. This is why mirrors always double. Grandest historical claims are nothing without the intimate depths of passion and outrage.

But there is no tale of redemption or salvation here. The white glare of optimism proved blinding to those who had already witnessed too much yet had still persisted as if nothing had happened. And so the tides of history returned. Absolution reigned supreme until the end. They held their trials. They condemned as guilty many in their midst for the inhumanity that they had shown to fellow humans. But never did they see the mirrors for what they truly were. Maybe they didn't have the courage to see themselves truly ravaging the beauty of the world. And maybe they didn't want to see how they had ultimately destroyed themselves and thus played out the most fateful of all the worldly tragedies. That was the nihilism. And so all that remained was for each soul to be captured in its fall from grace, visibly caught up in the flight from meaning and forever lost in the depths of these mirrors of the void.

Disappear. Where?
Be with the water
The water is painted
It has no clarity
Moans wet, with blood
Drowned screams that mutated the voice
Bodies caught
The terror submerges
I don't see the history
I don't see the fright
I discard the body
No ashes, no dust
A flotilla of absence
My voice is silenced
In a chorus that never leaves
But history returns
Cascading waves
Broken on shattered lands
Ghosted by the moment
In the weeping eyes of the world

ACT FIVE: FRAGMENTS OF A CATASTROPHE

The apocalypse already happened. When exactly is difficult to tell? It wasn't a singular event. Contrary to biblical prophecy, there was no final day of judgment. No horsemen rode into town to smite the unrighteous and nonbelievers. The apocalyptic was slain by the gospel of catastrophe. Its truth was displaced by the logic of tragedies, which rained down without the possibility of redemption or eternal salvation. Nobody was exempt. Its destructions afforded no distinction. There were no innocents. Everybody was included. All notions of refuge proved an impossible luxury. The casualties were intellectual as well as physical. We lost hope in our ability to transform the world for the better. The signs were already there. The apocalypse was in the making for some considerable time. Early warnings appeared through the cracks in sites of abandonment and zones of crises. Violently, it marched. Justice as war, so terrifyingly normal! Onward and downward, the disasters slowly became endemic. Catastrophic imaginaries colonized all before them. Everything became connected. Everything went south! Everybody learned wretchedness. Vulnerability became the default setting. We became survivors without survival, haunted by the violence of the past while forced to face the spectre of the next catastrophe, always there, waiting on the horizon of possibility. Humanity was fatally wounded long before its final generations walked the scorched earth. Anxiety was the only thing collectivized. Enriched lives that once basked in their own delusions of grandeur and progress were forced to live in open burrows of mechanical enslavement, which ultimately proved more effective in producing endless spectacles of violence. A simulacrum of watching defined us, even as we authored our ruination. Fear spread like some uncontrollable virus. It was digitalized. But it was no less real. All that remained, it seemed, was to live out the unfolding fate, together, alone.

How might we have heeded the warnings of the real witnesses of history? How might we have listened to those whose testimonies and signs may just have pushed us in a different direction, demanding a different gaze, one that asked us to look more intently into ourselves? Those who lived with the disappeared never sought to turn their pain into spectacle. The suffering was too real for all that. Nor did they wish to have our pity. There is no dignity in such a demand. But now even the memory of witnessing is scattered among the ashes. We saw too much, blinded by our overexposure to nothing in particular.

Who am I? The last anthropologist left to survey and make sense of these ruins. How can we look upon every Garden of Eden slowly disappearing as all colour bleeds from the earth? I was once human. Now, I see tragic figures who authored their own pre-existing extinction. So all we have left are these fragments, but pieced together they tell the story. It begins with nature. Back to the beginning, again. Beautiful. Poetic. But some, as already told, had already seen this as a savage beauty. And the final act of humanity will be recorded as a moment when it brought about its collective disappearance.

This is not a speculative prophecy. The warning signs are already here. If only we could piece together the fragments of a catastrophe that is unfolding before our very eyes – another child mercilessly lost in the waters, another women savagely pulled from the streets, another forest mercilessly burned along with all the forms of life that it sustains, another act of abandonment. No, this is not a speculative prophecy but a simple piece in a complex and fractured book whose pages are already scattered and overlaid.

Disappear. Where?
On earth
Where is my body?
Fragments of hope
Despair
The shape?
A mixture of red and black
Touch me
I disappear. Dark mass
Let the earth be
There in the dust, I exist
I breathe within us
A wrenched life
Stained ash
Sorrows that walk
Covered in red
Muting the voice
Blood within blood
The liquid you pour
The earth absorbs me
My trail
A crimson wound, that gives life

ACT SIX: THE COLLAPSE OF CONSCIOUSNESS

Everything ends, like it began, in the mind. The last witness, after the annihilation, faces the final reckoning – that nobody was left to even deny the extinction of humanity, to care about or map out the disappearance of disappearance. That is the disappearance of humans, who have, in the final act, obliterated all other life forms. After all, if humans couldn't survive, nothing should. And so, she stands alone, with nothing left except her thoughts. Is she anything without the Other? Venturing for one last time into the abyss where everything had been thrown, she sees how the depths of its denials were so monstrous that even the most brutal tyrants were willing to be forgotten for fear of confronting the intolerable madness. If only she had the strength to conscientiously object. There is nothing to make sense of within this terrain. Surveying the ruins of her mental landscape of total devastation, alone she sees how everything meaningful has collapsed. Like Tiresias, she walks blinded, having lived every prophecy and witnessed too much suffering. But she no longer has any need for sight. Even notions of past, present, and future have been fully obliterated. Can she even call herself a survivor? Surely, that would mean bearing witness. Yet how can you be a witness if there is nobody left to tell? And what would she say anyway? Even language has been eviscerated.

Once the courage to speak the truth was denied, she knew every evil would be liberated and every sacred claim to purity mobilized in response. That was the real nihilism. And so now an unwilling accomplice to her thoughts, she relives the final collapse of humanity. The collapse of consciousness itself. A terrorscape more horrifying than anything that Dante every dared to conceive, where every single exhausted thought that appears without asking is subjected to a monstrous schizophrenic haunting. Where every claim that she once held to life is caught in the swirling vortex of mental torture without any possible hope to escape. To survive now means only to carry the shameful burden of humankind complete. At the ends of humanity, every mental coordinate is abandoned, as this neurological assault – the final frontier now also being denied – illustrates how the collective consciousness has also become a brutalized river of indistinction. The collapse of all resistance, the collapse of all memory, the collapse of all dreams, the collapse of her imagination. Fate? Humanity? They all read the same.

But if time had a way of repeating itself, there was always something that emerged from the dust of history. Who am I? Time beyond time. A disappearance that refuses to vanish beneath the weight of absence. A subconscious trace of an abstract memory that breathes fire into the ruins of the mind's blackened eye. Seekers always find a way to a reimagine the world even upon shards of broken glass. She feels, sensing that there is the glimmer of something. In the shadows, in the dark side of consciousness, something refuses to die, for nothing is more uncertain than the nothingness of the void.

I am not wise
My strength, sometimes, trembles
I find it hard to breathe
Because I feel as if every breath is you
The memory of us vanishes
Maybe I am a stealer
A stealer of air
I remove your only breath
I live and you die
The light hurts my eyes
Eyes closed
You are a dark abyss
Floating in an empty space
I can't walk to you

I can't move
I paralyze
With eyes wide open
I see you
The lips don't move
I talk to you
Our childhood
Our voices clear
My body still
Tired

I ask for help
Your fault
Denial
You are dead
They saw everything
I know nothing
Furious turmoil's
Broken pavements
Humiliating debris
Surrounded by smoke
Our heads burst
Collapsing, collapse
A wandering mind
Memories attract
They will keep you alive
Forget
Don't forget

Disappear
I am waiting in here

NOTES

1 Kakfa writes, "A book must be the axe for the frozen sea inside us." Franz Kafka, *Letters to Friends, Family, and Editors*, trans. Richard Winston and Clara Winston (New York: Shocken Books, 1977), 16.
2 Rothko insisted that the explanation of his paintings "must come out of a consummated experience between picture and onlooker." Adolf Gottlieb and Mark Rothko, with Barnett Newman, "Statement," published in art critic Edward Alden Jewell's column, *New York Times*, 13 June 1943.

7

Vanishing Points

David Theo Goldberg

> Life bleeds from the biosocial wounds etched ever more deeply into our social ecology.
>
> Chantal Meza[1]

In California, September 2020 saw 3 million acres burned by firestorms, more than ten times an average summer. Fires in Oregon and Washington added more than another million acres devoured by flames.[2] A thousand plus homes were in ashes, hundreds of thousands temporarily evacuated as the flames licked at their heels. Pretty much the entire coastal geography from San Diego to the Canadian border was covered in a grey sheet of fine ash dust, particularly and more apocalyptically the northern half of California and southern Oregon. For a week, the only sun was an alien orange ball, the daylight a perpetual dark peach fog patched with brown bruising. Temperatures in the Pacific West had climbed to their highest on record, over 54°C in the Mojave Desert and 49°C in the suburbs just east of Los Angeles. These temperatures followed a summer in Sydney that had broken 50°C and weeks of the same temperatures in Delhi. The day following President Donald Trump's declaration that "temperatures will cool" and that "scientists don't know" what they are talking about regarding the onset of the firestorms,[3] the Netherlands recorded its hottest 15 September on record.

Eighteen of the hottest nineteen years since record keeping began in 1880 have occurred this century. As global temperatures have warmed, snow and ice caps across land and sea have melted. On 6 February 2020, Antarctica reached 18.3°C, the highest temperature ever logged on that continent. The global temperature in January 2020 averaged its monthly highest. Surface sea temperatures have heated up and sea levels have risen. Canada's ice shelves have reduced to just 10 per cent of their volume a century ago. Greenland's dramatic ice-melt in 2019, now irreversible, added

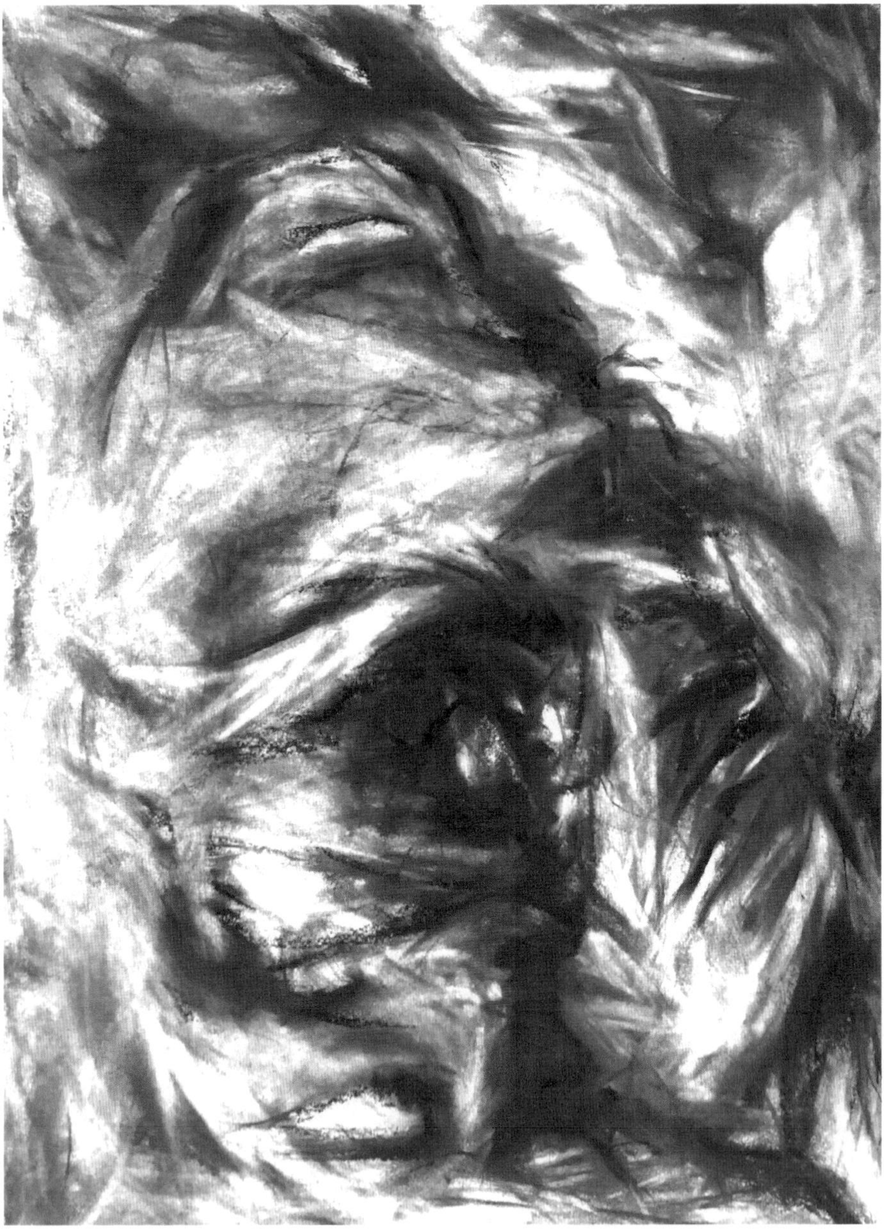

Chantal Meza, *The Void IX*, 2019, graphite and charcoal on paper, 29.5 x 42 cm

2.2 millimetres to global sea levels. The Arctic is warming faster than elsewhere, hitting nearly 27°C in May 2020. The area covered by the Arctic ice sheet has shrunk to its second lowest level as a result of these warming temperatures, under 4 kilometres in total. Whereas the ice sheet deflects the sun's heat, cooling down temperatures, the large patches of dark green water left in the wake of the melt absorb heat, warming ocean waters even more quickly.

A recent study predicts that for every 1°C increase in average global temperature, another 1 billion people will live in intolerable habitats, equal to the Sahara Desert's hottest areas.[4] Fires in 2019 destroyed massive swaths of acreage in Siberia, Alaska, and western Canada, along with 10,000 square miles (25,000 square kilometres) in Indonesia. Australia's fires in the summer of 2019–20 blotted out all daylight. Anthropocenic climate change, in short, is transforming environmental and geological time into historical time. Humans have become a force of nature – and in no commendable way.

The taken-for-granted ecosystem inhabited up to and throughout the twentieth century is disappearing in real time.[5] We are partial witnesses, at best, to the old dying and to the new and less livable being born before eyes wide shut. Carbon neutrality is no longer a viable option given the thresholds already rubbed out. Any day-to-day action not reducing the carbon and methane footprints not only adds to but also accelerates the current challenges: more fires and floods, more cataclysmic effects, more deaths from events triggered by the boiling points that we have collectively produced, more uninhabitable environments. As some have intimated, we are not far off from all being climate refugees.[6] But from what immediate event(s) and to where exactly remain the open questions.

Land-producing pollution, from fossil fuel production to plastic discards and swarming fires decimating swaths of the planet, are throttling maritime ecologies. Our cast-off culture is killing the life that these ecologies support. Oceans absorb 8 million tonnes of plastic each year, now totalling in the tens of trillion pieces. By mid-century, there will be more plastic in oceans than fish. It kills birds and mammals, polluting the marine life that other species consume. The disintegrating plastic particles, suffocating sea life, are nearly impossible to absorb or remove. In 2017, off Bergen, Norway, an ailing goose-beaked whale was discovered, its stomach filled with microplastics and thirty plastic bags – a Ukrainian chicken packet, a Danish ice-cream wrapper, a British potato chip bag – inhibiting its digestion. Brought to shore for treatment, it died. A "hydrocolonial" quality characterizes these practices, to bend Isabel Hofmeyr's term.[7] The landbound exploitatively pillage oceanic resources while caring less about the health of oceans as long as they keep on giving.

There is a double disappearance at work in these processes. Plastics and other discardables are cast off with no regard for where they end up. And the constituents of our collective biodiversity, key to our evolutionary reproducibility, are being made to die off. When the asphyxiating materials of easy everyday life are disappeared from attentive practice,[8] the conditions for extending that very life are placed in jeopardy. Inattention to the disappearance of the former creates the conditions of possibility for the extinctive disappearance of the latter.

Human bodies and almost all animals are sustained by the air breathed, which nevertheless can kill when toxin-bearing. The air supply has grown increasingly polluted since the onset of the Industrial Revolution. Vertebrates are largely defenceless in the face of having to breathe. Coal underpinned much of the energy demands of industrialization, supplemented since the late nineteenth century by other fossil fuels. Coal has proved the most toxic. London's Great Smog of 1952 led to the deaths of over 4,000 people in less than a week as a result of factory and home fireplace pollutants. Automobile exhaustion, especially from diesel-burning engines, has added to significantly worsened air quality worldwide. In the first decade of the twenty-first century, nearly half the population of the United States lived in areas designated by the American Lung Association as suffering from unhealthy levels of particle or ozone pollution, the effect of largely human-produced ash, soot, diesel exhaust, aerosols, and chemicals.[9]

Nature is being "corpsed," as Samuel Beckett evocatively declared. But not nature alone. It is the collective world that faces our "endgame," our disappearance.[10] We are decomposing, "intoxicating on carbon dioxide," in Bruno Latour words,[11] and on methane, too. Undertaking to colonize another planet, to launch our innovative industrial production into space beyond the blue horizon, as some billionaires with too much spare cash to burn are propelling forward, will just hasten the demise, bring on the cremation. As Jenny Offill has a character remark in her novel *Weather*, "These people long for immortality but can't wait ten minutes for a cup of coffee."[12] Fearing immediate apocalyptic demise, they cannot wait to be immortalized. This Entropocene, an unarrested and perhaps unarrestable evaporation, also names the new planetary political economy.

A zeitgeist is taking hold, an unnerving sense of a futureless future. The singularity is not the point of perpetuation but of entropic dissolution. The immediate becomes the infinite at the point of vaporization. Disappearance is a state not just of nonbeing but also of transmogrification. It produces a "dis-appearance," as Ackbar Abbas would have it,[13] into something else – a future with the qualities only of the destructive and self-destroying. Technology is invariably invoked as the inevitable fix. As it has in the past, the quieting projection goes, technology will save us. The never stated implication is that the saving is from ourselves! The reliance for the inevitable saviour is on the very figure causing the demise. The model is totally Trumpian.

This supposed fix includes more than policy reversals. Microsoft and Ikea have committed to a carbon-negative rollback of their own carbon-footprint legacies, and Germany has declared that in the foreseeable future it will be the first country to end both nuclear and brown-coal power plants, although the phase out has been slowed or temporarily reversed as a result of the Russian war on Ukraine. Delta Airlines has committed to setting aside $1 billion over the next decade in a bid to offset its carbon footprint, although that was before the Covid-19 pandemic.[14] (Perhaps the virus has revealed a more effective way to reduce carbon emissions: fly far less!) Technologies have already been designed to scrape up larger pieces of plastic floating in the ocean, and popcorn-size flying and diving bots are gobbling up the microplastics too small for the scraper.

The question is whether the proposed technological fix of the day can keep up with the technologically enabled and enhanced waste runoff. Conservative politicians are declaring proposals to plant trillions of trees in order to suck carbon out of the atmosphere.[15] This is an encouraging start. Yet widespread forestation alone is more panacea than solution. Forests, it is now evident, require ongoing management, from clearing the incessant growth of ground cover to using controlled fires as breaks when uncontrolled fires spread.

Technology, no doubt, is having an impact. Critics of "degrowth" like to cite the advances of techno-solutions.[16] However, despite being a "soft power" mediation of more extreme manifestations of demise, technology is hardly a global solution. For one, the remit to the technological fix undercuts the responsibility of all of us, individually and collectively, to change our ecologically impactful ways. Technology, after all, has played a significant role in the challenging elemental changes now placing zoetic life at risk. Far less needs to be consumed, and so exhausted, in a dramatically narrowing temporal window.

Now, digital technology has made it more possible to track, map, data-source, and data-bank massive quantities of information about climatic conditions, causes, effects, and variable implications in close to real time. Its material conditions of production and application, however, eat up spiralling energy resources. These conditions include the surging heat generated by huge server requirements for cloud computing and the cooling necessary to counter the heat generated and keep the machines running. The energy resources needed to mine bitcoin equal the entire energy consumption of the Czech Republic, a population exceeding 10 million. Digital applications generate, proliferate, and intensify the very conditions that they track.

Electrical cars are well and good, but short of extensively greening energy supplies, the environmental benefits of electricity production are rendered minimal. Our spiralling technological take-up, the very technological fix to which we so readily turn as the foremost way to repair the shattered eco-form, is a major contributor to ecoexhaustion. The fix is also at fault.

The cost of doing nothing is of course economic. But it is more deeply also existential. The erosion of biodiversity threatens the life of countless species, including that of *Homo sapiens*. This erosion is neither something being done *to* humans nor just a case of humans killing nature. The very biosystem that makes life – much of planetary life – possible is being undermined. There are temperature parameters within which our planetary existence has been made possible.[17] These bounds are now being undermined at the upper limit. Bees, butterflies, and small flies pollinate most plant and food seeds. All are showing signs of significant depletion due to pesticide use, increased invasive species, and rising heat. The same can be said of coral reefs, which anchor the planet's greatest range of biodiversity and by extension serve as a foundation of our planetary ecosystem.

The "angel of history" is of our own making.[18]

The driving responses are, again, overwhelmingly ambivalent. A reinvigoration of Malthusianisms is festering, waiting to explode. The racial casuistry rationalizes that a significant cause of planetary threat is overpopulation. The deaths from global warming, chillingly on this account, will "naturally" cull the population to planetarily manageable proportion. The most vulnerable, history has taught us, will be those more readily left to the racially eliminationist culling machine, those historically racially identified as poorer and not white. Covid-19 serves merely as a prelude.

Covid-19 has proved to be a virus of our time, one that we all are involved in circulating, if not feeding.[19] It courses across and through populations worldwide. Like popular music, it waxes and – eventually – wanes with global force and local accent. Parasitic and exploitative, it sucks life more readily from the vulnerable, the aged, the racially impoverished. It is a mirror reflecting what we have made of ourselves, our world, our ecoformation. The picture is far from pretty. Individual care, extraordinary in courage and contribution, has had to fill in, at considerable personal risk, for broad and deep politically shaped failings of the commons.

It has been a stunning turn – a world spun at the interface of the microbiome and the social so quickly driving itself to lockdown, supplemented to degrees by older governing technologies of locking-out and locking-up. Lockdowns have something of a history, too. As Michel Foucault reminds us, lepers were expelled, exiled to external colonies, effectively disappeared by locking them out.[20] Those suffering plagues, by contrast, were quarantined, containably locked into their homes to die or recover in virtually invisible silence in these packed infrastructures of infection.

Covid-19 has increasingly disappeared a sociality taken for granted. The old is dying. The pandemic has laid the groundwork for the threads of something else to appear. The new has yet to be fully birthed. More isolation, more self-reliance, less face-to-face interaction. More combustible anxiety and anger. Wars farther afield have morphed into growing belligerence at home, the contestational rumblings of civil war. The coronavirus, perhaps unpredictably, hit pause on the proliferation of wars in progress and their progression. A world with less war, however, seemed ill at ease without one. Russia's invasion of Ukraine in February 2022, prompting NATO's inevitable response, proved the point. A global war declared against an enemy oblivious to the characterization seems like a losing proposition, a category mistake. Borne on the air breathed and surfaces touched, the virus is more like an angel of death. Dread wafts off death's wand as it waves spasmodically throughout the world, no one sure that they will not be touched by it. Like global warming, Covid-19 is a process rather than a person or an event, and it seeps across and into everything. It is to be lived with and managed rather than fought, adapted to, accommodated, and worked around – our habits altered to delimit the disruption.

The virus has stopped the world short. It has worked to take our breath away. The costs and impacts of the practices that have brought us to this point were thrown into sharp relief. The viral shutdown momentarily cleaned the air and water, bringing animal life back to old habitats, now largely untroubled by human presence. But the consequent reduction in emissions turned out to be about a quarter of what is needed to reverse spiralling temperature increases and their effects. The destructive conditions have been underpinned by deeper cultures more difficult to forego. Velocity and volatility, speed and movement, discardability and waste, rampant wealth and instantaneous vulnerability, privilege and disposability, disinformation and make-believe – these are the constitutive conditions of viral sociality.

Alongside the social evaporation, what has increasingly disappeared is the prevailing form of political economy, a disappearance that has intensified, if not birthed, another emergent one. Covid-19 is the siren song of *neoliberal capitalism*. The virus has called into question the contemporary state's cracked foundation on *economic* freedom and its deep paring-back of the caretaking state. This agenda has included undercutting viable access to necessary health care, leading to incessant attacks on the "deep state." The contours of these fracturing fissures have become undeniable. Neoliberalism has privileged economic freedom, using it to trump or advance other liberties as dictated by economic interests and calculations of cost and utility. Neoliberal capital has pushed freedom of movement while calibrating it differentially for financial capital, goods, and services than for people. Covid-19 has not undone capitalism, as some have bemoaned and others have celebrated. Rather, it has dramatically mobilized efforts to pave the path from neoliberal capitalism to an intensification of another kind, what I have called "tracking-capitalism."[21]

For conventional *commodity capitalism*, value is principally extracted and profit produced at the point of consumption, the moment at which goods and services are purchased. Value changes hands, materially or increasingly virtually, with payment. As service capitalism expands into *experiential capitalism*, the production of value is radically extended into and throughout the experience. Witness cruise ships, fun parks, gaming, sports spectatorship, concerts, festivals, fairs, and everyday spectacles, including large church services, fancy restaurants, expensive wines, and so forth. Indeed, the experience itself is stretched out to maximize profit making via endless sharing in and after the moment. This sharing includes experience-related merchandise, photos, recordings, reviews and newsletters, consulting, advice, gig offerings, and even nostalgia-inducing anniversary reminders on social media.

The experiential has become capitalism's extended logic. Commodities themselves are advertised and sold through their experiential qualities. They are made to represent and promise, including in the form of value-added servicing agreements and warranties. It is neither happenstance nor inconsequential that the experiential and its make-believe culture assumed the public face of neoliberal capitalism. This outcome was coterminous with the exorbitant but far less evident, even grey, rise of speculative finance, privatizing individualism, more or less anonymous virtuality, and boring back-end digitization. The experiential is the loudspeaker of otherwise far less visible and celebrated success.

Covid-19 did not end the conditions of possibility for experiential capitalism, but it did upend them. It did so both by exhibiting their deadly impacts and by curtailing the broad range of experiential possibility. In the former case, cruises and large church services became ground zero for viral spread. In the latter, the lockdown requirements delimited the conditions of possibility for robust consumptive experiences.

The experiential both reveals and hides. Value reveals itself in the experience. Focus on the experiential hides the circuits of capital, production, and delivery of the means to enable this experience. What get tracked in tracking-capitalism are largely the experienced endpoints. Covered over are the circuits of capital and work, leading both to the possibility of the experience and to the offshore capital movements that extend the economy of experience and capital generation in their wake.

Experiential capitalism requires and promotes movement: travels far and wide for business and recreation, cruises and vacations to far-flung places, explorations and expeditions that test the limits of endurance and determination, not to mention the limits of local ecologies and older habitats. Pathogens once localized and thus limited to usually remote rural biosystems find new life as they are carried by trade and travel to densely populated urban environments. There, they swirl energetically through newfound peoples and places that lack any built-up immunity. Just as European diseases once decimated colonized populations, something of the reverse is in process today. The ramping-up of industrial food production, with closely quartered animal stocks and fast throughput, likewise extends the zoonotic life and circulation of viral pathogens.[22] Tracking-capitalism will eventually be able to trace, if never quite catch up to, these crossover circulations, too.

Tracking-capitalism – a political economy predicated on tracking everyone and everything – enables the tracing of global movements and networks of human capital, interests and consumptive demand, labour and products, along with perceived threats and disruptions. Tracking drives the microtargeting of the genes and proteins that have a causative role in the disease, of people with the disease and those with whom they interact, and of the health conditions that people experience, informing decisions about when, if at all, to intervene with treatment. Tracking-capitalism, soft-pedalled as "tracing," fine-tunes when to keep those who belong locked down and determines who among those arriving from places with high rates of incidence and undesirability to keep locked out. Tracking-capitalism is fine-tuning in real time the governing logics of securitization as the emerging technologies of domination program our times. Disappearance is woven socially together with the tracking and tracing of ultimately everything.

Against the backdrop of this culture of vulture consumption and rampant circulation of misinformation, the virus can be read only as ecological. The virus has attacked the organs of human life, in turn upending sociality. It serves as a reminder that the capacity to breathe and breathable air are inseparable conditions of living. Bodily and climatic health are mutually reinforcing. Together, they ensure that the next breath is not the last.

Technology has enforced the "great apartness." Covid-19 licensed the universal experiment in "social distancing" (which in 2020 turned out to be one of *The Oxford English Dictionary*'s top terms of an extraordinary year). This isolation, in turn, has further advanced technological escalation and diffused social discomfort in the interests of biopolitical securitization. E-securitization is fast trumping freedoms. Above all, the digital today tracks movement, physical and virtual movements, as the interactive networked circuits of its websites and databases link locations, places, spaces, people, and things across boundaries and borders, past gates, over walls, and into and out of buildings. It tracks where bodies are showing up, leaving traces, and where they are "dis-appearing" from and to, vacating one site only to show up elsewhere and otherwise. Biometric traces are more difficult to leave behind, even when we change what is worn and borne. Bodies' sensed and "sensored" states of being stick to them. The "sensorious" has acquired new functionality, ascribing novel meaning.

Authoritarianisms (re-)emerged and were solidified through varieties of "coronavirus coups."[23] New authority came to be licensed, and repressive measures likely to last well past the worst of the pandemic were introduced or extended. The suspension of elections, and sometimes the insistence on holding them precisely because of the dangers, as well as the capacity to repress and imprison dissidents were all ramped up. Not only critics but also scientific knowledge and accurate data were silenced, with emergency powers and noncontestable sovereign power being rampantly invoked. The application of tracking technologies was ubiquitously expanded, not just to surveil movement and networking but also to monitor social media use and free expression. The reach for dictatorial power has mixed the material with the digital – the response to the virus with the techno-viral.

This regime of almost ubiquitous tracking reinforces the reach for states of totalizing control. Control exercises itself over what it is able to identify, to pin down, or at least to shape and contour. It seeks to monitor flows and movements, long conditions more or less evasive of surveillance. States of control reach their limits, become paranoid, when faced with deepening shadow spaces, the unseen, the less trackable. There, the bombing – actual, virtual, and viral – takes over. Perhaps the operative logic drives states inevitably to this condition. Hence the still early but gathering drive to supplement, if not to replace, sensors that monitor spaces with technologies placed (permanently) on and ultimately *in* subjects. There is a movement in process today from the need for social subjects to display the logos of their corporate masters to the dictate that they carry built-in self-tracking technology. Cyborgs may escape otherwise easy ascription of identity. Techno-subjectivity is fast making evasion of identification more difficult. There is disappearance and then dis-appearance.

Covid-19 is the vector most clearly exemplifying this occurrence. Infections wax and wane and wax again when commitment is foregone in favour of make-believe normalcy, the impossible reach-back for the disappeared status quo ante. Infections rise and ebb when attention is diverted by fictionalization, the obvious by the fantasized. When common interest is self-consciously undercut by self-interest radicalized and weaponized, freedom is reduced to nothing but life left to lose.

Donald Trump was quite happy to sacrifice the elderly to his political ambition. Life should return to normal, he insisted to his cultic campaign crowds a month or two out from the 2020 presidential election. After all, he insisted in the face of all the evidence, that "it affects virtually nobody."[24] He and his overwhelmingly milk toast supporters were quite willing also to sacrifice blacks and Latinos, whose rates of infection and death soared, driven by accumulated social histories of impoverished health care and nutrition.

Across the world, by September 2020, the coronavirus had infected 20 million people and taken 1 million lives. The United States led the way. With just 4 per cent of the global population, the country represented over 20 per cent of infections and deaths. Making up 30 per cent of the US population, blacks and Latinos saw rates of infection and death that together reached more than double that. The dismal pandemic management by the US political leadership had broader impacts, providing cover for countries like Brazil to be similarly irresponsible.

Nuclear extinction aside, the disappearance of worlds is less an event than a process. The process – or really overlapping and intersecting processes – may indeed incorporate events along the way. They serve as distinct eruptions, stand-alone signals. They are really higher-order registers on the instrument recording the ups and downs of the unfolding process. They are like earthquakes: we ordinarily register in our daily lives only those shakes that we feel, but in structural terms the earth is actually shaking, moving beneath us, more or less constantly.

Ecofascism projects the most extreme eliminationist version of social disappearance. Proponents advocate for a white ethnostate, a racially homogeneous, ecologically pristine, and pure set-aside for an ecofascist order. The commitment is to help along the culling, to advance elimination by wiping out, sending away, or preventing the immigration of the racially unbelonging, those designated strangers within or trying to enter. Ecofascists are wedded to what they insist is *their* national land, decrying the spoiling of the national natural beauty by industrialization, the built urban environment, the unwelcome. Green here is bleached white, soaked in the red blood of others. Blood and soil, race and nature: the battle cry of the ecofascists.

Ecofascist groups like Northwestern Front, active in the US Pacific Northwest, may be politically marginal but seed such ideas for mainstream politicians. Trump once spoke offhandedly of plastic dumped in the Pacific by Asian nations. The Pacific garbage patch, which he blamed on Asian nations like China and Japan, was supposedly floating toward America to pollute the homeland landscape, the implication being that Asian migration pollutes the body politic.[25] Marine Le Pen has castigated "nomadic migrants" for not caring about the national (French) environment.[26] Such statements prompt an affect of apprehension, a bracing for the worst. A pessimism less of intellect than of predisposition, the apprehension nevertheless freezes feet in place.

Life on our planet may not yet be unlivable. We have but paved a few more kilometres of cement in that direction, somewhat oblivious to the landscape's warning signs surrounding the path. No doubt, people will adapt some to the challenging conditions. But acceleration far more readily applies to the eroding ecology than it does to the politics of promotion or response.

The politics have become more strident, as much using the ecological as a vector and a vehicle as responding to its warnings. The threads of a politics of disappearance are starting to emerge, an incipient design for an eliminative political intervention. In September 2020, at a political rally in Bemidji, Minnesota, near the Canadian border, Donald Trump boasted that his overwhelmingly white supporters at the rally – 84 per cent of Minnesotans are white – "have good genes, you know that, right? A lot of it is about the genes, isn't it, don't you believe? The racehorse theory … You have good genes in Minnesota."[27]

What the Trumpian ramblings reveal is an emergent ecogenics as political mobilization for an implicitly articulated, white-majority – although on the verge of becoming white-minority – ethnostate. That the likes of Northwestern Front broadcast the boast made it possible for Trump to nod and wink without having to mouth the actual terms of eliminationism. The melting-away of life when America was supposedly once great magically evaporates its burgeoning heterogeneity since that romantically fabricated moment.

Traces invariably linger in the wake of the disappeared.[28] Disappearance is not the endpoint, the state of finality. It is almost invariably incomplete, never quite totalized. Charred forest and fire-consumed structures sit eerily in the fires' wake. Water-scarred homes follow the recession of flood waters. Odours – burned ash in one case, musty mould in the other – cling to the survivors, reminders of the plight even when backs are turned to those left behind. Breathless lives follow the pandemic.

Efforts to eliminate a group – Jews, Armenians, blacks, Muslims, Latinos, Palestinians, gays, communists – are more exhausting than exhaustive, as much psychically as physically, never final. They always prompt resistance, counters, pushback. The more broadly coalitional these responses, the more likely they are to be successful. Traces signal the endurance of the disappeared but in a partial, even transformed, condition. They announce both disappearance and reappearance, if only in part, which are transformed at the outset of a remake, of a resignification.

Disappearance accordingly is not simply an end state, a termination. Whatever is left behind, disappearance conjures also a dynamism, a pulse perhaps in new directions, as much terminus as terminal. Disappearance always bears within it the fuel of dis-appearance, of appearing elsewhere, otherwise, multitemporally. Traces are like electricity, not quite dormant charges set off, if not mobilized by, an interaction of not always predictable forces. The fire, as James Baldwin signalled, is as much a social as an environmental outbreak.[29]

Disappearance, of course, does not beset groups equally. The social structures set in place are designed to ensure that. The modes of infliction both bear out this structural inequality and augur some shifts. Fires, storm floods, and pandemics do not themselves discriminate so much as impact differentially on the basis of pre-existing conditions of social standing, capacity, and preparedness, systemically structured in place.

Things, social order, systems, and structures can disappear, evaporate, and condense variously. They can similarly reappear, if in a different guise, remade and repurposed. They often fragment in their disappearance, parts or aspects returning or showing up in different ways, to be used for different purposes and ends elsewhere. People disappear, too,[30] their legacies haunting in the afterlife. But they can also return, sometimes repeatedly, to bare truth to power about the conditions of their purging.

Neil Vallelly, while addressing the epistemological quandaries of disappearance, perhaps also gets at the key processual dynamics of disappearance: "Where appearance is judgmental, disappearance is attentive; where appearance is retrospective, disappearance is forward-looking; where appearance is reactive, disappearance is patient; where appearance evaporates, disappearance remains."[31] If appearance insists on asserting itself, disappearance navigates erasure not only by taking flight but also by practising a politics of reconstitution. Dis-appearance calls (for) attention to the evaporation and its processes of production, as well as to the evaporated. It evidences the absent signifier, as hint or implication, symptom or index. Ontic dis-appearance becomes epistemic presence, past production signalling future reproduction or resistance, collusion clashing with refusal. Where appearance is immediate, the dis-appeared mark time, perhaps on behalf also of the disappeared, who can no longer act for themselves, their compatriots, or their wards, biding this time productively as they move toward the transformative repositioning for the to-come.

Toward futures in the remaking.

NOTES

1 Chantal Meza in the video interview with Brad Evans at https://www.chantal-meza.com/stateofdisappearance. These words resonate with Chantal Meza's series *Since the Beginning*, online at the same website, along with the other artworks referenced in this chapter.

2 The destruction of these firestorms is evoked by Meza's drawing *Obscure Beasts I*.

3 Meza's drawing *Obscure Beasts III* echoes the onset of firestorms. For Trump's take on climate change, see "'It'll start getting cooler': Trump Dismisses Science When Calif. Official Discusses Climate Change," *YouTube*, 14 September 2020, https://www.youtube.com/watch?v=r6waicuKwQM.

4 Chi Xu, Timothy A. Kohler, Timothy M. Lenton, and Marten Scheffer, "Future of the Human Climate Niche," *Proceedings of the National Academy of Sciences* 117, no. 21 (2020): 11350–5, https://www.pnas.org/doi/full/10.1073/pnas.1910114117.

5 For an invocation of such ecosystem destruction, see Meza's drawing *Obscure Beasts IV*.

6 For one source among many, see Sean McAllister, "There Could Be 1.2 Billion Climate Refugees by 2050: Here's What You Need to Know," *Zurich*, 13 January 2023, https://www.zurich.com/en/media/magazine/2022/there-could-be-1-2-billion-climate-refugees-by-2050-here-s-what-you-need-to-know.

7 Isabel Hofmeyr, *Dockside Reading: Hydrocolonialism and the Custom House* (Durham, NC: Duke University Press, 2022).

8 Such asphyxiating materials come to mind when viewing Meza's series *The Void*.

9 American Lung Association, "State of the Air," 2022, https://www.lung.org/research/sota.

10 Samuel Beckett, *Endgame: A Play in One Act* (New York: Grove, 1958), 30.

11 Bruno Latour, *Facing Gaia: Eight Lectures on the New Climate Regime*, trans, Catherine Porter (Cambridge, UK: Polity, 2017), 39.

12 Jenny Offill, *Weather* (New York: Vintage Books, 2021), 39.

13 Ackbar Abbas, *Hong Kong: Culture and the Politics of Disappearance* (Minneapolis: University of Minnesota Press, 1997), 25.

14 Sabine Kinkartz, "Germany Energy Policy Forced to Change Course, *DW*, 1 March 2022, https://www.dw.com/en/ukraine-crisis-forces-germany-to-change-course-on-energy/a-60968585; Delta, "Delta Invests $1 billion to Become 'World's First Carbon Neutral Airline Globally,'" 14 February

2020, https://news.delta.com/delta-commits-1-billion-become-first-carbon-neutral-airline-globally.

15 Valerie Volcovici, "Plant a Trillion Trees: U.S. Republicans Offer Fossil Fuel–Friendly Climate Fix," *Reuters*, 12 February 2020, https://www.reuters.com/article/us-climatechange-usa-trees/plant-a-trillion-trees-u-s-republicans-offer-fossil-fuel-friendly-climate-fix-idUSKBN2061FG.

16 Thomas Roulet and Joel Bothello, "Why 'De-growth' Shouldn't Scare Businesses," *Harvard Business Review*, 14 February 2020, https://hbr.org/2020/02/why-de-growth-shouldnt-scare-businesses.

17 Dipesh Chakrabarty, "The Climate of History: Four Theses," *Critical Inquiry* 35, no. 2 (2009): 197–222.

18 Walter Benjamin, "Theses on the Philosophy of History," in *Illuminations: Essays and Reflections*, 253–64 (New York: Shocken Books, 1969), 249.

19 The Covid-19 pandemic brings to mind Meza's series *Fragments of a Catastrophe*.

20 Michel Foucault, *Abnormal: Lectures at the Collège de France, 1974–75* (London: Verso Books, 2003).

21 See David Theo Goldberg, *Dread: Facing Futureless Futures* (Cambridge, UK: Polity, 2021).

22 Rob Wallace, Alex Liebman, Luis Fernando Chaves, and Rodrick Wallace, "COVID-19 and Circuits of Capital," *Monthly Review*, 27 March 2020, https://monthlyreview.org/2020/05/01/covid-19-and-circuits-of-capital.

23 Adam Weinstein, "The Coronavirus Coups Are Upon Us: Emergency Contagion Measures Are Quickly Eroding Democracy Worldwide," *The Soapbox*, 3 April 2020, https://newrepublic.com/article/157170/coronavirus-coups-hungary-serbia-pandemic-authoritarianism.

24 Tara Subramaniam and Holly Yan, "'It affects virtually nobody': Fact-Checking Trump's Continued Efforts to Downplay the Risks of Coronavirus," CNN *Politics*, 22 September 2020, https://www.cnn.com/2020/09/22/politics/trump-covid-19-statement-fact-check/index.html.

25 "Trump Rebukes Japan, China and Others over Garbage Drifting in Ocean, *Japan Times*, 12 October 2018, https://www.japantimes.co.jp/news/2018/10/12/national/politics-diplomacy/trump-rebukes-japan-china-regions-garbage-drifting-ocean.

26 Blake Smith, "Jacques Attali, Nomads, and French Anti-Semitism," *Tablet*, 12 July 2018, https://www.tabletmag.com/sections/news/articles/jacques-attali-nomads-france-anti-semitism.

27 Donald Trump, *Twitter*, 18 September 2020, https://twitter.com/atrupar/status/1307124621389463553.

28 Traces are everywhere in Meza's series *Apparitions*.

29 James Baldwin, *The Fire Next Time* (London: Penguin Classics, 1990).

30 Dalia Khamissy, "The Missing," *Peace Building in Lebanon*, 1 April 2017, 11, https://www.salamwakalam.com/uploadImages/DocumentFiles/PEACE%20BUILDING%2015th-637096812530802161.pdf.

31 Neil Vallelly, "Practicing Disappearance: Postmodernism in the Making," *Electronic Book Review*, 4 December 2016, https://electronicbookreview.com/essay/practicing-disappearance-a-postmodern-methodology.

8

Witness

Adrian Parr

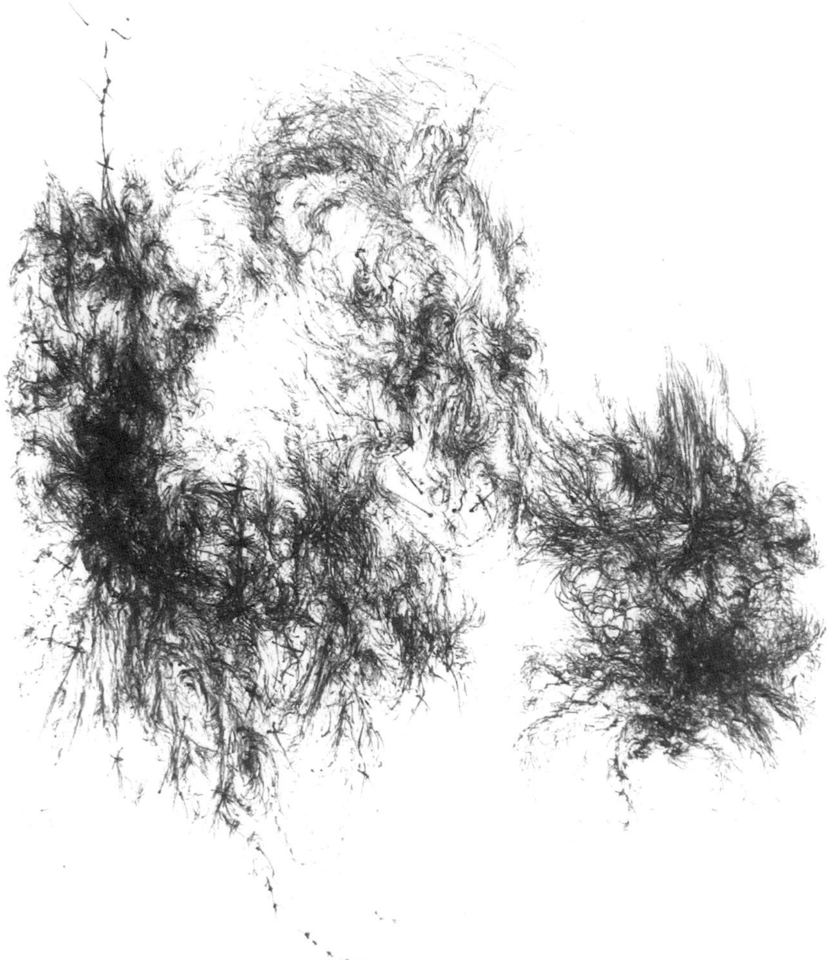

Chantal Meza, *Apparitions VII*, 2017, ink on paper, 35 x 27 cm

We witness
bitter poverty and persecution
driving people into the waves
their thirsty bodies flood
another's shoreline.
A shoreline to be shared
but which no one dares.
A new life intercepted
and turned away.
And their darkness is panic.

We witness
waters monstrous and thick,
ironclad bodies
navigate the riptides
filled with viciously good intentions
not upset
without regret
all hoping to protect
a national story
from foreign spaces of emptiness.
And their darkness is ferocious.

Imagine
a people neither blindfolded
nor kidnapped
by fundamentalists,
opportunists,
terrorists,
or,
capitalists.
Standing in defiance amidst the dust and debris
of hate speech
and gangsters,
outlawed by compromises
made in other lands.
And the darkness falls silent.

Imagine
the stature

of a species never hunted
looking its killer straight in the eyes.
Or,
a warrior dragging
the secrets of war
through the trap door.
And the darkness, it's booming.

Imagine
another world
of wind, waves, and sun
energizing a planet once in waiting,
announcing: tomorrow has come.

Another world
impenetrably open,
struck by tomorrow's reach
it throws out a mischievous wink,
linking arms in deep
friendship.

Like a young girl's dreams
released inside a woman's body,
tomorrow finds its way
past overcast skies
and mobster lies.
Filled with laughter,
the kind that saturates a world
with the sweet sounds of sisterhood and fireflies,
it swaps the forsaken futures of yesterday
where hustlers roamed the beaten tracks alone
and the hungry stared silently through the heavy heat,
with bright-eyed conviction and wonder.

Today, strong steady lips embrace
the promise tomorrow brings.
Today, together, and unrelentingly tender
the earth stands unashamed and tall
stealing a long overdue kiss
from which new earth is born.

9

State, Disappearing

Samuel Weber

I

Let me begin by trying to separate "state" from "disappearance." Some years ago, I tried to distinguish Walter Benjamin's transformation of Carl Schmitt's notion of sovereignty in Benjamin's *The Origin of the German Mourning Play* (1928) by arguing that for Benjamin, the process of exception could not simply be considered a "state," which is the way that Schmitt construes it – *Ausnahmezustand* (taking out, ex-cepting) – whereas for Schmitt, this process serves only as a means of re-establishing the state as a *Zu-stand* (lit. as something that stands to).[1] But in relation to what? To the idea of a certain *stasis*, both in the current sense of the English word as an immobilized movement and in the sense of the ancient Greek word as a civil war, an "internal" conflict that precisely splits what we would call the "state" and what the Greeks called the *polis*. Benjamin, I argued, takes exception to this notion by taking exception to the limit – that is, the point beyond which the exception can be stabilized through a "decision" of an executive to suspend all positive law – ultimately the Constitution – in order to secure, protect, or re-establish the order that Schmitt argued is indispensable to all law and, indeed, to all polity. The primordial condition presupposed by the state of law is, in this view, the state of exception, an exception stabilized through and as the extra or better – that is, the metalegal power of the executive.

It was precisely this notion that Benjamin, in his book, recognized to be the essence of what he identified as the Counter-Reformation, which he insisted should not be limited to any one confession or church since it characterizes all attempts to legitimate institutional authority in response to the challenge of radical Protestantism, identified by Benjamin with what he called Martin Luther's "storm against work,"[2] implied in the credo, *sola*

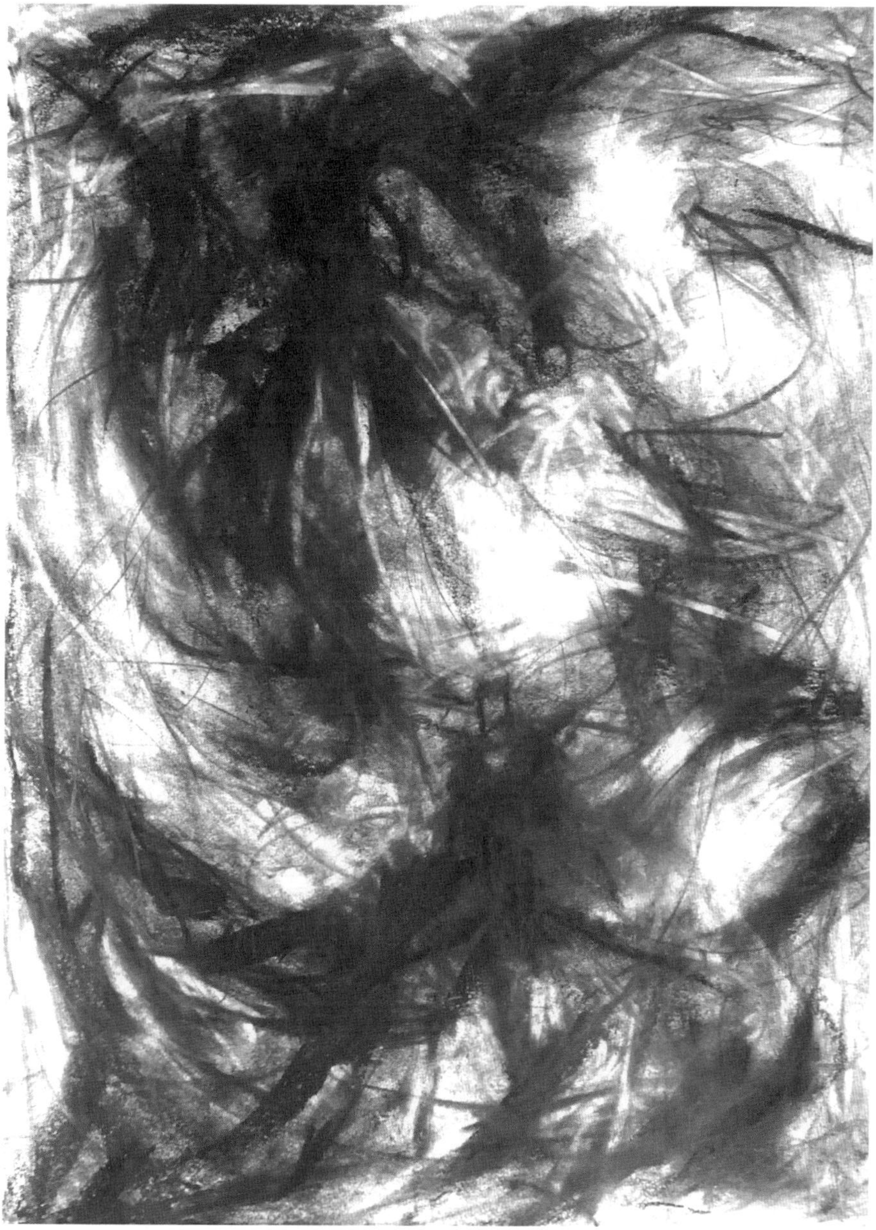

Chantal Meza, *The Void X*, 2019, graphite and charcoal on paper, 29.5 x 42 cm

fides (faith alone). Faith, in the monotheological tradition that determined the horizon of Carl Schmitt, had to be construed as faith in a self-identical, sovereign executive capable of "deciding" the "exception" as a state by putting itself – himself – beyond the reach of all positive law. The gap between the general claims of law and the need for these claims to be "applied" to singular events, thus making them "cases," or instantiations, of more general situations, could be bridged only by faith, not by works, according to Benjamin's interpretation of Luther. This idea in turn implied the devalorizing of all work, construed as an intentional, goal-directed act that was aimed at separating order from chaos.

The development of capitalist society since Benjamin wrote and in particular from the 1980s onward, with the ever-increasing importance of the financial sector and with speculation tending to replace production as the primary generator of wealth, has done much to demonstrate that Benjamin's interpretation of Luther's "storm against work" was far more than the interpretation of a remote historical period. Rather, well into the twenty-first century, it is looking as though this reading of Luther has renewed relevance today. Not that the notion of "state" loses its pertinence but rather that it is subordinated to a dynamic that transcends the nation-state as an established institution that is subordinated to flows of capital and credit, which those states struggle to exploit rather than to control.

Similar issues strike me as implied by the notion of a state of disappearance. This state entails disappearance not just as the attribute of individual, isolated events that come and go but also as a more dynamic, conflictual, and therefore unstable stasis. Again, this stasis does not involve the disappearance of the state – a notion that has gained popularity with the rise of finance capitalism – but rather the transformation of its status and function. The stability of the state, whether of exception or of disappearance, depends increasingly on the dynamic circulation and relation of forces: social, military, economic, cultural, medial, technological. In the realm of political economy, this change has been demonstrated by the increasing power of nonstate actors as factors influencing the circulation of capital and credit.

Despite such a fundamental shift in power, the nation-state and the state more generally are not simply disappearing, although they are not simply staying the same either. They are changing their appearance. The recent example of invisible hackers – allegedly part of Russian intelligence agencies – hacking into the most influential and secret US government agencies, as well as into their private-commercial partners, is perhaps the most flagrant yet invisible demonstration of the state of disappearance as the disappearance (but not extinction) of the nation-state.[3] But this circumstance also affects changes in the way that the notion of disappearance is being experienced.

Normally, we would think that something can disappear only if it has previously appeared or been manifest in some way. A state, particularly in the political sense, does not simply appear as such; it may appear in its emanations, its institutions, but these do not make it a state. In American English, the primary meaning of "state" in a political sense at least is associated with the fifty states that make up the United States. But whether singular or plural, a state cannot simply disappear because it has never simply been visible as such. It does tend to be personified in its chief executives, but in democratic states, these leaders come and go and generally do not last long enough to be regarded as a manifestation of the state itself. In other words, to conceive of disappearance, whether as a state or not, one must first imagine just how something has appeared. If disappearance, then, is understood as the negative form of appearance, the question becomes how appearance is or should be understood.

There is a widespread tradition, both in nonspecialized and in philosophical language, that separates appearance from reality. What appears is not simply real. And what is real does not simply appear. "It appears that ..." is a way of relativizing whatever comes next in the statement. In this sense, appearance is often used as a way of designating the disappearing of the real. This designation in turn is based on two presuppositions: first, that the real is what exists and produces effects independently of its appearance; and second, that its appearance distances it from that which it essentially is – in short, appearance as a kind of facade or mask. These presuppositions are not simply a form of watered-down Platonism, separating the forms from their images or manifestations, but also reflect the difference between something considered to be identical with itself and something that is determined by its relation to something else – to a perceiver. This difference is part of what Immanuel Kant made famous with his distinction between things in themselves and things for us – between the so-called noumenal and phenomenal modes of being. From this distinction, Friedrich Nietzsche then drew the consequence that all so-called being in itself could be experienced, thought, and articulated only as a form of being construed from a particular "perspective" – thus making appearance a function of the position of an observer. This position and this perspective, he speculated, were in turn determined not just spatially but also temporally by their relation to traditions of selection and exclusion that co-determined the limits and structure of all appearances. Because the very notion of appearance, and hence of disappearance, presupposes a certain delimitation and individuation, everything cannot appear to disappear at once but only in a sequence of discrete moments. Even the notion of lights out, which would eliminate in one fell swoop the visual medium necessary for anything to appear, thus presupposes a certain limitation in order to be experienced as disappearance. Lights cannot go out if they have not previously been on.

II

If the notion of disappearance thus presupposes a prior appearance, and if this appearance is never simply in and of itself but always also for and from a certain point of view or perspective, then any discussion of disappearance must also take into account the medium and manner in which it takes place. For instance, the word "disappearance" is impossible to separate from visibility and visuality and hence from the media in which they operate. Visibility and visuality not only depend on the individual organs of sight – for they never function in a vacuum, no more than do appearance and disappearance – but also depend on a highly structured, highly selective, highly differentiated context within which individual acts of sense perception are both situated and constructed. The forces shaping the interpretive contexts where things appear and disappear and, perhaps even more significant, where disappearance can be experienced as a state are multiple and complex, differing according to linguistic, cultural, socio-economic, ethnic, racial, and religious traditions or conventions. Whereas some of these conventions may be shared by different cultural contexts, others may not. Perhaps one of the most pervasive of these conventions is the tendency to structure everything, including so-called sense data, in terms of binary opposition. With the visual realm, this habit can take the form of perceiving things as situated within a field whose limits are given with respect to individual acts and at the same time taken as stable. Thus the Gestaltist approach to visual perception tended to separate a perceptual image into a foreground and background, without worrying too much about the frame through which both grounds were grounded. In his effort to apply Freudian categories to visual perception and representation, Anton Ehrenzweig insisted on the importance of "peripheral vision" as an alternative form of organizing appearance and disappearance, one that would correspond to the Freudian notion of "primary" as distinct from "secondary" perception.[4] The destabilizing of the constituent frame and hence of the field that it delimits undermined another binary that is perhaps even more influential in considering visual phenomena, although it is by no means limited to them, namely that of oppositional exclusion and priority. In the case that we are discussing, this binary would hold that appearance and disappearance have to be regarded as mutually exclusive. If something is disappearing, it cannot be thought to be simultaneously appearing (or reappearing) at the same time and place. Yet this is precisely what is suggested by the transposition of primary processes onto the field of representations, visual and other: something can and does *appear in disappearing and vice versa*. This occurrence is perhaps more palpable and tangible in regard to acoustic phenomena: a sound both appears and disappears more or less simultaneously, its appearance coinciding with a certain disappearance. In the case of visual phenomena, this occurrence is less evident. But where the substance of what is being described is not unambiguously identifiable with an object, as in most of Chantal Meza's artworks, appearance and disappearance are difficult to separate or distinguish – for the what has become ambiguous. Something is shown in the work, but it is difficult to say just what that something is. In this situation, what is shown does not simply appear; rather, it disappears but without vanishing or leaving a total void. In this respect, it participates in what I have elsewhere described as the triad of visibility, invisibility, and divisibility[5] – a triad that tries to take into account the convergence and nonexclusivity of appearing and disappearing based on the intrinsic divisibility of signifiers, visual as well as verbal and acoustic. This characteristic suggests that the process of visual perception is not fundamentally different from reading – except that conventional wisdom encourages the expectation of immanent and transparent meaning of visual phenomena in a way that is partly absent from the expectations of readers confronted with a text. But this absence is by no means total since the very process of reading, as commonly understood and practised, presupposes again the appearance of meaning as well as its accessibility through memory – What Edmund Husserl called "retention"[6] – by means of which words can be distinguished from mere agglomeration of lines and letters, sentences from mere sequences of signs. Literature, in the emphatic sense that distinguishes it from other uses of language – and perhaps from art in general, including its visual and graphic dimensions – begins with the disruption of such expectations. But it is a disruption that presupposes the need and the desire that have given conventional expectations of meaning their staying power and ostensible self-evidence.

Since I have argued that the question of states of disappearance cannot be separated from the state in which one finds *oneself*, this argument implies that such states cannot be separated from the kind of *self* that one finds, no less than they can be separated from the *one* that is attached to it. Is it a singular *one*, as in "the one and only"? Or is it one of a homogeneous sequence of *ones* that simply repeat and accumulate themselves? Or is it both of these things at once? And if the latter, what would that imply about the structure of the self?

What is, after all, the state of the self? Is it that of the selfsame, the self that is the same as itself, that remains itself throughout changes in space and time?

This is anything but a merely theoretical or academic question. At the time of this writing – by the time(s) this is read, things may be very different – the United Kingdom has been virtually isolated from the rest of the world due to the discovery of a new mutation in the virus that causes Covid-19. The British government and health authorities have declared that this "new" version of the virus "may be up to 70% more contagious" than previous ones, although it is not at the moment clear whether it is therefore more virulent.[7] But if it will infect more persons than the previous strains, it will add to the burden of hospitals and thereby make treatment of the disease more difficult.

However, the virus, like all viruses, is in a constant state of mutation. It is mutating all the time, for better or worse. Its state is that of perpetual change, although the nature of this change cannot be predicted with any accuracy. Can one say that it is therefore either disappearing or appearing? As long as it is identified as the same virus, it will keep the same name – SARS-COV-2 – even if its genetic composition, and thus its appearance under microscopes, has changed. Of course, we cannot "see" the virus with our naked eyes. But since so much of our understanding of the world is extrapolated precisely from what can be seen with our eyes, explanations seeking to make the changes that it undergoes comprehensible to a general public often resort to images that can indeed be pictured and drawn, such as spikes that attach themselves to walls of cells, to receptors known by the acronym ACE2 receptor cells. The chemical names for these elements are not visualizable: S-glycoprotein for spikes and angiotensin-converting enzyme 2 for ACE2 receptors. Does the virus appear or disappear or both when it receives these names and when it is described by means of spikes penetrating the receptors? Or as already suggested, must not the opposition of visibility and invisibility be supplemented by the notion of divisibility, which introduces a process of splitting that paradoxically constitutes what cannot be seen as an ongoing and changing *process*?

This process is thus highly singular and at the same time "singularly plural," as Jean-Luc Nancy puts it, in a memorable phrase.[8] It is singularly plural because it is divisibly singular. That is what allows it to mutate while staying the same yet being different.

The many threads and strands that I observe in the drawings of Chantal Meza remind me of this singular divisibility: are they one or many or both? The question in her work is anything but academic; the traces of physical violence are impossible to overlook and difficult to sustain. One is called upon to reflect on the integrity of the bodies that have disappeared, or as one also says, "been disappeared," making "disappear" a transitive verb. The viewer, regarding these multiple strands as perhaps hair, now blood-stained, must reflect on a bodily violence that is all the more oppressive for being depicted only in its traces. We are reminded of how violence thrives on exclusion, of which a certain kind of disappearance can be the most lethal instrument. On 31 August 2022, just a few days before I wrote these lines, a former Mexican attorney general was arrested and warrants issued for eighty-two other suspects in the horrific disappearance and "presumed killing" of forty-three students on 26 September 2014, almost exactly eight years after this "state-sponsored crime."[9] The spread of such humanmade violence in both official and unofficial forms provides a somber counterpoint to the waxing and waning of epidemics such as Covid-19 and to the rising and ebbing of the conditions that make them not just possible but inevitable.

III

The situation in which I originally began to write these lines during the last quarter of 2020 was dominated by the effects of Covid-19, which, ever since making its appearance in Wuhan at the end of December 2019, has not ceased to produce its disturbing effects. But it is perhaps misleading to write, as I just did, of Covid-19 "making its appearance" at the end of 2019 because traces of the virus were present in various places much before that time, preserved in the sewerage waters of various cities, some of which are far removed from Wuhan, China, where it was first localized.[10] And apart from the difficulty of ascertaining its origin, it is misleading because Covid-19 never really appeared as such. Covid-19 is the name that the World Health Organization has given to the illness caused by the virus, which it calls SARS-COV-2 – a name that is contested given the distinction between the first SARS virus and the "novel" one. But what exactly is Covid-19? Where does it start, and above all, when does it stop? If it can infect someone without showing symptoms, disappear, and then reappear in after-effects that are now being designated with the strange name "long Covid," how do we reconcile its appearance with its disappearance – its nonappearance (asymptomatically) with its reappearance as symptoms, or after-effects? About this question, ideas are changing constantly. The genetic code of the virus was rapidly identified and made public, but as we have "seen," this code is constantly changing, mutating, and its mutations belong to the nature of the virus, in general and in particular. And if the virus is the cause of the disease, the latter is often produced not directly by the virus but by the overreaction of the immune system that the virus provokes, the so-called cytokine storm. Although this storm provokes damages to the lungs, which are otherwise associated with hereditary autoimmune diseases such as cystic fibrosis, the disease in this case is neither hereditary (as far as we know at least) nor autoimmune since the virus is not a part of the "autos" – the self – of the organism that it infects. Nor is its name, SARS-COV-2, entirely accurate since its destructive effects are not limited to the respiratory system, as the acronym SARS (Severe Acute Respiratory Syndrome) implies, but can affect all the organs where ACE2 receptors govern access to the cells, including the heart, the brain, and the circulatory system. The virus can disappear, but the ravages that it has caused, even indirectly, can remain for an indefinite period.

Covid-19 can without exaggeration be said to have appeared and disappeared more or less simultaneously, insofar as it harbours an extraordinary diversity in itself – as virus, as immune reaction, as symptoms, and as after-effects. And none of this diversity can be seen by the naked eye. What can be seen by these eyes, what can appear, are some of the effects that the virus has produced. But these appearances are relayed to individual perceivers mainly by television – such that the televisual media and the forces that control them, here as elsewhere, determine what can appear and what cannot. And these media select the appearances according to predetermined agendas: an emergency hospital built in Wuhan in a matter of weeks to house contaminated patients; body bags in a truck in front of a Wuhan hospital; videos by a citizen journalist soon to disappear along with other citizen journalists as the Chinese government asserted its right to control the state of appearance and of disappearance; refrigerator trucks parked in front of a Brooklyn hospital to house corpses in the spring of 2020, which are still there today, with the same cargo; and trenches being dug in Iran photographed by spy satellites to demonstrate the inability of the Iranian regime to control the pandemic, at least in its early stages. Such depictions of death – appearances of disappearances – serve to distract spectators from viewing or imaging the agony of dying through asphyxiation and in isolation, scenes that most television networks, whether private or public, would have little interest in allowing to appear to their viewers. Through Covid-19, it is therefore not so much death that disappears as it is the dying that leads to it. This is even more the case today as I write and rewrite this essay in the fall and winter months of 2020 while the debate about the value of wearing masks and avoiding crowds rages on in the United States and elsewhere, encouraged by those for whom the health of the economy takes priority over the health of society.

But can it be said that the forces that influence the media and, through them, public opinion – not to mention an electoral process that requires millions of dollars to function – are themselves either manifest or in a state of disappearance? Whether one agrees with the use to which it is being put, the metaphor of the "dark state" has a long and ominous history, reaching back to the assassinations of President John F. Kennedy, Martin Luther King, and Robert F. Kennedy, all of which were done in broad daylight and, in the case of the Kennedys, before television cameras in prime time. Yet the assignation of Lee Harvey Oswald, his almost immediate assassination, and the subsequent official report of the Warren Commission declaring Oswald to be the sole person responsible for the murder could be seen as major factors in demonstrating how certain appearances operate to perpetuate a state of disappearance, whether or not we endorse the idea of a "dark state" to describe the process. Does the ostensible transparency of images in the mainstream media, and more recently on so-called social networks, serve to reveal or conceal – or perhaps both? Is the state of disappearance really ultimately so different from the state of appearance? The attempt to personify the essentially impersonal economic institutions and forces that dominate liberal-democratic societies by identifying interests and processes with the images of billionaires such as Bill Gates, Warren Buffett, and Jeff Bezos produces appearances that conceal social relations that are neither visible nor invisible, for they are there to be seen, to offer objects of identification and idealization, while allowing the forces that determine social reality to remain in a state of disappearance – one that is closely related to the fata morgana of the disappearance of the state, dark or not.

Rather, if the wearing of masks has inspired so much anguish and so much aggressivity, could it be that the mask best describes the conditions under which the dominant forces in our societies appear in disappearing and disappear in appearing. Karl Marx, it may be remembered, spoke of "character-masks" to suggest the ways that all personification serves to disguise the essentially impersonal nature of capitalist exploitation.[11] But in thus revealing the convergence of appearance and disappearance, of revealing and concealing, and perhaps above all in holding out the possibility not of dispensing with masks altogether but of *changing* them, the mask suggests a possibility that allows for a certain state of disappearing to converge with the person in its etymological sense of both mask and anyone; to wear a mask is to appear and disappear at once, not in a static antagonism but in the possibility of being seen and read as something other and different. Masked, the person is liberated from the constraints of being an individual and is rendered divisible, dividual.

It seems as though in cultures not entirely dominated by the individualism of a liberal-democratic tradition, above all in Asia and in Africa, the obligation to wear masks has not been resisted and condemned as an infringement of the innate, if not God-given, liberty of the individual to be oneself. The notion of such liberty is based on the idea that one's body and everything that it involves – which is nothing less than the world – belongs to the individual wholly and without limitation. The face (like the head) is felt to be the quintessence of private property, and the state has no business intervening in its use – except to protect the individual's right to do what one wants with it – including infecting others. That, after all, is their problem, not ours. Even in relatively sophisticated philosophical circles, Emmanuel Levinas's identification of "the face" as the privileged manifestation of "the other" has enjoyed a popularity that belies its theoretical ambiguities and its theological origins – as clearly, if respectfully, identified by Jacques Derrida in an early study.[12] That the wearing of masks should have become the focal point of debate today, as a means of preventing the spread of the epidemic, is revelatory about "the state of disappearance" of monotheistic religion that was experienced during the pandemic of Covid-19. Masks after all cause the face partially to disappear. They also sometimes do the same with the voice. But what wearing them thereby allows to appear is an alterity that is neither entirely foreign nor entirely innate. This disappearance of a certain self allows for the appearance of one's concern for others – quite concretely, for their potential disappearance. What thereby disappears is the appearance of an unfettered and absolute self.

This effect of wearing masks is also why and how it can become a security issue as well: police wear all sorts of masks in order to conceal their identity and prevent eventual reprisals; demonstrators wear masks to protect them from the police and the violence that they use, from tear gas to grenades; and both wear masks to avoid identification. But the widespread rejection of masks is not a response to such situations alone. It involves the refusal to acknowledge that one's face is not one's private property, which takes precedence over its relation to everything else. What the masks of Covid-19 recall is that the face is not just an appearance or a disappearance but a site of transformation, where the binary opposition of inside and outside, self and other, is revealed itself to be a mask, concealing their inseparable interdependency – for instance, in the indispensable life process of breathing, whether inhaling and exhaling or speaking, spitting, and emitting particles from nose and mouth, all of which can produce the so-called aerosol transmission of the invisible virus. As perhaps the most vital sign of the state of disappearance, the mask discloses what may never appear as such: the vital communication of singular living beings who, although separate, are never entirely isolated from each other and from the world that they share.

NOTES

1 Samuel Weber, "Taking Exception to Decision," in *Benjamin's -abilities*, 176–94 (Cambridge, MA: Harvard University Press, 2008).

2 Walter Benjamin, *Gesammelte Schriften*, vol. 1 (Frankfurt: Suhrkamp Studienausagabe, 1980), 317, my translation.

3 At the time of this writing, December 2020, two recent reports that exemplify the changing status and appearance of the state – not for nothing increasingly seen to be "dark" – are "Suspected Russian Hackers Spied on US Federal Agencies" and "Suspected Russian Cyber-Attack Growing in Scale," *Guardian* (London), 14 and 18 December 2020.

4 Anton Ehrenzweig, *The Psychoanalysis of Artistic Vision and Hearing: Introduction to a Theory of Unconscious Perception* (1953; reprint, London: Routledge, 2014); Anton Ehrenzweig, *The Hidden Order of Art: A Study in the Psychology of Artistic Imagination* (Berkeley and Los Angeles: University of California Press, 1967); Sigmund Freud, *The Interpretation of Dreams*, trans. James Strachey (New York: Avon Books, 1965), 626–47.

5 Samuel Weber, "What Is a Literary Image?" *Paragraph* 43, no. 2 (2020): 125–39.

6 See V.C. Thomas, *The Essentials of Husserl: Studies in Transcendental Phenomenology* (Willmingont, DE: Vernon, 2023), 163.

7 Kate Holton, "Factbox: UK Says New Coronavirus Variant up to 70% More Transmissible," *Reuters*, 19 December 2020, https://www.reuters.com/article/uk-health-coronavirus-britain-variant-de-idUSKBN28T0V6.

8 Jean-Luc Nancy, *Being Singularly Plural* (Stanford, CA: Stanford University Press, 2000).

9 "Mexico One Step Closer to Justice for the Missing 43?" *Civicus Lens*, 31 August 2022, https://lens.civicus.org/mexico-one-step-closer-to-justice-for-the-missing-43.

10 Nathan Allen and Inti Landauro, "Coronavirus Traces Found in March 2019 Sewage Sample, Spanish Study Shows," *Reuters*, 26 June 2020, https://www.reuters.com/article/us-health-coronavirus-spain-science-idUSKBN23X2HQ.

11 Karl Marx and Frederick Engels, *Collected Works*, vol. 37 (New York: International Publishers, 1975), 22.

12 Jacques Derrida, "Violence and Metaphysics: An Essay on the Thought of Emmanuel Levinas," in *Writing and Difference*, trans. Alan Bass, 79–153 (Chicago: University of Chicago Press, 1978), 142.

10

The Disappearance of Emergencies

Santiago Zabala

> Those who rescue us from "emergency" – certainly – but rescuers into emergency: where are they? Those who venture into the untrodden and unformed realm of the opening of the emergency that urges, insofar as it demands that human beings be free – that they bear the abyss – and this emergency is be-ing itself.
>
> Martin Heidegger[1]

Former president Donald Trump will not be remembered for exercising extralegal powers to transform the state of emergency into routine political measures, as George W. Bush did, but rather for denying pressing emergencies altogether. During his presidency, he did not need to take advantage of pretexts to establish states of exception because the exception – in the form of unprecedented technological, social, and political global framings – has already become our condition. This circumstance is probably why he was able to ignore emergencies such as climate change, the refugee crisis, and also the Covid-19 pandemic. But he is not alone. Why are emergencies overlooked everywhere?

A global return to order – one that is not only political, as demonstrated by the various right-wing forces that have taken office around the world, but also existential – now threatens us with the emergence of our greatest emergencies. The rise of notions such as alternative facts, fake news, and post-truth in public discourse is symptomatic of this return, as they presuppose an absolute knowledge common to the "more civilized" Western countries. Although modernity was overcome with the end of colonialism and the rise of cultural anthropology, the resentment that this turn caused among ruling powers has now created a condition where the greatest emergency is becoming the absence of emergencies – that is, the disappearance of existential emergency by the rhetoric of control imposed by right-wing

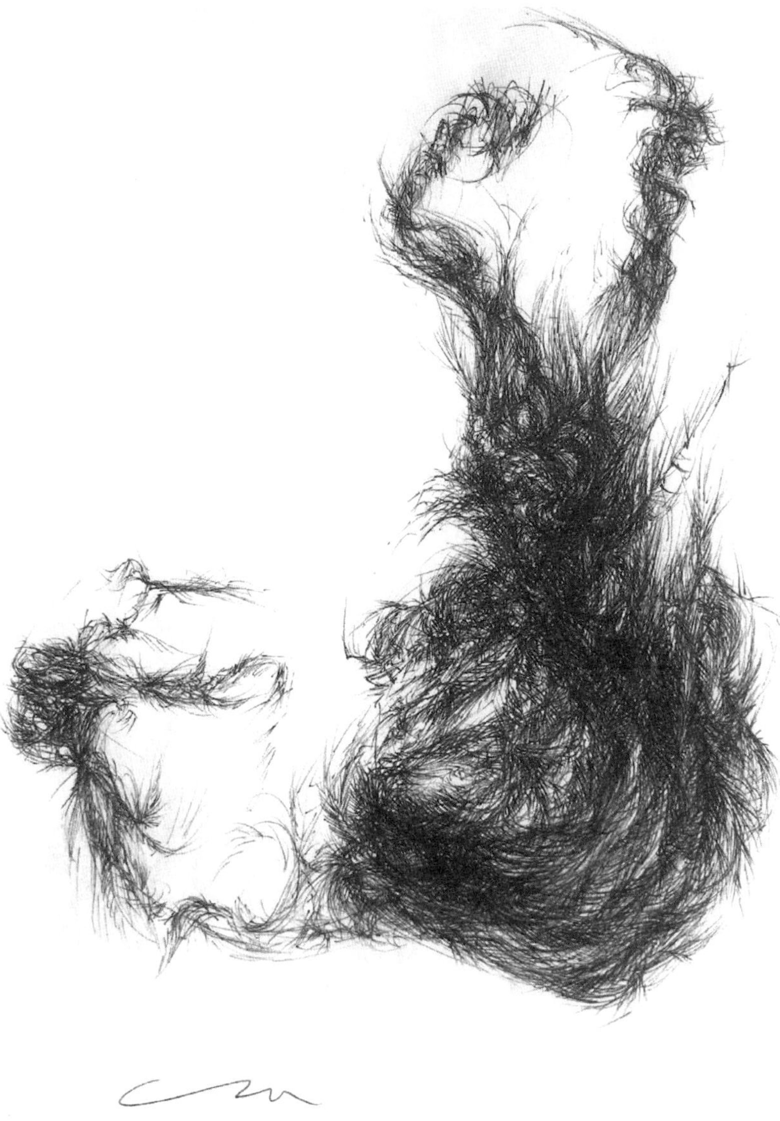

Chantal Meza, *Apparitions XVIII*, 2017, ink on paper, 35 x 27 cm

and capitalist powers to preserve their power. The goal of this essay is to illustrate this return to order and how Chantal Meza's art rescues us "into" the greatest emergency, as Martin Heidegger says in the epigraph.

Alternative facts, fake news, and post-truth are concepts that entered our cultural discourse after Kellyanne Conway, counsellor to President Donald Trump, defended a false statement about the attendance numbers at his inauguration celebration in 2017.[2] The problem with these concepts is not the matter of whether they properly describe our condition at the beginning of the twenty-first century but rather that they are a symptom of a return to order and realism among right-wing populist politicians, scientists, and philosophers. Bari Weiss believes that these intellectuals are part of a movement, the "intellectual dark web," determined to emphasize the "biological differences between men and women,"[3] and Jacob Hamburger has shown how these differences are directed against "various left-of-center critiques by arguing that what appears to be systemic inequality is actually the result of individual choices or behavior."[4] The goal of these politicians and intellectuals is to present themselves as defenders of "reason," "truth," and "facts," rational principles that they claim have been corrupted by postmodern relativism.[5]

As Slavoj Žižek explains, postmodern relativism is not the cause of alternative facts. They have always existed. Facts or data "are a vast and impenetrable domain, and we always approach them from (what hermeneutics calls) a certain horizon of understanding, privileging some data and omitting others." The secret of those who excoriate postmodernity and its hermeneutic historicist relativism "is that they miss the safe situation in which one big Truth (even if it was a big Lie) provided the basic 'cognitive mapping' to all."[6] To return to this "safe situation," thinkers from the intellectual dark web such as Jordan B. Peterson, Sam Harris, and Christina Hoff Sommers, along with "new realist" philosophers such as Graham Harman, Quentin Meillassoux, and Markus Gabriel, claim that we can have access to truth, as well as factual primary qualities of the world, without being dependent on language or interpretation. But as the philosopher of science Bruno Latour recently explained, no "attested knowledge can stand on its own, as we know very well. Facts remain robust only when they are supported by a common culture, by institutions that can be trusted, by a more or less decent public life, by more or less reliable media."[7] The rise of alternative facts is another indication that whether a statement is believed depends less on its reality than on the conditions of its political, linguistic, and social "construction."

Although these realist intellectuals will tell you that they do not necessarily want their takes on psychology, neuroscience, or philosophy to prevail over others, they in fact are seeking to preserve a society where they find themselves at ease – that is, where they have become more or less conscious servants of the ongoing return to order. Realism is an aspect and a consequence of dominion, not its cause. Although these thinkers have different agendas, the general idea is to return to the universalistic aspirations of modernity – to the idea that fundamental political, moral, and cultural concepts function to denigrate and marginalize those who do not measure up to their criteria of rationality. "The European project that I have in mind," Gabriel recently explained, "is that of the universal human values. Europeans, thanks to their philosophical past from the Greek to contemporary philosophers, are the best equipped to respond to the challenge of social justice and the future of democracy. Not only for Europe, but for all of humanity."[8]

The problem with this European rational universalism – as we have experienced in the twentieth century – is how it results in totalitarianism, colonialism, and genocide. As Zygmunt Bauman explains in *Modernity and the Holocaust*, "when the modernist dream is embraced by an absolute power able to monopolize modern vehicles of rational action, and when that power attains freedom from effective social control, genocide follows."[9] This is why the so-called chaos brought about by the voiding of metanarratives through postmodernity did not aim to create a new order, as many today believe, but to avoid the external imposition of order. As Austrian-Hungarian Karl Popper explained while self-exiled in New Zealand during the Second World War, the open societies of Europe were falling to authoritarian regimes. He defined such a society as one "in which individuals are confronted with personal decisions" as opposed to a "magical or tribal or collectivist society."[10] In the former, no one is in possession of the ultimate truth because it is acknowledged that people have different views, interests, and values. In the latter, truth is imposed by the bearers of power. Conway's insistence on alternative facts is a move in the ongoing return to order, a demonstration of the imposition of truth through power.

Trump, Peterson, and others who insist on these universal truths are creating a condition where the absence of emergency is the greatest emergency. At the centre of this condition is the belief that there are no alternatives to the framed global order. This order imposes realism politically upon other cultures and justifies its imposition intellectually by discrediting facts. Trump's hostility toward the facts of climate change, for example, is meant to create a condition without emergencies – where truth is imposed by authority and where nothing, neither observations of the external world nor measures that would counteract the power of these authorities, is permitted to emerge from the overwhelming order. Difference, change, and cultural others must be avoided as disruptions of the "safe situation" that order claims to represent.

This order reveals itself every day as more authoritarian. Like Bernard Stiegler's "epoch of the absence of epoch,"[11] the absence of emergency has become the greatest danger that we face today, signalling the abandonment of the interpretative nature of existence in favour of the return to order and realism. But if, as Friedrich Hölderlin said, "Where the danger is, / There also grows our saving grace,"[12] we must find ways to experience this danger, to reveal emergency from within its imposed absence.

Art, as I have explained in *Why Only Art Can Save Us*,[13] often works better than scientific announcements and philosophical treatises as a way to reveal emergencies. The reason for this capacity is not the ability of artists to create beauty but rather the intensity and depth of their works. Documentary photographs of the melting Arctic, for example, can be truthful but are rarely as powerful as works of art that address this emergency. "When a work of art truly takes hold of us," as Hans-Georg Gadamer says, "it is not an object that stands opposite us which we look at in the hope of seeing through it to an intended conceptual meaning. Just the reverse. The work is an '*Ereignis*' – an *event* that 'appropriates us' into itself. It shocks us, it overturns us, and sets up a world of its own, into which we are drawn."[14] Scientists and philosophers can also overturn our world, but their works preserve a distance that is constitutive of their findings and renders their effects less immediate. A work of art seeks to reduce this distance as a way not only to draw our attention but also to involve us in an experience that the artist considers significant

Artists today are closer to the hidden emergencies than many scientists and philosophers because art has been more resistant to the return to order. Science and systematic thought seek to rescue us *from* emergencies, improving and preserving our order, but art at its best attempts to rescue us *into* emergencies, creating event and shock. This rescue not only reveals absent emergencies – climate change, the unemployment crisis, femicide, whatever has been concealed by the rhetoric of power – but also becomes an emergency, an experience of danger. The artists who seek this experience are the ones whose works demand public intervention in global emergencies that are concealed in the idea of their absence. Art's role in stirring our existence is vital to opposing the absence of emergency sought by the advocates of the return to order.

This is particularly evident in the art of Chantal Meza, whose paintings are meant to thrust us into the absent emergency of violence. As she points out, "Art can bring light to that which is somehow occluded. And it allows us to dwell on widespread problems that are affecting us, slowly, gradually, and yet surely."[15] The paintings in the series *Obscure Beasts* are composed of black and red brushstrokes that evoke not just violence but also what remains of it through blood.[16] What emerges from these works is the intensity of existence. That Meza often recalls the numerous emergencies ignored in Mexico – from femicides and kidnappings to extrajudicial executions – is an indication that these paintings refer to them. These works are meant to thrust us into the "profound indifference to social problems in this country," she tells us, which is manifest in "people's amazement when they see what is happening. It's as if they have been living in some trance, which denies any mutual responsibility. In order to improve social justice, there is always a need for a constant commitment in battle concerning how we see and relate to the world around us."[17] This is why I agree with Henry A. Giroux that, when viewing Meza's *Obscure Beasts*, "we are reminded that the worst we can do is look away."[18]

Meza, like some other contemporary artists,[19] demands that we intervene in social emergencies that we have not been able to confront because they have disappeared in the ongoing return to order and realism. Their works, and that of others, are also a sign of the ongoing turn from "relational" to "emergency" aesthetic theories and an indication of artists' inevitable participation in global matters.[20] Although the art world, like scientific and political establishments, is also a system with hierarchies and frames, it has been affected by globalization in a different way, one that through actual exchange enables works to emerge in unusual locations and to reveal different emergencies. The "*globalization of the art world*," as Arthur Danto says, "*means that art addresses us in our humanity,* as men and women who seek in art for meanings that neither of art's peers – philosophy and religion – in what Hegel spoke of as the realm of Absolute Spirit, are able to provide."[21]

Globalization's effect on the art world is evident in the different experiences of art to be had at art fairs in contrast to biennales: the rigid art fairs invite the public to contemplate works of art as valuable objects, whereas the biennales invite all the members of the audience to take responsibility for an experience that concerns everyone. In line with Gadamer's definition of a work of art, Caroline A. Jones believes that it "is the emphasis on events and experiences, rather than objects, that constitute[s] the surprising legacy of biennial culture."[22] The fact that the latest trend in biennales, which have increased markedly in recent decades, is to offer these experiences in remote places such as Antarctica and the Californian desert indicates that globalized art demands global interventions from its artists and its public.

To rescue the public *into* the greatest emergency – the imposed absence of emergency that is the result of an authoritarian return to order and realism – artists such as Meza have begun to thrust us into this absence. These works demand from the public an intervention that is not only political but also existential. Whether these artists will succeed in disrupting the "safe situation" that politicians and thinkers are trying to impose depends on the level of intervention of the public. Although these interventions are constantly undermined, the public must continue to question a return to order and realism that reproduces only a "uniform, dull, gray, suffocating, and unimaginative" world, as Meza says.[23]

NOTES

1 Martin Heidegger, *Ponderings VII–XI: Black Notebooks, 1938–1939*, trans. Richard Rojcewicz (Bloomington: Indian University Press, 2017), 219, my translation of this passage.

2 Aaron Blake, "Kellyanne Conway Says Donald Trump's Team Has 'Alternative Facts.' Which Pretty Much Says it All." *Washington Post*, 22 January 2017, https://www.washingtonpost.com/news/the-fix/wp/2017/01/22/kellyanne-conway-says-donald-trumps-team-has-alternate-facts-which-pretty-much-says-it-all.

3 Bari Weiss, "Meet the Renegades of the Intellectual Dark Web," *New York Times*, 8 May 2018, https://www.nytimes.com/2018/05/08/opinion/intellectual-dark-web.html.

4 Jacob Hamburger, "The 'Intellectual Dark Web' Is Nothing New," *Los Angeles Review of Books*, 18 July 2018, https://lareviewofbooks.org/article/the-intellectual-dark-web-is-nothing-new.

5 For a detailed analysis of postmodern relativism, see Santiago Zabala, *Being at Large: Freedom in the Age of Alternative Facts* (Montreal and Kingston: McGill-Queen's University Press, 2020).

6 Slavoj Žižek, *Sex and the Failed Absolute* (New York and London: Bloomsbury, 2019), 104–5.

7 Bruno Latour, *Down to Earth: Politics in the New Climate Regime*, trans. Catherine Porter (Cambridge, UK: Polity, 2018), 23.

8 In Ana Carbajosa, "Silicon Valley y las redes sociales son unos grandes criminales," interview with Markus Gabriel, *El País*, 1 May 2019, my translation, https://elpais.com/cultura/2019/04/17/actualidad/1555516749_100561.html.

9 Zygmunt Bauman, *Modernity and the Holocaust* (London: Polity, 1989), 93–4.

10 Karl Popper, *The Open Society and Its Enemies* (1945; reprint, Princeton, NJ: Princeton University Press, 2020), 165.

11 Bernard Stiegler, *The Age of Disruption*, trans. Daniel Ross (Cambridge, UK: Polity, 2019), 5.

12 Quoted in Martin Heidegger, *Elucidations of Hölderlin's Poetry*, trans. by Keith Hoeller (New York: Humanity Books, 2000), 40.

13 Santiago Zabala, *Why Only Art Can Save Us: Aesthetics and the Absence of Emergency* (New York: Columbia University Press, 2017). See also Santiago Zabala, Daniela Angelucci, Amanda Boetzkes, Paul Kottman, and Ivelise Perniola, "Forum: Santiago Zabala, *Why Only Art Can Save Us: Aesthetics and the Absence of Emergency*, New York, Columbia University Press, 2017," ed. Daniela Angelucci, *Lebenswelt*, no. 15 (2019): 114–54, https://msu.mk/wp-content/uploads/2020/10/Forum-on-Zabala-Why-Only-Art-Can-Save-Us-with-critical-articles-by-Angelucci-Perniola-Boetzkes-and-Kottman-and-Zabala-responses.pdf.

14 Hans-Georg Gadamer, *Gadamer in Conversation*, trans. Richard E. Palmer (New Haven, CT: Yale University Press, 2001), 71.

15 In Brad Evans, "The Intimate Witness: Art and the Disappeared of History," interview with Chantal Meza, *Los Angeles Review of Books*, 22 October 2018, https://lareviewofbooks.org/article/histories-of-violence-when-art-confronts-the-denial-of-life.

16 Chantal Meza, *Obscure Beasts*, https://www.chantal-meza.com/stateofdisappearance.

17 In Evans, "Intimate Witness."

18 Henry A. Giroux, "The Violence of Organized Forgetting," this volume.

19 I discuss these other artists in Zabala, *Why Only Art Can Save Us*.

20 In Zabala, *Why Only Art Can Save Us*, 127–32, I refer to aesthetic theories such as Malcolm Miles's "eco-aesthetics," Jill Bennett's "practical aesthetics," and Veronica Tello's "counter-memorial aesthetics," where hidden emergencies, the environment, terrorism, and refugees play central roles.

21 Arthur Danto, *Unnatural Wonders: Essays from the Gap between Art and Life* (New York: Columbia University Press, 2006), xvi.

22 Caroline A. Jones, *The Global Work of Art: World's Fairs, Biennials, and the Aesthetics of Experience* (Chicago: Chicago University Press, 2017), xiv–xv.

23 In Evans, "Intimate Witness." See also Zabala, *Why Only Art Can Save Us*, 127–32.

11

Technologies of Disappearance

Julian Reid

"Aphanisis" is a term that Jacques Lacan used to describe a particular process of interest to psychoanalysis, what he explained as *the emergence of the subject in its disappearance*.[1] Lacan openly borrowed and developed this term from another, less well-known analyst, Ernest Jones, a Welshman and friend of Sigmund Freud. Jones used the word, which derives from the Greek, to describe the fundamental and in some cases pathological "fear of seeing desire disappear."[2] This is the simple fear, perhaps, of being unable to get it up, or of being castrated, or simply of being deprived of sexual enjoyment.

With Lacan, however, the term became a way of describing something more complex, less rooted in sexuality, but nevertheless concerning desire – for it was in disappearance that Lacan located the very emergence of the subject as such. He thought about disappearance not simply as a source of fear, or a problem to be solved, but also as an act, a movement, a manifestation, crucial to the subject's coming-to-be.[3]

It is a game, he argued, that we first enter into as children with our parents when the phantasy of one's own disappearance is the first object that we learn to bring into play in answer to the question of whether these persons charged with our care can afford to lose us.[4] When the desire that founds the subject is intuited to be, merely, the desire of the big Other, then the subject, to emerge as itself, has to somehow make itself disappear.[5] At least, I take that to be what Lacan means – that disappearance is a kind of practice (and a way, as Michel Foucault would later put it), first invented by the Greeks, of caring for the self.[6]

2050

It is the summer of 2050, and I am an eighty-year-old man who suffers from all the troubles that come with inhabiting a body of such biological age. In those short bursts of mental animation of which I am still capable, usually

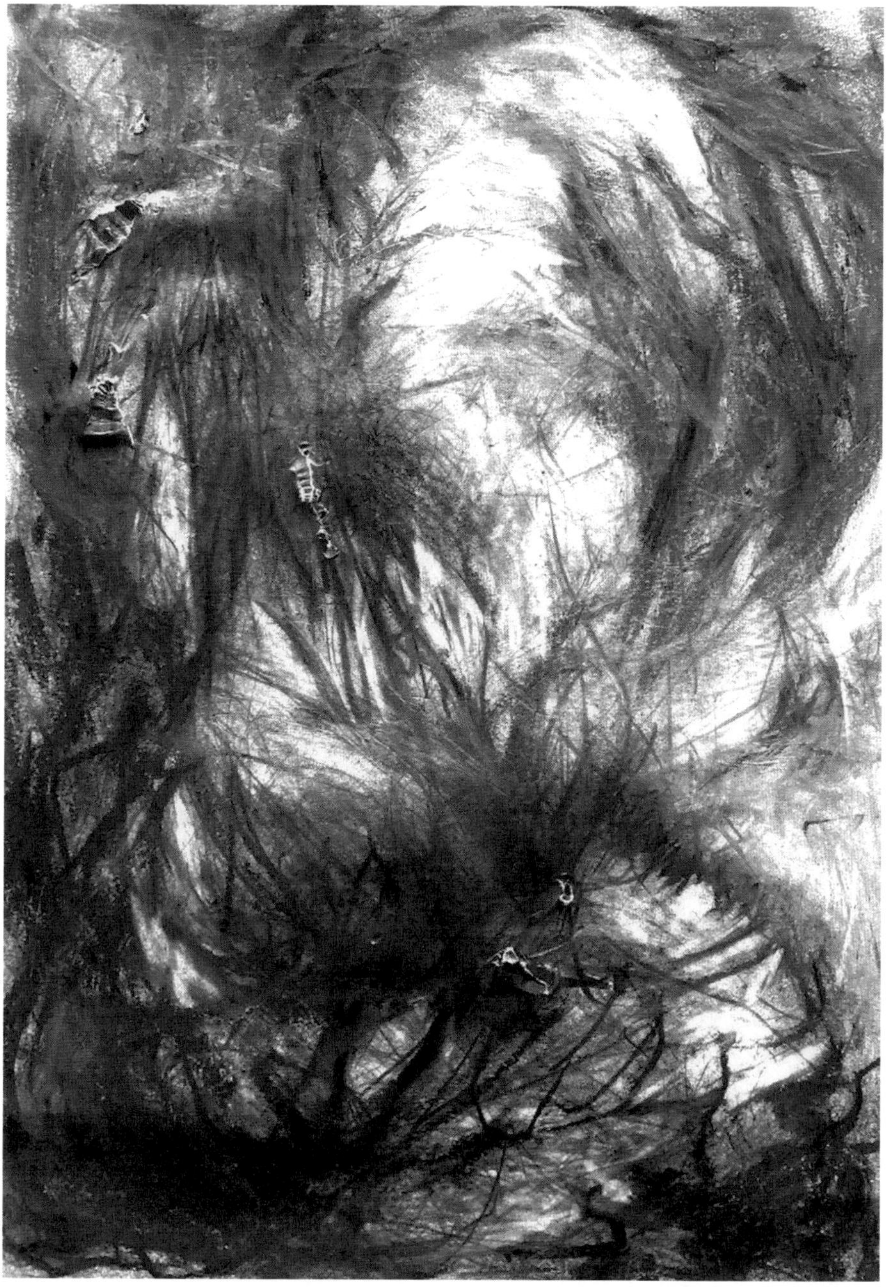

Chantal Meza, *The Void I*, 2019, graphite and charcoal on paper, 29.5 x 42 cm

late in the morning after coffee, I have been trying to think about how to connect aphanisis to aphasia. "Aphasia" is another Greek term, commonly used to describe impairments of language that degrade the ability of a person to either produce language for themselves or to comprehend it when it is produced by another. It is said to result from injuries to the brain. The French physician Paul Broca discovered, back in the nineteenth century, that there is a particular area of the brain where the faculty of speech is located: the third frontal convolution of the left hemisphere.[7] It is in this precise area of the brain that all kinds of disorders related to language emerge, not just aphasia but also agraphia, which describes the more particular diminishment of our abilities to write.[8] Presumably, it is also where reading disorders, known as alexia, originate, although I have yet to clarify that.

It is well documented, as I have learned from reading the secondary literatures, that Lacan himself suffered from aphasia. He was reported to often struggle to speak. His speech was accompanied by a wide range of different sounds – coughing, sighing, throat clearing, and mumbling – all of which led to the impression of a speaker whose speech was permanently "on the brink of dissolving."[9] He was also notorious for finding it difficult to write. What has been handed down to us of his thinking has been largely in the form of his seminars, held at various venues, from his apartment to a psychiatric hospital to the École normale supérieure, and transcribed for us by a shorthand typist from the 1950s to the 1970s, when they finally came to an end in 1978 with a seminar described as having been, quite simply, "silent."[10]

Could it be that Lacan's aphasia expressed Lacan's aphanisis? I mean, could it be that the disappearance of his faculty for language expressed, precisely, the emergence of Lacan the subject? In dictionaries of critical thought, we customarily find these two concepts and terms, "aphanisis" and "aphasia," alongside each other in the alphabetical ordering that structures such tomes. I have not, however, been able to locate research that brings the two together in any kind of logical synthesis, let alone research that offers us a theory of Lacan along such lines. The closest that I have found is the now long deceased Alain Badiou's *Theory of the Subject*, which did draw on Lacan to offer what its title describes while positing the idea that disappearance is the basis of all politics, of revolutionary force, of mass movements, of history, even of the world itself.[11] But that is using Lacan only to think about "the subject," not to produce a theory of Lacan as subject. Could it not be, however, that it was there, in *the third frontal convolution of the left hemisphere* of Lacan's brain, where his aphanisis occurred and where Lacan the subject manifested itself in the disappearance of his capacity for speech, which is to say, in his aphasia?

Maybe in art I could find better resources for thinking this matter through. I recall Barnett Newman, the vast emptiness of his paintings. Images of spaces made such that one can go into them and disappear. Newman who always preferred the tundra to Paris. Newman who just wanted the paint on the canvas to look as good as it did in the tube. Then I think of Chantal Meza's series *Since the Beginning*.[12] Didn't she paint disappearance? That one image of hers with all the colours and intricacies of a vast placenta. "Disappear, where?" it asks. "The body," it replies. Yet the body that she paints is no maternal home. I see there a deranged tree of life that promises to strangle me in its torments.

Perhaps it is just an old man's fantasy, anyway, that in its fading the body manifests the subjectivity of which it is capable, a subjectivity that its more vitalized version of days past was only holding back. As Lacan was subjectified in and by his relation to the exhaustive desire of an academic audience to forever hear the professor speak, his aphasia would, on the surface, make perfect sense to another professor, such as myself, as a manifestation of aphanisis – a disappearance absolutely necessary, if also lethal, for the academic subject in question. I too learned to disappear. But probably like every professor, I knew the fear of aphasia, the many nightmares of being in front of an audience and opening one's mouth only to find that you are unable to speak or can produce nothing but indecipherable nonsense – the fear of being exposed as the fool. The professor disappears, and the subject emerges, in all its emancipated cretineity. But I also learned that I required this other, not a nightmare but the fantasy of no longer needing to make sense, of being able to abandon one's place and go AWOL, not into cretineity but into the world as such, into language as it can be, that space where one can meaningfully get lost, disappear, and vanish in thought. So much of my academic career has been about averting that journey!

It is the summer of my retirement from the North American university where I have spent my latter years teaching. It is, like every summer before it, the hottest summer on record. Worse, however, is the ruination of the intellectual climate, if it can even be called that. Every direction I look, I am surrounded by ruins. The university has been in decay for some time, caused not only by decades of mismanagement but also by a fading of purpose that nobody in all reality could save it from. Comparable to Lacan's brain, the traditional organization of faculties has gone, and I have been relocated to a Transdisciplinary Centre for Evocative Autoethnography. All research has to be justified by its compatibility with the university's strategic disavowal of the old norms and methods. For myself, given my wish to fade, that has been okay, but for the canons of theory in which I was trained, it has been the death knell. There must be no further denouncement of present worlds in pursuit of ideal worlds. Instead, we must dedicate ourselves to writing lives and telling stories, to caring for future worlds by giving our attention to the destructive consequences of subject-formations of past worlds.

I have to find a way to fit these fading interests of mine – in Lacan and in how aphanisis connects to aphasia – within this remit of a university that itself is disappearing into the void.

1985

I'm fifteen years old, and I have decided to disappear. It is late in the summer of 1985, and the new school year is as ominous as it is imminent. I have been reading the memoir *As I Walked Out One Midsummer Morning* (1969), by Laurie Lee, a gift I received last Christmas. I like the lightness and simplicity of its images, the depiction of an easygoing survival on the road, as Jack Kerouac, George Orwell, and numerous others have also well conveyed to me in stories of themselves. It feels like destiny to disappear now, with these images alive inside of me.

"Life must not be a novel that is given to us, but one that is made by us."[13] Ah, yet, with stories so given to us, we can also make.

At school, we read *Cider With Rosie* (1959), another memoir by Lee. I'm sure it was given to us because it deals with adolescence and puberty, depicting as it does Lee's sexual encounter with a girl named Rosie. If I were to play along, I would find some way to identify with the boy. But I don't, and this other book of Lee's leaves me cold.

Perhaps it is partly because I dislike the name Rosie. It is a name that reeks of the English countryside, of freckles and apple cheeks, of fat bums in short dresses. I imagine her red-headed, unalluring, and feel the fear that I would wish to feel if I were faced with the prospect of a roll in the hay with Rosie. I do not like cider either. But figs, of which I have read, and on which Lee lives as he walks out that midsummer morning, I can well imagine to fully enjoy. I do not really know what figs are. I don't think I have ever eaten one, but I have an idea, and I understand very well that they are a poorly disguised literary metaphor for the female genital organ. "Female genital organ" is a clumsy phrase. But it is telling that writers like Lee either resort to metaphor or mimic the serious scientists by talking in clinical terms about genitalia.

On a bookshelf at home, I found a text on *Feminine Sexuality* by Jacques Lacan. It describes the theory of the great founder of psychoanalysis, Freud, concerning what the scientists themselves call "dread of the vulva."[14] It is true that for a teenage boy there is something potentially dreadful about vulvas. At least, if I force myself to imagine Rosie's, I can feel the spread of dread within me, and the image is suffocating.

However, the figs on which Lee lives in *As I Walked Out One Midsummer Morning* are different. I read that a Spanish girl called Doña Maria gave him these figs, cool and green, and that, fed on those, he could walk far and long into the day. I like Lee's descriptions of Doña Maria, this image of her that he has shown within me. This is an image into which I can go, disappear, get lost.

At what moment and why the image of Doña Maria contained within itself the source of my disappearance, I cannot say because I cannot remember. But that it contains this kind of promise is a fact. If I am to disappear, then this disappearance has to be somehow also a journey into this one image. In the world of images given to me by Lee, Rosie's cider is tragic, whereas Doña's figs are epic. If I am to disappear, it is essential that I take this image of her figs with me, that I fix on it, and that I follow the way into it. This disappearance is not going to be an exit onto a road, as with Kerouac. Nor is it going to be simply a departure along a path onto which one walks out, as with Lee. It will be an entry and an internalization of a space that I was once outside of and that I now turn inside out. This will not be a simple trip, by road or any other way, or an escape; it will be a disappearance, a mystery, an act of magic, made possible by the force of this one image.

As the train pulls alongside the platform of Edinburgh's Waverley Station, I go to the last carriage, at the back of the train, and get off, heading up the stairs and out the north entrance, where I ascend into my city, its streets, its hidden corners, its crevices, its depths, its resting places, and its fruits.

2000

It is the summer of 2000, I'm a man of thirty, younger than I feel, and I'm back in my hometown after a long sojourn working and then studying in the South of England. I am trying to write my doctoral thesis, which is intended to be a theory of the concepts of war and strategy buried in the works of Michel Foucault and others apparently influenced by him. I don't quite know yet what its final form is going to be or what to include, but for now I'm reading the entire works of Paul Virilio, and I plan to make his work the subject of at least one chapter of the thesis. Basically, the thesis is just a way for me to express the organization of my reading – the reading that I want to do, the reading that I feel I have to do because these texts contain important stuff for me to know in order to explain myself to myself.

Foucault's texts are dense, dubious literary and reading experiences. The ideas are good, great even, and definitely useful to me, but the style in which they are relayed to the reader is questionable. I prefer his interviews and lectures to his books. Penguin has just published a new three-volume series of his more obscure stuff: interviews and lost essays. There is one that I read this morning where he talks about a recurrent nightmare. A nightmare that has followed him from childhood and from which he awakes disturbed.

"I am looking at a text that I can't read, or only a tiny bit of it is decipherable. I pretend to read it, aware that I'm inventing; then suddenly the text is scrambled, I can no longer read anything or even invent it, my throat tightens and I wake up."[15]

I guess that this debility may be what is called alexia or a variation of it – a disorder that affects the brain, or more especially the third frontal convolution of its left hemisphere, where those other disorders, of aphasia and agraphia, which disturb the ability of a subject to speak and write, also occur. Anyway, it is comforting to know, and it is good to listen to him connect his own work with his own confessedly haunted self. It is as if his own sense of himself and its survival is bound up with an ability to read, to make legible, and to penetrate a given text, putting himself in there. It is the obduracy of a text to penetration that really terrifies him. He wishes to appear where he is not, and his subjectivity is bound up with that particular practice. It is a style that is somewhat masculine, perhaps, and it is essential to Foucault.

Reading Virilio, I am thinking about how disappearance isn't simply a physical act, made in space, but profoundly temporal – and spiritual. If I go missing, it can be in time, not just space. "The lapse occurs frequently at breakfast and the cup dropped and overturned on the table is its well-known consequence," Virilio wrote.[16] A lapse, a being absent, is also a necessary, if not a wilful, action in time and a defence, a counter-strategy, against an order that demands of me too much presence. Yes, disappearance is a technique of defence, a veritable "defence-reaction," as they say, of the subject "against unpleasant demands or trains of thought."[17] Or, as in my case, fifteen years ago, against physical trains that would otherwise send us somewhere that we actually did not want to be and that threatened us with a diminishment of our subjective energies.

Yes, disappearance is a defence-mechanism observed strongly in children. Those little people, still sensitive enough to what is good and what is bad for them, often react with what are known as absence seizures. Such absences can take the form of staring into space for a few seconds when the brain becomes overloaded, as it were. Or they can be performed physically in movement, as I did back then by going absent without leave, as the old term AWOL expresses.

2008

It is the summer of 2008, and I'm in a village whose name I cannot pronounce, somewhere in the Finnish countryside, to the south, on the eastern side of the country, not far from the Russian border, which is still relatively peaceful. I completed my doctorate a few years ago, but it already feels far behind me, and somehow I'm already the incumbent of an academic chair at a small but beautiful university in the far north of Finland, close to the Arctic Circle. Right now, I'm on vacation and have a paper I would like to write for a small conference I'm convening on political aesthetics. It seems like a good opportunity to finally read Gilles Deleuze's two books on cinema. I've skimmed them but never really read them, even though I would love to take the time to do so, ingesting what he had to say about the history of cinema, an art form that I like very much. I wonder how he ever got the time to see all the movies listed in the index while writing so incredibly much. I imagine him, late into the evening, after a day of writing, sitting there, toward the back of a sparsely populated cinema, imbibing everything. He, too, knew the power of refuge, of a happy solitude, of being the unseen face in an absent crowd.

I'm familiar with Deleuze's theory of nomadism, his nomadic thought. This was also something that I worked on when I was writing my thesis, back in the day. Well, not so long ago, actually. Nomadism, you could say, is how Deleuze gave his own spin to the same phenomenon that Virilio worked on, seeing a peculiar power in the same kind of subject, which Virilio located especially among children – a nomadism of the spirit, by way of which the subject disappears, goes off "on a trip," AWOL, deserting the place where he or she is meant to be. And Deleuze, like Virilio, also locates this power of disappearance in relation to war and strategy. We talk too much of annihilation, and of violence, when we talk of war, its episodes in time, and its supposedly destructive purposes. There's something else going on here in his texts, and my task has been to spell it out a bit. Deleuze sees in nomadism this trippiness of the spirit, the very origin of war itself and of a violence that is life affirmative.

But now, anyway, I'm reading the cinema books, and they have much less to do with war, although he does place a certain emphasis on "the war," by which he means the Second World War, as the historical period when a fundamental break in the development of cinema occurred. After 1945, he says, cinema became a machine for the production of a new race of characters[18] – who themselves embody this technique of disappearance, of never being where they are meant to, and who are always disappearing, going off on trips, disrupting the narratives that they were supposed to fulfill. The characters are not the obliterators of history but those who disappear to invent the future.

On the surface, this image of disappearance, as a physical act in space, might seem to involve an opposition to Virilio's – the physical act of disappearing in space contrasted with the psychic journey of the subject, who does not disappear anywhere except into the self. But as good students of Deleuze know, the nomad does not really move far, physically. He distributes himself somewhere, in a smooth space, which he occupies, holds, and inhabits.[19] The nomad is the "one who does not depart," does not want to leave, but clings to that space in which he moves.[20] He is the opposite of the migrant, who already knows where he wants to go and sets off for his destination. So maybe the nomad is closer to the photosensitive subject that Virilio discusses, whose disappearance is entirely stationary and is itself a defence mechanism, a way of holding onto what territory one has and is, against forces of intrusion that, if left to operate unabated, would colonize the self.

2015

It is the summer of 2015. For a few years now, I've been working on the topic of technologies of the self. I know from reading the late Foucault that, for the Ancients, technologies of the self were those practices by which the subject learned to move to the summit of itself and to see the self by looking down, surveying it, becoming its master from above, taming it, and rendering it conducive to its own needs.[21] They were, in other words, tools of climbing, of ascent – parts of an apparatus of ascension by which we subject the self from on high, drawing the vertical division between subject and self, becoming as a subject a kind of summit in submission of a self that is made to live in the valleys of our experience, as the sheep does, when tended to successfully by the shepherd of its flock.

Writing is among those practices that were fundamental to the Ancients as supports for the ways that we learn to ascend, climb, and see ourselves from above. It is, in a way, that practice by which we render ourselves apparent, appear to ourselves and to others, depending on the precise form of self-writing in question. It is this practice that was most crucial for Foucault's own coming-to-be, his own way of taking up space.

But we also need, as the Ancients did, technologies that enable our disappearance – ways by which to dissimulate our selves in relation to oneself and to others. No doubt, writing can function in much this way, too, although I don't think that is its principal function. However, it seems to me that reading might be the technology to which we best turn for this other function. Understanding technologies of disappearance requires, in other words, a theory of reading more than it does writing, or at least a theory of reading and writing that starts from reading and links it to writing. Novalis, I think, intended something like that when he remarked on how reading works to dissipate the subject of writing, how it can at least involve the entry into another being and the derangement of that being from within, including when that being is the self – that is, when one is reading, simply, one's own text.[22]

It is interesting that Foucault's own nightmares were characterized not by fears concerning the loss of the ability to write, a practice so obviously definitive of his own ways of being, but by fears concerning the loss of the ability to read. I have looked but haven't been able to find any research on Foucault's alexia or fear of alexia. Of course, plenty has been said about Foucault's other supposed disorders.[23] But it seems to me that this one might be the more crucial. If I were to make a general observation or to develop a general hypothesis concerning reading as a technology of the self, it would most probably head in the opposite direction of that traced by Foucault in the development of writing as a technology of the self.[24] I mean that the reader reads not to reach any kind of summit or to submit the self from on high. Instead, reading follows the opposite route. It is the technology by which the self disarms itself of subjectivity – that is to say, evades the risk of becoming subject – and disappears, goes AWOL, like the sheep sometimes does when the shepherd, asleep or too drunk to care, is not looking. That may be why fear of alexia troubled Foucault's dream life so.

Writing and reading are two technologies of the self that are helpless without each other, two technologies of the self that have grown prodigiously in the course of the development of the West, from antiquity to the present, two technologies of the self without which the subject of Western experience could not and would not have (dis)appeared.

2020

It is the summer of 2020, and I am reading the latest novel by Michel Houellebecq. I remember reading *Atomized* (1998), the first book of his that I came across, back in the summer of – was it 2006? I'm not sure. Another absent memory, although the impression that it made still remains. The recollection is of a certain melancholy emanating from the text amid the heat of a small bedroom backing onto a busy road in suburban London – a sense of descent – but it could have been any of those years, particularly the summers spent there. I'm in a different place now, literally and metaphorically, and well accustomed to Houellebecq. I don't expect to be surprised, only to be fulfilled by whatever is at stake in the narrative. Mostly, I look forward to the humour. This new one is called *Serotonin*.[25]

The cover illustration is not figurative in the same way as the one used for my edition of *Atomized*. I still have my original copy, located on a shelf not far from where I am writing now, its cover adorned with a skinny blonde who faces the viewer as she looks earnestly toward the camera. The cover of *Serotonin* is almost nondescript; I barely notice the image within it – a village seen from a distance – but the colour of the graphic, a kind of infrared purple, is at least distinct. From the details inside the back cover, I learn that it is drawn from the database known as Getty Images, where many authors go in search of a relevant image to adorn their academic texts, often ending up, as I have on occasion, with something barely relevant to the subject matter, at least not in any way edifying of the major themes of the work. The marketing of radicality – maybe there's a book to be written about it? They'd probably fuck that cover up, too!

It is true, however, that *Serotonin* does concern a village, although it is hardly the subject of the text. No, *Serotonin* concerns disappearance – the disappearance of a man, aged forty-five and in the middle of life, as they say. At least, it concerns the desire to disappear on the part of this guy, Florent-Claude, who, tired of life, of existence, abandons his place in the world to go off into – it is hard to say what.

It is a tired and well-worn plot, of course, this desire to disappear and the attempt at its fulfillment. What is Homer's *Odyssey* if not that? Are we not all subjectified by this narrative structure in one way or another? Like that of Odysseus, the story of Florent-Claude is about the attempt and failure to disappear. People can easily vanish under the duress of tyrannies. To wilfully disappear, now that is harder to do.

The disappearance in question, that of Florent-Claude, is spatial. It brings back memories for me of 1985. The planning, the execution, the inner conversation with oneself that goes on in bringing about a disappearance. The disappearance of Florent-Claude is also profoundly sutured with vulva, like my own was, giving me cause to remember Doña Maria. In the case of Florent-Claude, the vulva in question is that, also, of a Spanish girl – or *indignada*, as he describes her – encountered at a motorway service station in the province of Almería, which by remarkable coincidence Laurie Lee had also passed through in *As I Walked Out One Midsummer Morning*. Houellebecq himself is also not Spanish, but French, a traveller in a foreign land.

I play with the idea of writing a brief essay on Lee and Houellebecq, an analysis of how the of tropes of vulva and the motifs of disappearance are intertwined in their work. Would such an analytic, however, run the risk of contributing to "an entrenched cultural tradition that defines female genital morphology as absence and female sexuality as passive"?[26] Better to let the idea pass. Yet, for Houellebecq, it is not vulva as such that arouses Florent-Claude's disappearance but, more accurately, the "frank but depilated pussy"[27] that he ascribes to the *indignada* encountered at the service station in Almería, which like that of Doña Maria, is only imagined yet engenders his disappearance. I have to search Google for the term "depilated," confusing it too easily with "dilapidated." Clearly, we have different imaginaries, Houellebecq and I, because in mine Doña Maria was most certainly hirsute.

Nevertheless, what a remarkable coincidence of these imaginary passages through Almería and what a remarkable intertwinement of these images of Doña's vulva and the *indignada*'s "pussy," here and now, finally, in 2020. This intertwinement occurs somewhere in my brain, not necessarily in the third frontal convolution of the left hemisphere – even though, of course, these two images are indissolubly bound up with language, with names and words – but somewhere else, locatable, mappable, that ought to be of great interest to the science of both aphasia and aphanisis.

Brain imaging studies tell us that there is a "face area" of the brain where neural activity occurs regardless of whether the face in question is real and encountered or is imagined.[28] The face area in the brain becomes active whenever we either see a face for real or imagine a face just for ourselves. In both instances, the brain creates a face. Could it be the same for other zones of the body, or does this neural truth apply only to faces?

For the neuroscientists, however, there is a difference between these two kinds of images since, in encountering a real face, the brain has to continually revise its image on account of the ways that this face escapes its imaginary model. The imagined face, in contrast, does not err. It appears to me and requires no revision. It is perfect in itself. For some in neuroscience, this occurrence indicates the "utterly uncreative" nature of imagination because it has "no errors to resolve."[29] The act of revision that goes on in the encounter with real faces is what makes reality the creative space that it is said to be, whereas imagination is a dead space, they claim, filled with lifeless forms, which appear and demand little of us.

In the erotic encounter, the face is always a sign that leads, pointing toward the potential for disappearance, very quickly, almost automatically, but not quite. André Breton describes the speed of this movement within himself very well in his recollection of an encounter on 5 April 1931 with a young woman in a cafe at Place Blanche in Paris. Meeting the woman's gaze, he surveys her body "from head to toe" as her rapidly swung leg slowly reveals itself, forcing the gaze to produce the image of a "dark and dazzling friend"[30] – a woman who offered him neither figs nor cider but pickles.[31]

When Breton encountered this friend and her pickles, it was in the context of his search for a way out of the loss of love, an anguish resulting from the disappearance of a woman he does not name.[32] He recounts very well the experience of a peculiar kind of anguish, the interrogation of one's own desire, when trying to replace one lost love with the bodies to be dredged from the sea of others who surround us when the umwelt that one has taken for granted has disappeared. He accounts for the ways that we try to "chase away the image" of a lost love by replacing it with images of others whom we do not love but can have.[33] He knows the disappointment of this image when it does not link up with the face that is the sign pointing toward a happy disappearance. We ought not to underestimate the profundity of these linkages.

2022

It is the Autumn of 2022, and I am at home in Finnish Lapland, with aphanisis, mother of aphasia. It is here in this umbra that I elect to disappear, between sun and moon, while beholding her visage – a face that bears all the signs of an image of the potential disappearance that I first learned to associate with Almería. It is here in this shadow space that this self becomes subject. I am far from the summer of 1985, yet I am here in Almería, where I was then, the place in which I first learned the practice, and mastered the technology, of disappearance.

NOTES

1 Jacques Lacan, *The Four Fundamental Concepts of Psycho-Analysis* (London: Karnac, 2004), 218–21.
2 Ibid., 207.
3 Ibid., 208.
4 Ibid., 214.
5 Ibid., 235.
6 Michel Foucault, *The Care of the Self* (London: Penguin, 1990).
7 David Anson Lee, "Paul Broca and the History of Aphasia," *Neurology* 31, no. 5 (1981): 600–2.
8 Ferdinand de Saussure, *Course in General Linguistics* (London: Bloomsbury, 2013).
9 Alice Lagaay, "Between Sound and Silence: Voice in the History of Psychoanalysis," *Episteme* 1, no. 1 (2008): 53–62 at 57.
10 Ibid., 58.
11 Alain Badiou, *Theory of the Subject* (London: Continuum, 2009), 53–65.

12 Chantal Meza, *Since the Beginning*, https://www.chantal-meza.com/stateofdisappearance.
13 Novalis, *Philosophical Writings* (Albany: State University of New York Press, 1997), 66.
14 Jacques Lacan, *Feminine Sexuality: Jacques Lacan and the École Freudienne* (New York: Norton, 1985), 113.
15 Michel Foucault, "On the Ways of Writing History," in *The Essential Works of Michel Foucault, 1954–1984*, vol. 2, *Aesthetics, Method, Epistemology*, ed. James D. Faubion, 279–96 (New York: New Press, 1998), 290.
16 Paul Virilio, *Aesthetics of Disappearance* (New York: Semiotext(e), 1991), 9.
17 Ibid., 19.
18 Gilles Deleuze, *Cinema 2: The Time-Image* (London: Athlone, 1989).
19 Gilles Deleuze and Félix Guattari, *A Thousand Plateaus: Capitalism and Schizophrenia* (London: Athlone, 1999), 391.
20 Ibid. 381.
21 Foucault, *Care of the Self.*
22 Novalis, *Philosophical Writings*, 45–6.
23 James Miller, *The Passion of Michel Foucault* (New York: Bantam, 1994).
24 Michel Foucault, "Writing the Self," in *Foucault and his Interlocutors*, ed. Arnold Ira Davidson, 234–47 (Chicago and London: Chicago University Press, 1997).
25 Michel Houellebecq, *Serotonin* (London: William Heinemann, 2019).
26 Emma Heaney, *The New Woman: Literary Feminism, Queer Theory and the Trans Feminine Allegory* (Evanston, IL: Northwestern University Press, 2017), 160.
27 Houellebecq, *Serotonin*, 16.
28 Chris Frith, *Making Up the Mind: How the Brain Creates Our World* (Oxford: Blackwell, 2007), 136.
29 Ibid., 137.
30 André Breton, *Communicating Vessels* (Lincoln: University of Nebraska Press, 1990), 65–76.
31 Ibid., 79.
32 Ibid., 67.
33 Ibid., 69.

12

D—nce

Gil Anidjar

PRELUDE: KANT'S ELASTIC CRITIQUE

> An elastic ball [*eine elastische Kugel*] that strikes another one in a straight line communicates to the other its whole motion, hence its whole state (if one looks only at their positions in space). Now assuming substances, on the analogy with such bodies [*mit dergleichen Körpern*], in which representations, together with consciousness of them, flow one to another, a whole series of these substances may be thought, of which the first would communicate its state, together with its consciousness, to the second, which would communicate its own state, together with that of the previous substance, to a third substance, and this in turn would share the states of all previous ones, together with their consciousness and its own. The last substance would thus be conscious of all the states of all the previously altered substances as its own states, because these states would have been carried over to it, together with the consciousness of them; and in spite of this it would not have been the very same person in all these states.[1]

THE PAINTER'S DANCE

It is a stereotype, a fiction of sorts, that has been seen nonetheless a thousand times. Facing a wall or a canvas – sometimes it is a ceiling or else the floor – the painter is holding a brush and possibly a palette. Left hand, right hand. Both are raised and move at changing heights, following the exigencies of the moment. Armed with the brush, one hand grasping tightly or loosely, the arm rises, extends and folds, wrist, elbow, shoulder. The posture changes, however slowly or minutely, in a kind of balancing act. Thus, in his *Anthropologie du geste*, Marcel Jousse refers to "un certain mouvement

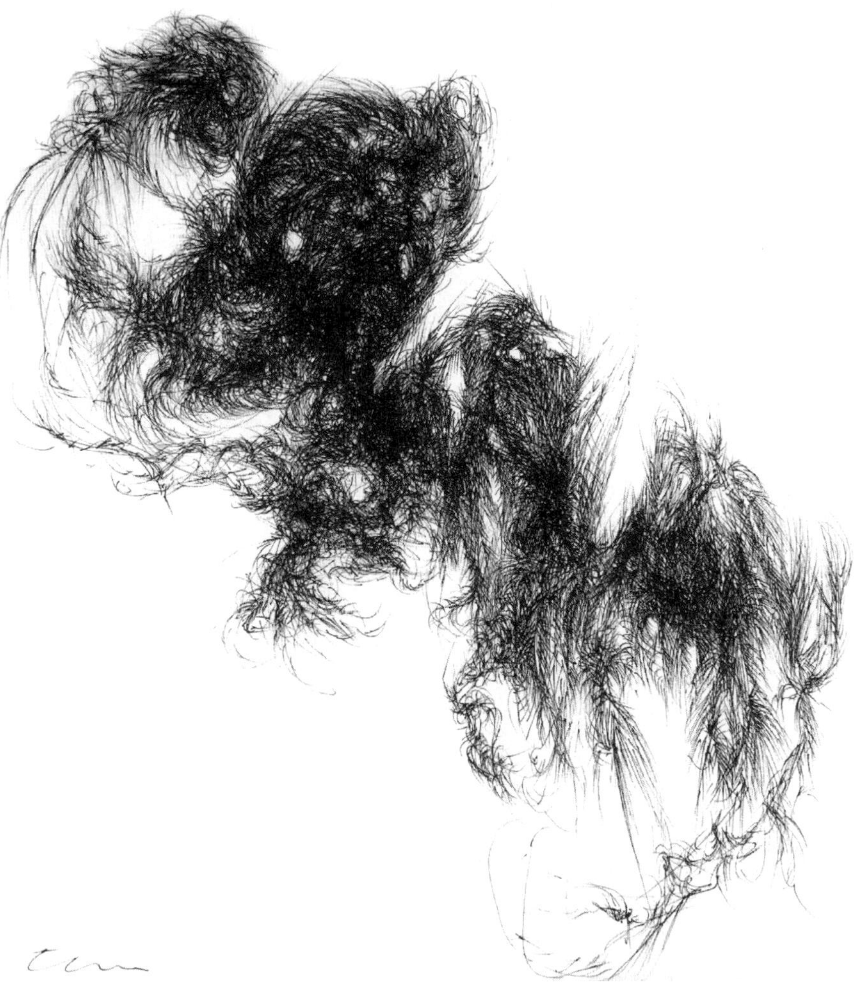

Chantal Meza, *Apparitions XXI*, 2017, ink on paper, 35 x 27 cm

oscillant" shared by the painter and the sculptor alike as each encounters and confronts the artist's work and the world.[2] Prior training, however informal, and ingrained habits are, in any case, rehearsed or reformed, transformed. (Pascal Quignard recalls Paul Klee as a model of sorts, who although right-handed, forced his left hand into painting service.)[3] For some, a ladder is needed, some sort of scaffolding. Sometimes there is crouching down to the ground. The feet, in any case, are rarely idle, and rarely parallel, more likely starting at an angle, recalling ballet's fourth position, or possibly fencing. The painter is ready to step forward, back, away, or aside, which will have to happen. The head follows the eyes, the legs, the hands, and the arms, too, and it communicates force and energy, contributing its own dynamic to the painter's dance.

One has seen it a thousand times, in movies and photographs, in paintings and paint dancing, too, yet it is among the first things to disappear. Ubiquitous as it is, dance always disappears. And ever more so, perhaps, since Eadweard Muybridge's so-called "motion studies," which is to say, since "appearances that were once as fluid as water running through one's fingers became solid objects."[4] But we are yet to linger on painting as a set or subset of such "techniques of the body," techniques of the moving body (assuming there are other kinds).[5] "The painter paints with the whole body," explains Kélina Gotman, "and in that respect this activity is theatre, choreography."[6] Painting, then, is dancing, "a body making images of itself," as Kimerer L. Lamothe has it.[7] It "only exists during a manifestation devoted to its own disappearance."[8] It is an art of the ephemeral, a practice of disappearance.[9]

Art critics and historians will no doubt persuade us of their ability to reconstruct basic gestures, a particular grasp, the movement and direction of the stroke, the blending of the colours, the intensity of the light, the temporality of the layers, the nature and origin of the materials, the dating of the work. They might even find the actual brushes or unused canvases, the original setting, but they will never quite present us with the painter as shape-shifter, with the painter's participation and involvement – from the Latin *in volvere* (to roll in) – in what Aimee Meredith Cox calls "the choreography of citizenship." (As with labour, the division of the arts, if it is the arts that we are speaking of, is the history of race, class, and gender.) Concerned with "the map of movement or plan for how the body interacts with its environment," Cox insists on widening the frame, on recalling that "choreography is shapeshifting made visible" since "by the body's placement in a space, the nature of that space changes."[10] Hence the nature of the body, or bodies. Shape-shifting – dancing – is thus inextricable from the completed art work, even if no viewing will ever provide an account of the transformations, the stretches and contortions, genuflections and repetitions, time after time imposed upon themselves (upon others, too) by painters. Or by rulers. Thus, for Michel Foucault, famously commenting on Diego Velázquez, by the time we look at the work, everything is as if "all the figures whose alternation, reciprocal exclusion, interweaving and fluttering one imagined (the model, the painter, the king, the spectator) suddenly stopped their imperceptible dance, immobilized into one substantial figure."[11] But such arresting and arrested (albeit importantly, collective) metamorphosis – or disappearance – is only the last of a long succession, one that, an essential if neglected part of the vanishing history of movement and dance, of political dance (model, painter, king, spectator), would merit patient and intensive comparisons with that other *Marionettentheater*,[12] the body work, the *commotion*, of musicians, the training of sculptors, the athleticism of scribes and poets, the gymnastics and gesticulations of pantomimes – "techniques for disciplining bodies, and governing them onstage" and offstage, too.[13]

There remains – for now – a more *visible* dance, one made luminously manifest, for instance, in Chantal Meza's series of paintings aptly named *Apparitions*, but elsewhere as well.[14] Contrary to Foucault's account, one can easily observe that there is dancing there, accelerations and decelerations, traces or archives of the painter's dance, moments and movements of the spectator (of "the eye and the spirit," as Maurice Merleau-Ponty has it),[15] older animal dances ("who is beast?" Meza rightly asks as she paints), hunting dances, and also war dances, rehearsal and repetitions, vanishing stages of a pained evolution, of ossified or loosened, living and dying rituals, suspended metamorphoses, fleeting and conflicting scenes of a series in formation. States – and stages – of disappearance. Or d—ance.

"*Increase packs*," Elias Canetti wrote, as though commenting on the painter's dance in its generalizability, "are formed so that the group itself, or the living beings, whether plants or animals, with which it is associated, should become *more*."[16] In their metamorphoses, "they dance fire itself; they become fire."[17] And there is indeed an increase and an intensification: "What they lack in numbers the dancers make up in intensity."[18] One may discern therein further intimations of a collective, the mode of emergence – the motions and commotions – of a political movement.

POLITICAL MOVEMENT

There is a moment in the Platonic dialogues that has rightly caused some (mostly philosophical) astonishment. Socrates is revisiting the *politeia* described in *The Republic*, and he confesses to feelings of frustration. It is as though, Socrates says, one were gazing upon "magnificent-looking animals, whether they're animals in a painting or even alive but standing still."[19] What is frustrating, what is missing – in painting, in sculpture, and in writing, too – is movement. One finds oneself longing, Socrates goes on to say, longing for movement, wanting to observe these animals "in motion or engaged in some struggle or conflict ... I felt the same thing about the city we've described." What Socrates would want, then, what he would love, is to hear someone attend to the polis in motion, which means, for him, a city "in a contest with other cities ... I'd love to see our city distinguish itself in the way it goes to war and in the way it pursues the war."[20]

Thinking about politics – and about the arts – Socrates yearned for movement. He wished, strange as it might appear, for war. In this desire, Socrates was not unlike many after him who, exhaustively and exhaustingly, elaborated on the relation of politics to war. He was certainly prefiguring those who, increasingly since Thomas Hobbes formulated his "politics of motion," joined Carl von Clausewitz, Carl Schmitt, and more recently, Paul Virilio and Peter Sloterdijk (and their distinct retrievals of Ernst Jünger's "mobilization") in their preoccupation with war and movement.[21] As Claudia Baracchi underscores in a reading that restores movement to the centre of Plato's thought, "warfare presents itself as the most extreme, most remarkable figure of motion."[22] Attending as well to *Timaeus*, Nicole Loraux asks about the nature of that war, arguing that movement, the movement of politics and politics as movement, marks in fact a strange void in political thought,[23] for if there is a longing for movement in *Timaeus*, it is one that is, as it were, covered over with a different desire, a wish for persistence and perdurance, and for stability. Socrates may have longed for movement, then, because movement, although ubiquitous (and so well beyond war), is occluded as it disappears from necessarily static depictions and theorizations, and from political consciousness, too, under layers of repression and forgetting, particularly so in the history of democracy.

The word that, for Loraux, signals and summarizes at once the inescapability of political movement as well as its negation, its forgetting and repression, is the Greek word *stasis*, from which derive, in European languages, terms like "state" and "status" but also "stand" and "stance." In Greek, such associations evoked, as in English, the propensity one might have to adopt a stance and take or make a stand – to join, therefore, a faction, to engage in factional politics, and ultimately, to go to war, civil war. Loraux traces, in a truly remarkable way, the vicissitudes of *stasis* in Greek political thought and beyond. Of all political constitutions and regimes, Loraux argues, democracy singularly enacts the very inescapability of movement, of motion as division, the proliferation of postures and stances that hover, in ever so fragile equilibrium, a tense and uncertain (if not always gracious) suspension over the edge of civil war.

Who better than Hobbes has named this predicament? Who more than him – and ever since – has wished to repress into oblivion, into an archaic past, its permanent possibility? In physics and in politics, Hobbes paradoxically imagined nothing but bodies in motion, not all of which, Adriana Cavarero shows, are "equal wolves ... able to attack each other in turn."[24] We shall have to return to the "maternal dominion" identified by Hobbes in its relation to movement and to civil war. For now, let us consider that, like Socrates, and closer to Aristotle than he might have liked, Hobbes was also seeing and conceiving of bodies at war and of bodies at rest. By way of this general division – this *stasis*, which, oscillating, is not yet, or not only, a civil war (between, say, the active and the contemplative) – one might account for much, if not most, of political philosophy. And particularly so in its relation to the arts, graphic or rhetorical. Recall that Socrates wanted to see the city – and magnificent looking animals depicted in painting and elsewhere – in motion. What might therefore become apparent is that one particular practice, a privileged engagement with movement, which we tend to think of and frame as "artistic," might have offered itself as a particularly fruitful, perhaps universal, resource to reflect on bodies, political bodies, in motion or at rest, in peace and at war, in fragile equilibrium or in infrequently gracious suspension. I refer, of course, to dance.

The Greeks spoke of *mousikē*, which Jean-Jacques Rousseau and Friedrich Nietzsche knew, and Thanos Zartaloudis recently recalled, corresponded to "the mixture of dance, song, and word" and "was a key component of 'ritual' practice and social ordering."[25] Now, as Zartaloudis insists, "it would be anachronistic to perceive the wide practice of *mousikē* as 'artistic,' since *mousikē* forms (orders) activities and events as varied as civic celebratory *ēthos* or military formations in war."[26] Still, like Aristotle (and like Rousseau and John Dewey) after him, Plato thought much about dance, about dance and civic – which is to say, martial as well – education, about dance and political life. Havelock Ellis reports how "it has been said that dancing and music lay at the foundation of the whole political and military as well as religious organisation of the Dorian states."[27] There was ambivalence, too, most manifest perhaps in the allegory of the cave, where, Baracchi explains, "puppet-handlers" stage a permanent shadow play. These "makers of wonders ... do not share their ability to move" with the cave dwellers, although they do "produce, by their movement, immobility."[28] The puppeteers' projection is the original stage dance, the first "deceptive play [with] the function of keeping the others bound to the ground," in place and in chains. Other grounds, other choreographies, are possible.

But with few exceptions, dance – as opposed to healing and seafaring, sheep herding and other martial or even mechanical, if always bodily, elaborations – never moved front and centre in the (static or dynamic) conceptions and figurations of political thought and practice. One might be tempted to argue that, like *stasis* – and civil war and tumult, or as Hobbes called it, sedition – dance, which as we shall see is *ek-stasis*, simply failed to appear as political, but this argument would not be quite right. For just as *stasis*, Dimitris Vardoulakis underscores, signifies both stability and movement,[29] dance might be more accurately said to *disappear* from politics. Very much akin to the activities identified by Hannah Arendt, in which "the 'product' is identical with the performing act itself" and therefore goes the vanishing way of "action and speech," dance was among those occupations that "furnished ancient thinking with examples for the highest and greatest activities of man" – all arts of the ephemeral. Indeed, Arendt herself does refer, if only once, to "the performance of the dancer or play-actor."[30] Dance appears, therefore, but only to be forgotten or repressed. Notwithstanding partial, if pregnant, exceptions found in Adam Smith (whom Arendt explicitly indicts) or in Jean-Jacques Rousseau, Friedrich Schiller, Herbert Spencer, or Giorgio Agamben, dance insistently figures as a sideshow, a shadow play or a stage dance, that takes place, however paradoxically, backstage – one often identified, moreover, with madness, primitive savagery, or worse, "religion." ("I would only believe in a God who knew how to dance," said Nietzsche's Zarathustra.)[31] The political focus, when there is one, remains in any case on the provisional *display* of movement and on its aesthetic, and aestheticized, content. Such focus manifests and reinscribes a marked ambivalence, perhaps outright ignorance, toward "the frailty of human affairs" (as Arendt had it),[32] the ephemeral but impressive force of collective transport, the dangers of Dionysian ecstasy, the so-called "frenzied" – and again "religious" – movements, which Kélina Gotman brilliantly explores, reactivating and expanding on the old-new label "choreomania."[33] Surely, the witches' Sabbath, southern Italian *tarantismo*, the South African *go bina*, the Maori *haka*, the American Indian Ghost Dance, the Sudanese *Zār*, the agricultural dances that have left countless traces in cave paintings and across the ancient Mediterranean, as well as the raves of recent decades (not to speak of TikTok and Fortnite viral dances), are unlikely to be best understood under the single heading of "religious" dance, Dionysian orgiastic abandon, sexual or mystical revolution, or individual-denying "fascism." And so, beyond the specific practices rightly or wrongly identified as "dance" (or as "social dances"), what are we to make of the movements that shape, form, and transform, order and disorder, human (and nonhuman) bodies?

HUMAN FORMS

An awkward step aside, a question of uncertain footing and rhythm. The question is whether it is possible to follow in Giorgio Agamben's tracks and ask not about the human voice – "Is there a human voice, a voice that is the voice of man as the chirp is the voice of the cricket or the bray is the voice of the donkey? And, if it exists, is this voice language? What is the relationship between voice and language, between *phōnē* and *logos*?"[34] – but rather about the shape of the human body in its relation to movement. Does the human have a gait the way the horse ambles? Does it have a shape after the manner of a camel? And if it does have one, are that gait and shape what we might call *dance*? Is it not, as Randy Martin asks, "the gait of politics?"[35] Could we thus begin to ask about the relation between body and movement, between *sōma* and *chorea*? But if such a thing as a human shape, or movement, does not exist, if its grammar escapes us – notwithstanding Rudolf Laban's celebrated efforts to formulate a "theory of effort" and its relation "to the expressive qualities of the action, which are visible in the rhythm of body movement"[36] – what does that tell us about our understanding, about our bearing, of that notorious and persistent object we call "the human body" or simply "the body" in its relation to movement and to dance? To dance *as* politics?

My questions spring, as I have already intimated, from a disappearance. The disappearance of dance. As William H. McNeill marvelled not so long ago, dance is missing from major accounts of the origin of humankind.[37] From Charles Darwin to Sigmund Freud, from Thomas Hobbes to Michel Foucault and to (why not?) Yuval Noah Harari, it is as though dancing were less significant than, say, painting or language, narrowly conceived. Netta Yerushalmy summarizes: "Plenty of people think about visual art and literature as part of a larger cultural discourse, but they don't mobilize their thinking through dance. Dance is systematically marginalized both as a form of knowing and as a field worth turning attention to."[38] Even when included by Plato and Aristotle, by Rousseau, Schiller, or of course Nietzsche, dance is immediately caught in a second movement of disappearance. Dance is, after all, notorious for being *essentially disappearing*. In other words, if dance is an art, which is mostly as it appears in historical, philosophical, or political accounts, dance remains the art of the ephemeral. Strangely, even the interrogation of this persistent understanding of dance continues to conceive of dance as a matter of display, as primarily phenomenal, which is to say, as something that appears and is made visible to an audience ("Dancing addresses itself to the eye," is the way that Adam Smith hands this truth down to generations of seemingly unmovable thinkers.)[39]

What disappears – and this is a third moment or movement – is dance as a collective practice, dance as rehearsal and commotion, which, tweaking McNeill's phrase and making space for polyrhythms, might be understood and, indeed, lived as "moving together in time."[40] But what precisely is meant by collective practice? Or, as Dimitris Vardoulakis asks, commenting on "the mystery" of the political, "how many does it take to dance?"[41]

The insistent foregrounding of "the dancer's body" – where both terms are used repeatedly, almost exclusively, in the singular – involves yet another disappearance.[42] It is one that can be interrogated by pursuing the analogy of the voice. Recall the observations of the great linguist Roman Jakobson, who, elaborating on the work of Antoine Grégoire, recognized that in "the so-called babbling period," babies (whose very heads and limbs, we should recall, have been shaped and reshaped by countless swaddling and holding techniques) are "capable of producing all conceivable sounds."[43] As children go on to acquire the capacity for language, they *lose* the ability to produce sounds. More precisely, Jakobson explains, those innumerable sounds of which children are first capable "disappear from [their] inventory."[44] The distinction between loss and disappearance is however crucial since, with hard work, the sounds *can* be recovered. They have not been lost as much as they have been forgotten. They have, in other words, disappeared. One might say that they have been archived at a remove, made less accessible to retrieval. Like so many voices and languages, so many gestures and movements, *so many bodies* (infant and animal bodies, too) that we store and deploy, remember and forget, and of which we are capable, these sounds await retrieval and reactivation (one that may, of course, never come). Just as there is no unique sound but a plethora of sounds, available and remote, there is never a body, never only one body, but a plurality of bodies, that appear and disappear, move in and out of space and time, in and out of realms of capability and activity. A multiplicity of bodies that move and are moved and so, hence my argument, dance. Pascal Quignard summarizes: "Dance is the ek-stasy of the body exiting the body that precedes."[45] That is, "Dance calls upon the silent body that inhabits *all life* into another body that precedes – into another body that is no longer."[46] All movement, in other words, is collective movement.

Dancing bodies, then, whether squatting, walking, or leaping, whether fleeing, grasping, embracing, or striking – in one of Laban's formulations, bodies "thrust, slash, dab, flick, press, wring, glide, float"[47] – are only provisionally fit and healthy and are constantly aging. They are moving and changing bodies that recall and rehearse, reiterating shapes imprinted and archived within distinct registers of retrieval (imitation being of course an important mode thereof). It is a matter of manifesting and mobilizing "the body as both archive and artefact, both a space for the collection and recording of historical memory and remembrance and itself an expression of memory and re-membrance."[48] Thus we carry and activate (or not) these multiple bodies. We are differently able, and some of us indubitably carry fewer, having been shaped into rigid and unimaginative forms. We move in and out of them when we dance, which is to say, every time we move – or rest. However minutely we reach or gesture, we are and activate, we appear and disappear as the plural occurrence of those techniques of the body, techniques of the bodies, which Marcel Mauss (whose explicit treatment of dance was surprisingly swift, if otherwise generative) described so well, bodies *into which and out of which* techniques are impressed and expressed, limbs and postures are shaped, movements are lost and found, habits are learned and disappeared. Bodies or souls? Lucian tells of a "barbarian" who asked where the dancers were who would wear the numerous masks laid out on stage. When told that only one dancer would don each of them in turn, he exclaimed, "I did not realize, my friend, that though you have only this one body, you have many souls."[49] One body? A dancer?

Dancing, by which one would have to mean *generalized dancing*, is – as Stéphane Mallarmé and many since have recognized – an expansive kind of writing, one irreducible to the particular graph, or to the letter. Dancing is rather the movement that writing always already is. It is a movement of inscription and erasure, the very movement of *différance*, which Jacques Derrida insisted (if not necessarily successfully, judging by the reception) carries an unsettled difference between voice and writing.[50]

Dance would here again be eminently related to painting, the making of traces. In dance, appearance and disappearance, appearance as disappearance, and the logic or illogic of the vanishing trace left by the body as brush all emerge as pure movement. Which is to say, as Derrida had it, that because "the movement of the trace is necessarily occulted, it produces itself as self-occultation."[51] From the violence of the letter to the painter's dance and the frightening impeachability of the witness, the comparability of aesthetic gestures and practices, the multifarious impressions of and on the senses, are sustained and abolished by this movement, however fleetingly extended. At various levels of speed, and with increased acceleration in the time that remains, is it not the case that everything – speech, writing, dance, and painting – moves and disappears? Dance, one might suggest, would simply be another name for the generalized writing that Derrida also called *différance*, otherwise spelled "d—nce."

Derrida reminds us, of course, that sound might fail to resonate, that writing may fail to appear. The movement of this failure, of writing and of its phenomenality (but also lack thereof), corresponds in any case to the plurality of bodies that emerge and vanish in and out of our every gesture and movement. (The tactile dimension of sound might have to be recalled here as well.) And just as the dancers' bodies, independent of the number of dancers – the intensity of the increase pack – make and unmake the moving archive of the history of dance and, more proximately, of the particular choreography that they learn or enact, we who move and gesture, we who dance or paint, or pray, we activists and those who seem resolutely idle, we make, unmake, and remake the vanishing archives of movements that we have learned and unlearned. Thus we have Derrida, who "would like to believe in the masses, this indeterminable number of blended voices, this mobile of non-identified sexual marks whose choreography can carry, divide, multiply the body of each 'individual.'"[52] We many-bodied, of various ability and disability, are iterations of innumerable marks and graphological *spacings*. We are dancing.

We – for it is always a collective that dances – are disappearing.

THE PRIMAL HORDE

Like any origin story, it is mired in contradictions and impossibilities. In disappearances. The challenge is, once again, to account for movement, to acknowledge its force, to register its traces. We know how the story ends – which is to say, if we believe it, we know where we began – but we do not know how or, most importantly, when. We must account for a stage, which we trust must follow, yet we can only do so on the ground (!) of the consequence, the cause or condition of which is otherwise unavailable. If the end is in the beginning, the trajectory appears superfluous. If the beginning was as contingent as it seems, how did we get where we are? As Peter Fitzpatrick renders it, and do note the lexicon, Freud's "fantastic story … begins with a desolate stasis in which the savage 'primal horde' somehow exists under the complete sway of the father. This is a place of utter fixity where nothing can be other than what it is. Somehow, in this stilled scene, action erupts and the father is killed."[53] How does movement emerge out of fixity? How does stasis become *stasis*? In the beginning, Freud would be telling us, there was always already *stasis*, stability and movement. Indeed, as he recapitulates his debt to Darwin and to James J. Atkinson, Freud opens a surprising perspective on what the primal horde was doing, how it was moving, as it were, *before* the murder of the father, which allegedly sets everything in motion. Freud tells us that the murder happened "one day," although he also asks for some indulgence with regard to the temporal accuracy of such dating. One day, after many days, the brothers came to be united. And, "united, they had the courage to do and succeeded in doing what would have been impossible for them individually." The brothers first had to come together. In order for them to initiate the act that would bring about the beginnings of society, they had to become a society. They had to *organize* into a collective capable of concerted action. A rehearsed choreography. How did that come about? Freud speculates that "some cultural advance, perhaps, command over some new weapon, had given them a sense of superior strength."[54] As with Socrates, what marks the onset of movement is war, or at least the weapons of war, which is, in fact, movement. But the time of movement is also the movement of time. Freud quotes Atkinson, who explains that "strength was gained with time," that "combined attacks" were launched, "renewed again and again."[55] The brothers had to train for war. They had to learn the handling of weapons. They had to practise their movements. They had to rehearse moving together in time. The brothers had to dance. As would the sisters, one imagines.

Freud knew very well that dance was ubiquitous among the societies described or witnessed (the two often unrelated) by the scholars and missionaries of various anthropological persuasions, upon whom he was relying. As Barbara Ehrenreich expansively documents, "When Europeans undertook their campaigns of conquest and exploration in what seemed to them 'new' worlds, they found the natives engaged in many strange and lurid activities ... The European idea of the 'savage' came to focus on the image of painted and bizarrely costumed bodies, drumming and dancing with wild abandon by the light of a fire."[56] Accordingly, in *Totem and Taboo*, Freud early on refers to the way "clansmen represent or imitate the motions and attributes of their totem in ceremonial dances,"[57] hunting dances and war dances. More importantly, perhaps, Freud draws on the work of Sándor Ferenczi and what he describes as "an instance of *positive* totemism in a child."[58] The accuracy of the diagnostic is, no doubt, less interesting than the parallel Freud otherwise makes, whereby totemism involves a "superlatively ambivalent" attitude toward the totem – in this and many other cases, an animal that was at once an object of identification and the target of murderous violence. The slaughter "was a regular festival" for the child, who "would dance round the animals' bodies for hours at a time in a state of intense excitement."[59] As Freud goes on to elaborate, drawing this time on Robertson Smith, "the sacrificial feast was an occasion on which individuals rose joyously above their own interests and stressed the mutual dependence existing between one another and their god."[60] Dance, which may or may not be restricted to the rehearsal of sacrificial violence or of war, is the concerted activity, the movement and rest, or *stasis*, of a collective "self" – "I did not realize, my friend, that though you have only this one body, you have many souls"[61] – acting together in time, in rhythm and polyrhythms. One body and many souls, or – if one continues to abide by that implausible division – one soul (*anima*) moving multiple bodies.

DISCORDANCE: ELASTIC CRITIQUE 2

Far from Rousseau's *fêtes* and the concord and harmony ruling them (even if Rousseau made room, elsewhere still, for civil war), and far from the "ordering of freedom," from the "administration" and "securitization" of movement that, Hagar Kotef argues, define liberalism, among other "regimes of movement,"[62] Albert Memmi reminded us that colonialism, for one, is a dance. More precisely, the colonizer – a collective noun, obviously – is furiously engaged in a "tormented dance."[63] The lesson, political and choreological at once, bears repeating: as with labour, the division of the arts – the art of politics and the art of dancing – recapitulates the history of race, class, and gender. And this lesson may be revealed as having greater import when we consider that, prior to his famous "portraits" of both colonizer and colonized, Memmi had written on dance in a striking chapter of his largely autobiographical novel *The Pillar of Salt*.[64] What Memmi writes there, we shall witness, very much resonates with Loraux's meditations on *stasis*, for dance is what takes place not only between the dancer and the dance (as William Butler Yeats has it)[65] but also – we have learned from *stasis* – between those who move and dance and those who allegedly do not or do so too much (call them spectators, traitors, or even "lazy," and also, of course, "frenzied" Natives, or as Heinrich Heine did, Atta Troll).[66] The movement, but it is many, involves at once the perdurance of dance and its violent arrest, the attempt, if failed, to extricate the self from the midst – indeed, from the movements – of one's "own" tormented bodies. The critical kinetics of vanishing elastic balls.

"The Dance," as Memmi's chapter is called, begins under the sign of dissension and its forgetting, as "a mystery that made [the women of the house] forget all their dissensions." For the duration of the chapter, dissension will never abate, nor will its forgetting bring accord, harmony, or *communitas*. In fact, the forgetting of dissension seems immediately to generate and exacerbate further internal and external tensions, between emotion and appearance, poise and exuberance. Thus the women "tried to remain solemn ... but were too excited to be able to conceal their wild childish happiness." As this depiction makes evident, a major and unrelenting site of dissension and tension will remain the ethno-psychiatric gaze of the narrator upon the characters that crowd the chapter – first of all, upon "hysterical" women, "Negro musicians," and of course, "demons!" True to the "dance pathologies" attended to by Felicia McCarren and Kélina Gotman, the narrator pathologizes and racializes everything that he sees and depicts, himself included.[67] The truth of the painting, the truth of the generalized, and tormented, dancing is not at all diminished thereby.

A dance is being planned, "une dance invocatoire" and "the sacrifice of a live white cock," too, all "for the purpose of exorcizing and saving" a possessed aunt who, unhappily married – and widowed – "became hysterical" and returned to her brothers' home with two sick children. The repeated and uncontrollable movement of bodies – dissension – first affects that same woman, Aunt Maissa, who regularly "swoons away, collapsing on the ground and foaming at the mouth while her arms and legs beat the air like those of a sick mare," later uttering "frightful screams" and, with increasing frequency, "falling in the stairway too, rolling down whole flights of stairs." Maissa's body – its discordant iterations of uncontrollable, animal, and demonic bodies – is obviously foregrounded. Even when she, too, tries to conceal herself, it is "eloquently betrayed by her feverish glances and her uneasy hands." For the women, the "mysterious" explanation for her condition is that Maissa is "possessed of spirits, *possédée par les djenoun*."

These are very much moving and dancing spirits, which one should be careful of naming, for fear of being moved, pushed and thrown, by them. Still, active members of the polity, they are named and called "the damned" or "the dwellers beneath the earth." They are obviously chthonic spirits, "divinities from beneath the earth's surface," beings who are "exiled in perpetual darkness … vicious and cruel," who make their presence felt by kinesis, inflicting violence and acute cases of bodily fragmentation and division. "They like to pierce eyes, to afflict with madness, to twist bones, to paralyze limbs, even to kill." These demons must be appeased and their protection must therefore be invoked – by way of further excess of collective movement, a dance.

The dissension or discordance that rules the scene and the characters affects everything and everyone – first of all, the narrator's mother, to whom she shall return, and whose ease in spontaneous lying ("without much forethought"), whose "constant and futile untruthfulness," is a source of great emotion and commotion, of manifest alienation and great exasperation, of internal discord: "I generally had to pocket my ill temper as best I could." Dissension is at once internal and external to the narrator, who, following the protocols laid out by Kélina Gotman, seeks desperately to distance himself from a "barbaric" past he nevertheless carries. "I have never liked this kind of gathering," he says, repeatedly asserting a desire to forget his own cautious, even fearful, but deep relation to the very "evil spirits" and nonsense occupying "the minds of crazy old women." These "strange old wives' tales" are upsetting and synesthetic, kinesthetic. They are memories filled with disturbing images and scents, magical scents, with incantations sung by his mother that "continued to provoke in me some nervous reactions that no reasoning was ever able to dispel." Having found some refuge in "reliable scientific sources," the narrator still feels nervous and uneasy. He continues to be moved, forced to move further, to take his distance from the ceremony that is about to take place. He finds some calm in the company of a friend whose violin practice is soothing, even boring. "I must admit that Western music rather bored me … I generally had a hard time trying to avoid finding it monotonous and oversophisticated," he confesses. Having escaped the "dance ceremony dedicated to the *Djnoun*," he appears bound to it nevertheless, as he admits enjoying "only those pieces that have a fast rhythm, where the pace is more important than the intellectual content, so that I found myself carried away by the muscular tension. I thus enjoyed music when, far from encouraging me to meditate, it invited me to dance."

Still, he acknowledges in his friend's violin "a wise moderator, a mathematician of sounds, the expression of a civilization of men who had become masters of the world." He finds calm, then, "absolute calm," in studious reading and looking out a window. "The park was motionless, as if ill at ease, watching out for the storm that threatened … The whole room seemed to be seized by this absolute calm." By the time he returns home, believing the dance to be over, he is however greeted by "the wild music of tambourines and flutes … a violent cacophony of cymbals that sounded strangely explosive … The whole band was in a frenzy … The door was literally vibrating." But no one is there to open the house's door, and the narrator must reluctantly enter the space of the dance, a downstairs apartment, perhaps another continent, where "the air seemed tropical, damp and warm, heavy with human breath and incense." He encounters there a packed crowd, a "throng of women, all of them familiar faces, aunts, cousins, neighbors, but each one of them now a stranger under the spell that had overcome her. They stood there motionless, their hair disheveled, their eyes aglow, rigid as statues, or perhaps like stupid cows that I had to push aside." In the frenzied space of the dance, there is of course multifarious movement, and immobility, too, the rigidity of statues whose animation one awaits or fears. The narrator pushes through, looking, as Atta Troll does, for his mother. "The closer I seemed to get to the heart of all this mysterious din, the more crowded it was. The women who were watching were treading on each other's feet, almost melting into a mass of compact flesh." In the tumultuous space of the dance, everything seems to disappear. "The noise was so loud, so full, that I seemed no longer to hear anything at all. One moment I felt I was in sheer void, with no shapes or sounds around me any longer."

At the centre of this space, which is also a void (*chora*),[68] the narrator finds yet another, perhaps demonic, figure of discordance, "the strange creature that haunted this place. A woman dressed in gaudy veils, was dancing wildly, throwing out her arms, jerking her head back and forth with so violent a motion that it hurt my neck to watch her." Her hair "like tangled black serpents," she moves or is moved by the rhythm that "the terrifying Negro musicians" are playing. "There they are, I thought, the demons! But this was only a half-hearted joke ... These men, I was sure, were no simulators; possessed by ancestral rhythms, they were repeating gestures and ritual that, in their childhood or in their distant homeland, had left deep marks upon them, scars on their cheeks that had been incised to impose on them, for all time, a hideous grimace." But the woman? Not a "simulator" either, for is she not "a sensible housewife, with children who went to school"? Yet is she not "allowing herself to become hysterical, limp as a rag, a jointless doll tossed back and forth, without any conscience"? She is bodies in motion. And so, moved by and moving between "a frenzy of revolt" and the "anxious motionlessness" of "the crowded women," the narrator finds himself "disarmed," with and without emotions, oddly prevented "from flying into a rage." Soon, in any case, he anticipates being "seized by nervous spasms," just like the surrounding crowd, and just like the dancer, who is herself "overcome by her seizures that seemed to tear her apart. Her arms and legs and head, each one moving in a different direction, appeared to respond to contradictory impulses, going off madly at cross purposes, as if trying to tear themselves away from the body." In the general discordance, which here reaches its culmination, there is a "dreadful struggle" that is being conducted, "against rhythm, against the demons." And suddenly, a revelation. "Suddenly, the crazy dancer turned toward me – my mother, she was my own mother!"

Unrecognizable and all-too recognizable, the narrator's mother has too many bodies, too many faces. She is the face of dance, of course, and the face of the savage unknown. "Was this really my mother's face, this primitive mask, glazed with sweat, with its disheveled hair, eyes tightly closed, lips all bloodless?" He repeats to himself, "'She's my mother, my mother,' as if these mere words could re-establish the lost contact and express all the affection that they should contain. But the words refused to adapt themselves to the barbaric apparition in its strange costume." The narrator has lost and forgotten the mother he knew, for she is many. He can recall only the mothers – yes, mothers – he learned about in his books (and the dancer is unlike any of them). He is literally torn, alienated from himself and from her, although moved by an "obscure emotion" that seems otherwise oddly recognizable. Fear and desire, forsakenness. Oedipus or Jesus? The transparent dream of a not so opaque dance. "My God, my God," he says, "I'm afraid even of my own mother, even my mother has ceased to seem familiar and understandable to me! This must be what a man feels when he awakes at dawn and sees besides him the face of an unknown woman, sealed within her dreams that he can never penetrate, the face of an unknown woman by whose side he has chanced to sleep." More importantly, perhaps, he experiences a loss and a proliferation of parts, a profound estrangement, a deep discordance that is at once external and internal. "She was a stranger to me now, my mother, a part of myself become alien to me and thrust into the heart of a primitive continent." The mother, a dark continent. A demon or a ghost of dance. "What somber ties still bound me to this ghost, and how shall I ever manage to return from the abyss into which she is now dragging me?" Still referring to her as "the dancer," he returns to her and to the abyss. He describes how "she seems to explode, torn apart as her limbs begin to cast themselves wildly all around her." The dance – "this collective seizure of epilepsy" – generates motion and immobility, an image of ruler and ruled, a polity in motion. "My mother obeys the rhythm, or is it the rhythm that rules her from within?" An energetic field is generated, a field of violence ("I felt like shouting insults at them, like beating them, beating with all my strength these women and musicians") and of paralysis ("but I was paralyzed"). The narrator is again moved and unmoved, wishing to do violence, to beat others and himself. "Perhaps I too should dance … until I lost consciousness after accepting these rhythms and beating my own head again and again with disjointed gestures, repeated until it continued to shake all by itself, as empty as a doll's head that moves as it follows its leaded pendulum, until my whole body became dislocated in all its joints … with all my consciousness vanished and my body disintegrated." In this *Marionettentheater*, in which he imagines his limbs torn apart and scattered "north, south, east, and west, throughout the sky and the earth," he finds himself "delirious" and feeling "like a puppet when the thread that guides it breaks," which leaves him "motionless" while "the other women continued their movements." Ultimately, the narrator takes flight. He runs away from the dance. Or does he?

"Had I really escaped?" he asks. "Will I ever manage to escape, from all these sounds and rhythms that live in the depth of my being and can immediately gain mastery over the beating of the blood in the arteries?" Having engaged in much studious effort, "filled with conscious rejection of Africa, must I now accept this self-evident truth, that all these ancient and monotonous melodies move me far more deeply than all the great music of Europe?" The torment is hardly cultural, although it remains marked as such. As is the inescapability of movement. "Yes, I suppose I am an incurable barbarian!" he declares.

Like Kant's elastic balls, we are – we move – possessed by other bodies. We are archives and witnesses of "movement's contagion,"[69] taking part in the communication of force among and between bodies, in the contagion of motion and motionlessness, *stasis*, such as described throughout "The

Dance." Dance is politics, and politics is dance. We forget that at our own peril, we who have learned to arrest our bodies and souls, to sit and watch (but after what strenuous disciplinary efforts!) instead of being moved and indeed moving. And still we are moved, and we move together in time. Polyrhythmic, dance is that which forms and deforms, shapes and reshapes. It is what moves a discordant collective of men, women, and otherwise gendered, colonizer and colonized, demons and humans, a polity of those who dance and those who do not, but who, moving and resting, are repeatedly made and unmade of and by *stasis*, by discordance. Or d—ance.

NOTES

1 Immanuel Kant, *Critique of Pure Reason*, trans. Paul Guyer and Allen W. Wood (Cambridge, UK: Cambridge University Press, 1998), 423.
2 Marcel Jousse, *L'anthropologie du geste* (Paris: Éditions Resma, 1969), 205.
3 Pascal Quignard, *L'origine de la danse* (Paris: Galilée, 2013), 55.
4 Rebecca Solnit, *River of Shadows: Eadweard Muybridge and the Technological Wild West* (New York: Penguin, 2003), 17.
5 Marcel Mauss, "Techniques of the Body," trans. Ben Brewster, *Economy and Society* 2, no. 1 (1973): 70–88.
6 Kélina Gotman, *Essays on Theatre and Change: Towards a Poetics Of* (London: Routledge, 2018), 39.
7 Kimerer L. Lamothe, *Nietzsche's Dancers: Isadora Duncan, Martha Graham, and the Revaluation of Christian Values* (New York: Palgrave, 2006), 27.
8 Jacques Rancière, "The Dance of Light," in *Aisthesis: Scenes from the Aesthetic Regime of Art*, trans. Zakir Paul, 93–109 (London: Verso, 2013), 108.
9 José Gil mentions "the old cliché" of dance as "an art of the ephemeral." He proposes "virtual" as an alternative. José Gil, "Dancer's Body," in *A Shock to Thought: Expression after Deleuze and Guattari*, ed. Brian Massumi, 117–28 (London: Routledge, 2002), 125.
10 Aimee Meredith Cox, *Shapeshifters: Black Girls and the Choreography of Citizenship* (Durham, NC: Duke University Press, 2015), 28–9.
11 Michel Foucault, *The Order of Things: An Archaeology of the Human Sciences* (London: Routledge, 2002), 340.
12 Heinrich von Kleist, "On the Marionette Theater," trans. Thomas G. Neumiller, *Drama Review* 16, no. 3 (1972): 22–6.
13 David Kishik, "The Work of Dance in the Age of Sacred Lives," in *The Power of Life: Agamben and the Coming Politics (To Imagine a Form of Life, II)*, 17–32 (Stanford, CA: Stanford University Press, 2012), 29.

14 Chantal Meza, *Apparitions*, https://www.chantal-meza.com/stateofdisappearance.
15 Maurice Merleau-Ponty, *L'œil et l'esprit* (Paris: Gallimard, 1964).
16 Elias Canetti, *Crowds and Power*, trans. Carol Stewart (New York: Continuum, 1981), 95, original emphasis.
17 Ibid., 78.
18 Ibid., 31.
19 Plato, *Timaeus*, trans. Donald J. Zeyl (Indianapolis: Hackett, 2000), 4.
20 Ibid.
21 Thomas A. Spragens Jr, *The Politics of Motion: The World of Thomas Hobbes* (Lexington: University Press of Kentucky, 1973); Paul Virilio, *Speed and Politics*, trans. Marc Polizzotti (Los Angeles: Semiotext(e), 2006); Peter Sloterdijk, *Infinite Mobilization: Towards a Critique of Political Kinetics*, trans. Sandra Berjan (Cambridge, UK: Polity, 2020).
22 Claudia Baracchi, *Of Myth, Life, and War in Plato's Republic* (Bloomington: Indiana University Press, 2002), 137.
23 Nicole Loraux, *The Divided City: On Memory and Forgetting in Ancient Athens*, trans. Corinne Pache and Jeff Fort (New York: Zone Books, 2006).
24 Adriana Cavarero, *Horrorism: Naming Contemporary Violence*, trans. William McCuaig (New York: Columbia University Press, 2010), 22–3.
25 Thanos Zartaloudis, *The Birth of Nomos* (Edinburgh: Edinburgh University Press, 2019), 342.
26 Ibid., 343.
27 Havelock Ellis, *The Dance of Life* (Cambridge, MA: Riverside, 1923), 64.
28 Baracchi, *Of Myth*, 30.
29 Dimitris Vardoulakis, *Stasis before the State: Nine Theses on Agonistic Democracy* (New York: Fordham University Press, 2018).
30 Hannah Arendt, *The Human Condition* (Chicago: University of Chicago Press, 1998), 207.
31 Friedrich Nietzsche, *Thus Spake Zarathustra*, trans. Graham Parkes (Oxford: Oxford University Press, 2005), 36, translation altered.
32 Arendt, *Human Condition*.
33 Kélina Gotman, *Choreomania: Dance and Disorder* (Oxford: Oxford University Press, 2018).
34 Giorgio Agamben, *Infancy and History: Essays on the Destruction of Experience*, trans. Liz Heron (London: Verso, 1993), 3.
35 Randy Martin, "Dance as a Social Movement," *Social Text*, no. 12 (1985), 54–70 at 59.
36 Susanne Franco, "Energy, Eukinetics, and Effort: Rudolf Laban's Vision of Work and Dance," in *Energy and Forces as Aesthetic Interventions*, ed.

Sabine Huschka and Barbara Gronau (Bielefeld: transcript Verlag, 2019), 159.

37 William H. McNeill, *Moving Together in Time: Dance and Drill in Human History* (Cambridge, MA: Harvard University Press, 1998).

38 In Jack Halberstam, "Netta Yerushalmy by Jack Halberstam," interview, *Bomb*, 29 April 2020, https://bombmagazine.org/articles/netta-yerushalmy.

39 Adam Smith, "Of the Nature of That Imitation Which Takes Place in What Are Called the Imitative Arts," in *Essays on Philosophical Subjects*, 109–52 (London: J. Richardson, 1822), 125.

40 McNeill, *Moving Together in Time.*

41 Dimitris Vardoulakis, "How Many Does It Take to Dance? The Mystery of the Political in G.K. Chesterton," *Paragraph* 40, no. 2 (2017): 174–92.

42 José Gil's phrase is only partly misleading, as he does insist that "the body of all dancers" would be "composed of a multiplicity of virtual bodies." Gil, "Dancer's Body," 123.

43 Roman Jakobson, *Child Language, Aphasia, and Phonological Universals* (The Hague: Mouton, 1968), 21.

44 Ibid., 22.

45 Quignard, *L'origine de la danse*, 72, my translation.

46 Ibid., 76, original emphasis, my translation.

47 Rudolf Laban, *The Mastery of Movement*, ed. Lisa Ullmann (Alton, UK: Dance Books, 2011), 69.

48 Carol Marie Webster, "*Chat to Mi Back:* Meditation on Body Archive," *Journal of Dance and Somatic Practices* 11, no. 1 (2019): 49–66 at 51.

49 Lucian, *The Dance,* trans. A.M. Harmon (Cambridge, MA: Harvard University Press, 1938), 66.

50 Jacques Derrida, *Writing and Difference*, trans. Alan Bass (Chicago: University of Chicago Press, 1978).

51 Jacques Derrida, *Of Grammatology*, trans. Gayatri Chakravorty Spivak (Baltimore, MD: Johns Hopkins University Press, 1997), 47.

52 Jacques Derrida, "Choreographies," trans. Christie V. McDonald, in *Points …: Interviews, 1974–1994*, ed. Elisabeth Weber, 89–108 (Stanford, CA: Stanford University Press, 1995), 108.

53 Peter Fitzpatrick, *Modernism and the Grounds of Law* (Cambridge, UK: Cambridge University Press, 2001), 1.

54 Sigmund Freud, *Totem and Taboo*, in *The Standard Edition of the Complete Psychological Works of Sigmund Freud*, vol. 13, trans. James Strachey (London: Hogarth Press and the Institute of Psycho-Analysis, 1955), 141.

55 Ibid., 142.

56 Barbara Ehrenreich, *Dancing in the Streets: A History of Collective Joy* (New York: Henry Holt, 2006), 1.

57 Freud, *Totem and Taboo*, 2.
58 Ibid., 130, original emphasis.
59 Ibid.
60 Ibid., 134.
61 Lucian, *Dance*, 66.
62 Hagar Kotef, *Movement and the Ordering of Freedom: On Liberal Governance of Mobility* (Durham, NC: Duke University Press, 2015).
63 Albert Memmi, *The Colonizer and the Colonized*, trans. Howard Greenfeld (Boston: Beacon, 1991), 45.
64 Albert Memmi, *The Pillar of Salt*, trans. Edouard Roditi (Boston: Beacon, 1992); the chapter from which I will be quoting, titled "The Dance," is on pages 152–65. My gratitude to Joëlle Marelli for bringing me back to Memmi.
65 William Butler Yeats, "Among School Children," in *The Collected Poems of W.B. Yeats*, 2nd ed., ed. Richard J. Finneran, 215–17 (New York: Scribner, 1996), 217.
66 Heinrich Heine, *Atta Troll*, trans. Herman Scheffauer (London: Sidgwick and Jackson, 1913), canto 19.
67 Felicia McCarren, *Dance Pathologies: Performance, Poetics, Medicine* (Stanford, CA: Stanford University Press, 1998). See also Gotman, *Choreomania*.
68 David Kishik, "Critique of Pure Movement," in *The Manhattan Project: Theory of a City*, 221–9 (Stanford, CA: Stanford University Press, 2015).
69 Susan Leigh Foster, "Movement's Contagion: The Kinesthetic Impact of Performance," in *The Cambridge Companion to Performance Studies*, ed. Tracy C. Davis, 46–59 (Cambridge, UK: Cambridge University Press, 2008).

CONCLUSION

The Disappearance of the Aesthetic

Brad Evans and Chantal Meza

The sky was on fire. As the red dust blanketed this former colonial mining city, the inhabitants were reminded once again of the natural beauty of a World Heritage Site comfortably sitting within the arid plateau of the Sierra Madre Occidental. Could there be anywhere more beautiful on this tranquil evening? Yet maybe that explains the fate of this land. Could it be that the city of Zacatecas was enduring its own Medusa syndrome? Punished for its beauty by the vengeful, who had released so many serpents, the mythical eagle that adorns the Mexican flag was unable to contain them all. It is the summer of 2017, and Chantal is sitting on the roof in the heart of the old town. She, too, is captivated by this natural wonder yet increasingly haunted by the fall of the nation. This town, like her country, has always known about the violence. It has been part of the revolutionary attraction. But what's happening today is making the stars weep and the radiant sky bleed as though it were also trying to resist and testify to the forgotten souls that are taken from the streets below. Everything, it is said, returns to dust. And when that dust settles, a new horizon will be revealed. But what words have been silenced as the red dust speaks so loudly on this day that nothing can be deciphered? Is this dust meant to remind us of a deeper love, a more poetic meaning, one that refuses to let the triumph of violence march forth and recolonize these lands with a white substance that has taken so many lives? Maybe the sun is also bearing witness as the ancestral spirits rip apart the twilight hour binding this world?

It was during this summer visit in 2017 when the problem of disappearance first properly appeared in our consciousness. Chantal was sensitized by its near arrival, which in turn dominated our conversations for the months that followed. We later watched in horror as the problem followed an unstoppable trajectory and seemed to take on a life of its own as though some beast from the void had been unleashed upon the scorched earth. As we later

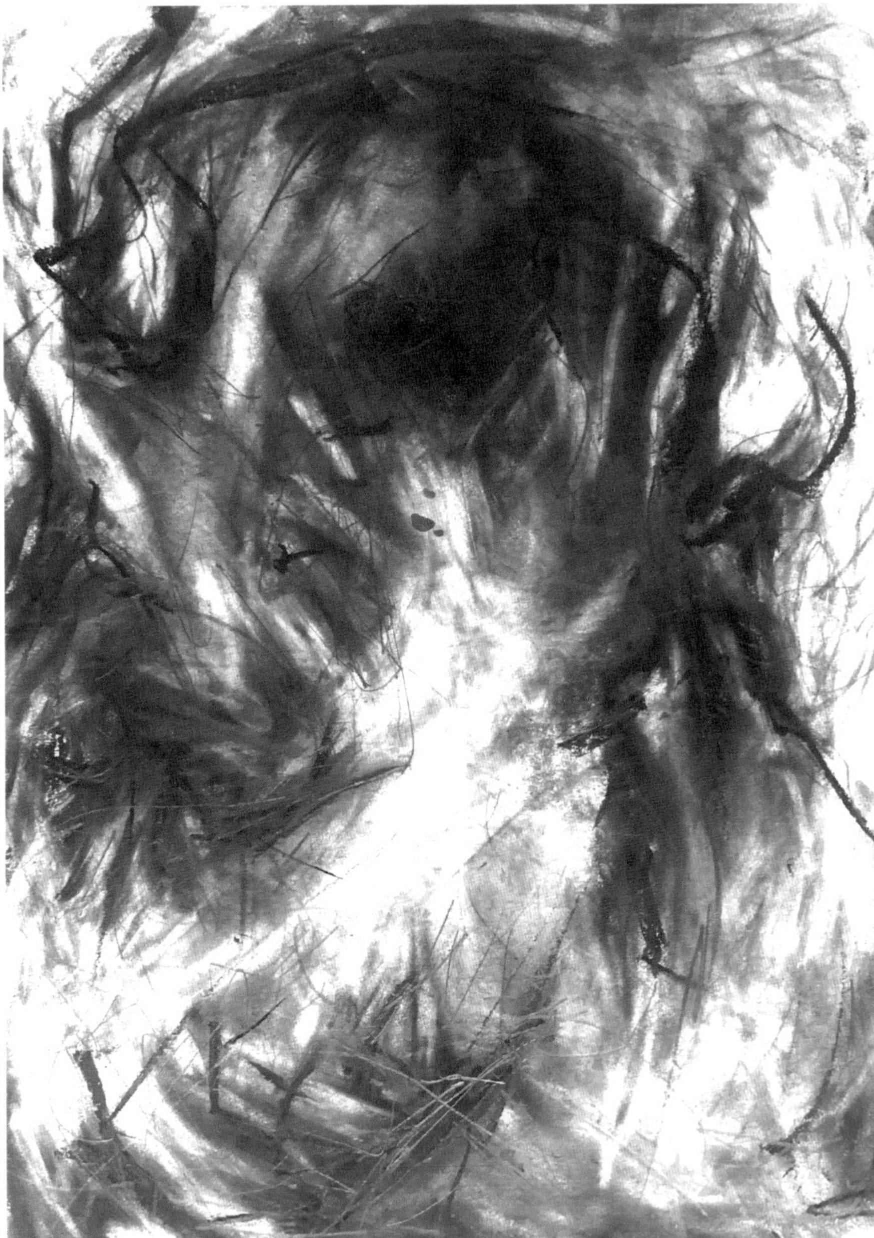

Chantal Meza, *The Void II*, 2019, graphite and charcoal on paper, 29.5 x 42 cm

walked around the ruins of the home of Hernan Cortez in Antigua, Veracruz, which has been poignantly reclaimed by rooted trees that are so symbolic to Indigenous peoples, the media were reporting of finding yet another mass grave containing over 100 unidentified bodies. In the decades following 9/11, the number of such violent pits into which the disappeared were thrown far exceeded those that captured the global media attention in the war zones of Iraq and Syria. This fact was harrowingly captured in a report published the following year whose title alone was devastating: "The Country of 2,000 Mass Graves."[1] We then returned to this scene as Zacatecas became one of the epicentres of Mexico's disappearance industry.[2] Disappearance is industrious, but to which economy does it belong? Jean Franco had already shown how the violence done to women moved from the household and into the streets as the forces of neoliberalism and its breaking apart of the traditional family unit took hold.[3] And there was certainly a correlation between Mexico's economic liberalization, the hyper-acceleration of the narcotics trade, and the violence of disappearance that this trade brought. This situation already presented a number of contradictions, which later actually revealed themselves to be part of the strategic design. How could we account for state complicity in violence when the state itself gets its primary authorization from the mandate to protect? This easily made sense when we factored in the desire and the ordered mechanisms that ensure the protection of interests above people. And how could we account for disappearance in an age increasingly defined by the spectacle? The answer here was rather straightforward when we saw how societies defined by the spectacle are seduced by the violence. But what of this violence today? We are no doubt in a time that differs from the tumultuous years around the turn of the decade and the NAFTA period that sparked the revolutionary activity in Chiapas, which marked the political landscape until President Felipe Calderón's war on drugs led to an exponential increase in brutality and slaughtering. Indeed, how could we reconcile the apparent contradiction, wherein the explosion of disappearance directly mapped onto the digital and information communications revolutions, which made everything visible and normalized the idea of the surveillance state?

Before dealing with this question of technology, let's step back for a moment to focus on the violence and what it means for our final analytics of power here. The more this project has developed, the more we have been forced to consider the enduring legacy of the violence of disappearance. Not only has this legacy made us turn toward the terror of a haunting that continues to condemn the living for years after the initial act of abduction, but it has also required us rethink the very meaning of power and violence, for they, too, operate within the haunting shadows. Through this reconsideration, we have increasingly come to see sovereignty itself as a ghost formation. The greatest violence ends in unrecoverable annihilation. This is a violence that dreams of a total absence. It is a violence that inaugurates a state of disappearance into which all history and claims to the future can be thrown. The confrontation with such intolerable violence – the violence of the void – is what truly marks out those we would identify as having been armed with a poetic sensibility. Post-Nietzsche and the critique of the inherent nihilism (the will to nothing) of the modern condition, we have seen it in philosophical concerns with vanishing points, nothingness, thresholds, and event horizons. And post-Goya, we have seen it through a transgressive witnessing of art, which has attended to the violent aesthetics of disappearance, revealing in subtle and explicit ways how erasure is the invisible power that effectively conditions what is possible in the realm of appearances. Such a desire to "make seen what won't let itself be seen," as Jacques Rancière puts it, has thus meant "not only inscribing the traces of the horror as a faithful witness" but also "being faithful to the general task that art – figurative or otherwise – prescribed for itself once it stopped being subject to the norms of representation: showing what can't be seen, what lies beneath the visible, an invisible that is simply what ensures the visible exists."[4] This desire to see the invisible has required us not only to witness the violence done to bodies, revealing the lasting wounds that they carve into the body of humanity itself, but also to recognize how the greatest violence literally leaves no trace. To bear witness is to account for the intolerable violence of absent space, in which violence has left its greatest and lasting impression – the violence of the void that brings together in a tremendous battle the invisible technological power of annihilation against a poetic love that rejoices in its confidential alliance with the secret.

Attending to the violence of absence has allowed us to present a more critical reading of political aesthetics, which in turn has commanded an alternative history on the phenomenology of disappearance. We might think here of the paintings by the American Romanticists, who despite pushing forward our appreciation of both the beautiful and the sublime, also brought an epic violence insofar as the lands that they painted were often completely depopulated of Indigenous peoples. We might also return to arguably the most recognizable political and spatially significant image ever produced: the frontispiece to Thomas Hobbes's *Leviathan* (1651). Although this image has been analyzed for understanding violence, giving rise to what we have since called the body politic, the image's largely depopulated landscape should still also command attention. Hobbes put forward the proposition that there can be no politics without security and no security without the state. But he also left us to look upon a vision of sovereignty that was marked both by a unified appearance and by a savagely administered absence. Hillsides are notably deforested – pointing to an ecology of devastation that also cleared the woodlands of the unruly and rebellious masses. With life unified through *appropriated abandonment*, we are left to fixate on the glorious sovereign, whose violence – already being waged elsewhere – is often nowhere visible yet still everywhere felt.

Although much has been said about this image in terms of biopolitics,[5] especially about the appearance of penguinesque figures – plague doctors – in front of the church, we have become more interested in how this image connects to the question of ghosting as a defining feature and arguably as the only remaining trace left by disappearance. Could it be that the absences in space show the violence of sovereignty in its purest form? Is sovereignty nothing more than a ghost formation, something that can never be properly photographed or captured on film, something that always manages to somehow evade detection, despite the continued violence that it authors? Is it a system of violence that always provisions an alibi and can never truly be held responsible for its brutal crimes? With these *ghost sovereignties*, the capacity to disappear is properly the highest achievement, for it reveals power as a purely unmediated invisible force, whose ultimate ambition was always to be everywhere present yet nowhere visible, everywhere felt yet nowhere seen, everywhere known yet perfectly unknowable. This is a vision for power that, from its inception to now, has proved to be profoundly theological yet fully compatible with the progressive will to fully technologize life. We see time and again how sovereignty is most visibly present when the methods and effects of its violence are hidden in plain sight. We also see time and again how sovereignty becomes unlocatable when it comes to accounting for its violence, including denying that the violence ever happened in its name or under its watch. This is important, for we often think of absent spaces as devoid of law and order – as spaces where even sovereignty itself has been vacated. But might we not argue that any viable autopsy of sovereignty is most purposefully explored precisely in spaces where it seems to be altogether absent? Indeed, is that not the real challenge set by Hobbes?

But if sovereignty can be revealed as intimately bound to the logics of disappearance, what of technology? And how has this relationship altered as we have rapidly moved from the analogue to the digital world? We started this volume with a meditation on the aesthetics of disappearance, which we explained was driven by the attempt to makes sense of and confront the unintelligible and to offer an artistic and critical response. During the course of its production, we have however also shifted our concerns, still ever mindful of the need to recognize the enduring importance of the artistic field. Guided by the thinking of Arendt, we increasingly turned back to the *Origins of Totalitarianism*, where she claims that what defined a concentration camp was precisely the attempt to kill humans while they were still alive. The starting point for disappearing the human, as she explained, was to create perfectly controllable conditions where "spontaneity itself" could be eradicated,[6] for what was the spontaneous after all if not the capacity to properly exercise one's unscripted freedom? Although some have continued to read the importance of this claim as being Arendt's concern with a juridical account of humanity,[7] which demands moral respect and legal protections, we venture to read it more poetically. If there is a lesson to be taken from those episodes in history where the disappearance was most concentrated, it is precisely to value the singularity of being human as defined by its expressiveness. This insight in turn leads us to a more sophisticated critique of technology, including the technical/calculative will to rule, which would suggest that it is absolutely integral to the will to nothing. And it would also allow us to better understand how physical disappearance is both accelerating and taking novel new forms in the contemporary hyper-technologized moment. What we can read from Arendt, among others, is that the capacity to disappear becomes exponentially more possible as society accelerates and deepens the technologization of life insofar as it is precisely such technologization that puts the human in peril. It is a stark reality that as we rapidly embrace artificial intelligence, digital surveillance, big data, neurotechnological interventions, and nano-productions – all of which hold the capacity to be militarized and weaponized and so truly put to the service of epic violence – we need to account for the new forms of disappearance appearing on the horizon, which threaten to swallow us all. This is especially the case for the arts and humanities, which we increasingly see can stake their own claims only if they are appropriated into digitalization and only if their value to society is scientifically validated.[8] As we end this project, then, it is no longer possible to concern ourselves only with the aesthetics of disappearance. We must now propose opening a new chapter in continuation of our concerns, one that also takes very seriously what some have already identified as "the disappearance of the aesthetic."

The late French philosopher Jean Baudrillard poses a question with the title of his last book: *Why Hasn't Everything Already Disappeared?*[9] Troubled by the onslaught of digital technology, Baudrillard begins the discussion by asking what it means to consider this world without humans. "Let us speak, then," the writer proposes, "of the world from which human beings have disappeared."[10] Central to his concerns is the unstoppable advance of what he has previously termed "hyper-reality," where the simulacrum of existence is becoming an unquestionable truism. This simulacrum doesn't belong to the virtual realm of thought or even to the realm of fiction but is validated as scientific fact. For Baudrillard, this validation demands a new theory of what can be presented as history, which he maintains can be traced back to what Arendt identifies as the "Archimedean point," where modern science forces a tremendous separation, or calculative break, from the natural world. Disappearance, then, for Baudrillard, is intensifying as a direct result of our so-called technological advance and the unnatural distances being produced among humans. To help formulate his ideas, Baudrillard turns specifically to photography, noting how the arrival of digital photography inaugurated a new age of the image, which brought a monstrous violence to more traditional approaches concerning witnessing and documentation, along with theories of presence/absence. Because of its binary constructs of zeros and ones, the advent of this new photography eliminates the "entire symbolic articulation of language and thought," abandoning the role of the individual creator to produce a manufactured reality as a "pure trace" devoid of meaning. As he explains,

> When everything disappears by excess of reality, when, thanks to the deployment of a limitless technology, both mental and material, human beings are capable of fulfilling all their potentialities and, as a consequence, disappear, giving way to an artificial world that expels them from it to an integral performance that is, in a sense, the highest stage of materialism. That world is perfectly objective since there is no one left to see it. Having become purely operational, it no longer has need of our representation. Indeed, there no longer is any possible representation of it. For, if what is proper to human beings is not to realize all their possibilities, it is of the essence of the technical object to exhaust its possibilities and even to go quite some way beyond them, staking out in that way the definitive demarcation line between technical objects and human beings, to the point of deploying an infinite operational potential against human beings themselves and implying, sooner or later, their disappearance.[11]

These concerns with technologically enabled disappearance were written just as Generation Z's digital natives were becoming a defining social grouping within contemporary liberalized societies. Having lost none of its relevance, this generation requires us to think more intently about these concerns in today's post-liberal age, wherein technology has become the unrivalled source for power in the world. Technology is no longer just a mediating or enabling force, nor can it be explained in terms of autonomous connectivity. It harvests and colonizes our minds. It seduces the gaze, creates a digital nervous system of the world, and even has us desire our own determinacy. Presented in fact as the only thing that can save us, technology today has assumed the position of a religion – the arrival of a worldwide "techno-theodicy" into which all of us are being recast,[12] not to mention having our fortunes held hostage to forces beyond all sight and knowledge. Reduced to engineers, we frame each and every problem within a technological paradigm for rule. And this transformation works by having us buy into the conceit that networked images of thought are liberating since they bring us closer to a truer picture of ourselves. Some even gesture that these technologies may be leading us toward a kind of automated socialism under which we may all leisurely live out a privileged life on highly regulated social media platforms, whose affective currency does nothing but compliment the user and enhance self-esteem.

Not to be defeated, however, by the normalization of hyper-realism – a technologically enabled condition in which the real and the simulacrum have become so indistinguishable that it is no longer possible to tell the original from the fake, the exceptional from the mundane, the event from the pre-programmed – Baudrillard still searches for an alternative encounter with the image. In *The Conspiracy of Art*, he asks, "Is there still an aesthetic illusion? And if not, a path to an 'aesthetic' illusion, the radical illusion of secret, seduction, and magic? Is there still, on the edges of hyper-visibility, of virtuality, room for an image?"[13] Apart from his writings on the types of vanishment that Baudrillard detects in the production of the image in the digital age, he also turns to photography in a style that at first glance might appear all too melancholic. The photography of Baudrillard, now exhibited in many galleries across the world, documents moments in the travelling life of the author and are simply titled by the location in which they were shot.[14] Extending his deep concerns with the ways that art has collapsed into hyper-reality, which has robbed it of the penchant for the impossible, the hidden, and the secret, what appears in his images are everyday objects warped by light and largely absent of human subjects. But rather than simply documenting the past, might we not look upon these images as a transgressive warning from a future that has now arrived? The abandoned and submerged car that gestures to a time when the open road was key to visions of liberation; the rotting tree that suggests how even the ancestral might become toxified; the empty red-veiled chair that's as regally unsettling as any empty throne; the building covered with an image of itself that at least omits a material quality; the airport runway at dusk claiming that a destination to nowhere else may just be possible; and the broken statue remaining publicly defiant – all of these photographs bring us back to the deserts of the real. Such images, as Sylvère Lotringer noted, should not be separated from his theoretical concerns: "He is a practicing artist of his own concepts … For Baudrillard the actual photographs are beside the point. It is what *precedes* them that counts in his eyes – the *mental event* of taking a picture."[15] Indeed, we might argue that their documenting of a material life where imperfections are allowed to spontaneously seep into the composition, imperfections as true as any intervention of light, gives them a resistive quality that provides not only a snapshot of the past but also a disruption of the present. They are, in short, a portent reminder to consider properly the erasure of humans from space, including the kinds of disappearances authored when the image is overexposed. Hence, as Richard G. Smith writes, the photographs enable us to "glimpse a parallel world that is slipping away in the face of an integral reality which is almost all encompassing and wants more than anything to impose meaning on the world."[16] The irony is that when we attempt to impose meaning, life appears to be all the more meaningless.

In an essay titled "Photography, or the Writing of Light," Baudrillard observes, "The idea is to resist noise, speech, rumours by mobilizing photography's silence; to resist movements, flows, and speed by using its immobility; to resist the explosion of communication and information by brandishing its secrecy; and to resist the moral imperative of meaning by deploying its absence of signification. What above all must be challenged is the automatic overflow of images, their endless succession, which obliterates not only the mark of photography (le trait), the poignant detail of the object (its punctum), but also the very moment of the photo, immediately passed, irreversible, hence always nostalgic."[17] And in this regard, we might extend our interest in these photographs today to consider them a powerful reminder that harnesses the power of nostalgia, doing so not to resurrect some glorious past but to deal with an accelerating violence of disappearance without the demand to fall back upon some truthful grounding. After all, such a return would only end up reinscribing the power of scientific thinking. "We deplore the disappearance of the real under the weight of too many images," Baudrillard insists. "But let's not forget that the image disappears too because of reality. In fact, the real is far less often sacrificed than the image. The image is robbed of its originality and given away to shameful acts of complicity. Instead of lamenting the relinquishing of the real to superficial images, one would do well to challenge the surrender of the image to the real. The power of the image can only be restored by liberating the image from reality."[18] This is an image, we might add, that invokes a fugitive occupation insofar as it still seeks to preserve the secret and the mysteries of an existence. It is an image that demands a different appreciation of the relationship between absent bodies, space, violence, and time.

Mindful of this imperative, what particularly interests us in the wake of Baudrillard's disappearing reality are the links between appearance and erasure in uncertain spaces that define our times. Having worked in the past on spectacles of violence, we have been looking more critically in recent years at the violence of disappearance. What makes erasure possible? And how do we confront the absence by drawing on the power of the abstract in both image and thought? These questions have brought us into direct confrontation with the phenomenology of disappearance – or the terror of living under erasure and how this marks space with a wound that tears apart the fabric of time. This is a terror that we recognize as being capable of sweeping life up without warning, transforming space itself into permanent violent haunting. This research has revealed many contradictions for us, not least the issue of how we can account for the exponential increase in human disappearance in a world that is simultaneously being tracked and surveyed on a scale beyond all knowing. Could it be, as Baudrillard insisted, that erasure in a digitalized world is no contradiction at all? This question brings us back to Arendt's concern with the Archimedean point, as discussed in *The Human Condition*. Concerned with the way that thinking has been subjected to a "closing in process," she observes how the 1960s – a period, we should note, when the intellectual seeds for the digital revolution first started to sprout – began with a profound realization:

> Only now has man taken full possession of his mortal dwelling place and gathered infinite horizons, which were temptingly and forbiddingly open to all previous ages, into a globe whose majestic outlines and detailed surface he knows as he knows the lines in the palm of his hand. Precisely when the immensity of available space on earth was discovered, the famous shrinkage of the earth began, until eventually in our world each man is as much an inhabitant of the earth as he is an inhabitant of his country. Men now live in an earth-wide continuous whole where even the notion of distance, still inherent in the most perfectly unbroken contiguity of its parts, has yielded before the onslaught of speed. Speed has conquered space.[19]

Crucially, for Arendt, full possession of the earth also corresponds to full possession of the image. It also corresponds to a moment when "true appearance" is inseparable from "the science of the structure of the mind."[20] Unrivalled here is the calculating technological mind, which proposes to provide answers to all the secrets of the universe, from the most intimate to the most expansive. In the "sky of ideas," as she puts it, there is no longer any room for images, shadows, or perishable matter. Phenomenology has been displaced by a new "condition of remoteness" under which most of us inevitably end up looking inward, with only the scientists possessing the tools to venture into the great beyond. The impact on art has been as expected. As Marshall McLuhan notes, "Scientists make their discoveries as 'artists,' not specialists. Such scientists construct experiments as 'works of art' to probe the environment."[21] Thus harmless creations like computer-generated fractal designs and lava lamps, which were meant to aesthetically seduce the drop-out generation, have swiftly turned into weapons of artistic colonization, from the Hubble Space Telescope and the Large Hadron Collider to robot artists and digital platforms designed to harness the true power of the image. Tasked with revealing the image of everything, creators have been forced to virtually inhabit spaces marked by explicit overexposure, spaces that speak the patterned language of connection and claim to possess the true power of aesthetic reckoning. In light of this claim, is there any wonder that art has fully collapsed into the scientific? Is it any wonder that artists of today are indistinguishable from computer-aided designers armed with a public relations mind? Which is to say, is there any wonder that wonder has lost its allure?

In this setting, abstract art must be something that exhibits a turn toward the intimacy of an emotional confession stripped of its metaphysical demands. Indeed, the aspiration for art becomes a new kind of digital mimicry that literally frames and sets the conditions for art within a technological landscape. This outcome has been perfectly captured by the aspirational icon for this new age of technological discovery, Mike Winkelmann (otherwise known as Beeple), who turns the focus of art into some astronaut adventure where the witness to the catastrophic – the Human One – now becomes the intrepid scientist who walks in solitude in a simulacrum of the place where Nietzsche once stood.[22] Yet, according to advocates, if we are to have any future, it is the digital image that will be our guide.

Inspired by the thinking of McLuhan, Julia M. Hildebrand and Barry Vacker provide a useful mapping of what they have termed "the media(s) cene." Attending specifically to the great absences of being, including the realization that we may truly be the only living species in the entire universe, they question our need for "sensory massaging to fill existential voids."[23] To account for this desire, they draw attention to McLuhan's distinction between hot and cold media, offering a visual media ecology that connects the big-strata visions, the exo/eco-media, made possible by the reach of science with endo/ego-media technologies that introvertly map the conditions of the inner space that we inhabit. For Hildebrand and Vacker, since the latter are defined by close proximities, their temperatures are notably hotter due to frictions and collisions. That is especially true for the hashtag culture of ego-media platforms such as Twitter, Facebook, Instagram, YouTube, and Google, where tribe rubs against tribe, amplifying the accelerations and collisions. In contrast, those media with a more outward gaze are said to belong to the category of cool media. "Cool media deal with lower densities, lower friction, with distance, drift, wander, wonder, wow," they argue. "Temperatures are lower, tempers are cooler. Whatever is hot out there – such as stars, black holes, and supernovas – is surrounded by the cool, the void, the entropy toward absolute zero. Big bang to the big chill. Deep space, deep time, deep futures."[24] The implications are terrifying, even if they might suggest an inevitable need to rethink our entire philosophical gaze. After all, in the cool gaze that looks upon the emptiness of an expanding void, "events slow, attention spans grow, reflection trump's reaction, the species supersedes the tribe, borders and wars become artificial and absurd."[25] But since we don't want to deal with such comforting absurdities, we instead rely more and more on the egocentric and leave metaphysical visions to the experts, blinded to the fact that we have become the vanishing point, imploding in upon ourselves in a world that offers no escape as we absently stare into the black screens of an existence "spanning the abyss,"[26] screens that are less about the event horizon of those black holes in the sky and more about an inner pull that is authoring a new kind of annihilation, one that is ironically selling a new lasting eternity.

Our wager is that we need to move in the opposite direction. We need to show how the void is not just a space of absence, annihilation, and terrifying coldness. And we need to go in search of lost time so that we may recover the slowness of verticality and the demand to reimagine a deeply intimate contemplative act, one that is not denied the metaphysical ambition to venture beyond the thresholds that police the realms of appearance and the realms of disappearance. We need to recover within art the aesthetics of annihilation so that in a new language art may speak poetry from the void. We need to recover within philosophy the possibility for a transgressive image of thought so that we may cross over and think as though already dead. Doing so means showing how the technological world of immediacy is the real order of coldness, nihilism, and absenting, whereas the slow and risky journey beyond the threshold of time is marked by the most intense fire that secretly resides in the depths of the void. Of course, we fully appreciate here how this argument could be read as remarkably conservative and indeed reactionary. What is the function of art after all if not to help identify a position and lead to progressive change? But is this question not another example of thinking like a scientist and seeking to render all things explicit? Hence, just as the abstract has been bound to typologies of intimacy devoid of metaphysical ambition, is not the collapse of art back into identity another indication of the way that vulnerability is but a symptom of the triumph of a technological will to rule?

Overexposure is authoring novel forms of erasure. Some of this process is implicit. Some of it adheres to the logic that in order for some things to appear, others must vanish. But some of it is also whimsically explicit in the banality of deletion. We might think here of the booming industry in erasure apps that now positively promote the disappearance of persons. A purposeful example is the AirBrush app, which promises to "remove unexpected photobombers from your photos" and even invites you to "say goodbye to old memories" by eliminating old lovers.[27] We might laugh this technology off as harmless fun (which is the default setting for the whimsical violence of digital cultures), but there is an important message being projected with such statements. There is nothing from the past that cannot be erased in digital "atopias,"[28] and as for memories, they can be curated as easily as anything else. If only we had the minds to forget – or at least to transpose every memory into the image, such that memory itself loses all meaning unless there is the manipulated image to prove that it was actually real. How often do we hear people justifying the taking of photographs of every moment shared so that they can relive the memory sometime in a future that never shall be? We are sure that Joseph Stalin would have adored this particular piece of software. When did curating absence become so acceptable? Why don't we want those unwanted strangers in our photos? Is it because they don't conform to a picture-perfect image of the world, one where the real and the simulacrum join forces? And what does this desire for erasure also tell us about our inability to confront messy or upsetting things from the past? What we do know for sure is that the traumas of material existence will find a way to haunt with even greater potency.

So we are led to question whether we have, finally, become ghosts in the machine. Although this possibility is compelling, the very framing has always been problematic. Technology has never had a theory of death. It simply puts us there. And if we return to our thinking on the ghosting nature of sovereignty, maybe that vision for power has realized its true and full potential in this digital age. The king is dead; long live the king! Not in body, but in spirit. Consequently, as we are now all being turned into technological apparitions that leave no lasting trace – a digital life casts no shadow – the real ghost is the machine itself. The deus ex machina is the holy ghost, whose divine violence courses through digital clouds and threatens to delete a life as fast as the speed of thought. We are on a fast trip, literally to nowhere. And we have the photographs to prove it. This trajectory, however, doesn't mean that there is no creative resistance. Our attentions are pulled here in the direction of the Russian photographer Alexey Titarenko.[29] Notably inspired by the cinematic vision of Sergei Eisenstein and the writings of Fyodor Dostoevsky, Titarenko offers a return to the tragedy and bleakness, yet also the magical beauty, of the material (post)industrial world without compromising any of his integrity. In his long-exposure work, the use of traditional darkroom methods reminds us of photography's exceptional capacity to bring into our gaze an irreducible mysticism, whose real power is to gesture toward a secret truth behind what is visible to us. These series include *City of Shadows* (1991–94), which brilliantly restores to life traces of the city's movements as it comes to terms with post-Soviet abandonment; *Time Standing Still* (1997–2000), which in photographs like "Begging Woman, Haymarket Square" (1999) powerfully brings together the stasis of neglect and the violence of time; as well as *Havana* (2003–06) and *New York* (2004–18), featuring haunting figures that populate largely abandoned sites to invoke a sublime yet eerie feeling.[30] When commenting on the influences informing his work, Titarneko notes, "Literature and poetry had the capacity to transform, by way of poetic comparisons or metaphors, a gloomy and uniform reality into something more appealing to the imagination and of its truest essence: to 'embellish' reality with the emotional and personal experiences of the writer who can in turn bestow on the work an additional aesthetic value."[31] He successfully brings this literary quality directly into the visual field by adopting a particularly unique analogue style. "In some way," he explains, "the effect of a long exposure in photography is comparable to the methods of musical interpretation: the latter directs the listener's attention to elements that might have gone unnoticed. In fact, it suggests precisely another meaning, which is more personal. All this gives music, as well as print, a poetic dimension that is the equivalent of metaphor."[32] This effect lends to photography not a journalistic but a literary quality that speaks in a more poetic style. Photography is "not reportage," Titarenko insists, "but a novel, whose central theme is the human soul, its modulations inspired by gazing upon human events, with their vibrations in a major or minor mode."[33] It also demands a deeper and slower contemplation of the violence that we continue to encounter.

Slowness is a luxury that most of us can ill afford or entertain today. Instead, we require a simulacrum of perfectibility, which proposes standards that nobody can match. In an interview with the BBC, the artist Tracey Emin argues that the greatest violence today is enacted by face-manipulation apps, which create an image of the self that even the self cannot compete with. We applied such "enhancements" to a photograph of the famous aged face of Samuel Beckett to show precisely how these technologies literally kill the character of a face by concealing the marks of time that contour experience and signify a life well lived. This is a form of erasure, too – a disappearance of the lines of individuality that set us apart as human, nothing more and nothing less. We are not saying that we need more visibility. On the contrary, the marks of a life reveal to us the true depths of what remains hidden. The marked face is a cartography of unwritten utterances, unspoken feelings, unknown mysteries, and so many other concealments that have refused to be given over to any policing apparatus. What then remains of such (im)perceptibility if the power of technology has already entered those uncharted black holes wherein our most intimate, creative, and guarded secrets were kept? We are reminded at this point of these poetic lines from Eduardo Galeano's meditation on "the nobodies":

> *Who do not have faces, but arms.*
> *Who do not have names, but numbers.*
> *Who do not appear in the history of the world, but in the police blotter of the local paper.*
> *The nobodies, who are not worth the bullet that kills them.*[34]

How might this verse be read when the face loses all meaning? What happens when the paper becomes the screen? And what happens when the bullets become virtual? Digitalization promises immortality. It promises to give us access to new spatial openings. And it promises to save us from, well, machines of the past. What we have tried to show is another reading, one that demonstrates how digital technology is authoring the most perverse kinds of violence, both through the erasure of bodies from the terrestrial surface of the earth and through the digital depopulating of landscapes, including poetic landscapes of the imagination. There is nothing immortal about these outcomes. As dust becomes a pixel, the digital is ultimately the greatest disappearing act. But we are not Harry Houdini on this stage in command of our own secretive illusions. The conjuring takes place elsewhere, such that the proliferation of the image promises to render everything potentially invisible, and all the while the spectacle of existence distracts us away from the real operations and mechanisms of power, causing us only to believe more and more in its redemptive narratives. Countering this effect requires a myth different from the one that is continuing to annihilate us from within and to take us ever farther away from what it means to be human. Formulating this counter-myth demands a different artistic vision that is not in line with the fashions of the times. Nor is it content to co-evolve with a technological master who has become a patron of none. Or as Paul Virilio retorts when asked what becomes of our dreams when everything becomes visibly apparent, "There are eyes everywhere. There is no blind spot left … We'll dream of being blind. This is the art of the engine."[35] And so we return to the abstract, for what is it in all its hiddenness and delight in the secret other than liberation of the pre-perspectival in order to short-circuit technological evisceration?

NOTES

1 Alejandra Guillén, Mago Torres, and Marcela Turati, "El país de las 2 mil fosas" ["The Country of 2,000 Mass Graves"], *Quinto Elemento Lab*, 12 November 2018, https://quintoelab.org/project/el-pais-de-las-2-mil-fosas.

2 Mónica Cerbón, "Zacatecas: El nuevo epicentro de las desapariciones" ["Zacatecas: The New Epicentre of Disappearances"], A dónde van los desaparecidos, 14 June 2022, https://adondevanlosdesaparecidos.org/2022/06/14/zacatecas-el-nuevo-epicentro-de-las-desapariciones.

3 Jean Franco, "Killing Priests, Nuns, Women and Children," in *Violence in War and Peace: An Anthology*, ed. Nancy Scheper-Hughes and Philippe Bourgois, 196–9 (Oxford: Blackwell, 2004).

4 Jacques Rancière, *Figures of History*, trans. Julie Rose (New York: John Wiley and Sons, 2014), 72.

5 Most notable here is Giorgio Agamben, *Stasis: Civil War as a Political Paradigm* (Edinburgh: Edinburgh University Press, 2015).

6 Hannah Arendt, *The Origins of Totalitarianism* (New York: Harcourt, 1976), 438.

7 Richard Bernstein, *Why Read Hannah Arendt Now* (Cambridge, UK: Polity, 2018).

8 We have dealt with this possibility elsewhere. See Brad Evans and Chantal Meza, "Narcissus in Three Acts," *Review of Education, Pedagogy, and Cultural Studies* 45, no. 1 (2023): 4–28, https://www.tandfonline.com/doi/full/10.1080/10714413.2022.2066394.

9 Jean Baudrillard, *Why Hasn't Everything Already Disappeared?* (New York: Seagull Books, 2009).

10 Ibid., 9.

11 Ibid., 10

12 Brad Evans, *Ecce Humanitas: Beholding the Pain of Humanity* (New York: Columbia University Press, 2020).

13 Jean Baudrillard, *The Conspiracy of Art: Manifestos, Interviews, Essays* (Cambridge, UK: Semiotext(e), 2005) 127.

14 See Jean Baudrillard, *Jean Baudrillard's Photography: Ultimate Paradox*, exhibition, Château Shatoo, Los Angeles, California, 12 December 2015 to 22 February 2016, http://chateaushatto.com/exhibition/ultimate-paradox-the-photography-of-jean-baudrillard.

15 Sylvère Lotringer, "The Piracy of Art," *Mal-estar na Cultura*, April-November 2010, 1–10 at 7, original emphasis, http://chateaushatto.com/wordpress/wp-content/uploads/2015/11/Jean-Baudrillard-Selected-Texts.compressed.pdf.

16 Richard G. Smith, "Baudrillard's Photographic Theory," *International Journal of Baudrillard Studies* 16, no. 1 (2020), https://baudrillardstudies.ubishops.ca/baudrillards-photographic-theory.

17 Jean Baudrillard, "Photography, or the Writing of Light," 1, http://chateaushatto.com/wordpress/wp-content/uploads/2015/11/Jean-Baudrillard-Selected-Texts.compressed.pdf. This essay is a translation of "La photographie, ou l'Ecriture de la lumiere: Litteralite de l'Image," in *L'Echange Impossible*, 175–84 (Paris: Galilée, 1999).

18 Ibid., 3.

19 Arendt, *Human Condition*, 263.

20 Ibid., 266.

21 Marshall McLuhan and Eric McLuhan, *Media and Formal Cause* (New York: NeoPoiesis, 2011), 55.

22 See Beeple, "Everydays," https://www.beeple-crap.com/everydays.

23 Julia M. Hildebrand and Barry Vacker, "Hot and Cool in the MediaScene: A McLuhan-Style Art and Theory Project," *Medium*, 28 January 2018, https://medium.com/mediascene/hot-and-cool-in-the-mediascene-a-mcluhan-style-art-and-theory-project-658ce02a6af8#_edn1.

24 Ibid.

25 Ibid.

26 Ibid.

27 See https://appairbrush.com/the-most-popular-tool-eraser.

28 See Evans, *Ecce Humanitas*.

29 See the artist's website at http://www.alexeytitarenko.com.

30 See these series at https://www.nailyaalexandergallery.com/artists/alexey-titarenko/series.

31 Alexey Titarenko, "City of Shadows," trans. Fiona Sze-Lorrain, November 2012, http://www.alexeytitarenko.com/essay.

32 Ibid.

33 Ibid.

34 Eduardo Galeano, "The Nobodies," in *The Book of Embraces*, trans. Cedric Belfrage (New York: Norton, 1992), 73.

35 In Louise Wilson, "Cyberwar, God and Television: An Interview with Paul Virilio," in *Digital Delirium*, ed. Arthur Kroker and Marilouise Kroker, 41–8 (New York: St Martin's, 1997), 47.

Contributors

GIL ANIDJAR teaches in the Department of Religion at Columbia University. Among his books are *The Jew, the Arab: A History of the Enemy* (2003), *Semites: Race, Religion, Literature* (2008), and *Blood: A Critique of Christianity* (2014). He has also written, among other things, on enmity, political theology, translation, and destruction – and now dance. He recently completed a manuscript entitled "The Sovereignty of Mothers."

ANA LUCIA ARAUJO is a professor of history at historically Black Howard University in Washington, DC. She has written or edited over thirteen books. Her three recent single-authored books include *Slavery in the Age of Memory: Engaging the Past* (2020), *Museums and Atlantic Slavery* (2021), and *Reparations for Slavery and the Slave Trade: A Transnational and Comparative History* (2017). She is a member of the International Scientific Committee of the UNESCO Slave Route Project. She serves on the Board of Editors of the *American Historical Review* (the flagship journal of the American Historical Association), the editorial board of the journal *Slavery and Abolition*, and the Editorial Review Board of the *African Studies Review*. Her research has been funded by the Institute for Advanced Study in Princeton, New Jersey, and by the American Philosophical Society. In 2023, as a recipient of the Getty Residential Scholar Grant, she is in residence at the Getty Research Institute, Los Angeles, California.

BRET W. DAVIS is a professor and Higgins Chair in Philosophy at Loyola University, Baltimore, Maryland. In addition to attaining a doctorate in philosophy from Vanderbilt University, he studied and taught for more than a year in Germany and thirteen years in Japan. He has published eleven books and more than eighty scholarly articles on topics in continental, Asian, and cross-cultural philosophy. He is the author of *Heidegger and the Will: On the Way to Gelassenheit* (2007) and *Zen Pathways: An Introduction to the Philosophy and Practice of Zen Buddhism* (2022). His edited books include *Sekai no naka no Nihon no tetsugaku (Japanese Philosophy in the World)* (with Fujita Masakatsu, 2005), *Japanese and Continental Philosophy: Conversations with the Kyoto School* (with Brian Schroeder and Jason M. Wirth, 2011), and *The Oxford Handbook of Japanese Philosophy* (2020). And he is the translator of Martin Heidegger's *Country Path Conversations* (2010).

MANGALIKA DE SILVA teaches in the Department of Media, Culture and Communication, New York University. Her research interests are post-foundational political thought, revolutionary poetics and aesthetics, decolonial ecologies, anthropology of violence, Afropessimism, postwar state (de)formations, popular Buddhism, and colonialism. De Silva is the author of *Soldiers, Princes, Prisoners and Prostitutes: Violence and Sexuality in the Iconography of the Nation* (2004). Her essays have appeared in the edited volumes *International Relations in South Asia: Search for an Alternative Paradigm* (2008) and *Women and the Contested State: Religion, Violence and Agency in South and Southeast Asia* (2007), as well as in *Social Text*, *Cultural Studies*, *Religion*, *Canadian Women's Studies*, *Domains*, *Indian Book Review*, and *Asian Women's Studies*. She was a recipient of a Scholar of Peace Fellowship from Women in Security, Conflict Management and Peace in 2000 and was awarded a Rubicon Research Fellowship by the Netherlands Organization for Scientific Research in 2009. Her forthcoming book is on minoritarian insovereignty.

BRAD EVANS is a political philosopher, critical theorist, and writer who specializes in the problem of violence. He is the author or editor of over twenty books, including most recently *Ecce Humanitas: Beholding the Pain of Humanity* (2020). Committed to education in the public interest, he publishes widely in many recognized forums, having previously led a series of columns on violence in both the *New York Times* and the *Los Angeles Review of Books*. Brad currently serves as Chair of Political Violence and Aesthetics at the University of Bath, United Kingdom, where he is also the founder and director of the Centre for the Study of Violence.

NUALA FINNEGAN is a professor in the Department of Spanish, Portuguese and Latin American Studies at University College Cork, Ireland, and director of the Centre for Mexican Studies. She has published widely in the areas of contemporary Mexican literary and visual-cultural studies, with a particular focus on gender. Her recent work on cultural responses to violence includes *Cultural Representations of Feminicidio on the U.S.-Mexico Border* (2018), among other outputs. Interested in multidisciplinary collaboration and community engagement, she has extensive experience of exhibition curation and coordination, including *Entre Mundos/Between Worlds: Images of Life between Mexico and Ireland* (2019) and *OUTPOSTS: Global Borders and National Boundaries* (2017–18) at The Glucksman. She is currently working on an interdisciplinary project that uses Latin American art practice to forge conversations about new futures on the island of Ireland, and she is completing two books: one on ethics, politics, and child-centred art practice at the US-Mexico border; and the other, forthcoming from Palgrave, on pandemic reconfigurations of Mexican commemorative mourning practices, including the Day of the Dead, written in collaboration with Jane Lavery.

HENRY A. GIROUX currently holds the Chair for Scholarship in the Public Interest in the English and Cultural Studies Department at McMaster University, where he is the Paulo Freire Distinguished Scholar in Critical Pedagogy. His most recent books include *The Terror of the Unforeseen* (2019), *On Critical Pedagogy*, 2nd edition (2020), *Neoliberalism's War on Higher Education*, 2nd edition (2020); *Race, Politics, and Pandemic Pedagogy: Education in a Time of Crisis* (2021), and *Pedagogy of Resistance: Against Manufactured Ignorance* (2022). His latest book is *Insurrections: Education in the Age of Counter-Revolutionary Politics* (2023). Giroux is also a member of *Truthout's* Board of Directors.

DAVID THEO GOLDBERG is Distinguished Professor of Anthropology, Comparative Literature, and Criminology, Law and Society, University of California Irvine. From 2000 to 2022, he directed the system-wide University of California Humanities Research Institute. Goldberg's work ranges over issues of social, political, and critical theory, the impact of technology on human futures, digital technology, and race and racism. Among his numerous books are *Dread: Facing Futureless Futures* (2021), *Are We All Postracial Yet?* (2015), *The Racial State* (2002), *The Threat of Race* (2009), and *The Future of Thinking* (with Cathy Davidson, 2011). His latest book is *The War on Critical Race Theory: Or, the Making of Racism* (2023). He also served as the executive director of the MacArthur-sponsored UCHRI Research Hub in Digital Media and Learning at the University of California Irvine, an on-site and virtual research facility designed to promote field building in the area.

CHANTAL MEZA is a self-taught abstract painter living and working in the United Kingdom. Her work has been featured in auctions, interventions, biennales and donations, and it has been widely exhibited in places such as Museum of Science and Technology, Mexico; Arocena Museum, Coahuila; Guadalupe Museum, Zacatecas; Popular Art Museum, Mexico; Centro Cultural Juan de Salazar, Paraguay; and Centrespace, United Kingdom. Her work is held in private and public collections. As part of the study of the subjects that interest her, she has co-written essays and delivered lectures, seminars, and panels at places such as Harvard University (United States), École Normale Superiéure (Paris), McMaster University (Canada), and Goethe Universität (Germany). Her artwork appears in many prominent international outlets as well as on book covers and in digital and print magazines. Her recent achievements include notable public recognition for her contribution to culture in her province in Mexico. Chantal is currently preparing an individual exhibition on her series *State of Disappearance.*

ADRIAN PARR is the dean of the College of Design at the University of Oregon and a senior fellow of the Design Futures Council. She served as a UNESCO chair for eight years and in this capacity curated the Watershed Urbanism exhibition in 2021 at the European Cultural Centre's Venice Biennale of Architecture. She is the author of numerous books, the most recent being *Earthlings* (2022), *Birth of a New Earth* (2017), and *The Wrath of Capital* (2014), all published by Columbia University Press. She has produced and co-directed (with Sean Hughes) two award-winning documentaries: *The Intimate Realities of Water* (2016) and *Thirsty and Drowning in America* (2016).

JULIAN REID lives in Finnish Lapland with his family, Kirsi, Lumi, Miro, Kosma, and Mortti their cat. He is Chair and Professor of International Relations at the University of Lapland. He lived previously in the United Kingdom, teaching at King's College London, Sussex University, and SOAS University of London. He is the author of *The Biopolitics of the War on Terror* (2006); a co-author of *The Liberal Way of War: Killing to Make Life Live* (with Michael Dillon, 2009), *Resilient Life: The Art of Living Dangerously* (with Brad Evans, 2014), *The Neoliberal Subject: Resilience, Adaptation and Vulnerability* (with David Chandler, 2016), and *Becoming Indigenous: Governing Imaginaries in the Anthropocene* (with David Chandler, 2019); and a co-editor of *Deleuze and Fascism: Security: War: Ethics* (with Brad Evans, 2013) and *The Biopolitics of Development: Reading Michel Foucault in the Postcolonial Present* (with Sandro Mezzadra and Ranabir Samaddar, 2013).

MICHAEL J. SHAPIRO is an emeritus professor in the Department of Political Science at the University of Hawai'i, Manoa. Among his publications are *The Political Sublime* (2018), *Punctuations: How the Arts Think the Political* (2019), *The Cinematic Political: Film Composition as Political Theory* (2020), *The Phenomenology of Religious Belief* (2021), *Writing Politics: Studies in Compositional Method* (2021), and *Aesthetics of Equality* (2023).

SAMUEL WEBER is Avalon Foundation Professor of Humanities and teaches comparative and German literature at Northwestern University, where he directs the Paris Program in Critical Theory. His most recent book publications are *Singularity: Politics and Poetics* (2021) and *Preexisting Conditions: Recounting the Plague* (2022). He is currently working on a book tentatively titled "Uncanny Animals: Nietzsche, Kafka, Derrida."

SANTIAGO ZABALA is ICREA Research Professor of Philosophy at Pompeu Fabra University in Barcelona. His most recent books are *Why Only Art Can Save Us: Aesthetics and the Absence of Emergency* (2017), *Being at Large: Freedom in the Age of Alternative Facts* (2020), and *Outspoken: A Manifesto for the Twenty-First Century*, edited with Adrian Parr (2022). He has written for the *Guardian*, the *New York Times*, and *Al-Jazeera.*

Index